BEYOND THE ROMANS

Posthuman Perspectives in Roman Archaeology

BEYOND THE ROMANS

POSTHUMAN PERSPECTIVES IN ROMAN ARCHAEOLOGY

Edited by

Irene Selsvold and Lewis Webb

TRAC THEMES IN ROMAN ARCHAEOLOGY
VOLUME 3

Series Editor: Katherine A. Crawford

OXBOW | books
Oxford & Philadelphia

Published in the United Kingdom in 2020 by
OXBOW BOOKS
The Old Music Hall, 106–108 Cowley Road, Oxford OX4 1JE

and in the United States by
OXBOW BOOKS
1950 Lawrence Road, Havertown, PA 19083

Hardcover Edition: ISBN 978-1-78925-136-4
Digital Edition: ISBN 978-1-78925-137-1

A CIP record for this book is available from the British Library

Library of Congress Control Number: 2020931810

Printed in Malta by Gutenberg Press

Typeset by Versatile PreMedia Services (P) Ltd

For a complete list of Oxbow titles, please contact:

UNITED KINGDOM
Oxbow Books
Telephone (01865) 241249
Email: oxbow@oxbowbooks.com
www.oxbowbooks.com

UNITED STATES OF AMERICA
Oxbow Books
Telephone (610) 853-9131, Fax (610) 853-9146
Email: queries@casemateacademic.com
www.casemateacademic.com/oxbow

Oxbow Books is part of the Casemate Group

Front cover: Foreground: The 'Great Artemis'. Trajanic period. Now in the Ephesus Archaeological Museum (Seljuk). (Courtesy of the Austrian Archaeological Institute (ÖAI). Photo credit: OeAW-OeAI/Niki Gail). Background: Marble pilaster with acanthus scrolls, Roman, first half of first century AD. Now in the Metropolitan Museum of Art. Accession number: 10.210.28a–c (Public domain [CC0 1.0 Universal]).

Contents

Series Foreword

Katherine A. Crawford

The Theoretical Roman Archaeology Conference (TRAC) is pleased to present the third volume within the *TRAC Themes in Roman Archaeology* series. The present volume engages with new and emerging debates about posthumanism and its study within Roman archaeology. Throughout this volume, the authors approach the topic in innovative ways and strive to push boundaries. We hope that their contribution will lead to advances in how posthumanism is applied and studied within the field of Roman archaeology. TRAC continues to be committed to engaging with and furthering the dissemination of theoretically informed scholarship relating to Roman archaeology. A testament to this success is that this year marks TRAC's 30th anniversary as an organisation. As the present chair of the TRAC Standing Committee, I am excited to reflect upon how we as an organisation have grown from what started out as a single conference and eventually evolved into an international organisation as well as considering the role that we will play in continuing to advocate for and influence the way theory is approached within the Roman archaeology community.

This series has sought to provide a venue for theoretically informed research themes, which has been successfully achieved in the first two volumes, of which the first volume covered different theoretical approaches as a way to understand 'barbarian' interactions within the Roman Empire's Northern frontiers, while the second volume considered the materiality and embodiment of Roman magic. The present volume represents the third volume in the *TRAC Themes in Roman Archaeology* series. This volume continues to demonstrate the ways in which theoretical topics are being engaged with and pushed within the Roman archaeology community. To this end, TRAC remains committed and passionate about evolving and developing with the ever-changing archaeological community. In particular, we as an organisation are focusing increased attention on the broader accessibility and dissemination of theoretically informed research through the venue of open access publications. Embracing this move, we launched the *Theoretical Roman Archaeology Journal* (TRAJ) in 2017, which is hosted by the Open Humanities Library. This journal will continue to leverage and act as a leading platform for the dissemination of theoretically informed debates and research within the field of Roman archaeology while complementing the research that has been produced within the three themed volumes of this series.

I am delighted to have acted as the series editor for this third volume and to see it to completion. Acknowledgements are owed to Thomas J. Derrick who oversaw the volume's inception. Further thanks go to the authors who willingly contributed to this volume and to the anonymous reviewers whose invaluable feedback has strengthened the presented research. Thanks are also owed to the team at Oxbow Books who have supported and ensured the successful release of this volume. Enormous gratitude is owed to Dr Sarah Scoppie (TRAC Standing Committee Treasurer) who provided tremendous support in helping me with the final copyediting. Finally, I would like to thank the volume editors Dr Lewis Webb and Dr Irene Selsvold – without their perseverance and dedication you would not be reading this volume now.

University of British Columbia
24 November 2019

Foreword: A Posthuman Call to Scholars

Francesca Ferrando

Being a scholar offers a great opportunity: to be an agent of change. Knowledge-production is one of the technologies through which social constructions and political hierarchies are created and maintained. We, scholars, produce what is valued as scientific knowledge, which constitutes the basis for laws, civic norms and social evolutions; this is why we also bear great responsibility. A good scholar is someone honest with themselves and with the world around them. A good scholar is someone who is aware of their own point of view so that they are not forcing it onto others. A good scholar is someone who can see what is happening and is able to say: *it does not have to be this way*. Karl Marx said it clearly: 'the philosophers have only *interpreted* the world, in various ways; the point, however, is to *change* it' (Marx and Engels 1976: 15; emphasis in original). As scholars, we can change the world, but first, we have to change ourselves, otherwise our own biases and bigotry will manifest in our writings and, without even realising it, we will be reinforcing injustice in static systems of power. In other words, if we just kept repeating the same prejudices that were developed and reinforced in previous eras, even if we were not aware of them, we still would not be rigorous scholars.

As scholars, we play a key role in social change. Society trusts us to produce scientific knowledge in order to advance not only general welfare, but also a fair system of regulations and ethics. Still, academic productions often reflect the biases of their era; thus, it is not surprising that great minds of the past could also be sexist and racist, such as the case of Aristotle, for instance, one of the fathers of Western philosophy, according to whom women were inferior and slavery was a natural condition. Scholarly productions that are still tainted with sexism, racism or ethno-centrism, among other discriminatory frames, are becoming less predominant (although still existing), thanks to the great work of intellectuals who dared to challenge mainstream views, and speak from perspectives that had been, until then, marginalised. As the black feminists Akasha (Gloria T.) Hull, Patricia Bell Scott, and Barbara Smith render it: 'all the women are white, all the blacks are men, but some of us are brave' (Hull *et al.* 1982). Yes, we have to be brave to dare to change social and intellectual trajectories that are perceived as 'normal', by showing with academic rigour and scientific honesty what is missing.

Today, for instance, most studies are still based on anthropocentric and human-supremacist assumptions. This has to change. It is vital that scholars in the twenty-first century understand their role and responsibility in informing, with their work and research, on the consequences, implications and impacts of living in the era of the Anthropocene. It is still common in Western academia for scholars to reiterate the outdated narrative, and symbolic paradigm, developed in Europe in the eighteenth century and known as the Enlightenment, according to which humans, through science and reason, can overcome any obstacle. Ironically, while some scholars still do not understand the significance and deeper ramifications of the current ecological crisis, civil society is stepping up, reminding us all that we can no longer ignore our location in space-time. The amplitude of climate protests against global warming is revealing. This is how *The New York Times* describes the reasons nurturing this growing ecological awareness, that has been fully embraced by the youngest generations, and that is giving rise to street marches worldwide, as experienced during the September 2019 climate strikes: 'Anxious about their future on a hotter planet and angry at world leaders for failing to arrest the crisis, masses of young people poured into the streets on every continent' (Sengupta 2019). Scholars can no longer ignore the call; it is time to change outdated worldviews based on false premises, such as human supremacy and the myth of unlimited resources. Posthumanism can help.

This book is a brave move towards a thorough development of the posthuman paradigm shift. It makes a clear statement: posthumanism has to do not just with the twenty-first century, but also with the history of planet Earth. Currently, the posthuman is mostly discussed in terms of the present and the future, by centralising the debate on speculative and emerging technologies. One area of reflection is often bypassed: the past. However, history is life's teacher. The Romans already knew that, as Cicero indicates: '*Historia* [...] *magistra vitae*' (Cic. *De or.* 2.36). Without a full acknowledgement of the past, there is a risk of persevering in species habits that no longer fit our social, political, and environmental understanding of the world. For instance, some of the issues that raise concern in the era of the Anthropocene developed in Antiquity. *Beyond the Romans: Posthuman Perspectives in Roman Archaeology* clearly shows that significant changes in the Earth's environment were already produced during the Roman period, and that some ethical debates on anthropogenic processes, such as terraforming, deforestation, and declines in animal population, were also being discussed among Roman philosophers, such as Lucretius and Pliny the Elder.

The editors of this book are at the forefront of academia. They are not only re-accessing archaeology from a posthumanist, post-anthropocentric and post-dualistic perspective; they are also taking archaeology to the posthuman. They show, through the case of ancient Rome, a point that is of key relevance to our discussion about changing outdated worldviews. A common type of resistance encountered when challenging the 'norm', relies on the false belief that 'things have always been this way'. In actuality, everything is constantly changing and shifting. Even systems of power that may seem invulnerable, at one point substituted other systems of power, which, previously, might have also deemed untouchable. This is the history of all empires, but also the history of hegemonic ideas and worldviews. More specifically, anthropocentric and supremacist accounts are neither 'original' to humankind, nor inevitably part of human mindsets; and still, they have been reiterated into the micro- and macro- narratives of major historical empires, religions, and philosophies. Consequently, assumptions based on human supremacy have significantly shaped and impacted international politics, species relations, ecological dominance, and habitat loss in recorded history, to the point that many current societies, and scholars, have not started to challenge them, yet.

This book unveils the material and ideological, as well as natural-cultural construction of history, not only of the past, but also of the present and the future. We are the results of billions of years of cosmic agency, and we are part of such agency. As Friedrich Nietzsche and Michel Foucault evocatively remind us: power is everywhere (Nietzsche 1901; Foucault 1975). We, scholars, have a great responsibility. We can no longer be silent and uncritical of human-supremacist narratives, since this kind of silence turns into complicity with a type of privilege that is neither neutral, nor favourable, to the human species. What can be of help to current human societies is understanding the human not as superior to other species, but as in relation to them, to the planet, to technology, and beyond. By underlining the intra-relationality of existence, scholars can facilitate and support the actual manifestation of multi-species justice and planetary co-existence. As scholars, we can now embrace our fields, from Archaeology to Philosophy, from Biology to Cybernetics, from Physics to Engineering, from Palaeontology to Anthropology, from a regenerated view that is honestly engaging with the posthuman call, in its posthumanist, post-anthropocentric, and post-dualistic premises.

This is a great time to rethink our habits as a species, and our biases, not only as individuals, but as scholars. It is time to stop, take a pause, and unlearn. It is time to learn from society, from our planet and from this book. It is time to ask ourselves, in all sincerity: what kind of assumptions are we taking for granted in our research and in our life? We cease to be animals of *habit* by realising that nothing is inevitable, and that everything we promulgate through our writings and teachings will affect and effect the generative network of social and species interactions. We are now aware that words shape the world, and thus, an integral understanding of our world should shape our words. We bear great responsibility, and now that we know it, we can make a difference. We are the brave ones, who can move through challenging times without losing our smiles, because we know that what we say is how we say it. We are the ones who dare to see, because what we see no longer frightens us. We are excited about the relevance of our role and the ontological power of originality, because we know that our envisioning is already shaping the sensitive body of space-time. We are: posthuman scholars.

Liberal Studies, New York University

Bibliography

Ancient Sources

Cicero, *De oratore*.

Modern Sources

Foucault, M. 1975. *Surveiller et punir: naissance de la prison*. Paris: Gallimard.

Hull, A., Bell Scott, P. and Smith, B. (eds) 1982. *All the Women are White, All the Blacks are Men, but Some of Us are Brave: Black Women's Studies*. Old Westbury: Feminist Press.

Marx, K. and Engels, F. 1976. *Selected Works. In Three Volumes. Volume One*. Moscow: Progress Publishers.

Nietzsche, F. 1901. *Der Wille zur Macht: Versuch einer Umwerthung aller Werthe*. Leipzig: C.G. Naumann.

Sengupta, S. 2019. Protesting climate change, young people take to streets in a global strike. *The New York Times*, September 20. https://www.nytimes.com/2019/09/20/climate/global-climate-strike.html [Last Accessed 30/10/2019].

1

Introduction: Posthuman Perspectives in Roman Archaeology

Lewis Webb and Irene Selsvold[1]

Nothing I beheld in that city seemed to me to be what it was, but all, I believed, had been transformed into another form by a fatal murmur: the rocks I encountered were hardened humans, the birds I heard were feathered humans, the trees that surrounded the *pomerium* were leafed humans, and the liquid in the fountains had flowed from human bodies. Soon the statues and images would start to move, the walls start to talk, the cows and other animals of that species begin to utter prophecies, and from the sky itself and the splendour of the sun would suddenly venture an oracle.

Nec fuit in illa civitate quod aspiciens id esse crederem quod esset, sed omnia prorsus ferali murmure in aliam effigiem translata, ut et lapides quos offenderem de homine duratos et aves quas audirem indidem plumatas et arbores quae pomerium ambirent similiter foliatas et fontanos latices de corporibus humanis fluxos crederem; iam statuas et imagines incessuras, parietes locuturos, boves et id genus pecua dicturas praesagium, de ipso vero caelo et iubaris orbe subito venturum oraculum (Apul. *Met.* 2.1).

The Roman author Apuleius' carnivalesque vision of the Thessalian city Hypata destabilises and blurs the boundaries between human and non-human beings, between the animate and the inanimate, questioning human ontology itself. Apuleius' vision prompts a question: what did it mean to be human among and with other living and non-living beings in the Roman world? The Romans were entangled in the divine, non-human animals, plants, material objects, and the wider environment: they were relational beings, as we are today. Such questions and entanglements propel this volume on posthuman perspectives in Roman archaeology. Fundamentally, posthumanism is concerned with the entanglement, interactions, and relations of beings. Or, to borrow an expression from the inimitable Donna Haraway, 'all the actors become who they are *in the dance of relating*' (Haraway 2008: 25; emphasis in original).

Gracing the cover of this volume is a material manifestation of such entangled interactions and relations: the so-called 'Great Artemis' (*Große Artemis*), a marble statue of the goddess Artemis from the Prytaneion in Ephesus dated to the Trajanic period. The 'Great Artemis' is crowned by a high *polos* depicting three temple façades with Ionic columns and a city gate flanked by two temple façades, winged sphinxes in the interstices of arches and columns and perhaps an altar flanked by crenellated ashlar walls, and winged griffins and torches. Her head is framed by a so-called nimbus with winged griffin protomes. Her neck and décolletage are adorned with diamonds, a pearl necklace with pendants, a heavy garland, a row of pine cones and button-shaped objects, and a row of berry-like clusters. On her midriff are three rows of egg-shaped objects whose identification is controversial (possibly bull testicles) and she bears a lion on each forearm. She wears a belt depicting bees, rosettes, and serpent-tailed sea creatures and a kind of apron inset with square panels depicting winged sphinxes, lion-griffins, *Rankenfrauen* (female deities whose torsos emerge from leaves or calyxes), does, bees, equines, lionesses, bulls, and rosettes (Steskal 2010: 205–206; *cf.* Fleischer 1973, 46–136; Steskal 2008). This statue of the Ephesian Artemis displays a mutually entangled assemblage of living beings (animals and plants), divine beings, mythical hybrid beings, and non-living beings (monuments and minerals): a vibrant microcosm of the Roman world. For us, the 'Great Artemis' and her entanglements are 'good to think with' in a volume on posthumanism and Roman archaeology. We will return to her throughout this introduction.

Our volume originated in a session held at the *Theoretical Roman Archaeology Conference* (TRAC) 2016

(La Sapienza, Rome) entitled *Beyond the Romans: What can Posthumanism do for Classical Studies?*, co-organised by Irene Selsvold and Linnea Åshede. The aim of the session was to explore the possibilities offered by posthuman theoretical perspectives for the development of Roman archaeology and Roman studies, both in relation to how we approach the Roman world and to our own positions as researchers. Our experience from the panel was that posthumanism offers valuable perspectives on Roman myth, art, and material culture, displacing and complicating notions of human exceptionalism and individualist subjectivity. We found these perspectives to be particularly relevant for Roman mythology and religion, with its emphasis on metamorphoses, hybrid creatures, and encounters between actors that are human, divine, monstrous, or a mix thereof. Roman religion is rife with animated landscapes and sacred groves, the oracular capacity of 'inanimate' objects and liquid boundaries between images of gods and the gods themselves. Our panel contributors engaged with themes as diverse as Priapic statues, Roman attitudes towards the Galli, posthuman emperors, and the agency of epigraphic funerary markers. In our volume, we take up a few of these and other case studies to a) explore the potential and utility of posthuman theoretical perspectives for Roman archaeology, to b) de-centre the human subject in Roman archaeology, and to c) think through the entanglement, interactions, and relations of humans with other living and non-living beings in the Roman world, as well as the ethical implications thereof.

In this introduction, we begin with an explanatory outline of posthumanism in order to provide a clear theoretical framework for our volume. We then map the state of scholarship on posthuman perspectives in archaeology and the study of the ancient world, the aims of the volume, and the outline of our chapters. As we will discuss, the use of posthuman perspectives in archaeology is well established but the use of these perspectives for the study of the ancient world has just begun. Our volume offers a new encounter between Roman archaeology and posthumanism.

TRAC has long been a leading forum for the exploration of new theoretical perspectives in Roman archaeology. The *TRAC Themes in Roman Archaeology* series offers a rich venue for such exploration and we are delighted to be its third entry. We would like to thank the former and current TRAC Standing Committee, particularly Katherine A. Crawford, Lisa Lodwick, Matthew Mandich, and Sarah Scoppie, as well as Thomas J. Derrick for their support and numerous efforts on our behalf. Especial thanks go to Linnea Åshede for her vital role in the inception and development of this project, to Sabine Ladstätter and the Austrian Archaeological Institute (ÖAI) for their provision of our cover image of the 'Great Artemis', and to Francesca Ferrando for generously agreeing to write our foreword.

Posthumanism

'Posthumanism' is an umbrella term applied to a multiplicity of theoretical perspectives that critique humanism, de-centre the human subject, reconsider the boundaries and relations among humans and the natural world, and frame the human as 'a non-fixed and mutable condition' (Ferrando 2013: 27; *cf.* Miah 2008; Nayar 2014: 15–22; Bolter 2016: 1). Such posthuman theoretical perspectives also consider the agency of 'non-humans', *e.g.*, living and non-living beings, landscapes, climate, and ideas, their entanglement, interactions, and relations with humans, and the situated nature of research. Fundamentally, these perspectives reject aspects of Western humanism, particularly anthropocentric, androcentric, and universalising assumptions, dualism, speciesism, transcendence, and the sovereign human subject (Miah 2008: 82–83; Ferrando 2012: 10–11; 2013: 29; Braidotti 2013: 56, 132; 2016: 23; Nayar 2014: 15–16, 19; Bolter 2016: 1). Many claim relational epistemologies and ontologies (sometimes termed 'flat ontologies') that are 'not anthropocentric and therefore not centred in Cartesian dualism' (Bolter 2016: 1), are grounded in a 'philosophical critique of the Western Humanist ideal of "Man" as the universal measure of all things' (Braidotti 2019a: 339), and focus on immanence (being within the world) (Ferrando 2012: 11; 2013: 29; Braidotti 2013: 56, 132; 2016: 23). Such epistemologies and ontologies are ostensibly divorced from human exceptionalism, the humanist assumption that 'the proper study of man is man' (Bolter 2016: 1), and the hierarchies that sustain 'the primacy of humans over non-human animals' and 'sexist, racist, classist, homophobic, and ethnocentric assumptions' (Ferrando 2013: 28). Posthuman theoretical perspectives are prominent in the humanities and social sciences, particularly in communication studies, cultural studies, feminist studies, literary criticism, philosophy, science and technology studies, and theoretical sociology (Ferrando 2013; Bolter 2016). A brief genealogy of posthumanism and an outline of these perspectives follow.

The terms 'posthuman' and 'posthumanism' were conceived by the postmodern theorist Ihab Hassan in his foundational article *Prometheus as Performer: Towards a Posthumanist Culture?* (1977). Using the titan Prometheus as an *exemplum*, Hassan challenged humanism and the human subject, and demanded a reconsideration of the relation of humans to and with other living and non-living beings. Drawing on antihumanist elements in Claude Lévi-Strauss' *A World on the Wane* (1961), Michel Foucault's *The Order of Things: An Archaeology of the Human Sciences* (1970), and other works, Hassan critiqued the humanist 'image of us, shaped as much by Descartes, say, as by Thomas More or Erasmus or Montaigne' and called for 'the annihilation of that hard Cartesian ego or consciousness, which distinguished itself from the world by turning the world into an object' (Hassan 1977: 845). He proposed a 're-vision of human destiny [...] in a vast evolutionary scheme' and charged posthuman philosophers with the task of addressing 'the complex issue of artificial intelligence' (Hassan 1977: 845). For Hassan, Prometheus was a kind of posthuman subject, a figure that went beyond humanist divisions and dichotomies such as 'the One and the Many, Cosmos and Culture, the Universal and the Concrete' and allowed for the entanglement of 'Imagination and Science, Myth and Technology, Earth and Sky', that is, he (Prometheus) was a fundamentally relational being who offered 'a key to posthumanism' (Hassan 1977: 838). Essentially, posthumanism began with an allusion to an entangled and relational being in Greek mythology. Hassan's critiques and core ideas laid the groundwork for the development of posthuman theoretical perspectives thereafter (Ferrando 2013: 26 n. 1; Bolter 2016: 1).

Beyond Hassan, posthuman scholars have been influenced by poststructuralist and postmodernist theorists, particularly Roland Barthes, Gilles Deleuze, Jacques Derrida, Michel Foucault, Félix Guattari, Fredric Jameson, Bruno Latour, Jean-François Lyotard, and Paul de Man (Wolfe 2010: xi–xxxiv, esp. xii, xv, xx; Ferrando 2013; Bolter 2016: 2–4), whose theories critiqued and subverted, *inter alia*, 'the [modernist] assumptions of universally applicable aesthetics and universally valid epistemology', structuralist analyses of 'language, literature, and culture', 'master narratives', and the perceived 'totalising practices and rhetorics of the modern era' (Bolter 2016: 2). The antihumanism of Michel Foucault has particularly influenced posthuman scholars, as his 'deconstruction of the notion of the human' and the 'death of Man' inform many posthuman enquiries (Ferrando 2013: 31–32). However, posthumanism is not antihumanism per se, as humans, human concerns, and human rights are not excluded from posthuman enquiries (Ferrando 2012: 20; Braidotti 2013: 23). Such poststructuralist and postmodernist critiques and subversions inform posthuman theoretical perspectives.

Prominent theoretical perspectives often identified as posthuman are 'critical posthumanism' (posthuman critical theory), 'cultural posthumanism', and 'philosophical posthumanism' (posthuman enquiries emerging from the fields of literary criticism, cultural studies, and philosophy), 'transhumanism' (the study of human enhancement through science and technology), and 'new materialisms' (the study of matter and materialisation in the field of feminist studies) (Ferrando 2013; *cf.* slightly different classifications in Braidotti 2013: 38; Nayar 2014: 15–22). Critical posthumanism, cultural posthumanism, philosophical posthumanism, and new materialisms are characterised by post-anthropocentric, post-dualistic, post-exclusivist, and relational epistemologies and ontologies (Ferrando 2013: 27, 30; Braidotti 2016: 13, 23–27). In general, these perspectives are also characterised by relational ethics, that is, ethics that value 'cross-species, transversal alliances with the productive and immanent force of [...] non-human life' (Braidotti 2016: 23) and ones that aim 'at enacting sustainable modes of relation with multiple human and nonhuman others that enhances one's ability to renew and expand the boundaries of what transversal and non-unitary subjects can become' (Braidotti 2016: 26; *cf.* MacCormack 2012). In other words, human relations with others, and the ethical implications thereof, lie at the heart of these posthuman perspectives. New materialist perspectives have a particular focus on developing research methodologies 'for the non-dualistic study of the world' and challenging the perceived reductivism of dualisms such as 'matter-meaning, body-mind and nature-culture' (Van der Tuin 2019: 277–279; *cf.* Ferrando 2013: 30–31). These perspectives developed in response to a perceived inattention to matter and materiality in 'the linguistic turn, the semiotic turn, the interpretative turn, [and] the cultural turn' (Barad 2003: 801), that is, 'the representationalist and constructivist radicalisations of late postmodernity, which somehow lost track of the material realm' (Ferrando 2013: 30). For new materialists, there is no division between 'language and matter', for 'biology is culturally mediated as much as culture is materialistically constructed' and matter is 'an ongoing process of materialisation' (Ferrando 2013: 31; *cf.* Barad 2003; Coole and Frost 2010; Van der Tuin 2019). While these four overlapping perspectives emerged from different fields and have different genealogies and foci, they share the same impetus to 'understand what has been omitted from an anthropocentric worldview' (Miah 2008: 72; *cf.* Ferrando 2013: 32). By contrast, transhumanism is a kind of 'ultra-humanism' that narrowly focuses on human enhancement and is characterised by a distinctly anthropocentric epistemology, what Cary Wolfe has termed 'an *intensification* of humanism' (Wolfe 2010: xv; emphasis in original). As such, some posthuman scholars argue that transhumanism should not be considered a form of posthumanism (Wolfe 2010: xv; Ferrando 2012: 11; 2013: 27–28; Nayar 2014: 16–18). We concur with Wolfe's claim that 'posthumanism is the *opposite* of transhumanism' (Wolfe 2010: xv; emphasis in original) and, as such, will not focus on transhuman perspectives in this volume. Prominent scholars of posthumanism and new materialisms whose theories have influenced this volume include Stacy Alaimo, Karen Barad, Jane Bennett, Rosi Braidotti, Diana Coole, Francesca Ferrando, Samantha Frost, Elizabeth Grosz, Donna Haraway, Susan Hekman, Patricia MacCormack, Pramod Nayar, and Cary Wolfe (*e.g.* Haraway 1991; 2003; 2008; Grosz 1994; 2017; Barad 2003; 2007; 2010; Wolfe 2003; 2010; Alaimo and Hekman 2008; Bennett 2010; Coole and Frost 2010; Ferrando 2012; 2013; 2016; MacCormack 2012; Braidotti 2013; 2016; 2019a; 2019b; Nayar 2014).

Francesca Ferrando provides an outline of the type of posthuman theoretical perspectives we use in this volume:

> Posthumanism, which should not be confused with Transhumanism, criticises anthropocentric humanism and opens its inquiry to non-human life: from animals to artificial intelligence, from aliens to other forms of hypothetical entities related to the physics notion of a multiverse. In so doing, it articulates the conditions for posthuman epistemology concerned with non-human experience as site of knowledge. [...] The posthuman refusal of the ontological primacy of human existence invites a review of practices such as uncritical omnivorism, overharvesting, and the unrestricted consumption of nonrenewable resources. Posthumanism reflects on the terms of human sustainability, but it does not dismiss the significance of human survival: in not rejecting human or individual rights, Posthumanism differs from Antihumanism. [...] Posthumanism offers a revisitation of the being as transcendent immanence, disrupting one of the founding splits of Western thought, the one between transcendence and immanence, which symbolically relates to every other traditional dualism, such as: the mind/body, subject/object, self/other, male/female, human/animal-alien-robot. [...] Posthumanism questions biocentrism and the concept of life itself, blurring the boundaries between the animate and the inanimate (Ferrando 2012: 10–11).

Posthumanism's post-anthropocentric, post-dualistic, post-exclusivist, and relational epistemologies, ontologies, and ethics open up new lines of enquiry for Roman archaeologists. By de-centring the human subject and affirming a relational ontology and ethics, new, entangled and interacting posthuman subjects emerge. A posthuman subject is a non-unitary (non-singular) subject that exists in relation to and with other living and non-living beings: it is what Rosi Braidotti terms a 'transversal entity, fully immersed in and immanent to a network of nonhuman (animal, vegetable, viral, technological) relations' (Braidotti 2016: 26). Such a non-unitary subject has 'an enlarged sense of inter-connection between self and others, including the non-human or "earth" others' (Braidotti 2013: 49). Posthuman subjects offer new ways of thinking about the Roman world. For example, if we turn a posthuman lens on Apuleius' Thessalian Hypata and the 'Great Artemis' statue, we can interpret these as posthuman subjects, for they are entanglements of relations and beings. The first is a city teeming with hybrid living and non-living beings, all in relation to and with each other. The second is a material assemblage of living and non-living beings, itself the product of living beings and technologies and, at the same time, a divine being materialised, whose material manifestation was part of religious life and relations for numerous living beings in Ephesus. By re-envisioning the Roman world through a posthuman lens, new research questions and results emerge, as the contributors in this volume will demonstrate.

We have not adopted a singular posthuman theoretical perspective for our volume. Instead, our contributors explicitly or implicitly draw on various strands of posthuman thought. Relational epistemologies, ontologies, and ethics, new materialisms, and the agency of non-human beings are prominent throughout their contributions.

Mapping Posthuman Scholarship

Roman archaeology is a node in the disciplinary meshwork that entangles archaeology with the study of the ancient world. This section maps the impact of posthuman theoretical perspectives in archaeology and in the study of the ancient world.

Posthuman theoretical perspectives have been embraced by archaeologists for some time. With labels such as 'symmetrical archaeology', 'entanglement theory', 'new materialisms', and 'multispecies archaeology', these theoretical approaches have not necessarily been explicitly referred to as posthuman in archaeological discourse. Yet, these theoretical directions have concentrated on radicalising the way we-as-archaeologists think about the relationships between humans and things, between humans and other species, and between things and other things, thus firmly situating them under the posthuman umbrella (Marshall and Alberti 2014; *cf.* Harris and Cipolla 2017: 134). The core posthuman objectives of challenging Cartesian dualisms and de-centring the human subject have been particularly influential in archaeology, and have provoked archaeologists to think about ways to discard common dichotomies within the discipline such as *nature/culture*, *male/female*, *body/mind*, *immaterial/material*, *humans/non-humans*, and *humanities/science* (Harris and Cipolla 2017: 31–32; *cf.* Olsen *et al.* 2012; Fredengren 2013; Conneller 2014). In the following, we briefly expand upon three main directions of archaeological thought in which posthumanist ideas have gained influence, namely symmetrical archaeology, new materialisms, and multispecies archaeology, before moving on to posthuman perspectives in the study of the ancient world.

In the archaeological discourse of the last decade or so, material agency and the relationships between humans and the material world have been in focus. A reaction to a longstanding anthropocentric attitude to artefacts (Olsen *et al.* 2012: 7–12), one central tenet of this 'material turn' was that things have agency: they affect humans and relationships among humans (see McKie and Parker 2017: 4–5). Within this framework, material agency can be attributed to objects or objects intended to act in certain ways according to human intent (*e.g.* Gell 1998), or as primary actors acting independently of human influence (*e.g.* Knappett and Malafouris 2008). The material turn was, therefore, an important step away from the human-as-subject/thing-as-object dichotomy that juxtaposed humans as autonomous actors and material things as inert (Robb 2010: 504–505). 'Symmetrical archaeology' and 'new materialisms' are both concerned with de-centring the human subject in human-thing relationships. Both directions emphasise that 'things and materials bring things to the table that go beyond what humans think, know, or understand about them' (Harris and Cipolla 2017: 146). As such, they can be understood as expansions and/or continuations of the material turn. Yet they both go further in de-centring the human subject.

'Symmetrical archaeology' is inspired by Bruno Latour (1993; 2005), particularly his critique of Cartesian dualism and his Actor-Network Theory (ANT). According to Latour (2005: 76) symmetry in ANT is not about *imposing symmetry*, but about *not imposing asymmetry* where humans act intentionally (as subjects) and the material world causally reacts (as objects). In symmetrical archaeology (*e.g.* Shanks 2007; Olsen *et al.* 2012) and the adjacent 'entanglement theory' (*cf.* Hodder 2012) humans are envisioned as but parts of larger networks with non-human material and immaterial actors that perform actions together. Important in symmetrical archaeology is the acknowledgement that things and non-humans exist, act, and affect one another apart from their relationships with humans, and that they do so whether or not they affect human life (Olsen *et al.* 2012: 11–14). Symmetrical archaeology is not exclusively relational, as things are recognised as capable of acting on others 'because of their own inherent properties': 'symmetry implies that qualities and relations are on the same footing; that we should treat them symmetrically' (Olsen *et al.* 2012: 13). Ian Hodder's 'entanglement theory' bears some similarities to symmetrical archaeology in its recognition of non-human lives, but it insists on the separation of humans and non-humans and does not go as far as symmetrical archaeology in removing dualisms (Hodder 2012: 94; *cf.* Harris and Cipolla 2017: 148). Instead, Hodder focuses on the entanglement of humans and things in what he terms a dialectic of dependence (enabling) and dependency (constraining) (Hodder 2012: 88–89).

As we have seen, 'new materialisms' are a 'return to matter'. The new materialist perspectives of, *inter alia*, Karen Barad (2003; 2007), Gilles Deleuze and Félix Guattari (1980), and Manuel DeLanda (2006) transform archaeology into a 'discipline of things', allowing archaeologists to delve even deeper into the role of material things in our understanding of the past (Harris and Cipolla 2017: 138). These perspectives offer new ways of thinking through the properties of materials and matter, their ontology, how they change and develop, and how they *become* together with others (Harris and Cipolla 2017: 141–143; *cf.* Conneller 2004; 2014; Ingold 2007; Fowler 2013; Marshall and Alberti 2014; Harris 2018). The properties of things emerge through relationships with the world around them. These set of relations are termed 'meshworks' by Tim Ingold (2007) and 'assemblages' by Gilles Deleuze (Harris and Cipolla 2017: 138–139). These assemblages are not only assemblages of *things* (such as ceramic assemblages, coin assemblages, etc.), but also assemblages of materials, ideas, beliefs, and beings (such as burial practices). A pot, for example, is an assemblage of the minerals and water that makes up the clay, the temper and heat, the potter, her ideas of what the pot should look like and do, and her ability to execute those ideas (Harris and Cipolla 2017: 139). Thinking of material things symmetrically, in terms of networks, assemblages, or meshworks, then, allows us to move away from thinking about material things solely as static things depending on humans and outcomes of human ideas, and demonstrating that humans are but part of these meshworks.

Akin to symmetrical archaeology and new materialisms, 'multispecies archaeology' challenges human exceptionalism and the mode of human relationships with non-human living beings such as animals and plants in the past. Just like material things, plants and animals have mutual relationships with other animals, and with humans, where they have agency, affect other beings and are affected thereby (Ingold 2000). Donna Haraway (1991; 2003; 2008) is an obvious influence, with her exhortation to think about and treat animals as companions rather than 'others' to dominate. Plants and animals have been integrated into archaeology in zooarchaeology and palaeobotany, but they are usually studied as traces of human activity, as subsistence, prey, and as human-domesticated species. Assemblage thinking and multispecies ethics challenge archaeologists to approach non-human species on a more equal footing, from multispecism in human bodies (Fredengren 2013), to animals as companion species in the past (Armstrong Oma 2013; 2016), to rethinking of agriculturalisation (Harris and Cipolla 2017: 168–169), to the Anthropocene.

This brief mapping has only skimmed the surface of recent posthuman publications in archaeology. Despite this surge of scholarship, posthuman perspectives have not yet influenced Roman archaeology significantly and there were, until now, no volumes on the subject. One notable exception to this scholarly silence is Astrid Van Oyen, whose work has demonstrated the great potential that relational epistemologies and ontologies have for the study of Roman pottery (Van Oyen 2015; 2016a; 2016b; Van Oyen and Pitts 2017). Yet, the vibrancy of the ancient world invites the scholar to posthuman enquiry, and posthuman perspectives have lately started to make an impact in other subdisciplines in the study of the ancient world. *Posthumanism and the Bible*, edited by Jennifer L. Koosed (2014), explored posthuman hybridities, relationships, and human-animal interactions in a Biblical context. Beate Pongratz-Leisten, Karen Sonik, and their contributors examined material aspects of divinity in *The Materiality of Divine Agency* and the relational aspects of materiality from a new materialist perspective (Pongratz-Leisten and Sonik 2015; Pongratz-Leisten 2015). Their volume focused on the ancient Near East and briefly dipped into Ancient Greece but did not engage with the Roman world. In her *Desiring Hermaphrodites: The Relationships of Hermaphroditus in Roman Group Scenes*, Linnea Åshede (2015) drew on the posthuman perspectives of Donna Haraway and Karen Barad to challenge the scholarly consensus about Hermaphroditus. Mario Telò, Melissa Mueller, and their contributors in *The Materialities of Greek Tragedy* applied new materialist perspectives to the study of objects and affect in Aeschylus, Sophocles and Euripides (Telò and Mueller 2018). Giulia Maria Chesi, Francesca Spiegel, and the contributors in *Classical Literature and Posthumanism* explored themes such as robots and cyborgs, the monstrous, human-animal relationships, heterogeneity, and machines (Chesi and Spiegel 2019a). Rather than focusing on the utility of posthumanism for examining ancient literature, Chesi and Spiegel and their contributors focused on what such literature could do for posthumanism (Chesi and Spiegel 2019b). In their *Antiquities beyond Humanism*, Emanuela Bianchi, Sara Brill, Brooke Holmes, and their contributors drew on posthuman perspectives to examine ancient literature, focusing mainly on ancient philosophy (Bianchi *et al.* 2019a). More work has been done in adjacent fields such as environmental humanities and the study of animals and their experiences in Antiquity (Campbell 2014; Fögen and Thomas 2017) with which posthuman enquiries often overlap (*e.g.* Schliephake 2017). The recent influx of posthuman publications in archaeology and in the study of the ancient world indicates that there is a rich body of evidence and great potential available for further posthuman enquiries in these fields. We propose that this potential extends to Roman archaeology itself. Our volume takes up these findings and perspectives and ventures into the Roman world.

Aims of the Volume

Our volume's primary aim is to explore the potential and utility of posthuman theoretical perspectives for Roman archaeology. In so doing, we intend to integrate Roman archaeology into wider scholarly and public debates on the entanglements and relations of humans with and to non-humans. Archaeologists have closely engaged with posthuman perspectives for some time, but these perspectives are relatively new in the study of the ancient world and absent in Roman archaeology. Oliver Harris and Craig Cipolla have demonstrated how symmetrical, new materialist, and multispecies theoretical perspectives allow archaeologists to overcome longstanding dualisms and preconceptions in archaeology, focus on new subjects, ask new research questions, produce new knowledge, and place 'science' and 'theory' on a level playing field (Harris and Cipolla 2017: esp. 130–131, 193–198). These perspectives are either explicitly posthuman (new materialism) or implicitly posthuman (symmetrical and multispecies archaeology). If they are fruitful perspectives for other archaeologists, might they not be also for Roman archaeologists? The TRAC conferences and publications are leading fora for the promotion of encounters between Roman archaeology and new disciplines and theoretical perspectives. We envision our volume within this tradition: an initial theoretical encounter, a beginning, and a provocation.

Our secondary aims are to de-centre the human subject in Roman archaeology – but not to eliminate it – and to think through the entanglement, interactions, and relations of humans with other living and non-living beings in the Roman world, as well as the ethical implications thereof. Similar themes and impetuses are prominent in the aforementioned posthuman scholarship and, to some degree, in the study of non-human animals, the environment, and the human impact thereon in the ancient world (*e.g.* Hughes 1996; 2003; 2014; Kalof 2011; Thommen 2012; Campbell 2014; Shelton 2014; Erdkamp *et al.* 2015; Fögen and Thomas 2017), but the posthuman framing is typically absent from these latter studies. Moreover, these latter studies are often in 'subfields of ancient philosophy and science' and are thus not well integrated into broader scholarly discourse (Bianchi *et al.* 2019b: 11). Notably, in their *Antiquities beyond Humanism*, Emanuela Bianchi, Sara Brill, and Brooke Holmes articulate similar aims, namely to examine 'the relations among the human and the animal, the divine and daemonic realms', 'take seriously the relationships between the human and the non-human worlds together with forms of non-human sociality', and 'expand beyond the animal and the divine to encompass, too, material objects, plants, and the cosmos as a whole' (Bianchi *et al.* 2019b: 11). While the contributions in their volume focus on ancient literature, their impetus is the same as our own.

In pursuit of these aims, our contributors examine a wide range of diverse themes, including the posthuman performances of the Roman emperors Caligula and Nero (Carlà-Uhink), the agency and relationality of Roman epigraphic funerary markers (Mihajlović), the ritual function and agency of votive figurines in Umbria (Zapelloni Pavia), the materiality of divine agency in the city of Rome (Iara), hybrid chicken-human coins (Feider, Hambleton, and Maltby), plant agency in the Roman world (Lodwick), the agency and nature of water in Roman urban infrastructure (Ingate), and the Romans and the Anthropocene (Selsvold and Webb). In all these contributions, the human subject is entangled with other non-human subjects (Carlà-Uhink, Selsvold and Webb) and/or de-centred (Mihajlović, Zapelloni Pavia, Iara, Feider, Hambleton, and Maltby, Lodwick, Ingate). Each contributor aims to explore a well-examined theme in Roman archaeology (emperors, epigraphic funerary markers, votives, divine objects, coins, plants, urban water infrastructure, and environmental impact) from novel, posthuman perspectives. We elaborate on their contributions below.

With this volume we hope to open up new, posthuman lines of enquiry in Roman archaeology and to show how entangled, interacting, and relational living and non-living beings were in the Roman world. Ultimately, we stress that humans and non-humans are entangled and imbricated in larger systems: we are all posthuman.

Outline of Chapters

The chapters in this volume engage with a diverse array of themes and are authored by archaeologists and ancient historians from a variety of disciplinary backgrounds. This diversity reflects our desire to illustrate the numerous possibilities that posthumanism offers Roman archaeology. While a reader may dip into a chapter as they please, we intend the chapters to relate and speak to each other: 'the whole is something beyond its parts' (ἔστι τι τὸ ὅλον παρὰ τὰ μόρια, Arist. *Metaph.* 1045a).

The chapters are arranged so that they progressively de-centre and move away from the human subject: they arc from posthuman emperors to the Anthropocene. Between these lie epigraphic funerary markers, votives, divine objects, chicken-human coins, plants, and water. Thematically they move from human beings engaged in posthuman performances (emperors) to artificial non-human beings/objects (epigraphic funerary markers, votives, divine objects, coins) to natural non-human living beings (plants) to non-living beings and environments (water, the Anthropocene). The chapters are bookended by our introduction and a concluding commentary by Oliver Harris.

Filippo Carlà-Uhink takes up the posthuman theoretical perspectives of Rosi Braidotti, Karen Barad, and others to examine several 'more-than-human' performances attributed to the Roman emperors Caligula and Nero in which they aimed at crossing or challenging boundaries of gender, nature, divinity, and animality in the Roman world. For example, textual and material evidence suggests Caligula accepted divine honours, appeared in public while impersonating male and female deities, commissioned (or others commissioned) statues, portraits, and coins with theomorphic representations of himself, terraformed environments, and aimed at elevating his horse Incitatus to the consulship and transforming prisoners into animals. Similarly, reputedly Nero (or others) commissioned statues, portraits, and coins with theomorphic representations (including the famous Colossus of Nero), terraformed environments and built artificial ones in Rome itself, performed on stage as female heroes and deities, aimed at transforming his male lover Sporus into a woman via castration, became a bride for his wedding with his freedman Pythagorus, perhaps aimed at transforming himself into an animal, and covered condemned human prisoners with animal fur to transform them into animals. Carlà-Uhink argues that these emperors made (ultimately unsuccessful) performative claims to a more-than-human nature: they were posthuman performers.

Vladimir Mihajlović draws on the ANT of Bruno Latour and posthuman theoretical perspectives of Karen Barad and others to explore the agency and relationality of epigraphic funerary markers (EFMs) in the Roman world. He argues that EFMs were more than just material means for personal and familial commemoration, display, or communication: they were also integral mediators and participants in the transformation of a living human being into a distributed deceased entity, in the constitution of a posthuman afterlife entity, and in the building of social relationships and realities. In other words, EFMs were vital beings within the ontological assemblage of deceased-ness. He illustrates such an assemblage with the example of a funeral mosaic from Salona for the deceased boy T. Aurelius Aurelianus, wherein Aurelianus' deceased-ness is constituted by an assemblage of intra-active elements (a depiction as pupil, a partridge, a herm, a grave, and a tombstone with biographical information), and which itself would have been part of an assemblage of, *inter alia*, the grave, immediate surroundings, and architectural features. Drawing on various other examples of present or absent EFMs in the Roman world, he argues that EFMs (along with other mediators of funerary assemblages) enabled and constituted the (perceived) ontological transition of living human beings into afterlife entities and that their absence disabled such a transition. EFMs articulated and determined the deceased and their relationalities: they were posthuman, relational beings.

Arianna Zapelloni Pavia uses the ANT of Bruno Latour, entanglement theory of Ian Hodder, and other theoretical perspectives to think through the ritual function and agency of votive figurines from Grotta Bella in Umbria. She argues that the Grotta Bella votive figurines – themselves artificial non-human beings/objects in the form of humans (anthropomorphic votives), non-human animals (zoomorphic votives), or human body parts (anatomical votives) – could represent parts or the whole of 'dividual' human beings. Such entangled objects were dedicated to deities: they were important material mediators between the human and the divine and vital to their interaction. Moreover, she suggests that the form and materiality of these votive figurines could have exerted an influence on the worshippers who deposited and observed them and the rituals of well-being they all collectively comprised. She argues that whatever their initial, intended function, these votive figurines could themselves have shaped human religious traditions and assumed alternative functions once they became enmeshed in social relationships involving themselves, humans, and deities. By moving beyond human exceptionalism, she reveals the agency of objects and some of the relationships among humans and non-humans in the Roman world.

Kristine Iara explores the materiality of divine agency in the city of Rome, that is, the agency of divine objects. She argues that there were many anthropomorphic and non-anthropomorphic objects that could 'presence' the divine in Rome, not simply anthropomorphic statues. Any object could be a suitable material means to presence the divine and facilitate religious communication and interactions between humans and deities. Indeed, as she demonstrates, numerous forms of media could be 'divine things' in the city of Rome, including temples and other architectural objects, aniconic and zoomorphic objects, and divine symbols and utensils. The boundaries between these objects, humans, and the divine were fluid and relational. Essentially, she proposes that we cease overvaluing anthropomorphic objects (*e.g.* statues) in the study of Roman religion and acknowledge the vitality and importance of non-anthropomorphic objects, that is, avoid anthropocentrism and move towards a richer, post-anthropocentric appreciation of divine things and their entanglements.

Mike Feider, Ellen Hambleton, and Mark Maltby unpack the posthuman implications of a series of *c.* first-century BC bronze coins from Belgic Gaul and south-east Britain that depict an unusual hybrid of a chicken with a human face on its stomach. They argue that these coins – the first to depict chickens in these regions – offer valuable insight into the entanglements of humans and non-humans in Gaul and Britain during a period of great social and political transition engendered by the Romans. Taking up the theoretical approaches of Alfred Gell on object agency and of Kristin Armstrong Oma on human-animal relations, the authors consider the various ways in which the numismatic hybrid chicken-human could have communicated and (re)produced meanings for communities in Belgic Gaul and Britain, including early chicken-human relations in the region and other solar, sonic, martial, religious, heroic, and ethnic meanings in an increasingly Roman world. These coins testify to the significant impact chickens had on Gallic and British human communities: chickens affected humans and humans commemorated them in bronze.

Drawing on the post-anthropocentrism present in posthuman theoretical perspectives, Lisa Lodwick evaluates the agency of plants in the Roman world. Her focus is on the effects of the 'weeds' (alien species) *Agrostemma githago* (corncockle) and *Atropa belladonna* (deadly nightshade) on human experiences in the province of Roman Britain, namely the changing human-weed relationships in a period of climatic amelioration and rapid urbanisation. She argues that the introduction of corncockle had significant effects on humans and other animals in Britain: it is a rapidly-growing, self-fertilising plant that is poisonous to humans and other animals, co-evolves with, grows with, and suppresses crops, and requires intensive human labour to detect and remove it from fields or during grain processing. Corncockle proliferated throughout Roman Britain, took advantage of the grain exchange by human beings, grew beyond human control, negatively affected human and non-human animal health, and forced human beings to engage in extra labour to avoid these negative effects. While corncockle took advantage of arable environments, deadly nightshade flourished in urban ones: it too is poisonous and capable of significantly harming humans and some non-human animals. Moreover, its distinctive appearance would have affected the multisensory experience of humans in towns and cities Roman Britain. Both corncockle and deadly nightshade communicated with other living beings through their toxicity and could have significant, negative impacts on human and non-human animals. Both expressed a kind of 'planty' agency in the Roman world.

Jay Ingate considers the agency of water in relation to urban water infrastructure (aqueducts, bathhouses, sewer systems, etc.) in the Roman world, particularly the waterscape of Roman Lincoln in Britain. By de-centring the human subject and avoiding human exceptionalism, he sheds light on the agency and complexity of water and its numerous influences on and relations with human and non-human beings in the Roman world. He argues that, for the Romans, 'waterscapes' had a significance beyond their roles in urban water infrastructure: water was entangled with deities and divine agency (*e.g.*, Tiberinus, Venus Cloacina, Oceanus), war, and burial practices, was considered sacred, and impacted the formation of urban spaces in Rome and beyond. For example, in the Lincoln area, the waterscape was a prominent and vital agent in the pre-Roman, Roman, and post-Roman periods: human beings depended on this waterscape for functional and religious reasons, interacted and negotiated with it, were influenced by it, and built their communities around it. He argues that water in the Roman world was not marginalised or subservient to human beings: instead, human beings were entangled with and dependent on the agency of water. Such a reinterpretation of water prompts us to think through our own contemporary relations with water and the environmental challenges we face.

Irene Selsvold and Lewis Webb take up the critical posthumanism of Rosi Braidotti to explore the intersections among the Anthropocene, the Romans, and posthumanism. They investigate a series of anthropogenic processes in the Roman period to situate the Romans within the Anthropocene and to demonstrate the need for posthuman perspectives in Roman archaeology. Their focus is on three case studies: Roman mining, human exploitation of non-human animal populations, and agricultural expansion. They argue that the Romans produced substantial changes in landscapes and ecosystems in the Mediterranean and beyond through these three anthropogenic processes. For example, Roman mining had a major impact on landscapes and living beings, as it led to deforestations, soil and air toxicity, terraformed landscapes, and atmospheric pollution. The exploitation of animals in animal spectacles led to declines in animal populations, possible local extinctions, and major cascade effects on ecosystems. Moreover, agricultural expansion had a major impact on ecosystems and environments, including modification of landscapes and declines in animal populations. Building on these findings, they argue the anthropogenic processes that contributed to the age of the Anthropocene can be found in the Roman period and that the Romans were significant contributors in its development. For these contributors, the age of the Anthropocene and its implications provoke new ways of thinking about Roman archaeology, about who and what Roman archaeologists study in the past, and how they go about it. They suggest that the relational ethics and ontology of Rosi Braidotti's critical posthumanism provides Roman archaeologists with a critical apparatus for facing the Anthropocene, for it encourages them to consider and value the entanglement of humans and living and non-living others in the Roman period, pose new questions of the past, produce new forms of knowledge, and move towards a post-anthropocentric worldview.

In his concluding commentary, Oliver Harris draws together the findings of our contributors and offers some reflections on the potential and utility of posthuman theoretical perspectives for Roman archaeology and beyond.

We return to the 'Great Artemis': herself a material assemblage of beings all entangled and interacting in Haraway's '*dance of relating*'. Artemis' manifold form invites, nay, commands us to consider the numerous possibilities posthumanism offers Roman archaeology and to ponder the posthuman nature of the Roman world.

Department of Historical Studies,
University of Gothenburg

Note

1. Irene Selsvold and Lewis Webb are equal co-editors and co-authors in this volume.

Bibliography

Ancient Sources

Apuleius, *Metamorphoses*.
Aristotle, *Metaphysica*.
(All translations by L. Webb)

Modern Sources

Alaimo, S. and Hekman, S. 2008. *Material Feminisms*. Bloomington/Indianapolis: Indiana University Press.

Armstrong Oma, K. 2013. Bronze Age horses: beyond dualist explanations. In S. Bergerbrandt and S. Sabatini (eds) *Counterpoint: Essays in Archaeology and Heritage Studies in Honour of Professor Kristian Kristiansen*. BAR International Series 2508. Oxford: Archaeopress: 141–146.

Armstrong Oma, K. 2016. Sheep, dog and man: multispecies becomings leading to new ways of living in Early Bronze Age longhouses on Jæren, Norway. In L.H. Dommasnes, A.T. Hommedal and D. Gütschmidl (eds) *The Farm as Social Arena*. Kornwestheim: Waxmann: 23–52.

Åshede, L. 2015. *Desiring Hermaphrodites: The Relationships of Hermaphroditus in Roman Group Scenes*. PhD Thesis. University of Gothenburg.

Barad, K. 2003. Posthumanist performativity: toward an understanding of how matter comes to matter. *Signs: Journal of Women in Culture and Society* 28 (3): 801–831.

Barad, K. 2007. *Meeting the Universe Halfway: Quantum Physics and the Entanglement of Matter and Meaning*. Durham/London: Duke University Press.

Barad, K. 2010. Quantum entanglements and hauntological relations of inheritance: dis/continuities, spacetime enfoldings, and justice-to-come. *Derrida Today* 3 (2): 240–268.

Bennett, J. 2010. *Vibrant Matter. A Political Ecology of Things*. Durham/London: Duke University Press.

Bianchi, E., Brill, S. and Holmes, B. 2019a. *Antiquities Beyond Humanism*. Oxford: Oxford University Press.

Bianchi, E., Brill, S. and Holmes, B. 2019b. Introduction. In E. Bianchi, S. Brill and B. Holmes (eds) *Antiquities Beyond Humanism*. Oxford: Oxford University Press: 1–30.

Bolter, J. 2016. Posthumanism. In K. Jensen, R. Craig, J. Pooley and E. Rothenbuhler (eds) *The International Encyclopedia of Communication Theory and Philosophy*. Chichester: John Wiley & Sons: 1–8.

Braidotti, R. 2013. *The Posthuman*. Cambridge: Polity Press.

Braidotti, R. 2016. Posthuman critical theory. In D. Banjeri and M.R. Paranjape (eds) *Critical Posthumanism and Planetary Futures*. New Delhi: Springer: 13–32.

Braidotti, R. 2019a. Posthuman critical theory. In R. Braidotti and M. Hlavajova (eds) *Posthuman Glossary*. London: Bloomsbury: 339–342.

Braidotti, R. 2019b. A theoretical framework for the critical posthumanities. *Theory, Culture & Society (Special Issue: Transversal Posthumanities)* 36 (6): 31–61.

Campbell, G.L. (ed.) 2014. *The Oxford Handbook of Animals in Classical Thought and Life*. Oxford: Oxford University Press.

Chesi, G.M. and Spiegel, F. (eds) 2019a. *Classical Literature and Posthumanism*. London: Bloomsbury.

Chesi, G.M. and Spiegel, F. 2019b. Theoretical introduction: the subject of the human. In G.M. Chesi and F. Spiegel (eds) *Classical Literature and Posthumanism*. London: Bloomsbury.

Conneller, C. 2004. Becoming deer: corporeal transformations at Star Carr. *Archaeological Dialogues* 11: 37–56.

Conneller, C. 2014. *An Archaeology of Materials: Substantial Transformations in Early Prehistoric Europe*. London: Routledge.

Coole, D. and Frost, S. 2010. Introducing the new materialisms. In D. Coole and S. Frost (eds) *New Materialisms. Ontology, Agency, and Politics*. Durham/London: Duke University Press: 1–43.

DeLanda, M. 2006. *A New Philosophy of Society: Assemblage Theory and Social Complexity*. London: Continuum.

Deleuze, G. and Guattari, F. 1980. *Mille plateaux*. Paris: Éditions de minuit.

Erdkamp, P., Verboven, K. and Zuiderhoek, A. (eds) 2015. *Ownership and Exploitation of Land and Natural Resources in the Roman World*. Oxford: Oxford University Press.

Ferrando, F. 2012. Towards a posthumanist methodology: a statement. *Frame Journal for Literary Studies* 25 (1): 9–18.

Ferrando, F. 2013. Posthumanism, transhumanism, antihumanism, metahumanism, and new materialisms: differences and relations. *Existenz* 8 (2): 26–32.

Ferrando, F. 2016. The party of the Anthropocene: post-humanism, environmentalism and the post-anthropocentric paradigm shift. *Relations* 4 (2): 159–173.

Fleischer, R. 1973. *Artemis von Ephesos und verwandte Kultstatuen aus Anatolien und Syrien*. Leiden: Brill.

Fögen, T. and Thomas, E. (eds) 2017. *Interactions between Animals and Humans in Graeco-Roman Antiquity*. Boston/Berlin: Walter de Gruyter.

Foucault, M. 1970. *The Order of Things: An Archaeology of the Human Sciences*. New York: Pantheon Books.

Fowler, C. 2013. *The Emergent Past: A Relationalist Realist Archaeology of Early Bronze Age Mortuary Practices*. Oxford: Oxford University Press.

Fredengren, C. 2013. Posthumanism, the transcorporeal and biomolecular archaeology. *Current Swedish Archaeology* 21: 53–71.

Gell, A. 1998. *Art and Agency: A New Anthropological Theory*. Oxford: Clarendon Press.

Grosz, E. 1994. *Volatile Bodies. Toward a Corporeal Feminism*. Bloomington/Indianapolis: Indiana University Press.

Grosz, E. 2017. *The Incorporeal. Ontology, Ethics, and the Limits of Materialism*. New York: Columbia University Press.

Haraway, D. 1991. *Simians, Cyborgs and Women. The Re-Invention of Nature*. London: Free Associated Press.

Haraway, D. 2003. *The Companion Species Manifesto: Dogs, People, and Significant Otherness*. Chicago: University of Chicago Press.

Haraway, D. 2008. *When Species Meet*. Minneapolis: University of Minnesota Press.

Harris, O.J.T. 2018. More than representation: multiscalar assemblages and the Deleuzian challenge to archaeology. *History of Human Sciences* 31 (3): 83–104.

Harris, O.J.T. and Cipolla, C.N. 2017. *Archaeological Theory in the New Millennium: Introducing Current Perspectives*. Abingdon/New York: Routledge.

Hassan, I. 1977. Prometheus as performer: towards a posthumanist culture? *The Georgia Review* 31 (4): 830–850.

Hodder, I. 2012. *Entangled. An Archaeology of the Relationships between Humans and Things*. Chichester: Wiley–Blackwell.

Hughes, J. 1996. *Pan's Travail: Environmental Problems of the Ancient Greeks and Romans*. Baltimore: Johns Hopkins University Press.

Hughes, J. 2003. Europe as consumer of exotic biodiversity: Greek and Roman times. *Landscape Research* 28 (1): 22–31.

Hughes, J. 2014. *Environmental Problems of the Greeks and Romans: Ecology in the Ancient Mediterranean*. Baltimore: Johns Hopkins University Press.

Ingold, T. 2000. *The Perception of the Environment: Essay in Livelihood, Dwelling, and Skill*. London: Routledge.

Ingold, T. 2007. Materials against materiality. *Archaeological Dialogues* 14 (1): 1–16.

Kalof, L. (ed.) 2011. *A Cultural History of Animals in Antiquity*. Oxford: Berg.

Knappett, C. and Malafouris, L. (eds) 2008. *Material Agency: Towards a Non-Anthropocentric Approach*. New York: Springer.

Koosed, J. 2014. *The Bible and Posthumanism*. Atlanta: Society of Biblical Literature.

Latour, B. 1993. *We Have Never Been Modern*. Cambridge, MA: Harvard University Press.

Latour, B. 2005. *Reassembling the Social: An Introduction to Actor-Network-Theory*. Oxford: Oxford University Press.

Lévi-Strauss, C. 1961. *A World on the Wane*. London: Hutchinson.

MacCormack, P. 2012. *Posthuman Ethics. Embodiment and Cultural Theory*. Farnham: Ashgate.

Marshall, Y. and Alberti, B. 2014. Karen Barad, ontology and archaeological bodies. *Cambridge Archaeological Journal* 24 (1): 19–36.

McKie, S. and Parker, A. 2017. Introduction: materials, approaches, substances, and objects. In A. Parker and S. McKie (eds) *Material Approaches to Roman Magic: Occult Objects and Supernatural Substances*. Oxford/Philadelphia: Oxbow Books: 1–8.

Miah, A. 2008. A critical history of posthumanism. In B. Gordijn and R. Chadwick (eds) *Medical Enhancement and Posthumanity*. Berlin: Springer: 71–94.

Nayar, P. 2014. *Posthumanism*. Cambridge: Polity Press.

Olsen, B., Shanks, M., Webmoor, T. and Witmore, C. 2012. *Archaeology: The Discipline of Things*. Berkeley: University of California Press.

Pongratz-Leisten, B. 2015. Imperial allegories: divine agency and monstrous bodies in Mesopotamia's body description texts. In B. Pongratz-Leisten and K. Sonik (eds) *The Materiality of Divine Agency*. Boston/Berlin: Walter de Gruyter: 119–141.

Pongratz-Leisten, B. and Sonik, K. (eds) 2015. *The Materiality of Divine Agency*. Boston/Berlin: Walter de Gruyter.

Robb, J. 2010. Beyond agency. *World Archaeology* 42 (2): 493–520.

Schliephake, C. (ed.) 2017. *Ecocriticism, Ecology, and the Cultures of Antiquity*. Lanham: Lexington Books.

Shanks, M. 2007. Digital media, agile design, and the politics of archaeological authorship. In T. Clack and M. Brittain (eds) *Archaeology and the Media*. Walnut Creek: Left Coast Press: 273–289.

Shelton, J.-A. 2014. Spectacles of animal abuse. In G. Campbell (ed.) *The Oxford Handbook of Animals in Classical Thought and Life*. Oxford: Oxford University Press: 461–477.

Steskal, M. 2008. Rituelle Bestattungen im Prytaneion von Ephesos? Zu den Fundumständen der Artemis Ephesia-Statuen. *Jahreshefte des Österreichischen Archäologischen Institutes* 77: 363–373.

Steskal, M. 2010. *Das Prytaneion in Ephesos*. Wien: Verlag der Österreichischen Akademie der Wissenschaften.

Telò, M. and Mueller, M. (eds) 2018. *The Materialities of Greek Tragedy: Objects and Affect in Aeschylus, Sophocles, and Euripides*. London: Bloomsbury.

Thommen, L. 2012. *An Environmental History of Ancient Greece and Rome*. Cambridge: Cambridge University Press.

Van der Tuin, I. 2019. Neo/new materialism. In R. Braidotti and M. Hlavajova (eds) *Posthuman Glossary*. London: Bloomsbury: 277–279.

Van Oyen, A. 2015. Actor-Network Theory's take on archaeological types: becoming, material agency, and historical explanation. *Cambridge Archaeological Journal* 25: 63–78.

Van Oyen, A. 2016a. Historicising material agency: from relations to relational constellations. *Journal of Archaeological Method and Theory* 23: 354–378.

Van Oyen, A. 2016b. Networks or work-nets? Actor-Network Theory and multiple social topologies in the production of Roman *terra sigillata*. In T. Brughmans, A. Collar and F. Coward (eds) *The Connected Past: Challenges to Network Studies in Archaeology and History*. Oxford: Oxford University Press: 35–58.

Van Oyen, A. and Pitts, N. (eds) 2017. *Materialising Roman Histories: Beyond Instrumentalism and Representation*. Oxford: Oxbow Books.

Wolfe, C. 2003. *Animal Rites. American Culture, The Discourse of Species, and Posthumanist Theory*. Chicago: University of Chicago Press.

Wolfe, C. 2010. *What is Posthumanism?* Minneapolis: University of Minnesota Press.

2

Posthuman Ambitions in the Roman Principate: The Cases of Caligula and Nero

Filippo Carlà-Uhink

Introduction

It is well-known that a series of Roman emperors were represented in ancient sources – and thus transmitted to posterity – as 'in-human', both in the sense of 'cruel', 'lacking mercy', and in the more literal sense of 'not worthy of or not conforming to the needs of human beings' (after Merriam-Webster 2019): through different anecdotes, authors such as Suetonius or Tacitus painted them as mad, uncontrollable, violent, and abusive tyrants. This – for instance in the case of Caligula – even concluded in scholarly attempts to 'diagnose' possible physical or psychological illnesses of the emperor from this information (*e.g.* Benediktson 1989; for a summary of some of these studies and their results, see Massaro and Montgomery 1978; Barrett 1989: 73, 214–217; Ronning 2011: 254–257). Scholarship has highlighted for quite a long time now that such representations cannot be taken at face value and that our sources are extremely biased, mostly controlled by the senatorial aristocracy. Thanks to Aloys Winterling's work in particular, Caligula, for example, is now recognised beyond the cruelty and madness attributed to him by the sources and summarised in Ludwig Quidde's concept of the *Cäsarenwahnsinn* (Winterling 2009; 2011; for a history of historiography on Caligula, see Yavetz 1996: 105–118; Ronning 2011: 254–262; on the image of Caligula in ancient sources, see also Schrömbges 1988; more generally, see Witschel 2006: 94–96). In the case of Nero, questions about the reliability of the stories about him were already being raised by Denis Diderot in the eighteenth century. The genesis and development of the image of the monster – rooted in the ancient tradition and transmitted to the following centuries – has now been thoroughly investigated (see Lefebvre 2017: 12–13 for a history of Neronian historiography).

Starting from the current state of research and from the idea that both the (much less extant) praise and the criticism of emperors such as Nero revolved around the idea of the transgression of boundaries, and interpreting such transgression from opposite perspectives (Cordes 2017: 1–5), this chapter aims to apply some aspects of posthuman theory. Following an investigation of the genesis of a series of anecdotes about 'mad emperors', this chapter will demonstrate that some, or even many, of them, should not be dismissed as pure slander and inventions to portray the protagonists in such negative way, but they can refer to actual performances. These had been developed to demonstrate the 'posthuman' divine nature of the ruling figures, to show that they were not bound by human norms and had thus been developed as crucial aspects of a 'positive' image-building of the emperors. Subsequently, these positive characterisations rebounded on the rulers when the public – or rather those members, who transmitted their opinions in the works we still can read – did not accept such authority to trespass and ended up in classifying these behaviours, therefore, as 'inhuman', as it will be more clearly shown below (Carlà-Uhink 2017b: 11–12).

Posthumanism, Crossing, and Performance

'The human is a normative convention, which does not make it inherently negative, just highly regulatory and hence instrumental to practices of exclusion and discrimination. The human norm stands for normality, normalcy and normativity' (Braidotti 2013: 26). This means that the 'human' is culturally constructed and always shifting; such an assumption is positioned within the intellectual tradition inaugurated by Michel Foucault and the *nouvelle histoire*: 'in our appeal to "historical specificity" we conceal the political valency of twentieth century's assault on a universalist conception of man' (Leonard 2005: 37). All this implies automatically also a – typically posthuman – rejection of the idea of a neat and defined boundary between 'nature' and 'culture', in favour of the idea of a 'nature-culture continuum' (Braidotti 2013: 2; see Derrida 2008: 35–36).

Defining the human consists thus of a process of territorialisation: in tracing a series of boundaries, which normatively delimit what is socially considered common to the human race and therefore acceptable to it. By defining these boundaries as 'human', they are reified and defined as 'natural', while anything that moves beyond them is discursively constructed as 'non-human', be it 'inhuman' or 'superhuman' (see also Baudrillard 1976: 137–138). As such, it is not and cannot be within human reach; as the human is, to this effect, 'regulatory', these boundaries are severely patrolled. Moving beyond such boundaries of the human is discursively presented, therefore, as a violation of the so-constructed rules, which brings upon whoever tries to breach them (or believes s/he has breached them) discrimination and stigma. This stigma can change broadly in its specific forms, according to the special characteristics of the boundary which has been violated: the trespasser can, for example, be presented as involved in self-humiliation, as 'bestialised' or 'monstrified', and/or they can be accused of hubris.

To be more precise, this applies to people who are perceived as having attempted to trespass the boundaries of the human; the situation is different for those who are indeed recognised as having already trespassed them (clear examples of both successful and unsuccessful performances of this sort are known for the Galli, the priests of Cybele, see Carlà-Uhink 2017a: 16–18). All boundaries are drawn exactly because without them, trespassing would be the norm. Every boundary can always be crossed in any direction. 'Crossing', a concept I adapt to provide a definition for this kind of performance and the consequent reaction of the public, deriving it from sociolinguistics (see Carlà-Uhink 2017b, and more generally Dresen and Freitag 2017 for a systematic explanation of this concept, its origins in sociolinguistics, and its application to other fields), is thus an action which requires a public to be meaningful. The boundary of the human can be trespassed, therefore, when someone acts in discourse and/or in performance in ways which are perceived by the specific public of that performance to be outside what they understand as such boundary, and this behaviour is recognised as legitimate by their public. Thus, breaking such normative definitions can either lead to stigma, discrimination, and exclusion or it can lead to the perception of the trespasser as 'non-human' or 'posthuman' in the sense of 'superhuman', if the trespasser is in a position to lead the public towards accepting their crossing. As Jacques Derrida famously stated in a seminar, which developed a clear and strong criticism of Cartesian humanism, the 'sovereign' and the 'animal' are unified in an 'ontologic-sexual attraction, a mutual fascination, a communitarian attachment, even a narcissistic resemblance', mostly through one aspect: their being positioned outside the law (Derrida 2008: 37–39, 59–60).

This thought was not extraneous to Classical Antiquity: Plato said that the demagogic politician could only be killed by his enemies, or become a tyrant, or become a wolf (Pl. *Rep.* 8.566a). Aristotle based his famous definition of the human as a political being on the assumption that living *apolis* characterises the animal and the god (Arist. *Pol.* 1253a; see Derrida 2008: 49–50), and he established with his statement the 'entire philosophical tradition of thinking the difference between human and nonhuman in terms of the human's ability to properly "respond" to its world rather than merely "react" to it, an ability made possible (so the story goes) by language' (Wolfe 2010: 63). Thus, he established the humanistic tradition and the human-animal divide, which posthuman theories try to overcome.

Everyone who claims a special divine nature, or a special contact with the divine sphere can, therefore, support this claim with performances that violate the boundaries of what is perceived as natural (*e.g.* through wonders) and the boundaries of what is perceived as human (as these figures are not bound by the rules and limits, which are characteristic of the human, they defy, for example, death). These are all acts of crossing, which are successful in front of a public accepting the authority of the actor to trespass; for those who do not recognise this authority, the trespasser is either a fraud and/or someone who abdicates human normativity and self-qualifies thus as 'non-human', but in the sense of 'inhuman' or 'less-than-human' – be it mad, beastly, or 'barbarian' (on the exclusion of other cultures from the norm of the 'human', see Braidotti 2013: 28). While this may sound weird to modern sensibility, it did much less so in an ancient world, in which the natural and the supernatural world were not as distinct as they are for us: 'posthuman' creatures and humans shared space and time, in spite of their otherness – including plants and animals, daemons, heroes, and gods (Lane Fox 1986: 84–146).

On this basis, I will show in the following that many anecdotes connected to 'mad' emperors can be explained as performances violating the boundaries of the human, which were not accepted by at least a part of the public; members of the latter group explained them thus as products of a 'deviated human' (*e.g.* due to mental illness) or even of a completely 'sub-human' nature. As proposed by Caroline Vout, the emperor's 'public displays of office could be turned on their head so that what was destined to spell distinction could – in the writing of a reign – make an emperor sub-human' (Vout 2009: 261). Posthuman theory facilitates locating the beyond-the-human in a non-hierarchical way, *i.e.* not structured into a super- and an infra-human. The posthuman understanding of performativity, in particular, allows us to understand better that the boundaries of the human are constructed and reinforced, but also destabilised, through the materiality of the acting body (Barad 2003: 807–808). Crossing the boundary of the human is the performative act. The 'interpretation' and the discourse around such performance (both also 'boundary-making practices', see Barad 2003: 820–821) as a movement up or down (and in the latter case as ridiculous or as monstrous, *ridiculum* or *tremendum*; see Cordes 2017: 309–315) are a matter of reception through the public and of discursive presentation. Therefore, if the act of crossing is not accepted and narrativised, it can be presented as a sign of terrifying craziness, or – as the violation of expectation generates ridicule – as a laughing stock (see Plass 1988: 90, see also 103: 'what they saw as mad disorder might in part have been an indispensable aspect of a different, but quite reasonable order which they disapproved'). Yet both reactions reveal at the basis a 'subversive' reading of imperial performance which aims at locating the emperor outside the sphere of the human.

In the Roman world, such forms of performance – and different reactions to them – can already be identified in Julius Caesar's actions. 'Caesar was a bounder: a person who operated on, and broke, the boundaries of his world' (Pelling 2006: 255). In his case, this becomes visible especially in two areas. The first is his disrespect of gender boundaries (see Carlà-Uhink 2017a: 20–21): 'Caesar may have manipulated habits of sexualised invective to create a new role for himself in Roman society'; thus he 'emerges as a radically individual figure', who 'had moved outside familiar social hierarchies altogether' (Hawkins 2017: 134–135). The second area, in which he was followed by many emperors (see *e.g.* Cordes 2017: 189–203), is the manipulation of nature, revealing a 'supernatural' power: in Caesar's case, the project of cutting the Isthmus of Corinth (Gerster 1884: 227 already realised that this project was connected in Antiquity with a claim of a superhuman nature) and the planned diversion of the Tiber (Plut. *Vit. Caes.* 58.8–10). Such claims by leading political figures are, quite obviously, strongly connected to monarchical stances and ideologies. Therefore, they could result in substantial tensions and conflicts of interpretation during the Roman Principate. As demonstrated by Winterling (2011: 16), the Principate was a complex communicative structure, in which a monarchy pretended not to be one. Senators had to act as if they retained a power they had lost; and the emperor had to exert his power as if he did not have it.

Due to limited space, in the following, I will concentrate on the two most prototypical examples of emperors represented as mad villains: Caligula and Nero – two emperors compared and considered similar already in the ancient tradition (*e.g.* Plin. *HN* 7.45, 36.111; Paus. 9.27.3–4; Dio 61.5.1; Eutr. 7.14.1; see Lefebvre 2017: 211–218). They are not just case studies: as members of the Julio-Claudian family, they acted within a context in which imperial power, as constructed by Augustus, was not completely institutionalised yet, and in which the forms of representation and performance of the emperor had yet to be clearly and completely negotiated. Both of them, I will argue, claimed a bigger-than-human nature, performing it in acts, which were perceived by the senatorial aristocracy not as a legitimate crossing but, on the very contrary, as desperate acts of a sub-normal, subhuman, and definitely less-than-imperial psyche, thus leading to the construction of the still very popular images of these two rulers as mad monsters.

As we have seen, ambitions to a superhuman status, their contestation, and their representation as actual manifestations of a sub-human status were nothing new when, in AD 37, Caligula became emperor. Tiberius had received his powers while Augustus was still alive; at his death, the situation was much less clear, and Caligula was the first to become emperor with a decree that established his role as an office. He thus had to find new ways of redefining and renegotiating his position *vis-à-vis* Roman institutions. Even if this now appears as an almost institutionalised conundrum of the Principate, it is therefore no surprise that an emperor decided to appropriate forms of self-representation, which – based on the centuries-long tradition of the Hellenistic monarchies – broke the communication strategy established by Augustus and displayed the nature of his monarchic power (Gradel 2002: 140–141). While the people of Rome – and even more of the provinces – did not necessarily object to explicit monarchic traits (and are recorded supporting Caligula and Nero: Suet. *Calig.* 13; *Ner.* 57.1; Dio 61.5.2), the senatorial aristocracy in particular – and especially in Rome – to which belonged most of the relevant authors, was keen on dismissing any imperial performance of power, which would – in the form and not only *de facto* – prove that *imperium* had become an autocracy.

Caligula

Breaking the gender boundaries and intervening on nature and landscape – as mentioned above for Caesar – appear also in Caligula's 'more-than-human' performances, accompanied by two additional aspects: challenging the boundaries between human and divine and those between human and animal. In general, Caligula demonstrates a consistent and varied set of performances which move far beyond the idea that the emperor might be above any rule, norm, or law binding the rest of society and aim to display his ability to break the boundaries perceived as natural (see, *e.g.* Joseph. *AJ* 19.202; or Caligula's answer to his grandmother Antonia in Suet. *Calig.* 29.1: 'remember that I have the right to do anything to anybody,' '*memento,*' [...] '*omnia mihi et in omnis licere*', see Plass 1988: 131).

The Human and the Divine

Caligula was the first Roman emperor to accept (and request) divine honours in Rome – something offered to his predecessors, who turned these honours down in an aim to display modesty and comply with senatorial tradition (and probably also because of the connection between divinisation and death since Caesar's murder: see Gradel 2002: 143–144). Caligula changed his attitude regarding divinisation quickly;

and while this did not result in direct divinisation and a cult, which would have been contrary to contemporary practice (*e.g.* Joseph. *AJ* 18.7.256; Dio 59.4.4; see Balsdon 1934: 157–173; Simpson 1981; Barrett 1989: 140–153; Gradel 2002: 140–159), it implies at least that 'it was his endeavour to resemble a god' (Yavetz 1996: 125–127; see Witschel 2006: 99–100). Caligula performed his claim of divine nature throughout his reign in different actions and forms of performances: from talking to the Moon (Dio 59.27.6), to lingering among the statues of the gods – and thus in their company – to his identification with *Jupiter Latiaris* and the way in which he posed his daughter on Minerva's lap, asking the goddess to raise her (or, following another tradition, on Jupiter's lap, claiming that the daughter had two fathers). According to Vout, aspects of Caligula's sexual life reflected this claim, or to be more precise, the 'serialisation of the emperor's private life is emphatically used to equate him and his treatment to a god' (Vout 2007: 5). Some of Suetonius' anecdotes relating to the emperor's insomnia and his night visions as well as his communication with the 'spirit of the Ocean' (Suet. *Calig.* 50.3) could also be a misinterpretation, which casts as imperial craziness a form of self-representation that aimed to reveal the superhuman nature of the emperor, who – in contrast to mortals – did not need sleep and could use the night to contact his divine peers.

Even the decision to build a house on the Capitol implies – considering the specific meaning of this area in Roman topography – an ambition to be recognised as an equal, neighbour, and colleague, but also as a rival and challenger of Jupiter (Sen. *De Ira* 1.20.8; Joseph. *AJ* 19.4; Suet. *Calig.* 22, 25.4, 33; Dio 59.26.5, 59.28.1–8). The rivalry with the god (highlighted, *e.g.* by Simpson 1981: 494–501) does not automatically exclude an identification with him; the emperor could be at different times one and the same with the god, his colleague and peer, his rival, etc. The perspective of this assimilation-shadowing-opposition to Jupiter should also be adopted when analysing the practice of sacrificing eagles to Caligula (Simpson 1996: 64–65). Nonetheless, the portraits known to us are rather conventional and do not display particularly evident divine characteristics (except for the 'Caligula and Roma' cameo in Vienna, showing Caligula as Jupiter (Fig. 2.1); cameos, however, had already demonstrated less restraint in such form of representation since Augustus, as clearly revealed by the *Gemma Augustea*). Coins, which adorned the emperor with a solar radiate crown only in near Eastern provincial mints, lacked such divine characteristics. As highlighted by Dietrich Boschung, yet, the 'most disturbing' statues were probably destroyed after Caligula's death, and some known representations of the emperor do hint at unconventional representations, in heroic nudity, colossal dimensions, or with the head turned in ecstatic contemplation, following the model of Alexander the Great (Boschung 1989: 102–103; Varner 2017: 76–78).

Figure 2.1: Caligula and Roma Cameo, Vienna, Kunsthistorisches Museum, Antikensammlung IXa, 59 (Courtesy of KHM-Museumsverband).

According to our sources, Caligula also wanted a statue representing him as Jupiter to be displayed in the Temple of Jerusalem (Philo *Leg.* 29.188; Joseph. *AJ* 18.261; *BJ* 2.10.1–8; Tac. *Hist.* 5.9); here is not the place to enter into the problematic discussion about this project and Caligula's relations with Judaism (see Balsdon 1934: 135–140; Bilde 1978; Simpson 1981: 492–494; Barrett 1989: 188–191; Wilkinson 2005: 53–61, is the only one to think that the story is made up, partially derived by rumours, partially invented by Philo); more important is to highlight its consistency with other anecdotes about the materialisation of the emperor as god in cult places: according to Philo, statues of Caligula were placed in many synagogues (Philo *Leg.* 20.134–135). In general, it is reported that Caligula wanted the heads of many statues of the gods to be replaced with his own. This belongs to the acts demonstrating his divine nature: by claiming for himself theomorphic representations: Caligula blurred, for his own persona, the boundary between the human and the divine.

As divine beings are both understandable in human terms (anthropomorphic, with human passions, etc.) and beyond human understanding at the same time, their appearance can indeed be perfectly human when under the human gaze and at the same time completely escape the human gaze (Squire 2011: 161–162). This not only allowed statues of the emperor to assume a theomorphic value but made it possible for the emperor to perform as a god, or as a living representation of divinity. It is indeed recorded that Caligula impersonated different deities in public, including Jupiter, Neptune, Mercury, Apollo, Bacchus, and Hercules (Philo *Leg.* 11.78–80, 13.93–97; Suet. *Calig.* 52.1; Ath. 4.148d; Dio 59.26.6–10). Roman generals of the Republic used to wear Jupiter's clothes and identified with Jupiter, but only during their triumph, and dressing up as gods had been a typical form of Hellenistic royal performances. It cannot, therefore, be dismissed as 'an exaggerated display of that love for exotic clothing and fancy dress which induced him to appear frequently in silk and in triumphal dress' (Balsdon 1934: 169). While it is true that such dressing up was 'an expression of status' (Gradel 2002: 146–149), it is important to expand rather than diminish this statement. Dio stresses that Caligula wanted to 'look like' the gods (*dokein*, Dio 59.26.6–7), he thus implicitly postulates that it was a mimicry, while Caligula firmly remained within the boundaries of his humanity. Closing the paragraph, the historian explicitly writes that 'the attire, now, that I have described was what he [*i.e.* Caligula] would assume whenever he pretended to be a god' (Dio 59.26.10). Dio's disdain and refusal (shared by his peers and by his sources) to accept Caligula's performance as an act of crossing (as explained above) – even at the distance of so many generations – becomes sarcastically burning when the historian relates the emperor's death in AD 41: 'Gaius [...] learned by actual experience that he was not a god' (Dio 59.30.1). Nor is it surprising that such claims to divinity were specifically highlighted by Jewish authors (Gradel 2002: 146).

The co-presence and at the same time absolute alterity of the divine and the human is the precondition for this form of 'posthuman' performance and ambition. Thus, statues and performances were a sign of the visibility of Caligula's divine nature, his anthropomorphism and presence within human society; yet, at the same time, they displayed his being beyond the possibilities of human understanding, for instance in the case of statues that show him switching figures, parts of the body and identity with different gods. While some contemporaries, even some senators, seem to have accepted Caligula's crossing (Gradel 2002: 155–156), Suetonius rejects the basic postulate that the emperor is not a human, but enjoys divine nature. From his point of view, Caligula is not expressing divine faculties, but laying claim to divine majesty (*divina maiestatem asserere*, Suet. *Calig.* 22.2); as the 'nature' of the person involved is not at stake, but just the externality of the honours attributed to them, Caligula commits hubris by wanting honours which do not belong to him.

As Winterling has shown, at least from AD 39, Caligula generally rejected the forms of communication, which had been established by Augustus, explicitly and directly, unveiling the contradictions of the relationship between emperor and Senate and the structural 'insincerity' of the senators in their way of handling the *princeps* (Winterling 2011: 94–96). This means that many of his actions and initiatives can be understood in the sense of bringing those contradictions to the fore and letting them explode, while solving the 'contradictory connection of Republic and monarchy' clearly through a shift towards monarchy (Winterling 2011: 96), and thus constructing – also in Rome – a new form of political communication, which was inspired by models and examples of Hellenistic kingship (*e.g.* wearing the costumes of the gods). Paul Plass states that 'in fusing religion with politics the emperor as a living representative of divinity was always perilously close to caricaturing and parodying himself' (Plass 1988: 71). This is somehow true; yet it must be highlighted that parody and caricature came from those, who did not recognise the divine role of the emperor and had thus to denigrate it, in a refusal to accept the emperor's act of 'crossing'.

Dio stresses the 'Roman' anxiety stemming from Caligula's friendship with the Hellenistic kings Agrippa I and Antiochus IX, who were considered 'tyrant-trainers' (*tyrannodidaskaloi*, Dio 59.24.1) – *i.e.* conveyers of Hellenistic forms of monarchical performance and political communication (on Caligula's friendship with Agrippa and Antiochus: Joseph. *AJ* 18.143–169; Suet. *Calig.* 16.3; Dio 59.8.2; see Barrett 1989: 36–37; Winterling 2011: 119–120). It is not a coincidence that Caligula had Alexander the Great's breastplate removed from the tomb of the latter. Caligula used to wear it, thus clearly displaying the political tradition in which he included himself (Suet. *Calig.* 52.1). Nor is it a coincidence when Philo records that Caligula's 'crossing' was particularly successful in Alexandria and Egypt. Although Philo pontificates against the atheism and the hypocrisy of the Alexandrians (Philo *Leg.* 25.162–165; see also 43.338 on Caligula's love for Alexandria), we can detect a greater adherence of the emperor's self-representation to the political language and to the performances of royal power known in Alexandria and Egypt. This does not require an Orientalist reading of the sources explaining Caligula's 'madness' as 'Oriental despotism' and arguing for a strong 'pharaonic Egyptian' influence on his style of government (for a summary of such interpretations, Barrett 1989: 219–221): beyond Orientalist stereotypes lingers the model of Hellenistic kingship (which was very well known in Rome), ready to be grasped by an emperor, who wanted to performatively demonstrate his absolute power. According to Suetonius, Caligula declared the Battle of Actium a ruinous day for Rome, thus not only re-establishing Antony's memory (Caligula was both Augustus' and Antony's great-grandson; Augustus' memory was celebrated since AD 39 on coins, through which Caligula reinforced his connection with the divine sphere by defining himself *divi Augusti pronepos*, *RIC* I², Gaius 39–54), but also praising his political plan and style (Suet. *Calig.* 23.1); according to Dio, 'he chose to pose as a descendant of Antony rather than of Augustus' (Dio 59.20.2 – even if Dio refers here to a plan to deprive the senators of their patrimony). His final plan to move the capital away from Rome, first to Antium and then to Alexandria (Suet. *Calig.* 49.2; see Winterling 2011: 156–160), matches his plans to recover Antony's 'political language'.

The explicit request and attribution of divine honours characterise the last part of Caligula's reign, during which he – after having unveiled the ambiguity and the structural feebleness of the Augustan Principate – moved towards the construction of an autocratic monarchy along the lines of a Hellenistic model. Surely, this is the moment when performances of a 'posthuman' kind become more frequent and increasingly ambitious. Caligula's movement towards autocracy was sped up by the conspiracies of AD 40, but elements of Hellenistic self-representation and the self-ascription of a divine nature had been present in the emperor's previous actions (as explicitly stated by Dio 59.26.5).

Control over Nature

The dynamics explained above also become visible in the performative acts meant to demonstrate the emperor's control over nature and his capacity to act upon and modify landscapes. The construction of a pontoon between Baiae and Pozzuoli in late May AD 40 must be read in this context, independent of a possible 'rivalry' with Xerxes, who bridged the Hellespont in 480 BC, as this was indeed not simply a bridge constructed of boats, but covered with earth to resemble a 'normal' land road (the *via Appia*, according to Suetonius), on which the emperor could ride up and down (Joseph. *AJ* 19.5–6; Suet. *Calig.* 19.1–2; Dio 59.17; see Balsdon 1934: 50–54, according to whom the bridge was built to impress Persian hostages; Barrett 1989: 211–212; Ronning 2011: 260–262). According to Dio's report, Caligula was wearing Alexander the Great's breastplate while crossing the bridge and celebrated the event as a military feat, stressing that the soldiers had been able to cross the sea on foot (Dio 59.17.3–7) – implicitly, thanks to his ability to shape the landscape. During the ensuing celebrations, Caligula wished 'to make the night day, as he had made the sea land' (Dio 59.17.9), revealing once again the reason for this complicated performance, which established the emperor's rule over nature: 'he built moles out into the deep and stormy sea, tunnelled rocks of hardest flint, built up plains to the height of mountains and razed mountains to the level of the plain' (*et iactae itaque moles infesto ac profundo mari et excisae rupes durissimi silicis et campi montibus aggere aequati et complanata fossuris montium iuga*, Suet. *Calig.* 37.3). As with Caesar before him, Caligula not only planned to cut the Isthmus of Corinth (Suet. *Calig.* 21.1; see Barrett 1989: 193–194; Winterling 2011: 85), but also to build a city in the mountains (Suet. *Calig.* 21.1) – again a sign of control over natural features. The construction of a giant boat, containing thermal baths, vineyards, and trees, can be ascribed to the same category of action, as the sign of a capacity to transform the sea into land (Suet. *Calig.* 37.2; see Winterling 2011: 74). This anecdote has been at least partially confirmed by the discovery of the ships of Nemi, one of which hosted an entire temple with marble columns and mosaic floors. These reports build upon and emerge parallel to a tradition of moralistic attacks against luxury that also portrayed luxurious buildings as a sign of living 'against nature' (Edwards 1993: 137–172); yet the stress is placed much more upon the god-like performance of the emperor re-shaping the terrain and mixing the distribution of land and water.

In this context should be read another episode from the life of Caligula, considered by ancient authors as a sign of his madness: when Caligula forced his soldiers to fill their helmets with shells on the coast of the English Channel (Suet. *Calig.* 46; Dio 59.25.2–3; only Bicknell 1968: 501–502, argues that the event took place on the coast of the North Sea in Lower Germany). According to John Balsdon, the reference to shells reflects either a mistake by Suetonius (and Caligula gave orders to collect *musculi*, 'a kind of sappers huts, which were used in siege works') or a punishment for the troops, who would have been thus humiliated (Balsdon 1934: 91–93; the second interpretation is also followed by Bicknell 1968: 505; Phillips 1970: 372–373). Further interpretations have been proposed, but without much success: thus, the theory that collecting these shells could have been part of military manoeuvres (Davis 1966, but see the confutation by Bicknell 1968: 499–504), or that Caligula ordered the gathering of captured British boats, but his words were later misinterpreted (Woods 2000).

Although Winterling agrees with the notion of a humiliation, he also establishes a connection with the episode in Baiae and adds that it might be read as a manifestation of imperial power beyond the traditional Roman system of signs. According to him, this was a 'triumph' outside of Rome and without the Senate (Winterling 2011: 112–113, 120–124). But a triumph over whom? It has been suggested that the gathering on the coast was part of a ceremony organised because Caligula had received the submission of the British prince Adminius (Barrett 1989: 135–138; Wilkinson 2005: 46–47). However, the assumption that a victory over Britain would automatically be understood as a victory over the Ocean by the Roman public cannot be evidenced through the existing sources. Only Bicknell identified this performance as connected to the control over nature, but assimilated it, in a strongly structuralist way, to 'the social interpretation of nature by primitive people' (Bicknell 1962: 73), adding that it was a ceremony aimed at impressing the Britons, who, in their Celtic mentality, personified the sea and considered it their ally and protector. And yet, the triumph – because as such it is indeed celebrated by Caligula – is exactly that: a triumph over the Ocean; the humiliation of the Senate is thus only a part of the story – and probably not even the most important one in this curious performance, which rather seems to aim at establishing the emperor as victorious over the seas and over nature, emphasised through the offering of the booty in the form of shells to the Capitol and the Palatine.

Gender Bending

A further area in which Caligula performatively breached the boundaries imposed onto the 'human' is the one of gender and gender roles. Suetonius highlights Caligula's clothes and shoes: 'in his clothing, his shoes, and the rest of his attire he did not follow the usage of his country and his fellow-citizens; not always even that of his sex; or in fact, that of an ordinary mortal' (*vestitu calciatuque et cetero habitu neque patrio neque civili, ac ne virili quidem ac denique humano semper usus est*, Suet. *Calig*. 52.1; see also Joseph. *AJ* 19.30; Dio 59.26.8; see Boschung 1989: 77–78). He subsequently lists different kinds of traditionally feminine shoes and clothes which Caligula used to wear. I have previously demonstrated that this must be understood as a performance aimed to demonstrate the superhuman, and indeed divine, nature of the emperor: gender boundaries are constitutive of the human and normative, while they can be overcome and broken by the gods, enacting one's own ability to switch between genders as a sign of faculties beyond the limits of the human or of a particular contact with the divine sphere (Carlà-Uhink 2017a; 2017b).

It becomes particularly evident that this is a special form of performance, when Caligula simultaneously breaches both the boundary between man and god and that between man and woman by appearing in front of his audience as a goddess, and more specifically as Juno, Minerva, and also Venus – the tutelary deity of the *gens Iulia* (Suet. *Calig*. 52.1; Dio 59.26.6–7). Caligula is not the first to perform in this way, and this is a further marker of a Hellenistic form of royal self-representation: Alexander the Great who, as we already highlighted, represented an important model and reference point for Caligula, is reported to have done the same regarding Artemis (Ath. 12.537e–f). Once again, such performances are acts of negotiation in front of a public. Thus, they can be either 'accepted', leading to the recognition of the superhuman nature of the performer, or 'rejected', leading therefore to their presentation as episodes of hubris, disrespect for the gods, or craziness – the form of interpretation which has been advanced by Suetonius (Carlà-Uhink 2017a: 20–21).

Humans and Animals

In his display of 'posthuman' faculties Caligula challenged a further boundary: the one between human and animal. He planned to make his horse, Incitatus, consul and this has generally been understood as a sign of craziness, as a further humiliation for the senatorial order, or as the enactment of the ultimate political faculty of the emperor: confer the consulship on any being he chooses (Suet. *Calig*. 55.3; Dio 59.14.5; see Barrett 1989: 45–46; Winterling 2011: 99–100. Plass 1988: 9 considers this a joke 'against the emperor or one by him' later taken seriously; this may be true but remains unprovable; a similar consideration may apply to almost all episodes of imperial history). All this misses one crucial point: through this action the emperor is also able to transform a horse into a human, a Roman citizen, and a consul. This aspect becomes even clearer if we consider that Incitatus should not only have become consul (and did indeed become a priest: Dio 59.28.6); the horse was regularly invited by the emperor for lunch, received – among other luxurious gifts – a house and slaves, and received guests invited in his name (Suet. *Calig*. 55.3; Dio 59.14.7). This is a performance of the emperor's capacity to 'humanise' at his pleasure an animal and, therefore, to act upon the boundary between human and animal in exactly the same way as upon the natural landscape, the boundary between human and divine and the boundaries between genders. This could also be applied in the other direction: according to Suetonius, Caligula forced prisoners into such small cages that they had to be on all fours like animals, thus being dehumanised (Suet. *Calig*. 27.3; see Curry 2014: 215, the meaning would be clear even if the anecdote was invented by Suetonius).

To this effect, we can share the opinion formulated by Hugo Willrich (1903: 461): Caligula's craziness was not craziness in a modern, medical sense, but a form of disrespect for the Roman tradition of power and of the will to impose the idea that the emperor had the power to move beyond the limits imposed on human beings – and, like the gods, act upon those boundaries also for other beings. Dio presents a Caligula angered with the Senate because the latter had not bestowed onto him 'divine honours' (Dio 59.25.5) – it does not matter whether this episode is true or not; it captures very well the spirit of Caligula's performances as claims to a superhuman nature, which is too reductive to simply consider as 'jokes', as suggested by Plass (1988: 82). Thus, Philo's judgement of Caligula appears much more precise than one could have thought: 'he no longer considered it worthy of him to abide within the bounds of human nature but overstepped them in his eagerness to be thought a god' (Philo *Leg*. 11.75). Even if Philo presents this as a sign of derangement, he attributes to Caligula an idea which, not by chance, would attract the attention of Rousseau and subsequently Derrida (2008: 32–34): kings are to people what humans are to animals, so that (so the emperor according to Philo), 'I who am in charge of the best of herds, mankind, must be considered to be different from them and not of human nature but to have a greater and diviner destiny' (Philo *Leg*. 11.76).

The Artist on the Throne

An analysis of the performative and discursive forms of self-representation of Nero shows that he, too, was crossing the boundary of the human, hoping for his subjects, meant as a public, to recognise his 'superhuman' authority, but failing to obtain such recognition among those groups which in the end shaped Roman cultural memory. Rolf Rilinger argues that, on the one side, Seneca constructed for Nero a theory of monarchic power based on the Hellenistic model, in which the emperor was situated between the human and the divine. On the other side, Nero found his own way to consolidate power through his artistic performances and his theatricality – a field in which he could dominate the public space (Rilinger 1996) and seek the acclamation of the masses (Maier 2008; *cf.* also Leigh 2017). Many forms of performance by Nero derived from the traditional celebrations of the winners of Greek and Hellenistic games (*e.g.* Suet. *Ner*. 25.1; on Nero's 'philhellenism' see Mratschek 2013: 46–47). Through such performances, which, as demonstrated by Edward Champlin, were often inspired by the model of the tyrant of Corinth Periander (but not exclusively, as Antony also played a crucial role: Champlin 2003a: 172–177), Nero aimed to appear as a 'man whose superior virtues and abilities absolved him from the moral constraints of society', *i.e.* someone not bound by the rules culturally enforced upon the human (Champlin 2003a: 107–111). Even outside the theatre, most actions by Nero can be interpreted as crossing performances, through which he tried to show his 'posthuman' nature in a way which Seneca probably disapproved, but which he contributed to formulate: 'we have a creative artist who was both a determined performer and the emperor of Rome. We should expect from his reign if not the triumph of art over life, then at least an assault on the boundary between the two' (Champlin 2003a: 83; see also Edwards 1994: 92–93; Curry 2014: 215).

Human and Divine

Nero was less explicit than Caligula in crossing the boundaries between human and divine (on Nero's 'divinity' in panegyrics and criticisms of the emperor, see Cordes 2017: 106–134). His respect for different deities is revealed in the sources. In an aim to criticise him, Suetonius must refer to specific cults, such as the one for Dea Syria and another one for an unnamed female deity (Suet. *Ner*. 56.1). Nero's dedication of his beard to Jupiter Capitolinus – after shaving it for the first time – and its enclosure in a golden sphere (Suet. *Ner*. 12.4; Dio 61.19.1) do not hint at any claim to a divine nature; nor does the (unrealised) proposal of dedicating a statue to Nero in the temple of Mars Ultor, which should have been as big as the god's (Tac. *Ann*. 13.8.1: it would not have been a cult statue, but see Varner 2017: 93 for its meaning); nor the proposal of building a temple to the deified Nero when he was still alive, presented in the Senate by Anicius Cerialis and rejected by Nero himself (Tac. *Ann*. 15.74.3; see Simpson 1996: 66–67). In the absence of any other sources, it is difficult to confirm or disprove whether Soranus was, among other things, accused of not sacrificing to the divine emperor's voice (Dio 62.26.3). Furthermore, it is here irrelevant that following his death Nero was worshipped by some (Champlin 2003a: 28–29). The idea that Nero – inspired by such comparisons – may have wanted to perform the twelve labours of Hercules on stage had he not died, as claimed by Suetonius (*Ner*. 53.1), could point to a development towards a stronger 'divine performance' as well as to a shift towards a bigger focus on Hercules (Champlin 2003a: 135–138). However, the statement is too generic to be able to draw any conclusions (and it is very unclear from where Suetonius received this piece of information).

Nonetheless, early portraits of Nero already represent him in theomorphic fashion, and he displays a radiate crown as early as a boyhood portrait (Varner 2017: 79). Since his accession to the throne, such theomorphic representations become dominant, not only on gems and cameos, but more generally in statues, and assimilate the young emperor to Jupiter (Varner 2017: 80–85; on the radiate crown, *cf.* La Rocca 2017: 196–200). Yet, in connection with his artistic interests, Nero linked himself mostly to the Sun and Apollo, who were part of a program of self-representation displaying him as the young reformer of the Empire, capable of beginning a new Golden Age (Sen. *Apocol*. 4.1–2, Suet. *Ner*. 53.1; see Bergmann 1998: 133–146; Witschel 2006: 102; Bergmann 2013: 340–346; Cordes 2017: 24–32; La Rocca 2017: 195–196; Varner 2017: 92–93). The link to Apollo also connected him to Augustus, for whom this god was of significance (Champlin 2003a: 140–144).

Even if these motifs appear right from the beginning of Nero's reign and even earlier (see Champlin 2003a: 112–116; 2003b, arguing for a start around AD 59; Varner 2017: 85–92, demonstrating that such motifs existed earlier), during later years, since AD 64, they become a central part of the forms of Neronian self-representation (Bergmann 1998: 214–230; Champlin 1998: 335–338; Bergmann 2013: 346–351). A colossal statue, first raised in the Domus Aurea, modified by Vespasian and later by Commodus, which gave the name to the Colosseum, represented him as the Sun god (Plin. *HN* 34.45; Suet. *Ner*. 31.1; see Hemsoll 1990: 29–31; Bergmann 1998: 190; 2013: 349–351; Mratschek 2013: 52; Cordes 2017: 71–75; La Rocca 2017: 200–201; Varner 2017: 95–96); an inscription from Acraiphia calls him a 'new Sun' shining upon the Greeks (*IG* VII 2713: see Witschel 2006: 112–113; Mratschek 2013: 48–50), and the Sun god represented in Rome on the so-called 'altar of Eumolpus' seems to have Nero's features (*CIL* VI 31033; see Bergmann 1998: 194–201; 2013: 351; Varner 2017: 98–100) (Fig. 2.2).

Tiridates – upon receiving from Nero the Armenian crown in AD 66 – is said to have addressed the emperor as his god, announced that he would worship him like Mithras and acclaimed him as his personal Moira and Tyche (Dio 63.4–6). On that occasion Nero presented himself as Apollo-Helios, using a huge display of light and gold, along

Figure 2.2: The 'altar of Eumolpus' (CIL VI 31033), Museo Archeologico di Firenze, Villa Corsini. (Courtesy of the Ministero per i Beni e le Attività Culturali – Polo Museale della Toscana – Firenze).

a depiction on the purple screens of himself riding a chariot surrounded by stars (Bergmann 1998: 181–185; Champlin 2003a: 221–229; Mratschek 2013: 52–53; La Rocca 2017: 201–202; Varner 2017: 97–98). Last but not least, since AD 64, coins represented the emperor with a radiate crown. While in the East Antony and Caligula had already been represented in this way, the Roman mint had previously used such iconography exclusively for Augustus – and only after his death, representing him as *divus*. Under Nero, such coins (*e.g.* Fig. 2.3) aimed to represent the emperor as both divine and assimilated to the solar deity (Bergmann 1998: 174–181; Varner 2017: 103–106), while further coins

Figure 2.3: RIC I², Nero, 215. Collection of the American Numismatic Society (Public Domain).

Figure 2.4: RIC I², Nero, 417. Collection of the American Numismatic Society (Public Domain).

showed him playing the lyre and thus assimilated him to Apollo (Bergmann 1998: 185–189; Varner 2017: 102–103) (Fig. 2.4).

When Nero established his famous Greek games at Rome, he called them *Neronia*. Miriam Griffin (1984: 119) notes that this is a breach in the tradition of naming such festivals after gods – but from Nero's perspective, this may well be the assertion of a self-ascribed divine nature. Among other things, Suetonius notices that Nero used to appear in public barefoot (Suet. *Ner*. 51.1). Except for a brief mention by Champlin (2003a: 170), who considers this a sign of the 'Saturnalian' attitude of the emperor, this has generally escaped scholarly attention. And yet, this could have been significant. As noted by Susan Curry (2014: 201–202), the last moments of the emperor's life – as told by Suetonius – consisted of a long series of quotations and reversals of other episodes of his reign. When Nero, desperate and destitute, runs away from Rome and retreats to the place, where he will commit suicide, he is barefoot (Suet. *Ner*. 48.1). Prior to this episode, appearing barefoot could have been a way for Nero to perform a form of heroic nudity, which would raise him to a more-than-human level – it has been generally assumed for the statue of Augustus of Prima Porta, for instance, that it represents the first emperor barefoot pointing at his heroic status. In this case, though, Suetonius would not accept the claim to heroism thus performed and presents Nero's barefootedness as a sign of sloppiness.

Terraforming

Nero provides us with good examples of claims to modify the landscape. In addition to the harbour in Antium (Suet. *Ner*. 9.1), which can be seen as a simple euergetic activity towards his place of birth, a channel was realised from Ostia to Rome, which surely had public utility, but is described by Suetonius as having the aim to let the sea reach the old city (*vetus urbs*, Suet. *Ner*. 16.1). This was followed by plans for a pool extending from Misenum to lake Avernus, to which the hot waters from Baiae should have been canalised and which was still called *stagnum Neronis* in Late Antiquity (Champlin 1998: 341), as well as for a channel from lake Avernus to Ostia (Suet. *Ner*. 31.3; Stat. *Silv*. 4.3.7–8; Plin. *HN* 14.61; see Griffin 1984: 107–108; Champlin 2003a: 158–159; Lefebvre 2017: 105–108). As Caesar and Caligula (and Periander) before him, Nero also planned to cut the Isthmus of Corinth; during his trip to Greece in AD 67, he even began the work himself (Suet. *Ner*. 19.2; Dio 63.16.1–2; see Gerster 1884: 229–231; Champlin 2003a: 137; Lefebvre 2017: 181–184). It will not come as a surprise that this – as a profound intervention aimed at changing 'nature' and thus expressing the emperor's ability to shape it – was an act which remained deeply impressed in ancient culture – up to being remembered as a relevant event in the Sibylline Oracles (*Or. Sib*. 5.214–219; 8.153–157; on Nero in the Sibylline Oracles, see Champlin 2003a: 12–17). The geographer Pausanias rejoiced that the project failed and that 'it is still mainland, as its nature is to be' (Paus. 2.1.5); the pseudo-Lucian of the *Nero* (possibly the first Philostratus) focuses from the very beginning on the cutting of the Isthmus, placing it in the tradition of Agamemnon (who would have cut the Euripus), Darius and Xerxes (Ps.-Luc. *Ner*. 1–4). This does not mean dismissing the idea that a channel may have had practical advantages, which Nero might have been very able to see (and are mentioned by the pseudo-Lucian). Nonetheless, limiting the interpretation of this act to purely utilitarian reasons, as facilitating communications, or adding onto it a value of imperial domination, through which 'the Romans' would have shaped 'their Empire' (see Alcock 1994: 101–103), would be too reductive. The parallels with other rulers, who attempted or claimed to attempt such an endeavour demonstrate how Nero wished to show his superhuman powers of shaping the world and nature.

The construction of the Domus Aurea after the fire of AD 64 – sometimes interpreted as inspired by Nero's connection with the Sun (*e.g.* Champlin 1998, reinstating an older theory by H.P. L'Orange; for a review of different positions, see Bergmann 2013: 354–355; Beste and von Hesberg 2013: 323–328) – clearly reveals this kind of performance of imperial power, expressed, for example, through the creation of a lake that was supposed to mimic the sea, and on whose shores cities were built. This is true besides and beyond the discussed 'Eastern' and Hellenistic inspiration of the Domus Aurea (see, *e.g.* Hemsoll 1990: 26–33, arguing for a dependence upon Eastern royal palaces, and in particular, the one in Alexandria; see also Ball 2003: 5–6), and would become even more relevant if it was true (as argued by Champlin 2003a: 185–191) that Nero was indeed responsible for the fire, following a pre-existing plan of rebuilding the city. The importance of light and its setting within architecture has been highlighted in this context on many occasions, for example in connection with the Octagon Suite: 'the visual effect of a feather-light dome, appearing to hover in a sea of light all around it, is almost mystical. [...] Obviously lighting was a design motif that Severus and Celer considered carefully' (Ball 2003: 219). Suetonius' description of the Domus Aurea, based on Ovid's description of the Palace of the Sun, does not contradict but rather reinforce the idea that the Domus Aurea was also a form of 'solar performance' of the emperor (Blaison 1998).

Throughout the Domus Aurea different landscapes were reproduced, from vineyards to woods, inhabited by the proper corresponding fauna; in the baths flowed seawater, and that of the Albula (see Voisin 1987: 517–518; Hemsoll 1990: 15–16; Edwards 1993: 158–159; Champlin 1998: 339–340; Ball 2003: 4; Cordes 2017: 67–73; La Rocca 2017: 203–212; Lefebvre 2017: 124–125, 133–138):

> what the visitor standing by the Colossus would realize immediately was that this artificial landscape was a microcosm of the world. More precisely, the 'sea' surrounded by 'cities', farms and wild countryside, humans and animals, may have represented the Roman Empire in miniature, with the Mediterranean at its center. Overlooking this world from the Oppian Hill was the glittering façade of the Palace of the Sun, while high above its entrance would stand the shining statue of the Sun, its master, holding the world in his hand (Champlin 2003a: 132).

In general, the project was 'a transgression of the discrete boundaries of *natura* approved by Roman custom and upheld by moral rhetoric' (Elsner 1994: 122; *cf.* Tac. *Ann*. 15.42; see also Griffin 1984: 139). This was exactly Nero's point: the most impressive feature was the main, circular room, rotating night and day and thus imitating the entire world, placing the emperor at the very centre of the universe and revealing his power over the entire cosmos (Suet. *Ner*. 31.1–2; see Hemsoll 1990: 31–33).

Some performances arranged by Nero also must be considered as a display of enormous powers: he organised a sea battle in a theatre, which had been filled with seawater (as well as with fish and 'sea monsters'); however, this was not enough, as his power was rather displayed by the speed with which, after the battle, the water was drained and a battle on land was staged (Suet. *Ner*. 12.1; Dio 61.9.5, 62.15.1). The famous 'banquet of Tigellinus', which included filling the area of the *stagnum Agrippae* with exotic animals and other interventions on the landscape could also be read to this effect (Tac. *Ann*. 15.37; see also Champlin 2003a: 153–157, connecting it with a wish of 'bringing Baiae to Rome').

Across Gender Boundaries

The theatre was also the first place in which Nero crossed gender boundaries, but here again with a twist, which moved his performance beyond the pure gender-crossing operated by other actors. According to Suetonius, he did not simply perform the roles of heroines and goddesses, but he used masks, which, in the case of male characters, had his features (thus reinforcing the idea of his protean qualities and his ability to identify with gods and heroes) and those of the women he was currently in love with in the case of female characters (Suet. *Ner.* 21.3; Dio 63.9.5, according to whom the female masks only represented Poppaea Sabina) – thus performing a capacity of switching gender and personality 'within the couple' and locating himself stably in the sphere of myth (Meier 2008: 592–593; *cf.* Leigh 2017: 28, whereas describing this as a merging of game and reality is reductive). In any case, Nero was stressing his position above the human also through his theatrical roles: 'by presenting himself as the heroes and heroines of myth, Nero of course raised himself above the level of ordinary action and responsibility' (Champlin 2003a: 111).

This aspect becomes much more evident at a later stage when Nero starts performing his ability at gender crossing within homosexual couples, of which one partner is 'made woman'. The first and most famous case is that of Sporus. Upon falling in love with this young man, Nero had him castrated and subsequently 'transformed into a woman'; Sporus was publicly acting as empress and Nero even married him, which meant that he had officially been 'declared' a woman. The emperor, thus, revealed his 'posthuman' nature by demonstrating his ability to create 'posthuman' figures through his intervention. It would be too reductive to consider this wedding a 'farce', meant to establish Nero as the 'prince of the Saturnalia' (see Champlin 2003a: 145–150): as highlighted by Vout, 'it fits with Suetonius' broader picture of a Nero who overturns the natural order of things' (Vout 2007: 152), and is 'a portent, a walking *prodigium*, who is constantly at the emperor's side' (Vout 2002: 496). Even more, a portent created by the emperor: 'Nero has played God and created his own hermaphrodite' (Vout 2002: 497). Vout's question, whether Nero champions 'the proclivity of emperors to "play god" and try to change nature' (Vout 2007: 152) should, therefore, be answered in the affirmative. Sporus would remain with Nero until his death, and continues to play a relevant role in the following years. On the other hand, Nero also married a freedman called Pythagoras (or Doryphoros? The latter name seems to be inspired by Polyclitus' sculpture, thus creating an implicit innuendo through its meaning of 'spear bearer', Vout 2007: 153). In this case, Nero himself was the bride (the idea that this marriage was an initiation rite to an Eastern cult, as supposed by Plass 1988: 10 or a parody of such an initiation, as argued by Vout 2002: 497–499; Champlin 2003a: 166–168, is unconvincing). The performative act revealing his capacity to change gender included that he '[even] imitate[d] the cries and lamentations of a maiden being deflowered [raped]' (*voces quoque et heiulatus vim patientium virginum imitatus,* Suet. *Ner.* 29.1; 28.1–2; see also Dio 62.28.2–3, 63.13.1–2; Sulp. Sev. *Chron.* 2.28.1; see Curry 2014: 217–218; Campanile 2017: 59–61; Carlà-Uhink 2017a: 21–22).

Animals and Bestiality

According to Suetonius, Nero also made himself an animal in performative acts, which are quite unbelievable: in a twisted version of a *damnatio ad bestias*, Nero, covered in animal furs and closed in a cage, would then jump out of the cage and bite the genitals of men and women, who had been tied to trees (Suet. *Ner.* 29.1; Dio 63.13.2). As Curry has shown, these episodes are an important part of representations of Nero as 'crossing boundaries' – and as she has shown, Suetonius turns all ironic when Nero, who performed the wild animal, involuntarily becomes one: at the very end of his reign, he has to enter the villa of a freedman on all fours (Suet. *Ner.* 48.3–4). Once again, Suetonius' (and his peers') judgement of Nero's acts of crossing – their 'posthumanism' – portrays him not as 'superhuman', but as 'subhuman': 'Suetonius implies that the emperor, already notorious for crossing so many other boundaries of acceptable human behaviour, has passed beyond the threshold of the "human" itself to become – not divine as he might have expected – but "animal"' (Curry 2014: 200). These acts may have been real and represent sexual games practised by Nero (Champlin 2003a: 169–170): in this case, Nero's way of crossing the boundary between human and animal must have been performed publicly enough to be known. But even if such performances were a pure invention by Suetonius (Curry 2014: 201–202), such invention would reflect the anxiety felt in coping with an emperor, who was repeatedly breaking the boundaries of the human. Suetonius might have been inspired by Tacitus' report of the first persecution of the Christians under Nero (Curry 2014: 212). In this context, Nero plays with the boundary between human and animal in a different, more Caligula-like way as the one, who would have the power to let other people cross the boundary. The condemned, so Tacitus, were covered in animal furs and torn apart by dogs (Tac. *Ann.* 15.44.4; see Champlin 2003a: 122–123, for an interpretation of this form of execution as 'fatal charade'). Dio reports that Nero, in his passion for races, disposed that elderly racehorses should be dressed as Roman citizens, 'with the regular street costume for men' (Dio 61.6.1); this can be a duplication of Caligula's Incitatus (Lefebvre 2017: 76–77), but even in this case, it reveals the same kind of anxiety seen in Suetonius.

Reconnecting Nero's ability at crossing with the theatricality of his performance of power, Curry argues thus that 'Suetonius's Nero allows neither class, nor gender, nor [...] even species to stand in the way of a role' (Curry 2014: 197). Beyond Suetonius, the historical Nero might well have felt the same, even if his ideas, aims, and even performances – once considered in detail – were very different from what Suetonius wants us to think – that Nero was a sick and depraved tyrant. Nero's reign was, as every reign, performance (in this sense, an emperor with a special predilection for theatre does not make a huge difference) – and performance of a kind that claimed for the emperor the ability to cross the boundaries imposed upon the human, and qualify thus as more-than-human, as divine. Suetonius is representative of a public dismissing such a claim and, therefore, viewing Nero's performances as blatantly mad: starting from the assumption that Nero is a 'normal' human being, indeed, his gestures are random; the contrary applies, once one accepts that Nero could do what humans cannot do – crossing the boundaries of gender, or even those between human and animal.

Conclusions

It is not necessary to believe that all ancient anecdotes about Caligula and Nero correspond to real performances – especially the idea of a barking Nero biting people's genitals can be dismissed as Suetonius' fantasy. However, this does not imply, on the other side, that everything written about these two emperors is simply slander and has been invented *ex nihilo* (Witschel 2006: 107–108). Behind many of the episodes described, one can indeed glimpse performative acts through which the emperors challenged the boundaries of the human – or better, tried to demonstrate that those boundaries did not apply to themselves. However, as with every act of crossing, it is the public, which in the end must define the trespass as successful. Many Romans probably agreed – considering the popularity that both emperors enjoyed; the senatorial aristocracy did not agree, and therefore interpreted these performances as failures, as mad acts of two depraved autocrats who received too much power when they were too young. Cary Wolfe writes:

> if the past is far more heterogeneous and complex – far more *ahuman* and strange, as the Annales school held – than the accounts of it we have inherited, it is also true that the present from which those accounts issue as products of specific practices and protocols is heterogeneous to *itself* in ways actively repressed by the recasting of a vast historical, cultural, and anthropological field within the protocols of humanism and the subject of knowledge it reproduces in and through those protocols (Wolfe 2010: 120).

From this point of view, Caligula and Nero qualify as posthuman, considering their ambition to move transversally through different spheres, ecologies, and expressions of matter. But this is only their prerogative – not contradictory with the idea that the 'posthuman political landscape is not necessarily more egalitarian', and on the contrary, it 'exacerbates power relations and brings them to new necro-political heights' (Braidotti 2013: 97). According to Rosi Braidotti, 'power is not a static given, but a complex strategic flow of effects which call for a pragmatic politics of intervention' (Braidotti 2013: 99). Thus, Caligula and Nero tried to build their power on a claim to a more-than-human nature; their failure, instead of bringing them back into the boundaries of the human, displaced them within the non-human sphere in which they had located themselves. In this way, they became *monstra* (Suet. *Cal.* 22.1): inhuman prodigies. To say it with Derrida, the sovereign showed in their case in a neat way his structural nearness to the beast.

Historisches Institut, Universität Potsdam

Bibliography

Ancient Sources

Aristotle, *Politica.*

Athenaeus, *Deipnosophistae.*

Dio Cassius (Translated by E. Cary and H. Foster). 1924. *Roman History, Volume VII: Books 56–60.* Loeb Classical Library 175. Cambridge, MA: Harvard University Press.

Dio Cassius (Translated by E. Cary and H. Foster). 1925. *Roman History, Volume VIII: Books 61–70.* Loeb Classical Library 176. Cambridge, MA: Harvard University Press.

Eutropius, *Breviarium Ab Urbe Condita.*

Josephus, *Antiquitates Judaicae.*

Josephus, *Bellum Judaicum.*

Oracula Sibyllina.

Pausanias (Translated by W. Jones). 1918. *Description of Greece, Volume I: Books 1–2 (Attica and Corinth).* Loeb Classical Library 93. Cambridge, MA: Harvard University Press.

Philo (Translated by F. Colson). 1962. *On the Embassy to Gaius. General Indexes.* Loeb Classical Library 379. Cambridge, MA: Harvard University Press.

Plato, *Respublica.*

Pliny the Elder, *Naturalis Historia.*

Plutarch, *Vitae Parallelae. Caesar.*

Pseudo-Lucian, *Nero.*

Seneca the Younger, *Apocolocyntosis*

Seneca the Younger, *De Ira.*

Statius, *Silvae.*

Suetonius (Translated by J. Rolfe). 1914. *Lives of the Caesars, Volume I: Julius. Augustus. Tiberius. Gaius. Caligula.* Loeb Classical Library 31. Cambridge, MA: Harvard University Press.

Suetonius (Translated by J. Rolfe). 1914. *Lives of the Caesars, Volume II: Claudius. Nero. Galba, Otho, and Vitellius. Vespasian. Titus, Domitian. Lives of Illustrious Men: Grammarians and Rhetoricians. Poets (Terence. Virgil. Horace. Tibullus. Persius. Lucan). Lives of Pliny the Elder and Passienus Crispus.* Loeb Classical Library 38. Cambridge, MA: Harvard University Press.

Sulpicius Severus, *Chronica.*

Tacitus, *Annales.*

Tacitus, *Historiae.*

Modern Sources

Alcock, S. 1994. Nero at play? The emperor's Grecian odyssey. In J. Elsner and J. Masters (eds) *Reflections of Nero. Culture, History and Representation.* London: Duckworth: 98–111.

Ball, L.F. 2003. *The Domus Aurea and the Roman Architectural Revolution.* Cambridge: Cambridge University Press.

Balsdon, J.P.V.D. 1934. *The Emperor Gaius (Caligula).* Oxford: Clarendon Press.

Barad, K. 2003. Posthumanist performativity: toward an understanding of how matter comes to matter. *Signs: Journal of Women in Culture and Society* 28 (3): 801–831.

Barrett, A.A. 1989. *Caligula. The Corruption of Power*. London: Batsford.

Baudrillard, J. 1976. *L'échange symbolique et la mort*. Paris: Gallimard.

Benediktson, D.T. 1989. Caligula's madness: madness or interictal temporal lobe epilepsy? *The Classical World* 82 (5): 370–375.

Bergmann, M. 1998. *Die Strahlen der Herrscher. Theomorphes Herrscherbild und politische Symbolik im Hellenismus und in der römischen-Kaiserzeit*. Mainz: von Zabern.

Bergmann, M. 2013. Portraits of an emperor: Nero, the Sun, and Roman *otium*. In E. Buckley and M.T. Dinter (eds) *A Companion to the Neronian Age*. Malden, MA/Oxford: Wiley-Blackwell: 332–362.

Beste, H.J. and von Hesberg, H. 2013. Buildings of an emperor: how Nero transformed Rome. In E. Buckley and M.T. Dinter (eds) *A Companion to the Neronian Age*. Malden, MA/Oxford: Wiley-Blackwell: 314–331.

Bicknell, P.J. 1962. Gaius and the sea-shells. *Acta Classica* 5: 72–74.

Bicknell, P.J. 1968. The emperor Gaius' military activities in AD 40. *Historia* 17: 496–505.

Bilde, P. 1978. The Roman emperor Gaius (Caligula)'s attempt to erect his statue in the temple of Jerusalem. *Studia Theologica* 32: 67–93.

Blaison, M. 1998. Suétone et l'ekphrasis de la *Domus aurea* (Suét., Ner. 31). *Latomus* 57: 617–624.

Boschung, D. 1989. *Die Bildnisse des Caligula*. Berlin: Gebr. Mann.

Braidotti, R. 2013. *The Posthuman*. Cambridge: Polity.

Campanile, D. 2017. The patrician, the general and the emperor in women's clothes: examples of cross-dressing in Late Republican and Early Imperial Rome. In D. Campanile, F. Carlà-Uhink and M. Facella (eds) *TransAntiquity. Cross-Dressing and Transgender Dynamics in the Ancient World*. London/New York: Routledge: 52–64.

Carlà-Uhink, F. 2017a. 'Between the human and the divine': cross-dressing and transgender dynamics in the Graeco-Roman world. In D. Campanile, F. Carlà-Uhink and M. Facella (eds) *TransAntiquity. Cross-Dressing and Transgender Dynamics in the Ancient World*. London/New York: Routledge: 3–37.

Carlà-Uhink, F. 2017b. Crossing gender. Transvestimus im römischen Kaisertum als Strategie zur Konstruktion von Ungleichheit. In A. Dresen and F. Freitag (eds) *Crossing. Über Inszenierungen kultureller Differenzen und Identitäten*. Bielefeld: Transcript: 11–38.

Champlin, E. 1998. God and man in the Golden House. In M. Cima and E. La Rocca (eds) *Horti Romani*. Roma: L'Erma di Bretschneider: 333–344.

Champlin, E. 2003a. *Nero*. Cambridge, MA/London: Belknap.

Champlin, E. 2003b. Nero, Apollo, and the poets. *Phoenix* 57 (3/4): 276–283.

Cordes, L. 2017. *Kaiser und Tyrann. Die Kodierung und Umkodierung der Herrscherrepräsentation Neros und Domitians*. Berlin/Boston: Walter de Gruyter.

Curry, S.A. 2014. Nero Quadripes: animalizing the emperor in Suetonius's Nero. *Arethusa* 47 (2): 197–230.

Davies, R.W. 1966. The 'abortive invasion' of Britain by Gaius. *Historia* 15: 124–128.

Derrida, J. 2008. *Séminaire La bête et le souverain. Volume 1 (2001–2002)*. Paris: Galilée.

Dresen, A. and Freitag, F. (eds) 2017. *Crossing. Über Inszenierungen kultureller Differenzen und Identitäten*. Bielefeld: Transcript.

Edwards, C. 1993. *The Politics of Immorality in Ancient Rome*. Cambridge: Cambridge University Press.

Edwards, C. 1994. Beware of imitations: theatre and the subversion of imperial identity. In J. Elsner and J. Masters (eds) *Reflections of Nero. Culture, History and Representation*. London: Duckworth: 83–97.

Elsner, J. 1994. Constructing decadence: the representation of Nero as imperial builder. In J. Elsner and J. Masters (eds) *Reflections of Nero. Culture, History and Representation*. London: Duckworth: 112–127.

Gerster, B. 1884. L'isthme de Corinthe: tentatives des percement dans l'antiquité. *Bulletin de Correspondance Hellénique* 8: 225–232.

Gradel, I. 2002. *Emperor Worship and Roman Religion*. Oxford: Clarendon.

Griffin, M. 1984. *Nero. The End of a Dynasty*. London: Batsford.

Griffin, M. 2007. Nero and the concept of imperial glory. In Y. Perrin (ed.) *Neronia VII. Rome, l'Italie et la Grèce. Hellénisme et philhellénisme au premier siècle ap. J.-C.* Brussels: Latomus: 15–25.

Hawkins, T. 2017. Pollio's paradox: popular invective and the transition to empire. In L. Grig (ed.) *Popular Culture in the Ancient World*. Cambridge: Cambridge University Press: 129–148.

Hemsoll, D. 1990. The architecture of Nero's golden house. In M. Henig (ed.) *Architecture and Architectural Sculpture in the Roman Empire*. Oxford: Committee for Archaeology: 10–38.

Lane Fox, R. 1986. *Pagans and Christians in the Mediterranean World from the Second Century AD to the Conversion of Constantine*. London: Penguin Books.

La Rocca, E. 2017. Staging Nero: public imagery and the Domus Aurea. In S. Bartsch, K. Freudenburg and C. Littlewood (eds) *The Cambridge Companion to the Age of Nero*. Cambridge: Cambridge University Press: 195–212.

Lefebvre, L. 2017. *Le mythe Néron. La fabrique d'un monstre dans la littérature antique (Ier–Ve s.)*. Villeneuve d'Ascq: Septentrion.

Leigh, M. 2017. Nero the performer. In S. Bartsch, K. Freudenburg and C. Littlewood (eds) *The Cambridge Companion to the Age of Nero*. Cambridge: Cambridge University Press: 21–33.

Leonard, M. 2005. *Athens in Paris. Ancient Greece and the Political in Post-War French Thought*. Oxford: Oxford University Press.

Massaro, V. and Montgomery, I. 1978. Gaius: mad, bad, ill, or all three? *Latomus* 37: 894–909.

Meier, M. 2008. 'Qualis artifex pereo' – Neros letzte Reise. *Historische Zeitschrift* 286 (3): 561–603.

Merriam-Webster 2019. Inhuman. https://www.merriam-webster.com/dictionary/inhuman [Last Accessed 19/11/2019].

Mratschek, S. 2013. Nero the imperial misfit: philhellenism in a rich man's world. In E. Buckley and M.T. Dinter (eds) *A Companion to the Neronian Age*. Malden, MA/Oxford: Wiley-Blackwell: 45–62.

Pelling, C. 2006. Breaking the bounds: writing about Julius Caesar. In B. McGing and J. Mossman (eds) *The Limits of Ancient Biography*. Swansea: Classical Press of Wales: 255–280.

Phillips, E.J. 1970. The emperor Gaius' abortive invasion of Britain. *Historia* 19: 369–374.

Plass, P. 1988. *Wit and the Writing of History. The Rhetoric of Historiography in Imperial Rome*. Madison: University of Wisconsin Press.

Rilinger, R. 1996. Seneca und Nero. Konzepte zur Legitimation kaiserlicher Herrschaft. *Klio* 78: 130–157.

Ronning, C. 2011. Zwischen ratio und Wahn. Caligula, Claudius und Nero in der altertumswissenschaftlichen Forschung. In A. Winterling (ed.) *Zwischen Strukturgeschichte und Biographie. Probleme und Perspektiven einer neuen römischen Kaisergeschichte*. München: Oldenbourg: 253–276.

Schrömbges, P. 1988. Caligulas Wahn. Zur Historizität eines Topos. *Tyche* 3: 171–190.

Simpson, C.J. 1981. The cult of the emperor Gaius. *Latomus* 40: 489–511.

Simpson, C.J. 1996. Caligula's cult: immolation, immortality, intent. In A. Small (ed.) *Subject and Ruler: The Cult of the Ruling Power in Classical Antiquity*. Portsmouth: Journal of Roman Archaeology: 63–71.

Squire, M. 2011. *The Art of the Body. Antiquity and Its Legacy*. Oxford: Oxford University Press.

Sutherland, C. and Carson, R. (eds) 1984. *The Roman Imperial Coinage. Volume I. Revised Edition. From 31 BC to AD 69*. London: Spink and Son.

Varner, E.R. 2017. Incarnating the *Aurea Aetas*: theomorphic rhetoric and the portraits of Nero. In S. Blakely (ed.) *Gods, Objects, and Ritual Practice*. Atlanta: Lockwood: 75–115.

Voisin, J.L. 1987. *Exoriente sole* (Suétone, Ner. 6). D'Alexandrie à la Domus Aurea. In *L'Urbs. Espace urbain et histoire (Ier siécle av. J.-C. – III e siècle ap. J.-C.)*. Paris/Rome: CNRS/École Française de Rome: 509–543.

Vout, C. 2002. Nero and Sporus. In J.M. Croisille and Y. Perrin (eds) *Neronia VI. Rome à l'époque néronienne*. Brussels: Editions Latomus: 493–502.

Vout, C. 2007. *Power and Eroticism in Imperial Rome*. Cambridge: Cambridge University Press.

Vout, C. 2009. Representing the Emperor. In A. Feldherr (ed.) *The Cambridge Companion to the Roman Historians*. Cambridge: Cambridge University Press: 261–275.

Wilkinson, S. 2005. *Caligula*. London/New York: Routledge.

Willrich, H. 1903. Caligula. *Klio* 3: 85–118, 288–317, 397–470.

Winterling, A. 2009. *Politics and Society in Imperial Rome*. Malden, MA/Oxford: Wiley-Blackwell.

Winterling, A. 2011. *Caligula. Eine Biographie*. Second edition. München: Beck.

Witschel, C. 2006. 'Verrückte Kaiser'? Zur Selbststilisierung und Außenwahrnehmung nonkonformer Herrscherfiguren in der römischen Kaiserzeit. In C. Ronning (ed.) *Einblicke in die Antike. Orte – Praktiken – Strukturen*. München: Utz: 87–129.

Woods, D. 2000. Caligula's seashells. *Greece & Rome* 47: 80–87.

Wolfe, C. 2010. *What is Posthumanism?* Minneapolis: University of Minnesota Press.

Yavetz, Z. 1996. Caligula, imperial madness and modern historiography. *Klio* 78: 105–129.

Abbreviations

CIL	*Corpus Inscriptionum Latinarum*.
IG	*Inscriptiones Graecae*.
RIC I^2	*Roman Imperial Coinage* = Sutherland and Carson 1984.

3

Roman Epigraphic Funerary Markers, Ontological Transition, and Relational Work-nets

Vladimir D. Mihajlović

Introduction

The perspective argued for in this chapter is derived from an earlier wave of 'thinking about and through things' and how they work (*e.g.* Appadurai 1986; Kopytoff 1986), and is further informed by recently developed 'posthumanist' perspectives. The latter term covers approaches variously named as 'new materialism', 'flat ontology', 'entanglement', and 'Actor-Network' theories (see Hicks 2010; Thomas 2015; Harris and Cipolla 2017: 71–189), and includes the works of Bruno Latour (2005), Karen Barad (2007), Bjørnar Olsen (2010; 2012; Olsen and Witmore 2015), Ian Hodder (2012; 2016), and others (*e.g.* Knappett and Malafouris 2008; Barrett 2014; Fowler and Harris 2015; see further Webb and Selsvold in this volume). While they are of different qualities and elaboration – and some of them seem like no more than semantic gymnastics or bare truisms – with severe problems of argumentation, a lack of methodological relevance, minimal applicability to studies of the past (Barrett 2016) and dubious ideological implications (Keil 2017), admittedly, many of their points have a capacity for opening more nuanced approaches in archaeological and historical research.

Notably, the posthumanist perspectives share the awareness that people have never lived and existed isolated and without diverse and dynamic co-relations with other entities (such as non-human organisms, materials, things, natural objects and phenomena, laws of physics and chemistry, spirits, concepts, ideas, etc.; see, for example, Feider *et al.*, Iara, and Lodwick in this volume). They also commonly assume that human lives, beliefs, practices, identity constructions, and transformations have always been permeated with, defined by, and dependent on modes of bond-creations with other entities. Consequently, the posthumanist outlook considers that the roles, positionings, performativities or, simply, living in the world could not have existed without such relations. No matter if we disapprove, partially or entirely accept the postulates suggested by the 'Actor-Network Theory' (Latour 2005), 'agential realism' (Barad 2007), 'speculative realism' (Shaviro 2014), 'entanglement theory' (Hodder 2012; 2016), 'symmetrical archaeology' (Olsen 2012; Olsen and Witmore 2015), or some other perspective of the 'ontological turn' (see Harris 2016), there is no doubt we have to change the viewpoints that have explained the past by focusing exclusively on the human part and simultaneously downplaying the significance of other agents in interconnectedness of various sorts.

It should be immediately stressed that I continue to hold the position that humans (in contrast to non-living entities) have a capacity to give meanings and create knowledge, ideologies, and modes of understanding and behaviour. Unlike non-living entities and most living organisms, humankind also possesses the power to produce things and invest them with purposes related to (human) needs and ideas. Crucially, people are differentiated from inanimate phenomena by intentionality/will, which directly affects other humans, things, and the world (*cf.* Barrett 2014). However, as it is undeniable that people are integrally linked with other ontological entities, a humankind unrelated to and separated from other biological species, material and immaterial things, factors of the natural environment, laws of physics and chemistry, materials, etc. simply never existed. This realisation has already made an impact on studies of the Roman world (*cf.* contributions in Van Oyen and Pitts 2017), albeit of relatively modest scope at the moment. Most notably, the work of Astrid Van Oyen urged us to think beyond objects as representations and their purpose. Instead, she suggests considering what they have done and how they did it inside the 'work-nets', in which they were involved. The term 'work-nets' is deliberately coined inversely (*cf.* Latour 2005: 132) to signify the connections made by the dynamic relationality of actors. It challenges the concept of networks that are generally understood as consisting of passive, preset, and distinctive elements, energised and manipulated only by human actors (Van Oyen 2015; 2016; 2017).

Following these general ideas and combining them in an idiosyncratic manner, the chapter re-examines what burial/funerary markers, specifically those made of stone and inscribed, did in the Roman Empire. More precisely, the following chapter considers the questions of: how exactly the Epigraphic Funerary Markers (hereafter referred to as EFMs) were associated with the ontological state of being dead; what kind of relations they were engaged in and how; what specific qualities and capacities they acquired through such associations; what effects and impact they produced; and what have they enabled and how they worked. The chapter entertains the possibility of understanding EFMs not only as artefacts invested with meanings by people but as things that had agency in their own right and participated in diverse and dynamic work-nets. Consequently, the discussion aims at opening the understanding of EFMs beyond the currently prevailing standpoints of commemoration as well as identity and status communication that treat them as mere embodiments of human conceptions and passive reflections of social drives. In short, this is a call for considering features of EFMs that are not yet fully acknowledged but could help us to gain some fresh and relevant understandings of the Roman funerary sphere and epigraphic-monumental practice.

However, what follows should be taken as a speculative exercise, an engagement of general theoretical views with the particular cultural phenomenon of the Roman world and, as such, a review, which necessarily bears limitations (such as, *e.g.* citing only selected and most illustrative examples to support the argument). Therefore, the subsequent sections by no means pretend to be all-encompassing, groundbreaking, and definite explanations of the matters in question. Rather, they should be comprehended in terms of an open-ended discussion of EFMs as a general category of things that were not fixed but had many and significant variations, differences, and specifics throughout the time-space-social coordinates.

Dead Humans and the 'Technology' of Becoming Distributed Deceased Entities

The death of a human is undoubtedly among the most obvious ontological transformations anybody can witness. Regardless of specific cultural attitudes towards the permanent cessation of one and the emergence of another state of an organism, the transition from life to death always leaves consequences for those who remain in 'this world' (see, *e.g.* Parker Pearson 2003; Fahlander and Østigård 2008) because death inevitably terminates the interconnections and relations that a person had made and was involved in while alive. Even if the dead are regarded as beings which can still interact with the living, their inability to do so in the former condition and manner (*i.e.* as a living body) inescapably underlines the changed state of existence. These kinds of shifts are usually accompanied by rites of passage (which are markedly but not exclusively related to humans *cf.* Fogelin and Schiffer 2015) that help the metamorphosis and re-establish the networks of associations among surviving humans, things, and other entities, and the newly formed after-death ontological category (however defined, experienced or imagined it might be).

If the previous notions are amplified with the arguments suggested by the Actor-Network Theory and agential realism, some striking features and perspectives surface. First, it is worthwhile considering that our world is constructed by and through effective associations of diverse human and non-human entities entangled in various ties that cannot be dissected to pure constitutive parts in any meaningful way (Latour 2005: 72, 108, 217–218, 240–241, 247). In simple terms, any phenomenon in our social reality is not a simple sum of its constitutive elements, where human actors necessarily play a primary role but, on the contrary, exists and functions only if the constituents in question mutually relate in specific manners and thus enable each other to create a phenomenon. Because each participator of some relational association – in synergy with others – influences the features of the structure by involving its agency, it acquires the qualities of a 'mediator'. In Bruno Latour's definition 'mediators transform, translate, distort, and modify the meaning or the elements they are supposed to carry,' while 'the word "translation" [now] takes on a somewhat specialised meaning: a relation that does not transport causality but induces two mediators into coexisting' (Latour 2005: 39, 108).

Furthermore, the distinct agencies of particular mediators do not precede but emerge through their mutual entanglement, while the specific 'intra-actions' of ontologically inseparable entities are what constitute any phenomenon (Barad 2007: 33–34, 128). Karen Barad's neat definition provides particularly helpful guidelines for the current topic under consideration: '[I]t is through specific agential intra-actions that the boundaries and properties of the components of phenomena become determinate and that particular concepts (that is, particular material articulations of the world) become meaningful' (Barad 2007: 139–141). 'Intra-actions', rather than interactions, stand here to emphasise that the constitutive components of phenomena do not have a preset, deterministic, and essential nature but acquire their qualities and are defined relative to other mediators (Barad 2007: 422, n. 15, 429, n. 14). Another instructive strand of thought – quite similar to the comprehension of phenomena cited previously – can be identified in the concept of 'assemblages'. This is understood as '[the] coming together of multiple different kinds of things...[which] operate at multiple scales...[and] are also always in the process of *"becoming"*... [as] they are the outcome of certain kinds of ongoing processes that involve particular kinds of histories, rather than being static and unchanging' (Harris and Cipolla 2017: 139, emphasis in original; see also Thomas 2015: 1293–1294 with bibliography). Stepping away from dense theoretical terminology, the following example can simplify the matter: instead of thinking that defined elements A, B, and C make X, by simply coming together, it is more productive to consider that the three particular elements – when related in specific manners – simultaneously constitute X and acquire the qualities-of and definition-as A, B, and C.

Recognising this, the mere notion of the deceased and what constitutes the state of being a departed entity start to unfold in an entirely different direction and take on a whole new meaning. The deceased as a phenomenon (or an assemblage) can be regarded as intra-actions of different entities, which in relation to each other make the state of deceased-ness come into existence. Specifically, the status of being deceased goes beyond the simple ending of biological life and turning into a lifeless body. To fully become deceased, the dead body has to 'plug in' or 'attach' (*sensu* Latour 2005) to various other entities. It needs to intra-actively determine with these entities the boundaries and properties of both the complete assemblage of deceased-ness and the role, feature and capacity of each of the interconnected components. More precisely, only through particular practices, beliefs, performances, attitudes, people, things, emplacement, funerary architecture, mechanisms of commemoration, natural objects, non-human organisms, or any other imaginable aspect of funeral and burial – all related in specific manners – is it possible for the dead human to fully emerge as the deceased and undergo ontological transformation from being alive to becoming the afterlife entity. More bluntly, in order for the dead human to change ontological states it is necessary to: 1) specifically process the body by associating it with particular (funerary) objects or activities (*e.g.* washing, incineration, ritual cleansing); 2) perform funeral rites; 3) invoke 'otherworldly' entities and concepts; 4) change the behaviour (*i.e.* grieving); 5) place the body (interconnected with other things such as, *e.g.* a burial container) into the resting place; 6) perform burial rites; 7) form the grave and mark it; 8) involve the ideas of afterlife; and 9) perform commemoration; etc. Of course, the listed components are cited for the sake of argument; in each particular case throughout space, time, and cultural dimensions, they certainly differ and have idiosyncratic characteristics. It is, however, essential that any given metamorphosis into being the deceased (and not merely biologically dead) is achieved only through specific relationalities of the diverse entities involved in the process that both determine the phenomenon (of becoming the deceased) and are determined by the formed mutual relations.

If the argument is pushed further and the concept of distributed personhood (Fowler 2004: 82–100; 2016) is introduced and adapted, the following picture emerges. Thanks to their distinctly made intra-relationalities, the components of the phenomenon of being deceased acquire the particular roles precisely by their relations to the dead person and/or the posthuman afterlife entity. Hence, the things, places, ideas, sounds, funerary markers and architectural features, graves, and other entities involved in the phenomenon of becoming/being the deceased begin to be determined through their relations with the dead human (*cf.* Miller 2010: 143–152). In this way, all interrelated intra-active entities can be understood as constitutive parts of the deceased-ness. They are elements, through which the deceased is distributed (albeit in qualitatively unequal manner since some of them play more critical part than the others) and constantly re-emerges upon the linking of those elements with the living (*e.g.* mourners, family, friends, community). At the time of 'becoming the deceased', a dead person ceases to be determined by the living acting body and the relations it had created. Instead, it is articulated through new 'rewiring' of the corpse and all other entities engaged in the funerary sphere.

Let me try to illustrate the point with the funeral mosaic found in Salona (Solin, Croatia), which shows the seated figure of the deceased T. Aurelius Aurelianus holding a scroll. He is accompanied by a partridge which gazes at him, a tombstone with the inscription naming the dead boy and a herm (of variously defined gender and identity: Apollo, Dionysus, the boy's teacher, a female poet, Sappho; Fig. 3.1; Duplančić 2017). It appears that the entire scene is situated at Aurelianus' own grave. Albeit, his resting place and the mosaic were located inside the mausoleum that upon discovery contained no herm or a tombstone (Duplančić 2017).

While the depiction did not correspond to the reality of Aurelianus' interment, it illustrates the point intended here. Aurelianus' state of deceased-ness emerges from the cross-relationality of: 1) the memory of him as a pupil or a boy interested in intellectual endeavours (the seated figure with a scroll); 2) the conceptualisation of his death through the mythical metaphor of metamorphosis (a partridge);[1] 3) the ideas implied by a herm (as a guardian of the grave? reference to some aspect of his personhood?); 4) the grave as a final resting place; 5) the tombstone with inscribed biographical information; and 6) lost elements represented in the damaged part of the mosaic (the bereaved?). Every entity in this depiction made Aurelianus a unique and specific deceased; any different combination of the intra-active elements would have made him a dead entity with quite different qualities, while the lack of certain mediators (*e.g.* the body, proper burial place, grave marker, and remembrance) would cause the incapability of becoming a 'complete' deceased. Going beyond the level of the content of the mosaic by taking into consideration Aurelianus' actual burial place, it can be argued that without this commemorative item he would have become an entirely different deceased entity, one without all the traits and potentials enabled by the inclusion of the pictorial-textual marker. In short, the

Figure 3.1: Funerary mosaic of T. Aurelius Aurelianus from Salona. Source: Archaeological Museum in Split. Inv. no. AMS-A-5723 (Photo by Tonći Seser. Courtesy of the Archaeological Museum in Split/Zrinka Buljević).

personhood of living Aurelianus was transformed by death into a deceased, whose ontological state was attained with and distributed among diverse kinds of participators (the grave, its immediate surroundings, the mosaic, the architectural features, etc.) that synergistically generated Aurelianus as a posthuman afterlife entity. The point can be additionally illustrated with the epitaph from Tibiscum in Dacia stating that 'the earth holds the body, the stone (holds) the name, while the air (holds) the soul of what once was better' (*terra te- | net corpus no- | men lapis atque | animam aer qu- | am melius fuer- | [at*, *CIL* III 8003 = EDCS-28600231), which clearly suggests the idea of dispersion of a living person into several interrelated components (Hope 2007: 213).

Indeed, similar cases are already known and discussed, although not by applying the same theoretical and analytical tools. In her study of personal mementos of the dead in ancient Rome, Valerie Hope turns attention away from the tombs and graveyards as places of public commemoration and points to a more private mourning and remembering the deceased, notably through 'objects which intertwined the names and images of the dead with the domestic and everyday settings of the living' (Hope 2011: 177). Hope presents the epitaph of Allia Potestas (*CIL* VI 37965), which had been dedicated by her (Allia Potestas') patron (and lover), who refers to the golden bracelet with her name he was wearing. By considering the image of Allia, which he intended to bring to his own grave, and the verses he addressed to the deceased women, Hope underlines that all of these suggest that the presence of the dead could also be found in personal contexts and not only in the tomb and activities associated with the final resting place (Hope 2011: 178). She emphasises that the portraits of the deceased could take different forms and could be found in diverse contexts, urging the living to commemorate the dead persons, imbue some potency to their images (which could in some ways make the dead person present or associate them with divine properties) and interact with such objects in habitual fashion. All of this makes the portraits of the departed persons much more than passive display objects and implies that they had greater potency than usually understood (Hope 2011: 180–185. See also Ackers 2019). Hope suggests that similar features could be assumed for jewellery and heirlooms or indeed any 'personal' item (*e.g.* clothes) somehow connected with the deceased (Hope 2011: 186–190; 2019). Although Hope focuses on triggering memory and emotions as the principal agency of the objects under examination and, following Alfred Gell (1998), considers only the so-called secondary agency of things (*i.e.* the potentials and capacities granted to or invested in them by humans), she rightly recognises the intimate link between the state of being deceased on the one hand, and various other entities (things, memories, emotions and divine powers) on the other. Hence, she states:

> The actions of the commemorator gave Allia Potestas a life after death, and this new 'life' was not tied to a spiritual afterlife (although the epitaph does give some space to that possibility), but primarily a 'life', or at least a sense of continuity, grounded in the everyday actions of those that survived her... Through these objects, the dead were given a sense of physicality. It was this physicality that was significant to the commemorator of Allia (Hope 2011: 191).

Another very instructive study comes from the work of Emma-Jayne Graham (2009), who directly utilised the concept of personhood (*i.e. dividual person*) to investigate the commemoration of Marcus Nonius Balbus, an Augustan senator and an important political figure and *patronus* of Herculaneum. Although Graham used the concept of 'dividual personhood', which has been revised since 2009 and less rigidly articulated than in its initial form (see Fowler 2016), the general theoretical framework and starting positions are well aligned with the perspectives cited above, and they are an invaluable reference for the points intended in this chapter. Thus, she notes:

> Memory and personhood are, then, both caught up in the same cycle of actions, relationships and performances involving people, objects and places. Both processes come to the fore within the mortuary context, where the physical body of the deceased provides a material metaphor around which processes of identity manipulation, dividuality and monumentalization revolve (Graham 2009: 54).

Building on these ideas Graham then explains that Balbus' personhood was dispersed between: his tomb; the altar dedicated to him, which served as a permanent memorial to his transformation (*i.e.* incineration) and also contained the buried part of his finger (that previously underwent the rite of cleansing by fire – *os resectum*, see Graham 2011); various places in the city's landscape linked to his deeds; and the honorary statuary (including the one behind the altar), which conveniently memorised and celebrated his life, achievements, and persona. It is of significance that processions on the occasions of public commemoration, which could lead from Balbus' grave through the cityscape to the honorary altar, actually facilitated his becoming the idealised civic ancestor. This enabled relational maintenance of his personhood that happened between his resting place, the altar as a spot of ontological transition, the places in the city permeated with his deeds/personhood, the various items linked to him, and the living community (Graham 2009: 60–65). As Graham puts it, this process, among other things, 'could keep Balbus alive within the sociopolitical community as a social being, with whom the living could continue to relate' (Graham 2009: 65). In other words, here again we encounter the realisation that the deceased is constructed through intra-activity of various kinds of entities, from the corpse, memories, and concepts of afterlife to objects, spatiality and living commemorating people/community, all of which were the mediators in Balbus' becoming the deceased of specific contents and qualities (compare Newby 2019 for consideration of the role of dolls as alter-egos of the interred girls).

What we see in such a clear manner in the cited example is valid in any other instance of the emergence of a deceased. The uniqueness of each and every case of transformation of a human into an afterlife ontological state stems from the idiosyncratic relationalities of the mediators that always create a singular distributed deceased entity. The term is derived from the concept of distributed personhood mentioned above (Fowler 2004: 82–100; 2016), and stands for the fact that deceased-ness always emerges and functions through different constituent elements of various sorts. If we consider the infinite diversity of funeral and burial practices, ways of commemoration, conceptions of afterlife, attitudes towards death and dying, and all other aspects in the sphere of an afterlife ontological change in the Roman world (see Pearce *et al.* 2000; Carroll 2006; Graham 2006; Hope 2007; Carroll and Rempel 2011; Hope and Huskinson 2011; Pearce and Weeks 2017), it becomes clear that every single dead human had to be transformed into a particular distributed deceased entity. Of course, there were also shared funerary features according to various differentiations such as age, gender, family affiliation, status, economic standing, local traditions, varied conceptions of religion and afterlife. However, if we understand the state of deceased-ness as an assemblage, each post-life ontological change created a specific set of relationalities that enabled the becoming of a particular distributed deceased entity. In this way, the particularity of the human actor inside work-nets while alive is transmitted after death and has a direct bearing on the kind of posthuman the actor would become, *i.e.* the precise distribution of the deceased entity among its constituent mediators. To simplify this point, the distributed deceased entity of an emperor, a slave, a boy fond of schooling in Salona, an unmarried girl in Rome, or a soldier killed in the battle of Abritus would differ precisely because they all emerge from particular sets of interconnections of various elements engaged in their ontological transition towards achieving the state of being deceased.

Nevertheless, it is crucial to stress that this perspective does not imply that people of the Roman world conceptualised their dead as phenomena distributed throughout things, ideas, memories, people, places, divine or spiritual entities, etc. The beliefs and ideas about the afterlife, other worlds, existence beyond death, souls, gods of the underworld, and similar important issues of the funerary sphere are not in direct focus here, nor have straightforward relevance for what I am trying to demonstrate. Any of these could have been but were not necessarily a mediator of the transformation into a departed ontological state, especially if we treat each case in its own rights and setting. In other words, the presented viewpoint considers the phenomenon of the distributed deceased entity as the 'technology' of emerging/becoming a deceased, as a mechanism of ontological transition, and not as some all-encompassing ideology or knowledge that was consciously utilised in Antiquity. This 'technology' (for lack of a better term) was more general than the mediators (including the ideological and religious aspects) involved in it. It was, of course, prone to change throughout space-time-culture coordinates, and some actors/mediators could acquire more significant potential inside the phenomenon. To a certain extent, it could be regarded as a subconscious habitual routine of at least some groups of people. The distributed deceased entity as an assemblage can be comprehended as a general methodology of dealing with the ontological change, which acquired distinctive features in particular cases. To be sure, we can also term this 'imagining the dead', but the approach suggested here gives more space for ruminating that 1) the deceased and any possible existence beyond death were a real ontological category to the living and were regarded as something that could and did affect the sphere of 'this world', and 2) it underlines the fact that any phenomenon cannot be reduced to one pure state or element that built it, but instead works as changeable relational web of various elements that enable constant (re)emerging in different states of existence, roles, positionings, identities, etc. All of this is thanks to the overall fact that humans are inevitably relational beings entangled with a wide range of other entities, both those which already exist in the world and those made (up) by people. With these thoughts, I turn to the question of what EFMs (Epigraphic Funerary Markers) did in the previously mentioned assemblages and what kind of effects they produced when related to other mediators of the distributed deceased entity.

The Agency of Epigraphic Funerary Markers

Epigraphic funerary markers are a particular kind of grave indicator distinguished by the employment of text that is often accompanied by various sorts of images (portraiture, scenes and motives of mythological or religious provenance, decorative schemes, etc.). Here they are referred to as markers and not monuments since the more general term allows for the inclusion of various types of funerary items (tombstones, built constructions with inscriptions such as mausoleums or memorials, mortuary containers intended for display, etc.) as well as those that were not necessarily monumental in the strict sense (*i.e.* exceptional in size and/or other qualities) but could nevertheless produce the effects discussed below. The focus here is primarily on EFMs made of stone since these survived and are well studied. However, this neither excludes the reviewed possibilities for EFMs constructed of other materials and in different manners nor does it mean that the discussed aspects apply only to the inscribed funerary markers.

It is important to note that the following builds upon a long line of research and groundbreaking changes in approaching the study of EFMs in the Roman world. Ever since the initial rethinking of the epigraphic-monumental practice as a consciousness and habit, as a question of social trends, and rhetorical device for establishing commemoration and communicating various identities (and most notably status), the number and quality of contributions in the field have been continually growing (MacMullen 1982; Saller and Shaw 1984; Mann 1985; Meyer 1990; Bowman and Woolf 1994; Woolf 1996; Häussler 1998; 2014; King 2000; Oliver 2000a; Bodel 2001; Cooley 2002; Mouritsen 2005; Edmondson 2007; Erasmo 2008; Mattingly 2008). Invaluable and compelling inputs, covering the entire range of aspects of the usage, understanding and meaning of EFMs came especially from the work of Hope (1997; 1998; 2000; 2001; 2003; 2007; 2011) and Maureen Carroll (2006; 2008; 2009; 2011; 2013), who undoubtedly transformed the general way of thinking about this sort of burial marker. Nevertheless, both Hope and Carroll mainly consider EFMs as objects of commemoration, representations of human identities, and a materially articulated echo of the Roman social structure. Although they underline the role, significance, and impact on people, they rarely explicate the more dynamic character and capacities of EFMs. In other words, there was a more generous focus on EFMs as (more or less direct but usually partial and passive) reflections of memory, identities, social order, and trends than as active components and enablers of the very phenomena they are thought to mirror or represent. The change in perspective recently came with the intriguing insights of Graham, who introduced approaches that go beyond the questions of representation and human component as the only relevant aspect of the funerary sphere (Graham 2009; 2011; 2018). This clearly indicates the fruitfulness of such moves. However, the implications are not brought to their full potential and, while treating the aforementioned endeavours of Hope, Carroll, and Graham as a reliable framework, there is room to stretch our viewpoints and further enrich interpretations.

First, it is relevant to highlight that EFMs of any particular type can be regarded as a 'category' of objects since (at least some) aspects of their qualities, intended roles, and ways of usage were determined and conformed to standardisation (at worst loosely and in a basic sense), regardless of their endless varieties throughout the Roman world (*cf.* Carroll 2006; Carroll and Rempel 2011; Hope and Huskinson 2011). This implies Van Oyen's definition of category 'as a relational constellation defined by its marked difference from other things' (Van Oyen 2016: 367; see Van Oyen 2015), meaning that EFMs could have been and were easily distinguished from other objects even if of very similar formal traits (*e.g.* stone slab, votive or honorary inscription, boundary stones, milestones). Additionally, by using the concepts of Igor Kopytoff (1986), it could be argued that EFMs evolved in their biographies from being commodities in a stonecutter's workshop or some other kind of acquisition setting (see Carroll 2006: 86–125) to becoming singularised objects. Furthermore and crucially, once an EFM received the name of its human (no matter if pre- or posthumously), often followed by some other biographical details such as age, kinship, social positioning, career information, name of a dedicator, etc., the marker became captured in the web of (that person's) relationalities as yet another mediator (see Carroll 2006: 33; Hope 2007: 75). By elaborating Kopytoff's perspective, it can be asserted that EFMs in this way were not becoming singularised but actually particularised and personalised objects, literally tied to the name and relations of their humans and thus determined as things in mutual permeation with the personhoods in question. Every single one of them was a unique item (regardless of the mutual resemblances characteristic for their category), which sets them apart from the majority of other material things in the Roman world. It is hard to think of any other single-form kind of artefact so obviously personalised: thanks to the carved biographical data, if not to other physical features, EFMs were assuming quality that resembled humans – all were mutually alike, but none exactly the same.

Moreover, when set at the grave an EFM was directly involved in the emergence of the phenomenon of a deceased entity as described above. It actively helped the transition and maintenance of the state of deceased-ness. Through the relations with its text and imagery, the human remains it stood for, and the role it played at the surface of a resting place, an EFM enabled the emergence of a particular kind of deceased entity that was (in the most cases) stripped of and cleansed of any characteristics other than the fundamental biographical particularities (see Hope 2001; Carroll 2006: 126–150). An EFM facilitated the distinctive interconnectedness of various elements, which then produced the deceased, in whose profile only some of the characteristics of the late human entered and had been displayed. Since no inscribed funerary marker is known to inform about the negative character traits of its human, it can be said that EFMs decisively participated in the elevation of the dead into a purified entity, deprived of wrongdoings – at least in official public commemoration. Formulaic in nature, funeral inscriptions are 'sin-free', divested from anything other than a 'sterile' social positioning, and thus associated with morally elevated and exemplary afterlife beings. In other words, highly selective representation of what the deceased was and what they became enabled their biography to be 'without a stain', which can be seen as a kind of symbolic capital desirable to refer to (as it was transmitting the part of reputation to the living associated with an EFM). Although this is, of course, the consequence of a rhetorical idealisation of the dead (Hope 1997: 58; 1998: 179; 2000: 178, 181) and a tendency to turn them into *exempla* (Erasmo 2008: 156), such an outcome would not have been entirely achievable if it was not for EFMs, which again stresses the productivity of the assemblage/phenomenon approach.

As the surviving Roman legal definition states (*Dig.* 11.7) and common practice shows, EFMs were intended for (as permanent as possible) preservation of memory of the departed through the engagement of a tombstone with anybody from the living population who could access it (Koortboijan 2005: 293; Carroll 2006: 18, 30–31, 48–51, 69–78; 2008; Hope 2007: 64, 71–84; Chioffi 2015: 627). Commemoration and memory were among the most significant ideas of the Roman Empire's communal sphere, a driving force behind different actions in public life and, conspicuously (but not exclusively – see Graham 2006), various levels of elites strived for a reputation (*fama*) that would surpass their lifetime, so posterity could admire ancestral accomplishments and enduring relevance. However, although the most researched and undisputed, this is but one of the effects that inscribed grave markers produced. Equally important is the aspect of EFMs in creating the deceased, and this is where we can see the full-fledged implications of the perspective urged for in this chapter. By intimate association with the burial place (regarded in the Roman law as *locus religiosus* – Carroll 2006: 4, 79; Hope 2007: 108) and the surface of a grave, as the most visible and tangible component of the funerary assemblage, the funerary markers played a pivotal role in establishing the afterlife ontological condition. One of the reasons for this can be identified in the temporalities of funerary assemblage: whereas the surface of a sepulchre, the marker and (optionally) surrounding architectural features were meant to last, to be on display and in ritual interaction, the burial pit, the container (in most cases) and the remains (with accompanying objects) became invisible just after interment. Correspondingly, without some kind of a grave marker, there is no way to know someone's final resting place (the remembrance of the living is limited if there is not some enduring indicator). Thus, since the departed could exist only through memories and objects (in some cases even in images, portraits, intellectual works, or other deeds) associated with the living person (*cf.* Carroll 2006: 60–61, 69–78), the importance of the funerary markers becomes even more apparent. The deceased-ness acquired quite a different constituency with and without a grave marker, while the employment of epigraphic ones enabled the emergence of unique afterlife entities, each distinguishable both by the marker itself and its text and imagery. An example cited by Zanker and Björn (2012: 180) can be particularly telling here: in the enclosed tomb of the Valerii in Rome, the *domini* of the house were commemorated both by inscriptions and portraiture, which determined them as the deceased of specified qualities. On the other hand, the ashes of some family's clients were put in urns or along the walls, while their slaves and freedpersons were granted burial places inside the tomb's floor but without any visible, durable material features. The point here is quite simple: the deceased a person could transform into with the help of an EFM is quite a different matter from the one without such a mediator.

Another illustrative case can be found in the exceptional discovery of seven burial markers in their original positions (Fig. 3.2) within the north-west necropolis of Scupi (Skopje, Northern Macedonia). Five of these are EFMs, of which two are published (Jovanova 2015a: 108–130, 131–158). In one case the stele (Fig. 3.2, a) was set ahead of (*i.e.* with its plain side above and facing) the grave (G1-04) of the locally well-known type that contained the remains of a cremated individual and was covered with tiles. Along the ashes and fragments of the burned bones, the grave inventory comprised two jugs (as a usual part of the regional burial custom), one ceramic lamp that possibly depicts a gladiator (although it is currently interpreted as Genius, Eros or Silvanus – Jovanova 2015a: 114–115, fig. 10–11) and two burnt (and thus unidentified) bronze coins. The tombstone is of the type common in Scupi and (highly likely) serially produced in a local workshop: it has a semicircular gable, which contains the relief of a rosette and a pinecone. The text in the inscription field runs as: 'To the shade-gods. Zmaragdus, who lived 40 years, lies here. The (society of) worshippers of the temple of Hercules, that is Valerius Satyrianus, under the aedileship of Valerius Eutichetis and quaestorship of Laevi Iuliani, made (the tombstone)' (*D(is) M(anibus) | Σmaragdus | vix(it) ann(os) XXXX | h(ic) s(itus) e(st) | cultore{n}s templi Her- | culis id est | Val(eri) Satyria- | ni sub aedili- | cio Val(eri) Eutiche- | tis et qu(a)estura | Laevi Iuliani | f(aciendum) c(uraverunt)*, Jovanova 2015a: 118). While the inscribed years correspond to the actual age of the cremated individual (Jovanova 2015a: 109, fn. 6), other elements of the grave do not match the textual information in any obvious way (except, perhaps, circumstantial correlation between the lamp depicting a gladiator and Zmaragdus'

Figure 3.2: North-west necropolis of Scupi with funerary markers found in situ; a: tombstone of Zmaragdus; b: tombstone of C. Iulius Arteas (Courtesy of the Museum of the City of Skopje/Lenče Jovanova).

membership in the society related to temple of Hercules). The treatment of the body, the form of the burial pit, and the elements of interment rituals fall within the general funerary trends in Moesia Superior, and they can be understood as a more-or-less standard procedure of dealing with the corpse and aiding the dead to transform into the properly buried deceased. In that sense, the funerary features hardly could contribute to 'specifying' the afterlife entity of Zmaragdus, and it was through EFM that he underwent 'particularisation' that created his unique deceased-ness. However, this was not only the matter of Zmaragdus escaping anonymity and being represented as a man of particular identity and social relations. Rather, it was by the entanglement of his persona and burial place with the EFM's materiality and text that he emerged as the deceased entity of distinctive qualities. The EFM enabled the afterlife entity of Zmaragdus in maintaining certain features and re-emerging as such upon every following interaction with the living.

The other published pairing of a grave (G1-06) and tombstone (Jovanova 2015a: 131–158) contributes to a similar conclusion. Again, the cremated remains of the deceased were placed inside the common-type grave covered with tiles (very similar to Zmaragdus') and accompanied with two jugs, a ceramic lamp, a bronze coin, and a fragmented iron strigil. The jugs, the lamp, and the coin belonged to the usual kinds of funerary goods and were part of a normative burial program. The lamp bears the depiction of a bust with draped clothing and some kind of a headgear, which perhaps alludes to Isis (although Jovanova 2015a: 139, fig. 9 presumes it is Minerva with a helmet), and could suggest the cult's possible significance within funerary ideas of at least some people in the town (since 22 graves in the south-east necropolis contained terracotta lamps with representations of Serapis or Serapis and Isis – Jovanova 2015b: 302–304). The placement of strigils in the graves was not an extremely rare practice in this part of the Roman Empire (Jovanova 2015a: 141–142), and possibly implies some specific but currently unknown characteristic of the buried person. Thus, judging by the traits and inventory of the grave, the only elements, which – to some extent – 'particularised' the interred person were the strigil and depiction on the lamp. In contrast, other features place the burial within the conventional funerary scheme. Nevertheless, the grave was marked with the stele of a typical shape (Fig. 3.2, b), with a rosette in a gable, that bore the inscription 'To the shade-gods. Caius Iulius Artiias, who lived 45 years. Members/brothers of the (society of) Genius of the market (made the tombstone) while the son-in-law Fortunatus looked after it (saw it done)' (*D(is) M(anibus) | C(aius) Iul(ius) Artiias(!) | vixit ann(os) XLV | sodales | a Genio ma- | celii(!) cur(a)n- | te gene(ro) For- | tunato*, Jovanova 2015a: 143–147). Accordingly, it was by associating the tombstone with the burial place and funerary customs that the buried individual became the 'specified' deceased entity. Of course, the interrelation of these mediators produced such an outcome, but since the EFM afforded the senses of materiality, visuality, textuality, and spatiality, it could be considered as a key enabler for the changed ontological condition.

Indeed, the evidence concerning cenotaphs convincingly demonstrates (Carroll 2009: 828–830) that funerals without the dead body (complete or partial) were possible, precisely because the other components of the assemblage of becoming the deceased, and notably the EFMs, allowed for it. The association of the EFM and the person it commemorated gave it the capacity to create the presence of the absent, to invoke and generate the afterlife entity anew in each interaction with the living (*cf.* Erasmo 2008: 10), and to literally stand as the most visible of the mediators through which the posthuman ontological assemblage was distributed. This fact seems to be reflected by a formula found on some EFMs stating that stone and name (*i.e.* monument) remain while other traces (of the departed) perish (*stat lapis et nomen vestigia nulla* – *e.g. AE* 2014, 1531 = EDCS-36400010; *AE* 1993, 1251 = EDCS-16100255; *CIL* VI 22215 = EDCS-13200502). Furthermore, not only did EFMs stand as a reminder of the inevitable dead (Carroll 2006: 53–54), but they had an autonomous potential to summon and even mentally transcend to the realms of the deceased as the story of Cassius Dio effectively reveals:

> Then he [Domitian] invited in his guests alone at night without their slave attendants. At first he set beside each of them a slab shaped like a gravestone, bearing the guest's name and also a small lamp, such as hang in tombs. Next, attractive naked boys, likewise painted black, entered like phantoms, and after circling the guests in an awe-inspiring dance took up positions at their feet. After this, set before the guests were all the things that are commonly offered at the sacrifices to departed spirits, all of them black and in black dishes. As a result every single one of the guests feared and trembled, constantly expecting his throat would be cut the next moment, the more so as everybody but Domitian was dead silent. It was as if they were already in the realms of the dead, and the emperor himself spoke only upon topics relating to death and slaughter (Dio 67.9.1–3, trans. Hope 2007: 119–120).

Indubitably, the entire grim atmosphere, performance, and staging the key funeral elements produced terror in the emperor's guests, but the installation of stones that emulated the EFMs and made the issue personal could be regarded as a triggering and underlining element within Domitian's 'fear factory'. A similar conclusion stems from Suetonius' story (Suet. *Ner.* 49.1) about Nero's preparation for death when the emperor hastily ordered his companions to dig a pit, bring water and wood, and to gather pieces of marble if any could be found (Erasmo 2008: 154). Again, even as substitution by the principle of *pars pro toto*, a burial marker was instrumental if the emperor was to be transformed into the proper deceased and not only a dead human. As a few pieces of undecorated and unengraved marble hardly can be seen as adequate or even sufficient means for commemoration, this episode shows that burial markers were more than just the reflections of identity and memory-savers of a dead person and, rather, played one of the pivotal roles in the ontological transition into an afterlife entity.

Opposite to the previous cases stands the example of a mass grave found in the south-east necropolis of Scupi that contained skeletal remains of around 200 male individuals (discovered so far). They were buried in a shallow trench at the southern outskirts of the necropolis in a naturally depressed area that served for deposing the waste debris from the cemetery (Jovanova 2017: 14–16). The dead were not accompanied by any objects, no traces of their clothes survived, and no evidence of any burial marker was found. The positions of the bones suggest that these people were dumped into the trench after meeting a violent death, with no intention that they would be remembered or interacted with in any manner (since they were covered with the same waste depot previously dug out to form the burial pit). Many of them probably had tied hands and presumably all were executed (most likely by decapitation), whereas it is beyond a reasonable doubt that the tendency was to outcast them both by the manner of killing and deposition of their dead bodies (Jovanova 2017: 16–18). No matter if we concur with the view that this group consisted of the soldiers of a defeated faction in the course of some inner conflicts during the third century AD (Jovanova 2017: 18–19), or we try to find some other explanation, certainly such treatments intended visible stigmatisation and marginalisation, first by deprivation of life and shortly after by denying a decent burial. This illustrates excellently both of the points made above: 1) there is a substantial difference between losing life and becoming a dead body on the one hand, or becoming a conventional deceased entity on the other hand; and 2) the lack of (some kind of) a burial marker disabled the proper and utter ontological transition. Even if the unmarked, vacant space, where the bodies were disposed of, could itself have served as a sufficient indication of the resting place of the executed (*cf.* Fowles 2010), its capacity to work in such a way was derived thanks to the absence of burial marker(s).

Another direct effect of EFMs is their spatiality, *i.e.* their role in making the burial place into a specific relational intersection of trajectories of various kinds (*cf.* Massey 2005 for general discussion on space as the relational dimension of reality). As a component in the ontological assemblage of deceased-ness, an EFM contributed in locating the afterlife entity, while the group of them – together with other sorts of funerary markers – determined the area covered by a necropolis as the separate realm of the departed (*cf.* Hope 2007: 237; Erasmo 2008: 158; Fig. 3.2). Even if the backside of the marker faced the surface of the grave as it was in the north-west necropolis of Scupi, the tight bond of an EFM and burial spot defined the physical limits of ritual activities and interactions between the living and deceased entities, which is evident in practices such as decoration, garlanding, food offerings, libations, feasting, and other activities performed in front and with EFMs (Carroll 2006: 25; Hope 2007: 235). Hence, an EFM (as well as other grave markers) was a thing that directly helped to define the affordance of location for varied performativities, their scope, and the immediate focus of participating humans (see Erasmo 2008: 2–3).

Furthermore, EFMs could be regarded, to some extent at least, as similar to the statues/portraits and their roles in the Roman world. While this association is evident for the grave markers that had sculptural or relief images of the deceased (see Koortboijan 2005: 293–294; Ackers 2019), the tangibility, interactiveness, association with the formerly living person, and distributed deceased entity, permit the supposition that any burial marker could acquire basically comparable traits. As with statues (Stewart 2003: 43, 70, 128–129, 189–190, 192, 275–276; Fejfer 2008: 63–67, 105), EFMs (no matter if they bore the image/figure of their human or not) could also allow for a sort of 'surrogate' or substitution for the deceased, some consolation for the absence of the human. EFMs enabled caring interactions, involving both a certain treatment of the marker (*e.g.* decoration, anointment, cleaning, repairing) and communication with it (conversation, tactile contact, mutilation), and could provoke various emotions and reflections (upon life, death, self, deceased, society, world). After death, relations between a deceased and the living could not be further achieved as exchange between humans, but instead as performative practices among the actors, one of which was an afterlife entity reified through an EFM.

Subsequently, all issues discussed in this section beg the question if EFMs were actually comprehended as an embodiment of the deceased themselves. Although only extremely scarce and circumstantial evidence suggests that the markers might have been regarded as a sort of direct afterlife materialisation of the humans, who lay below them (Hope 2007: 152 nr. 4.34, 237–238 nr. 6.49), we cannot completely exclude such possibility due to the formulaic character of epigraphic sources, the limited and biased nature of written accounts, and the thus virtually unknown beliefs/experiences of the majority of the population in the Roman Empire. On the other hand, in the majority of cases mentioning a grave marker in the epigraphic record (in any context other than who set the *titulus*), there is a clear distinction between the remains of the departed and their tombstones. This situation predominantly concerns the formula of calling the tombstone to lie lightly upon the deceased's remains (*te, lapis, obtestor, leviter super ossa residas*)[2] or, rarely, to wait for its human and then remain standing (*sta dum venio memoria superis*; *sta dum venio et cum venero stabes*, Šašel Kos 2014), both cases setting the conceptual boundary between the two.

However, how EFMs were understood and what beliefs accompanied them is of secondary importance for the questions in the focus of this chapter. The more relevant issue here concerns the role of EFMs inside the very fabric of the distributed deceased entity seen as an outcome of the transformed ontological state. Thus, what I have tried to show is not a matter of assumptions about, opinions on or experiences of EFMs, or how they were related to comprehensions of the funerary sphere, but an issue of what these things enabled and did in the cases when people associated with them. One speculative example may bring the point closer to a clear understanding: a warrior reaches the full capacity and state of the armed human force with/through engaging the skills and weaponry in acting against the enemy; although some warriors may believe that 'they are their armament and vice-versa', this is of lesser significance in comparison to the fact that they reach the full-scale status of fighters only by acting with their weapons. From the theoretical perspective of Actor-Network Theory and agential realism, the engaged human becomes a warrior while the involved object becomes a weapon only by active mutual relation and synergy, *i.e.*, their roles, effects, and the character of the constituted assemblage are defined only by the intra-action they produce. By analogy, the deceased reached their complete ontological metamorphosis only if burial markers, along with other mediators of funerary assemblage, were associated with them, while the ideas, lore, experiences, and explanations concerning the markers are yet another component that had no default priority over the rest.

Epigraphic Funerary Markers in the Webs of Interactions and Entanglements

All recent scholarship emphasises that EFMs operated through and with several interlinked manners of communication simultaneously: text, image, shape, size, location/placement, surroundings, colour, texture, and craftsmanship (Woolf 1996: 25–28, 32; Hope 1997: 245–258; 2003: 136; 2007: 75; Oliver 2000b: 4–5, 18; Bodel 2001: 25–26, 30; Carroll 2006: 18–58; Erasmo 2008: 159). EFMs were meant to address any living human in their proximity in order to convey various messages about the deceased's former life, their preferences and attitudes, emotions (of the departed and bereaved), ideas about the afterlife, etc. These characteristics made them multimedia communicative objects capable of articulating diverse connectivities between different kinds of actors. Thus, in addition to being the component within the ontological assemblage of distributed deceased, and thanks to this quality, they were involved and acted in other spheres of the Roman world as well. In other words, it is possible to assert that one of the essential features of their agency was creation, participation in, and perpetuation of diverse sorts of interrelations. If for the sake of clarity, we imagine an EFM positioned at the intersection of three axes, the following picture emerges (Fig. 3.3).

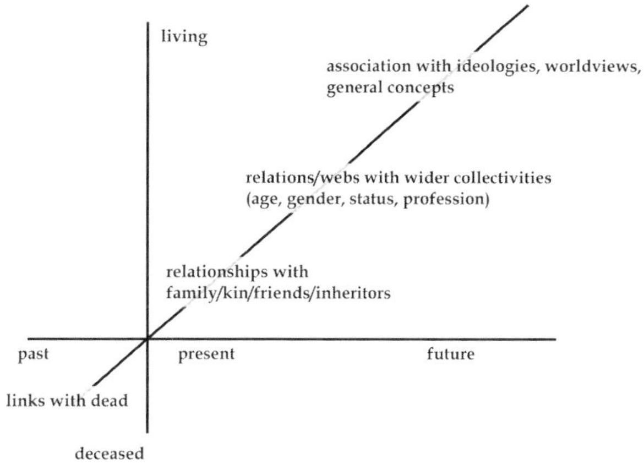

Figure 3.3: Axes of relationalities enabled by the Epigraphic Funerary Markers (Source: Author).

An inscribed funerary marker had a capacity of linking this world with variously conceptualised other worlds and realms of the departed. In this respect, it had the role of the salient material 'interface' that enabled the positioning of the living towards the dead and ensured the creation and maintenance of ties with ancestors. The Y-axis (Fig. 3.3) thus indicates the potential of an EFM to participate in defining the boundary of two separate ontological spheres at the same time mediating between them and acting as a channel for otherwise limited relationships. Sure, this effect is produced thanks to the synergy with other involved mediators, but the point is that the juncture of such a kind would not have been possible without the marker (remember the disposal of the executed in Scupi or other cases of unmarked 'deviant' burials). Therefore, to see and interact with an EFM could have meant to establish an as-close-as-possible link to the otherworldly realm, which was enabled by the straightforward association between an EFM and the deceased.

On the other hand, the X-axis in the illustration points to the marker's effect to transit the time. By commemorating, extending, representing, and enacting the share of the deceased's personhood and afterlife entity respectively, tombstones merged the past and present, simultaneously indicating the future (*cf.* Woolf 1996; Carroll 2006: 18–19; Hope 2007: 72; Graham 2009: 67–68; 2018: 12–13). The relation between the living and the afterlife entities was materialised through the markers that thus acquired the status of mediators, providing the sense of transience and change but at the same time continuity. The interaction with an EFM (or any grave marker for that matter) could have involved the feeling of generation succession and time flow, but simultaneously a fixity of (any kind of) a position and relationship between the living and deceased, both while the latter were alive and after their death. EFMs gave a sense of stability as they played a prominent part in generating the experience of continuity regardless of visible transitions and changes that were happening (*cf.* Graham 2018).

Together with these essential dimensions of the EFMs' multi-relationalities, we can consider the one represented by the Z-axis as well. This line stands for various relations that included the markers as mediators and was defined and functional precisely thanks to such association. First, an EFM was connected with other deceased entities due to its location inside a necropolis (or in other areas away from spaces of the living – Fig. 3.2). The 'cities of the dead' were constituted by grave markers and other components that stood for a populace of a different ontological state, *i.e.*, a separate collectivity of posthuman entities (however each of them was imagined in the afterlife). On an individual level, EFMs were also generating the links with specific deceased from the same kin group, especially if the relationships were explicated and the markers set in the proximity to burial places and tombstones of other members of a given family. Second, EFMs solidified and enacted relationships between the dead and their living associates (of varied types: family, kin, friends, members of a funerary *collegium*, colleagues/comrades, inheritors, etc.). This is apparent in the practice of stating who set up the monument and who was the closest relative to a buried person, which clearly indicated the importance, both for the passed away and the living, to publicly announce the relationships (Saller and Shaw 1984; Meyer 1990; Woolf 1996: 29, 33–34; Hope 1997; 1998; 2003; Mouritsen 2005: 61; Carroll 2006: 39, 180–196; Chioffi 2015: 635). Therefore, it could be argued that EFMs actively participated in the construction of personal relations and were one of the means by which these were determined, coming to existence, and lived. Just as EFMs were part of the phenomenon of distributed deceased, they were also the components of other assemblages involving the living. The announcing of family or other close relationships aided the material articulation and permanence of relevant social institutions (*e.g.* family, agnates, cognates, friendship, status, and other memberships, etc.) and made them real within the funerary sphere. Besides, the visits to a grave and EFM (or other grave markers) and 'keeping in touch' with the deceased could act/enable interactions with neighbouring burial places/markers and the living associated with them (see Zanker and Björn 2012: 29). In this manner, the deceased, localised and articulated through the graves and EFMs, urged their humans to interact with the surrounding departed entities and living people, no matter what kind of relationships might have been built (un/friendly or otherwise). The distributed deceased entities had a direct influence on making contacts in the world of the living, if not more than through their short-term and occasional but relatively regular gatherings around the grave/marker.

The same is true if we move from the level of closest personal ties to the broader social relationalities, which are next on the Z-axis. Communication of gender, age, family/lineage belonging, official status, titles, profession, political, or societal involvement, etc., as well as statements/expressions of cultural preferences through imagery, iconographical motives, poetry, literary quotations, colour, texture, size, and craftsmanship of EFMs, were undoubtedly re-establishing various sorts of relations the deceased had maintained in this world. The divergences among EFMs (and funerary markers in general) revealed distinctions among the deceased and by extension their living, whereas similarities suggested mutual resemblances. Consequently, EFMs were one of the defining factors of social connections, their articulation and performance, but also had a determinative part in the constitution and constant coming into existence of different groups of the living. For example, if we remember the two tombstones from Scupi, one has mentioned and hence reified the society of worshipers of the temple of Hercules and its inner organisation, whereas the other communicated and thus materialised the (funerary?) fellowship of Genius of *macellum*. These clubs and related buildings (the temple, the market) and cult entities (Hercules, Genius) came into being in yet another level (*i.e.* through funerary sphere), thanks to EFMs, which acted as additional mediators in creating them as distinctive phenomena. Generally speaking, EFMs contributed and enabled further means and methodology in the construction and perpetuation of various collectivities of peers, at the same time setting them apart from some other groups (Meyer 1990; Woolf 1996: 32–36; Hope 1997: 255, 257–258; 1998: 191–193; 2001; 2003: 85, 87; Carroll 2006: 19, 33, 58, 96, 128; Revell 2009: 179–181). The ties with EFMs and commemorative practice that they enabled were particularly critical to some social categories (notably in the urban and military settings and especially to soldiers and freed people: Woolf 1996: 36–37; Häussler 1998: 38–44; Hope 2001; 2003; Mouritsen 2005: 55–62; Carroll 2006: 39–40, 247–253; Mattingly 2008: 53–69), and it can be argued that inscribed funerary markers thus had a constituent role in allowing these groups, through particular mutual associations, to acquire specific qualities. In short, EFMs had a proactive role in creating not only the afterlife entities of the dead but also in creating personhoods, relations, and affiliations among the living. Finally, the last point on the Z-axis suggests that EFMs were interlinked with the concepts, worldviews, and ideologies of even wider order, ones that went beyond particular political, status, cultural, or some other categories and were circulating throughout the Roman Empire. These were primarily connected to the ideas of the afterlife, ways of commemoration and relationship with the deceased, overall political organisation, the conceptualisation of gender, and age roles. In this way, as material mediators, they were actively entangled within the general structuring networks and participated in the establishment and maintenance of the dominant order, roles, and relations.

Concluding Remarks

The association of some individuals and groups of people with the monumental-epigraphic practice and EFMs was not a mere outcome of adoption and adaptation of socio-political and cultural templates brought, imposed, and favoured by the imperial structure. Although EFMs were undoubtedly relevant for social strategies, (self)promotion, and individual/collective positionings, the involvement with them as a specific category of things primarily changed the technology of ontological transition. The usage of EFMs introduced new ways to correlate the mediators that created the phenomenon of being deceased, and added components that previously had not been part of the funerary sphere. By associating with an inscribed funerary marker, a dead human could be transformed into an afterlife entity which included particular kinds of memorisation and tangibility (*i.e.* by text, image, spatiality, and durable material), and hence enabled the construction of a specific sort of deceased-ness. The departed, who was transformed from a living human ontological state to a posthuman afterlife ontological condition became a specifically defined deceased, not merely because of their interconnection with an inscribed marker, but due to the EFM's effectiveness in providing relationalities of several different levels.

In other words, thanks to the EFMs' quality of working as tangible and visible components of the departed, these objects can be considered as critical mediators for the emergence of the deceased entities. This feature of EFMs was directly enabled by their entanglement with several aspects of the funerary sphere: 1) the remains and resting places of the dead; 2) epigraphy as a means of capturing and communicating social definitions and relations of the deceased; 3) the commemoration practice and its relevance for the living; 4) funerary rites, concepts of afterlife, and attitudes towards life and death; and 5) the spatial context of the necropolis as the place for the dead. Thus, EFMs acted as the material intersection of multilayered and multidirectional work-nets and as such were pivotal for achieving and maintaining the altered ontological condition. This is the reason EFMs cannot be interpreted only as material means for commemoration, the display of ideas about identities and status, or passive proxies of human society, but must be comprehended as potent objects that enabled the constitution of both the deceased-ness and majority of aspects of such an ontological state. Instead of being the things that mirrored the social features of the living and dead, whose essence supposedly resided in a purely human social domain, they were the integral texture that both accommodated and participated in the building of social relationalities and realities. Consequently, the differences in employment of EFMs, their types and other varieties across the Roman Empire, as well as their diverse relations with other actors in the funerary sphere, could point to particular technologies of becoming the deceased, *i.e.* reveal the diversities of conceptualisation/constitution of afterlife entities and their relationships with the living. In conclusion, the nuances of participation of EFMs as mediators inside the work-nets that articulated and determined the deceased, as well as their relationalities with other social dimensions, could offer us important insights into particular ontological perspectives that go beyond anthropocentric viewpoints.

Department of History, University of Novi Sad

Acknowledgements

I am grateful to Dr Sc. Zrinka Buljević, curator of the Archaeological Museum in Split, who kindly issued me the permission to use the photo of T.A. Aurelianus' mosaic. I also express sincere gratitude to Lenče Jovanova from the City Museum of Skopje, who allowed me to use her photo of tombstones found in the north-west necropolis of Scupi. The suggestions of two anonymous reviewers considerably helped me to improve the chapter and make it clearer. I thank Dr Irene Selsvold and Dr Lewis Webb for honouring me with the invitation to participate in this project and their endless patience and tireless efforts throughout the process of editing the volume. My gratitude also goes to Dr Katherine Crawford and Dr Sarah Scoppie, whose proofreading enormously helped the clarity of the chapter. Of course, the responsibility for mistakes and omissions remains mine exclusively.

Notes

1. The usage of mythical allegories as a way of expressing that the passed away did not really stop living but were taken by the gods (Zeus/Jupiter and Ganymede, Zeus/Jupiter and Europa, Pluto and Proserpine, Cybele and Attis) or fell asleep (Selene and Endymion) is well known in the Roman funerary sphere (Zanker and Björn 2012: 57–110). In this particular case, taking into account Aurelianus' untimely death at the age of 9, a partridge may refer to the story of a youth Perdix, Daedalus' nephew and pupil, who was transformed by Athena into this bird and thus saved from the deadly fall pushed into by the envious uncle (Ov. *Met.* 8.236–59). If accepted, this resonates well with the supposed tendency to commemorate Aurelianus as a pupil and boy of academic interests.
2. EDCS-08000796; EDCS-35200318; *CIL* II 1580 = EDCS-08700420; *AE* 1962, 55= EDCS-09000374; *CIL* III 2183 = EDCS-27700064; *CIL* III 12848 = EDCS-28100135; *CIL* XI 1616 = EDCS-20403092; CIL XI 7024 = EDCS-20700492; *CIL* II-14 1285 = EDCS-05503345; *CIL* XIV 316 = EDCS-05700315; *AE* 1966, 372 = EDCS-11800291; *CIL* III 12437 = EDCS-29100156; *AE* 1951, 251 = EDCS-15200120; *CIL* VI 6873 = EDCS-19300923; *CIL* VI 7872 = EDCS-18700297; *CIL* VI 25427 = EDCS-13801679; *CIL* VI 27728 = EDCS-14801683; *CIL* VI 27814 = EDCS-14801769; *CIL* VI 28523 = EDCS-14802481; *CIL* VI 29011 = EDCS-14802978; *CIL* VI 30116 = EDCS-17202217; *CIL* VI 30118 = EDCS-17202219; *CIL* VI 32311 = EDCS-20500136; *AE* 1958, 169 = EDCS-13500255; *CIL* V 7097 = EDCS-05400349;

CIL XI 654 = EDCS-31800084; *CIL* V 8485 = EDCS-01601304; *AE* 2006, 476 = EDCS-44100325; *CIL* V 470 = EDCS-04200557.

Bibliography

Ancient Sources

Digest (Translated by A. Watson 1985). *The Digest of Justinian, Vol. 1*. Philadelphia: University of Pennsylvania Press.

Dio (Translated by E. Cary 1925). *Dio's Roman History Vol. VIII*. London/New York: William Heinemann/G.P. Putnam's Sons.

Ovid (Translated by F.J. Miller 1951). *Ovid Metamorphoses, Volume 1, Books I–VIII*. London/New York: William Heinemann/G.P. Putnam's sons.

Suetonius (Translated by J.C. Rolfe 1959). *Suetonius Vol. II*. London/New York: William Heinemann/G.P. Putnam's sons.

Modern Sources

Ackers, H.I. 2019. The face of the deceased: portrait busts in Roman tombs. In Z. Newby and R.E. Toulson (eds) *The Materiality of Mourning: Cross-Disciplinary Perspectives*. London/New York: Routledge: 121–147.

Appadurai, A. 1986. Introduction: commodities and the politics of value. In A. Appadurai (ed.) *The Social Life of Things: Commodities in Cultural Perspective*. Cambridge: Cambridge University Press: 3–63.

Barad, K. 2007. *Meeting the Universe Halfway: Quantum Physics and the Entanglement of Matter and Meaning*. Durham/London: Duke University Press.

Barrett, J.C. 2014. The material constitution of humanness. *Archaeological Dialogues* 21 (1): 65–74.

Barrett, J.C. 2016. The new antiquarianism? *Antiquity* 90 (354): 1681–1686.

Bodel, J. 2001. Epigraphy and the ancient historian. In J. Bodel (ed.) *Epigraphic Evidence: Ancient History from Inscriptions*. London/New York: Routledge: 1–56.

Bowman, A. and Woolf, G. (eds) 1994. *Literacy and Power in the Ancient World*. Cambridge: Cambridge University Press.

Carroll, M. 2006. *Spirits of the Dead: Roman Funerary Commemoration in Western Empire*. Oxford: Oxford University Press.

Carroll, M. 2008. 'Vox tua nempe mea est': dialogues with the dead in Roman funerary commemoration. *The Accordia Research Papers* 11: 37–80.

Carroll, M. 2009. Dead soldiers on the move: transporting bodies and commemorating men at home and abroad. In A. Morillo (ed.) *Limes XX. XXth International Congress of Roman Frontier Studies, Léon 2006*. Madrid: Consejo Superior de Investigacions Científicas: 823–832.

Carroll, M. 2011. Memoria and *damnatio memoriae*: preserving and erasing identities in Roman funerary commemoration. In M. Carroll and J. Rempel (eds) *Living through the Dead: Burial and Commemoration in the Classical World*. Oxford: Oxbow Books: 65–90.

Carroll, M. 2013. Ethnicity and gender in Roman funerary commemoration: case studies from the empire's frontiers. In S. Tarlow and L. Nilsson Stutz (eds) *The Oxford Handbook of the Archaeology of Death and Burial*. Oxford: Oxford University Press: 559–579.

Carroll, M. and Rempel, J. (eds) 2011. *Living through the Dead: Burial and Commemoration in the Classical World*. Oxford: Oxbow Books.

Chioffi, L. 2015. Death and burial. In C. Bruun and J. Edmondson (eds) *The Oxford Handbook of Roman Epigraphy*. Oxford: Oxford University Press: 627–648.

Cooley, A. (ed.) 2002. *Becoming Roman, Writing Latin: Literacy and Epigraphy in the Roman West*. Journal of Roman Archaeology Supplementary Series 48. Portsmouth: Journal of Roman Archaeology.

Duplančić, A. 2017. *Membra disiecta* of a Salona's mausoleum. *Tusculum* 10: 71–94.

Edmondson, J. 2007. Funerary inscriptions and the development of local epigraphic cultures in Roman Lusitania. In M. Mayer, G. Baratta and A. Guzmán Almagro (eds) *Actas del XII Congressus Internationalis Epigraphiae Graecae et Latinae: Provinciae Imperii Romani Inscriptionibus descriptae*. Barcelona: Monografies de la Secció Històrico-Arqueològica: 461–468.

Erasmo, M. 2008. *Reading Death in Ancient Rome*. Columbus: Ohio State University Press.

Fahlander, F. and Østigård, T. (eds) 2008. *The Materiality of Death: Bodies, Burials, Beliefs*. Oxford: British Archaeological Reports.

Fejfer, J. 2008. *Roman Portraits in Context*. Berlin/New York: Walter de Gruyter.

Fogelin, L. and Schiffer, M.B. 2015. Rites of passage and other rituals in the life histories of objects. *Cambridge Archaeological Journal* 25 (4): 815–827.

Fowler, C. 2004. *The Archaeology of Personhood: An Anthropological Approach*. London/New York: Routledge.

Fowler, C. 2016. Relational personhood revisited. *Cambridge Archaeological Journal* 26 (3): 397–412.

Fowler, C. and Harris, O.J.T. 2015. Enduring relations: exploring a paradox of new materialism. *Journal of Material Culture* 20 (2): 127–148.

Fowles, S. 2010. People without things. In M. Bille, F. Hastrup and T. Flohr Sørensen (eds) *An Anthropology of Absence Materializations of Transcendence and Loss*. New York: Springer: 23–41.

Gell, A. 1998. *Art and Agency: An Anthropological Theory*. Oxford: Clarendon Press.

Graham, E-J. 2006. Discarding the destitute: ancient and modern attitudes towards burial practices and memory preservation amongst the lower classes of Rome. In B. Croxford, H. Goodchild, J. Lucas and N. Ray (eds) *TRAC 2005: Proceedings of the Fifteenth Annual Theoretical Roman Archaeology Conference*. Oxford: Oxbow Books: 57–72.

Graham, E-J. 2009. Becoming persons, becoming ancestors: personhood, memory and the corpse in Roman rituals of social remembrance. *Archaeological Dialogues* 16 (1): 51–74.

Graham, E-J. 2011. From fragments to ancestors: re-defining the role of *os resectum* in rituals of purification and commemoration in Republican Rome. In M. Carroll and J. Rempel (eds) *Living through the Dead: Burial and Commemoration in the Classical World*. Oxford: Oxbow Books: 91–109.

Graham, E-J. 2018. 'There buds the laurel': nature, temporality, and the making of place in the cemeteries of Roman Italy. *Theoretical Roman Archaeology Journal* 1: 1–16.

Harris, O.J.T. 2016. Becoming post-human: identity and the ontological turn. In M. Campbell and R. Pierce (eds) *Creating Material Worlds: The Uses of Identity in Archaeology*. Oxford: Oxbow Books: 17–38.

Harris, O.J.T. and Cipolla, C.N. 2017. *Archaeological Theory in the New Millennium: Introducing Current Perspectives*. Abingdon/New York: Routledge.

Häussler, R. 1998. *Resta, viator, et lege*: thoughts on the epigraphic habit. *Papers from the Institute of Archaeology* 9: 31–56.

Häussler, R. 2014. Differences in the epigraphic habit in the rural landscapes of Gallia Narbonensis. In W. Eck and P. Funke (eds) Öffentlichkeit – Monument – Text. XIV Congressus Internationalis Epigraphiae Graecae et Latinae 27.–31. Augusti MMXII. Berlin/Boston: Walter de Gruyter: 323–345.

Hicks, D. 2010. The material-cultural turn: event and effect. In D. Hicks and M.C. Beaudry (eds) *The Oxford Handbook of Material Culture Studies*. Oxford: Oxford University Press: 25–99.

Hodder, I. 2012. *Entangled. An Archaeology of the Relationships between Humans and Things*. Chichester: Wiley-Blackwell.

Hodder, I. 2016. *Studies in Human-Thing Entanglement*. http://www.ian-hodder.com/books/studies-human-thing-entanglement [Last Accessed 30/12/2018].

Hope, V.M. 1997. Words and pictures: the interpretation of Romano-British tombstones. *Britannia* 28: 245–258.

Hope, V.M. 1998. Negotiating identity and status: the gladiators of Roman Nimes. In R. Laurence and J. Berry (eds) *Cultural Identity in the Roman Empire*. London/New York: Routledge: 179–195.

Hope, V.M. 2000. Inscription and sculpture: the construction of identity in the military tombstones of Roman Mainz. In G.J. Oliver (ed.) *The Epigraphy of Death: Studies in the History and Society of Greece and Rome*. Liverpool: Liverpool University Press: 155–185.

Hope, V.M. 2001. *Constructing Identity: The Roman Funerary Monuments of Aquileia, Mainz and Nimes*. Oxford: British Archaeological Reports.

Hope, V.M. 2003. Trophies and tombstones: commemorating the Roman soldier. *World Archaeology* 35 (1): 79–97.

Hope, V.M. 2007. *Death in Ancient Rome: A Sourcebook*. London/New York: Routledge.

Hope, V.M. 2011. Remembering to mourn: personal mementos of the dead in Ancient Rome. In V.M. Hope and J. Huskinson (eds) *Memory and Mourning: Studies on Roman Death*. Oxford: Oxbow Books: 176–195.

Hope, V.M. and Huskinson, J. (eds) 2011. *Memory and Mourning: Studies on Roman Death*. Oxford: Oxbow Books.

Jovanova, L. 2015a. *Skupi – nekropoli: Storii za istaknati ličnosti spored epigrafski i arheološki svedoštva*. Skopje: Kalamus.

Jovanova, L. 2015b. On some of the oriental cults in the Skopje-Kumanovo region. In A. Nikoloska and S. Müskens (eds) *Romanising Oriental Gods? Religious Transformation in the Balkan Provinces in the Roman Period. New Finds and Novel Perspectives*. Skopje/Leiden: Macedonian Academy of Sciences and Arts/University of Leiden: 293–322.

Jovanova, L. 2017. Mass grave. In T. Mikulčić (ed.) *A Glance into the Dark Side of the Roman History. Scupi – A Mass Grave*. Skopje: Museum of the City of Skopje: 13–20.

Keil, D. 2017. The ontological prison: new materialisms and their dead ends. *Contradictions: A Journal for Critical Thought* 1 (2): 41–59.

King, M. 2000. Commemoration of infants on Roman funerary inscriptions. In G.J. Oliver (ed.) *The Epigraphy of Death: Studies in the History and Society of Greece and Rome*. Liverpool: Liverpool University Press: 117–154.

Knappett, C. and Malafouris, L. (eds) 2008. *Material Agency. Towards a Non-Anthropocentric Approach*. New York: Springer.

Koortboijan, M. 2005 *Mimesis* or *phantasia*? Two representational modes in Roman commemorative art. *Classical Antiquity* 24 (2): 285–306.

Kopytoff, I. 1986. The cultural biography of things: commoditization as process. In A. Appadurai (ed.) *The Social Life of Things: Commodities in Cultural Perspective*. Cambridge: Cambridge University Press: 64–91.

Latour, B. 2005. *Reassembling the Social. An Introduction to Actor-Network-Theory*. Oxford: Oxford University Press.

MacMullen, R. 1982. The epigraphic habit in the Roman Empire. *The American Journal of Philology* 103 (3): 233–246.

Mann, J.C. 1985. Epigraphic consciousness. *The Journal of Roman Studies* 75: 204–206.

Massey, D. 2005. *For Space*. London: SAGE

Mattingly, D. 2008. Urbanism, epigraphy and identity in the towns of Britain under Roman rule. In H.M. Schellenberg, V.E. Hirschmann and A. Krieckhaus (eds) *A Roman Miscellany: Essays in Honour of Anthony R. Birley on his Seventieth Birthday*. Gdansk: Akanthina: 53–69.

Meyer, E. 1990. Explaining the epigraphic habit in the Roman Empire: the evidence of epitaphs. *Journal of Roman Studies* 80: 74–96.

Miller, D. 2010. *Stuff*. Cambridge: Polity Press.

Mouritsen, H. 2005. Freedmen and decurions: epitaphs and social history in Imperial Italy. *Journal of Roman Studies* 95: 38–63.

Newby, Z. 2019. The Grottarossa doll and her mistress: hope and consolation in a Roman tomb. In Z. Newby and R.E. Toulson (eds) *The Materiality of Mourning: Cross-Disciplinary Perspectives*. London/New York: Routledge: 77–102.

Oliver, G.J. (ed.) 2000a. *The Epigraphy of Death: Studies in the History and Society of Greece and Rome*. Liverpool: Liverpool University Press.

Oliver, G.J. 2000b. An introduction to the epigraphy of death: funerary inscriptions as evidence. In G.J. Oliver (ed.) *The Epigraphy of Death: Studies in the History and Society of Greece and Rome*. Liverpool: Liverpool University Press: 1–23.

Olsen, B. 2010. *In Defense of Things. Archaeology and the Ontology of Objects*. Lanham: Altamira Press.

Olsen, B. 2012. Symmetrical archaeology. In I. Hodder (ed.) *Archaeological Theory Today, Second Edition*. Cambridge: Polity Press: 208–228.

Olsen, B. and Witmore, C. 2015. Archaeology, symmetry and the ontology of things. A response to critics. *Archaeological Dialogues* 22 (2): 187–197.

Parker Pearson, M. 2003. *The Archaeology of Death and Burial*. Stroud: The History Press.

Pearce, J. and Weeks, J. (eds) 2017. *Death as a Process*. Oxford: Oxbow Books.

Pearce, M., Millett, M. and Struck, M. (eds) 2000. *Burial, Society and Context in the Roman World*. Oxford: Oxbow Books.

Revell, L. 2009. *Roman Imperialism and Local Identities*. Cambridge: Cambridge University Press.

Saller, R.P. and Shaw, B.D. 1984. Tombstones and Roman family relations in the Principate: civilians, soldiers and slaves. *The Journal of Roman Studies* 74: 124–156.

Šašel Kos, M. 2014. A glimpse into stonecutters' workshops in Scupi, Upper Moesia. In A. Donati and G. Poma (eds) *L'officina epigrafica romana in ricordo di Giancarlo Susini*. Faenza: Fratelli Lega Editori: 507–524.

Shaviro, S. 2014. *The Universe of Things. On Speculative Realism*. Minneapolis/London: University of Minnesota Press.

Stewart, P. 2003. *Statues in Roman Society: Representation and Response*. Oxford: Oxford University Press.

Thomas, J. 2015. The future of archaeology. *Antiquity* 89: 1287–1296.

Van Oyen, A. 2015. Actor-Network Theory's take on archaeological types: becoming, material agency, and historical explanation. *Cambridge Archaeological Journal* 25: 63–78.

Van Oyen, A. 2016. Historicising material agency: from relations to relational constellations. *Journal of Archaeological Method and Theory* 23: 354–378.

Van Oyen, A. 2017. Finding the material in 'material culture': form and matter in Roman concrete. In A. Van Oyen and M. Pitts (eds) *Materialising Roman History*. Oxford: Oxbow Books: 133–152.

Van Oyen, A. and Pitts, M. (eds) 2017. *Materialising Roman History*. Oxford: Oxbow Books.

Woolf, G. 1996. Monumental writing and the expansion of Roman society in the Early Roman Empire. *The Journal of Roman Studies* 86: 22–39.

Zanker, P. and Björn, C.E. 2012. *Living with Myths. The Imagery of Roman Sarcophagi*. Oxford: Oxford University Press.

Abbreviations

AE	*L'Année épigraphique.*
CIL	*Corpus Inscriptionum Latinarum.*
EDCS	Epigraphik Datenbank Clauss/Slaby. http://www.manfredclauss.de/ [Last Accessed 15/10/2018].

4

Decentralising Human Agency: A Study of the Ritual Function of the Votive Figurines from Grotta Bella, Umbria

Arianna Zapelloni Pavia

Artefacts are not just clues to be decoded … instead, artefacts are integrant components of the past, which were shaped by, and in turn helped to shape, human behaviour (Jones 2004: 330).

Introduction

More than two-thousand votive figurines, representing offerors, warriors, animals, anatomical parts, and heads, have been retrieved from the sanctuaries of ancient Umbria. Although Guy Bradley notes that this material 'is a vital source of information for any picture of Umbrian religion' (Bradley 2000: 67) aside from a few site-based publications, this substantial body of evidence has escaped the attention of scholars. A common shortcoming of the few investigations into the Umbrian material that have appeared is a tendency to focus on the votives' socio-political meaning and to consider anatomical votives strictly as part of the 'Romanisation' package brought about by Rome during its expansion. Little attention, if any, has been given to the ritual meaning of dedicating votive objects in the region and how this changed during the third to the first centuries BC.

The present investigation has been influenced by recent approaches to cultural change in the Italian peninsula after the Roman conquest and by contemporary theoretical approaches to the study of ancient artefacts. The impact of Roman expansion on the sacred sphere of ancient Italy has only recently begun to receive focused attention in the field of archaeology (Stek and Burgers 2015). Scholars interested in the cultural process that is generally called Romanisation (in the absence of a better term) tend to overlook religious life. Moreover, when they pay attention to it, they discount the religious background of the local population and its material manifestation in the archaeological records and focus primarily on the outcome of the Roman expansion (Stek 2009; Jehne *et al.* 2013).

Votive religion can be a very useful tool for understanding patterns of change in the religious sphere of ancient Umbria. Taking up the sacred site at the Grotta Bella cave as a case study, I use a posthuman lens to de-centre human agency as a focal point in the study of votive figurines found in this cave. This approach sheds light on the cultural continuity, modification, and reinterpretation of ritual practices as a consequence of, and in response to, Roman expansion.

Archaeology of Religion

The archaeology of religion is a field of research that has a significant role in the exploration and understanding of past activities. For decades, however, archaeologists have struggled to find ways to recognise religious activity in the archaeological record. Religion was considered essentially metaphysical and abstract (Hawkes 1954) and therefore, difficult to detect in the material world.

Later developments in fields such as sociology, anthropology, and religious studies (Bourdieu 1977; 1980; Giddens 1984; Bell 1997) that paid progressively greater attention to religious practices and how religion is present in people's daily lives have contributed to archaeological studies on ancient ritual. The understanding that religion is emplaced in the material world has led many scholars to re-evaluate the material remains of ritual activities and to make increased efforts to bridge the apparent divide between the reconstruction of ancient rituals and archaeological data. As Evangelos Kyriakidis notes, ritual 'is most often a repeated activity, the material remains of which may create patterns' (Kyriakidis

2007c: 9). In the past two decades, an increasing number of scholars have attempted to reconstruct ancient rituals based on observable patterns, and they have contributed to making the archaeology of ancient ritual a dynamic and growing field of inquiry (Gebel *et al.* 2002; Insoll 2004; Kyriakidis 2007a; Barrowclough and Malone 2007; Whitley and Hays-Gilpin 2008; Steadman 2009; Hodder 2010; Insoll 2012; Laneri 2015; Swenson 2015). In light of this scholarship, my research aims to further enhance the debate regarding the intent and motivation attached by the dedicators to the materialisation of ritual activities.

Posthuman Theoretical Perspectives

Among the ongoing theoretical contributions to the field of the archaeology of ritual, the 'material turn' occupies a particularly important position. The material turn is part of a broad range of new approaches to archaeology that have been defined as relational or posthuman (Harris 2016: 17) and that reconceptualise categories of person and things and their relations. Following the lead of Alfred Gell's foundational book *Art and Agency: An Anthropological Theory* (1998) and Bruno Latour's 'Actor-Network Theory' (1990; 1999; 2005) much contemporary archaeological research highlights the active role of objects and articulates object agency by emphasising how human behaviour and cognition are influenced by the material world. Chris Gosden, for example, focuses on the replacement of Iron Age objects from southern Britain with Roman objects and analyses how the object's form and style influenced people. He draws from Gell's idea that objects have their own logic and that human behaviour and thoughts may 'take the shape suggested by the object, rather than objects simply manifesting pre-existing forms of thought' (Gosden 2005: 196).

Similarly, Ian Hodder (2012; 2014) argues that the materiality of things creates a set of dependencies between objects and people (entanglements), which he breaks down into four types: human-thing, thing-human, thing-thing, and human-human. Hodder, unlike Latour, considers the relationship between things and humans as asymmetrical, because the dependencies that one can have on the other lead 'to entrapments in particular pathways from which it is difficult to escape' (Hodder 2012: 19). Another central contribution to the recent 'material turn' in archaeological research is Carl Knappett's study of the relation between humans and objects (Knappett 2005). He concludes that humans and their artefacts 'bring each other into being' (Knappett 2005: 170).

Object theories and, more broadly, posthuman theories have recently been applied to archaeology of religion with increasing attempts to consider object intentionality and agency and to dissociate archaeology from complicated modern notions of human exceptionalism and individualist subjectivity. Among recent practice-based approaches in religious studies, research carried out by scholars such as Lynn Meskell (2004), John Barrett (1994; 2000), and Bill Sillar (2009), who work on Egypt, Greece, and the Andes respectively, emphasises that different objects – from human-made items to features of the natural landscape – have agency and intentionality that shape religious traditions. These scholars observe the inseparability of beliefs and other internal cognitive or emotional experience from material culture: objects express and shape symbolic meanings, identities, relationships, and perceptions. For these reasons, they argue that agency lies in the social relationship people have with the material world and that material objects can have social identities. These approaches emphasise the posthuman ethic of decentring the human: they enable us to consider the archaeological record as the visible materialisation of the interdependence between objects and human and challenge the limitations of modernist, western perspectives on the world.

Votive Offerings in Central Italy

In societies accustomed to giving gifts to transcendent beings, such as Italic and Roman societies, votive offerings represent the most prevalent evidence of ritual activity (Griffith 2013: 325). Any object could be vowed, but generally votives consisted of perishable items (*e.g.* grains and plants, milk, wine, honey, cakes); personal items (*e.g.* toys, amulets, jewellery); practical items (*e.g.* fish hooks, loom weights, tools, utensils, incense burners); statuettes/statues (*e.g.* gods, mortals, swaddled babies, animals); representations of body parts (*e.g.* miniaturised models of every description); altars, *cippi,* and bases; ceramic items (*e.g.* miniaturised pottery, lamps, temple models); and coins. These offerings are both abundant and ubiquitous. Votive offerings were left on display in urban, rural, extramural, extra-urban, spring, lake, mountain, cave, state, and private cult areas (Edlund-Berry 1988).

The quantity and variety of votive types inspired the term 'votive religion' since votives are tangible and long-lasting evidence for the principle of reciprocity. As Walter Burkert has emphasised, votive offerings embody the principle of exchangeability – *do ut des* ('I give so that you give') – that granted divine aid in exchange for the donor's vow (Burkert 1987: 43–44). As such, they are considered a visible expression of the interaction and communication between the donors and the deities. Thus, the beliefs and motives of the worshipper must have played an essential role in the selection of the dedication.

The function of votive offerings as gifts that bind men and gods makes this class of material an important tool for exploring cultural and ritual dynamics in ancient societies (Bradley and Glinister 2013: 173–191). First, votive offerings illuminate the complex relationship between people and things, and between people and gods (Osborne 2004). Second, votives can be used as a source of information towards the reconstruction of an ancient economy (Nijboer 2001), social and political aspects (Schultz 2006), and ritual practices (De Grummond and Simon 2006; Gleba and Becker 2009). Although the relevance of votive religion in Greek and Roman contexts has been recognised in recent publications (Glinister 2006a; 2006b; Kyriakidis 2007a; Pakkanen and Bocher 2015, Draycott and Graham 2017), this class of material presents challenges (Osborne 2004). Firstly, as any other class of ancient material, votive objects lend themselves to typological analysis. The consequence of devoting attention primarily to the classification not of assemblages but of objects, which are believed to provide chronological information, is to overlook the potential of artefact assemblages to elucidate ritual behaviours. Secondly, archaeologists struggle to differentiate between objects that have been dedicated and those that have been simply discarded. This is one of the primary complications of the interpretation of ritual in the archaeological record (Kyriakidis 2007b: 1–8; Pakkanen and Bocher 2015: 32–43). Finally, Robin Osborne rightly points out the hesitance among scholars to agree on a single term to refer to dedicated objects (Osborne 2004: 5–6): dedications, offerings, votives, hoards, or simply deposits, depending on what feature of the object the writer wants to emphasise (permanence of the gift/action of giving/connection with prior vow/quantity/ circumstances of the act of depositing). For the purpose of this chapter, I use the term 'votive'.

Within the context of the Italic peninsula, the study of votive offerings has suffered for decades from narrowly focused scholarly attention to anatomical terracottas and Etruscan rituals and beliefs. Even though recent work has highlighted that the exponential increase in the available material does not corroborate the orthodox view (Gentili 2005; Glinister 2006a; 2006b), much of the current debate still revolves around the ideological aspect of anatomical terracottas, considered as tools to track the process of Romanisation (Comella 1981; Torelli 1999; Stek and Burgers 2015; esp. De Cazanove 2000: 29–67, with strong correction from Glinister 2006a and 2006b). This scholarly insistence on anatomical votives as a sign of Roman cultural influence simplifies the interactions between Romans and locals and obscures the other possible categories of ancient Italic votive offerings.

Following the lead of Greek archaeology (Renfrew 1985; Warren 1988; Barrett 1994; Barrett 2000; Meskell 2004; Faro 2008; Sillar 2009; Pakkanen and Bocher 2015: 65–107), in recent years, archaeologists working on religious practices in ancient Italy have begun to look at how humans interact with material culture: how materials affect the behaviour of human beings and their complex networks, and how objects and their interconnections shape the experience of being in the world.

Emma-Jayne Graham's study of the anatomical votives from Gravisca and Punta della Vipera in Latium (Graham 2017) emphasises the multivalent nature of anatomical votives and focuses on how they affected the lives of their dedicants. She uses ideas of personhood, fragmentation, and enchainment to argue that votive offerings centred on the body can shed light on the understanding of human and divine personhood. More focused on the ritual practices is the recent work of Ilaria Battiloro on Lucanian sanctuaries (Battiloro 2018), which represents a milestone in the study of cult places and ritual practices in Southern Italy. Battiloro carefully analyses votive offerings from Lucanian sanctuaries and the ritual performances associated with them. Umbrian material has yet to receive similar attention. What follows is an effort to bridge the gap. After a brief methodological note, the first part addresses how votive deposits have been studied in this region, and the second presents the votive deposit from Grotta Bella.

The Ritual Function of Umbrian Bronze Figurines

Methodological Note

The majority of Umbrian cult places were excavated in the 1960s and 70s, with the result that stratigraphic analysis and techniques were not often applied. Furthermore, Umbrian votives have rarely been found in their original deposition level. In a manner similar to other parts of the peninsula and Greece, overtime votives were removed to make space for other offerings. However, their sacred value was not lost with their removal. Votive objects were accumulated in votive deposits in specific areas of the sanctuaries. For archaeologists, this means that the find context offers no stratification for a relative chronology. In addition to those found buried in secondary depositions, several Umbrian votives have been found distributed across the enclosure *temenos* or have been discovered accidentally on the surrounding surface, often due to the disturbance caused by more recent agricultural production. As is evident, the circumstances of votives' discoveries have an impact not only on their dating, which is often based on comparanda and stylistic criteria, but also on the reconstruction of the original purpose of their dedication. In my interpretation, therefore, both simplifications and generalisations are inevitable.

Approaches to the Study of Umbrian Votives

Studies of votive bronzes from Umbria have been largely influenced by Giovanni Colonna's *Bronzi votivi Umbro Sabellici* (1970). Colonna categorised the votives according to their stylistic affinities and labelled each group with the name of one of their principal find sites. He identified the figures of the warriors as the most common type and called them 'Mars in Assault'. Moreover, he recognised some figures as *oranti*, or worshippers, others as Hercules, walking figures, dancers, and devotees (Colonna 1970: 23–115). Bronze representations of parts of the body and bronze animals are not included in Colonna's work.

Umbrian bronze figurines have mostly been studied in order to shed light on the social and economic aspects of the communities that participated in religious activities. The likelihood that bronze figurines were publicly displayed in Umbrian sanctuaries has led scholars to see them as a means for the donors to compete within the context of sanctuaries. Paola Bonomi Ponzi for example, interprets the figurines of domestic animals and warriors as a representation of the basis of the aristocratic power (Bonomi Ponzi 1991: 64), while Bradley understands the more sophisticated types of bronzes as a sign of the active presence of Umbrian elite in the sanctuaries (Bradley 2000: 72). By the same token, Luana Cenciaioli interprets the presence of simple and schematic figurines as markers of the sanctuaries' frequentation by people from outside the social elite (Cenciaioli 1991: 212).

Scholars who focus primarily on the representation of animals and warriors favour an interpretation that considers the sanctuaries as the foci of rural populations. Daniela Monacchi, for example, has suggested that the more schematic bronzes of animals are thank-offerings for the protection of the donor's herd (Monacchi 1986: 81).

The same socio-economic approach can be noted for the votive deposits of the Roman period. Between the end of the fourth and the third centuries, as the Roman presence in Umbria spread and became a permanent fixture, bronze figurines that characterise votive deposits of the Archaic period noticeably decrease. In their stead, we find a wider array of votives among which the plastic figures include worshippers wearing a *corona radiata* (radiate crown) and anatomical terracottas, a type of offering whose popularity begins to fade in the first century BC.

Despite Fay Glinister's attempts to show that anatomicals existed in bronze also in the Archaic period and that terracottas do not necessarily coincide with the areas of Roman expansion (Glinister 2006a; 2006b), several archaeologists working in Umbria still regard anatomical terracottas as a sign of not just Romanisation, but in some cases of 'the physical presence of Roman colonists in the region', or of the arrival of new cults (Monacchi 1986; Roncalli 1989; Bonomi Ponzi 1989; Sisani 2013: 134).

All of this has, so far, overlooked the ritual function of this data: how do these bronze votives, which represent the primary ritual artefacts of Umbrian sanctuaries, define Umbrian religious ritual? Or, in other words, how does the analysis of these votives inform us about the character of the ritual associated with their deposition? The only attempt to address the ritual aspect of Umbrian cult places is Caroline Malone and Simon Stoddart's discussion of the results of the Gubbio Project (Malone and Stoddart 1994a). They suggest that the simplicity of the ritual enclosure at Gubbio points toward small-scale investment and low-key participation. However, they do not make any attempt to evaluate the type of ritual that the votives from this site may represent.

Case Study: The Sacred Cave of Grotta Bella

The Grotta Bella is a cave dug into the hard limestone of the Monte Aiola, located near Avigliano Umbro, eight kilometres from the town of Amelia (ancient Ameria, Fig. 4.1). The cavity is 10 m high, with the broadest diameter of 40 m. A corridor dug in the wall opposite to the entrance branches off in two tunnels, each about 50 metres long. The cave was discovered in 1902, and its main room excavated by the Soprintendenza Delle Antichità dell'Umbria (under the direction of M.S. Arena) with the collaboration of the Istituto di Paletnologia of the University of Milan (Arena 1975–1976: 481). It was inhabited from the Neolithic period (5000–3000 BC) until the late Bronze Age (1200–1000 BC) and became a cult place from the Archaic to the end of the Imperial period (sixth century BC to fourth century AD). The most superficial layers of the stratigraphy inside the cave have yielded a deposit of votive figurines dating from the sixth century BC to the fourth century AD.[1]

The sheer amount and variety of votive material found at Grotta Bella is representative of the abundance of ritual practices in the Umbrian region. As the Iguvine Tablets illustrate, Umbrian rituals included a variety of actions such as prayers, purifications, libations, sacrifices, and offerings (Rosenzweig 1937; Devoto 1948: 9–25; Poultney 1959: 15–23). Given the pivotal role sanctuaries played in the strengthening of communities' bonds and identities (Bradley 2000: 67; Zapelloni Pavia *forthcoming*), we should imagine that these activities could take place at the sanctuaries of the region virtually every day. Invaluable for our knowledge of Umbrian religion and cult practice, the seven bronze Iguvine Tablets were discovered in 1444 in the Italian town of Gubbio, in Umbria. Four of the tables (I, II, III, and IV) and part of the fifth (seven lines of table Va) are written using the Umbrian script, with the remaining text (line 8 of table Vb and tables VI and VII) recorded in the Latin alphabet. The former date from the third to the second centuries BC, the

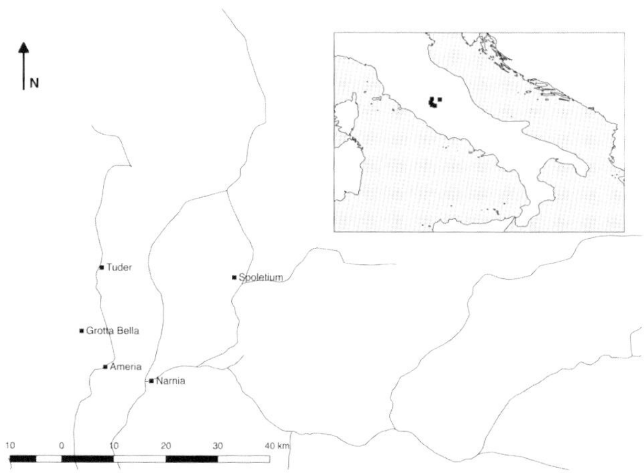

Figure 4.1: Location of the cave of Grotta Bella and the Umbrian and Roman cities mentioned in the text (Map by Irene Selsvold).

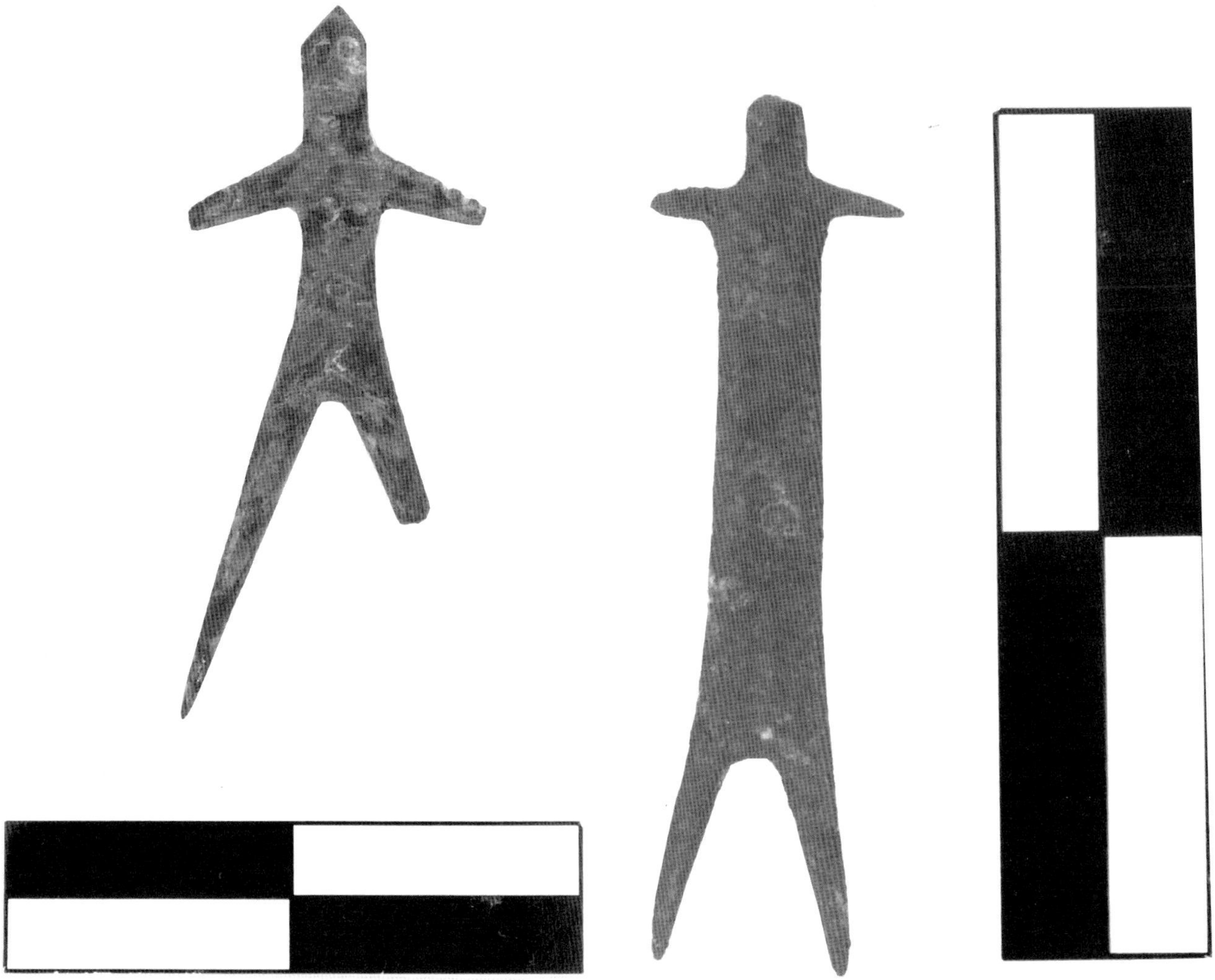

Figure 4.2: Esquiline figurines of worshipper. Fifth century BC, from the Grotta Bella. Archaeological depot of the Soprintendenza Archeologia Belle Arti e Paesaggio dell'Umbria (Photo by author by permission of the Soprintendenza ABAP dell'Umbria).

latter to the first half of the first century BC (for the absolute dating of the Tablets see Prosdocimi 1984: 151–161). The subject matter is a long series of rituals regularly conducted by a group of priests (the Aetian brothers) to protect the community of Iguvium, including taking of the auspices, prayers, the sacrifice of victims, and a procession around the walls of the city to purify it and its inhabitants and to execrate the neighbouring people.

Ritual activity in the Grotta Bella cave during the Archaic period is attested by a votive assemblage, partially published by Monacchi (1986), that comprises 207 bronze human figurines, 35 bronze warrior figurines, 7 bronze anatomicals, 15 bronze animal figurines, and 8 lead figurines. The human bronzes are under 10 cm in height, schematic in form, and are ascribable to the 'Esquiline type' codified by Giovanni Colonna (1970). They represent male and female figures in a frontal position, with outstretched arms, faceted modelling of the head, and slashes across the ends of the arms to indicate the fingers. The male types feature projections representing their sexual organs, while female types lack the projecting sex organs and have long clothing of some sort (Fig. 4.2). The warriors are identifiable by the presence of a highly schematic crest on the head and/or a hole in the right arm for a spear. Thirty-three belong to the 'Esquiline type' and are extremely small (under 5 cm in height), with legs spread wide and placed on the same level (Fig. 4.3), while two belong to Colonna's 'Nocera Umbra Group' and have a more filiform body (Fig. 4.4). As with the other male and female types, this warrior's body is also presented schematically, and only the crest on the head is rendered three-dimensionally. The anatomical bronzes range between 4 and 6 cm and consist of three small heads, one small leg, and two feet (Fig. 4.5).

The 15 animal bronzes (7 bovines, 5 swine, and 7 ovine) are similarly schematic in the rendering of the bodies; anatomical details are rendered by grooves or by small circles carved in the bronze (Fig. 4.6). All these types were

Figure 4.3: Figurine of warrior. Fifth century BC, from the Grotta Bella. Archaeological depot of the Soprintendenza Archeologia Belle Arti e Paesaggio dell'Umbria (Photo by author by permission of the Soprintendenza ABAP dell'Umbria).

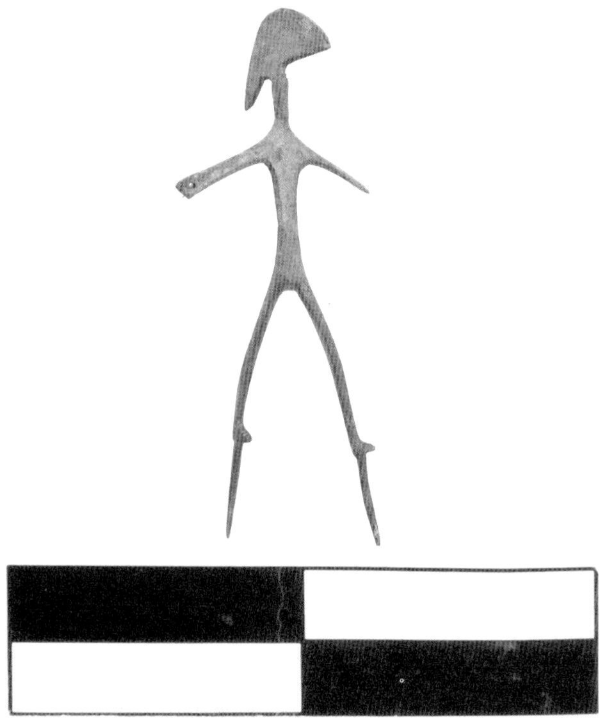

Figure 4.4: Warrior, 'Nocera Umbra'–group. Fifth century BC, from the Grotta Bella. Archaeological depot of the Soprintendenza Archeologia Belle Arti e Paesaggio dell'Umbria (Photo by author by permission of the Soprintendenza ABAP dell'Umbria).

Figure 4.5: Anatomical bronzes. Third century BC, from the Grotta Bella. Archaeological depot of the Soprintendenza Archeologia Belle Arti e Paesaggio dell'Umbria (Photo by author by permission of the Soprintendenza ABAP dell'Umbria).

Figure 4.6: Figurine of bovine. Fifth century BC, from the Grotta Bella. Archaeological depot of the Soprintendenza Archeologia Belle Arti e Paesaggio dell'Umbria (Photo by author by permission of the Soprintendenza ABAP dell'Umbria).

produced by simple processes of casting and filling in local workshops across Umbria and neighbouring areas of the Apennines (Bradley 2000: 68).

The 8 lead figurines are 7–12 cm high, dressed, and include 6 female and 2 male figures (Fig. 4.7). In the female types, eyes and breast are rendered in relief and the clothing, consisting of long tunics, is decorated with a zig-zag or wavy pattern. The male types are represented in the action of striding and armed with shield and shoulders straps. The right arm is lifted and suggests that the warriors originally held a spear or a sword. As Monacchi points out, lead votives are found in Umbria only at Grotta Bella and in the pre-Roman necropolis at Amelia, suggesting local production (Monacchi 1988: 83). Another peculiarity of both the bronze and the lead figurines from Grotta Bella is that they have sharp points on their lower surfaces. Malone, Stoddart, and Guy Bradley have hypothesised that such protrusions were intended to anchor the votives onto a wooden surface so that they could more easily be displayed (Malone and Stoddart 1994b: 128; Bradley 2000: 72).

During the fourth and especially in the third centuries BC, Umbria entered into the sphere of influence of Rome. As in the case of other rural sanctuaries of the Italian peninsula, the cave sanctuary of Grotta Bella continued to be used during and after the Roman conquest, despite being some distance away from developing urban centres (Bradley 2000: 175–178). Plastic offerings of the Roman period are dated between the end of the fourth century BC and the second century BC. They consist of two votive terracotta feet and one terracotta breast (Fig. 4.8), two bronze figures of an adorant of the Hellenistic type (Fig. 4.9), a terracotta model of a temple, 77 bronze coins, and black-slip pottery, mostly *paterae* and miniature vases. The broader range of votive material during the Roman period is not unique to Grotta Bella. As Bradley has indicated, the shift from archaic bronzes to a wider range of material was typical of much of central Italy, part of a more homogenised central Italian cultural koine (Bradley 2000: 176). The question arises as to how to interpret the ritual associated with the deposition of the bronze and lead offerings in light of the shift in votive deposition observed in the Roman period.

Toward an Interpretation of the Ritual Function of the Grotta Bella's Figurines

As mentioned above, recent studies of the spread of anatomical terracottas across the Italian peninsula have demonstrated that the traditional view linking their spread to the spread of Roman dominion is untenable. To counter the traditional assumption that votive terracottas are evidence of an 'obsession with health and fertility' that developed as a consequence of Roman conquest, Glinister points out that anatomical terracottas were dedicated to a wide range of deities and that only a few of them had a definite 'health' specialisation (Glinister 2006a: 93). Second, she emphasises that the presence of anatomical votives in pre-Roman sanctuaries illustrates that this type of votive preceded the spread of Asclepius' healing cult that is commonly associated with the diffusion of anatomical terracottas. Furthermore, shrines of Asclepius are barely attested in the peninsula in the fourth and third centuries BC. Although some anatomical votives from Latium and Etruria do seem to indicate specific concerns for health and body pathology, most anatomical votives do not exhibit a clear-cut connection with healing. Indeed, the presence of body part dedications representing open torsos or inner organs is limited to Latin and Etruscan areas – we can think of the polyvisceral plaques from Veii, Fregellae, Pozzarello, Manganello sanctuary at Cerveteri, or the internal organs from Tarquinia, Veii, Gravisca, Ponte di Nona and Lavinium: (Turfa 2006; Hughes 2017). In light of these considerations, Glinister's suggestion – that anatomical terracottas from the Roman period are most likely associated with a ritual of well-being, rather than with health in a medical way – is even more attractive. This broader connotation of the ritual connected to the deposition of these offerings implies wishes for a healthy, serene, and prosperous (physically as well as morally) life.

It is difficult to imagine that well-being rituals were performed in the Italian peninsula only after the Romans arrived in a given area. It is unlikely, in my view, that locals did not express their desire for happiness and comfort through ritual practices prior to their first intense cultural interaction with Rome in the fourth century BC. Furthermore, the presence of anatomical bronzes, not only at the site of Grotta Bella

Figure 4.7: Lead figures of female and male offerors. Fifth century BC, from the Grotta Bella. Archaeological depot of the Soprintendenza Archeologia Belle Arti e Paesaggio dell'Umbria (Photo by author by permission of the Soprintendenza ABAP dell'Umbria).

(Fig. 4.5) but at virtually all archaic sanctuaries of the region (Zapelloni Pavia *forthcoming*), strongly suggests that Glinister's interpretation should not be restricted to the Roman period. It seems possible to hypothesise that bronze (and lead) human and animal figurines from the sacred shrine of Grotta Bella were connected to the same ritual of well-being as the one identified by Glinister in the anatomical terracottas of the Roman period.

If the function of the votives from Grotta Bella was to request general well-being, a question arises as to whether this ritual function was assigned to the objects *a priori*, before their production, or not. As recent posthumanist studies have shown, human-made objects can shape religious tradition. This means that the ritual function of votives can be achieved by the objects themselves because they lend themselves to such function. To use a line of thought originated by Alfred Gell (1998), it is not a given that objects were created purposefully with their function in the mind of the maker, but rather they may assume a function once they became enmeshed in social relationships.

Indeed, the types/form of the objects comprising the Grotta Bella figurines represent the basic recognisable figures through which worshippers could identify themselves and their environment: the warrior – recognisable also as Mars, who for Italic populations had the two-pronged function of protector of the crops and against nature's plagues

Figure 4.8: Anatomical terracotta. Third century BC, from the Grotta Bella. Archaeological depot of the Soprintendenza Archeologia Belle Arti e Paesaggio dell'Umbria (Photo by author by permission of the Soprintendenza ABAP dell'Umbria).

Figure 4.9: Hellenistic offeror or adorant. Third century BC, from the Grotta Bella. Archaeological depot of the Soprintendenza Archeologia Belle Arti e Paesaggio dell'Umbria (Photo by author by permission of the Soprintendenza ABAP dell'Umbria).

(Sigismondi 1979: 48) – female and male figures; animals, which constituted the base of Umbrian economy; and, finally, parts of the body, which, through synecdoche, may stand for the whole male or female figure. The dedication of these votive categories may be related to the complex concept of personhood applied to archaeology by Chris Fowler and recently used by Emma-Jayne Graham (Fowler 2004; Graham 2017). In summary, parts of bodies are a 'visual abbreviation of the whole being of a suppliant' (Graham 2017: 51), and animal votive figurines are representative of the divisible part of a dividual human being (suppliant in our case), which in ethnographic studies means the part of their selves that can be detached and entrusted to the care of the gods (Fowler 2004: 7–8). As Graham argues with respect to anatomical votives, these votives offerings represent bodies, their extension, and the base of their subsistence. They can be considered a prime means of dedication to an intangible divine power.

In his investigation of the effect that objects have on people, Chris Gosden (2005) demonstrates that an artefact's form displayed *en masse* can suggest thought and mental representation. This means that artefacts influence the way people use them and that their use may have nothing to do with the human intention that created them. It is, therefore, possible that these figurines, made because they represented a familiar and recognisable association with the everyday life of worshippers, used together and displayed in the specific context of the sanctuary, influenced the meaning of the ritual they came to represent. As Glinister noted (2006a: 94), Italic and Roman religions were concerned with the gods' close interaction with humans and control of human fates, individual and collective. The images of worshippers and animals displayed in the sacred areas of the region contributed to creating a ritual whose teleological aim was the prosperity of the community and the worshippers. We can read the same association in the warrior type, as the figure of the soldier evokes maintenance of stability and more general protection. When considered from this point of view, the anatomical votives that are part of the votive assemblages at Grotta Bella during the Roman period do not represent a novelty, as many have argued. As we have observed, not only were anatomical bronze votives already in use at Grotta Bella during the Archaic period, but, together with male, female, warrior, and animal figurines they were used for the same ritual of well-being.

The possibility that the same ritual was performed overtime in two different media (bronze and lead figurines, during the pre-Roman period, and anatomical terracottas during the Roman period) falls in line with current ideas on the archaeology of ritual. Archaeologists working on ritual practices have demonstrated that the same ritual is not necessarily manifested through similar ritual material (Kyriakidis 2007b: 9–22) and that rituals can remain the same throughout time, even if the physical expressions change. Many of the contributions in the recent book edited by Tesse Stek and Gert-Jan Burgers (2015) successfully show that it was not uncommon in cult places of the Italic peninsula to add new votives to rituals that were already in existence.

Bronze figurines are not the only evidence of rituals of well-being in Umbria. The *Iguvine Tables* also highlight the well-being of the Iguvine community. For example, *Iguvine Tables* I.1–5 reads:

> Commence this ceremony by observing the birds, those from in front and those from behind. Before the Trebulan Gate sacrifice three oxen to Jupiter Grabovius. Present grain-offerings, place the ribs on a tray, sacrifice either with wine or with mead, for the Fisian Mount, for the state of Iguvium (*Iguvine Tables* I.1–5 = Poultney 1959, 158).

These tablets mention a ritual that, according to Bradley (2000: 75), remains invisible in the archaeological record of Umbrian sacred spaces. In the case of Grotta Bella, the bronze votives of humans and animals represent additional evidence of the presence of rituals of well-being, whose importance over time is emphasised by the presence of the Tablets during the Roman period in the Umbrian town of Iguvium.

The question remains as to why a ritual should persist, but its votive form should evolve. According to the anthropologist Anthony Cohen, it is in phases of significant social and spatial change that groups tend to emphasise and enhance old community borders, often in a ritual context, by reinterpreting the past (Cohen 1985: 87). The ability of ritual to articulate group identity and promote group cohesion, trust, and cooperation has been discussed in archaeology through various perspectives. Colin Renfrew emphasises that the experience of ritual activity creates links between people, and thus, ritual participation defines the membership of the participants in certain groups (Renfrew 2007: 109–123). The cave sanctuary at Grotta Bella was likely affected by 'the winds of change' brought about by the Roman conquest: it was located not far from the two newly founded colonies of Spoletium and Narnia and the allied communities of Ameria and Tuder. It seems possible that the persistence of the well-being ritual in the Middle Republican period may have helped the local people to define the identity of their community in the period that followed the Roman conquest and the formation of new cultural and political settlements, and thus unite their members.

The presence of new types of votives can be addressed by using Andrew Wallace-Hadrill's theory of code-switching (Wallace-Hadrill 2008). Code-switching has its roots in a theoretical linguistic model that explores the situational use of languages. It rejects traditional ideas about cultural superiority and hierarchy and focuses on the set of choices and practices by which a group constructs, interprets, and reproduces its own identity within simultaneous coexistences in diverse culture-systems. Situational switching between different 'languages' to best communicate your message may not only be confined to bilingualism/multilingualism but may also map onto expressions of material culture. In archaeological contexts, Wallace-Hadrill believes that it is possible to recognise cultural cues that survive alongside each other, as people can 'switch' from one code to another strategically according to the contexts (2006: 13).

Although, as already mentioned, a few anatomical bronzes are present in Umbrian pre-Roman cult places, it is undeniable that they replaced bronze figurines during the Roman period (Glinister 2006b; Scopacasa 2015). It is possible that anatomical terracottas replaced small bronze figurines by process of code-switching, according to which locals selected the terracotta votives as a new means of offering within the well-being ritual that they were accustomed to practice. As they represented an extension of the corporeal body, in all likelihood, the offering of parts of the body instead of full bodies may have seemed as more immediate and effective for a ritual whose teleological aim was the contentedness and wellness of the individual/group. Furthermore, the fact that anatomical terracottas were easier to make and more affordable to people of different socio-economic statuses (Scopacasa 2015: 7) justifies their popularity over figurines made of bronze. In addition, the sheer number of anatomical votives that were spread throughout Central Italy and Greece during the Middle Republican period (Van Straten 2000: 191–221; Hughes 2008: 217–236) may suggest that this class of material was looked upon as desirable and in line with the latest demands and preferences for votive objects. At the same time, the fact that in the third century BC at the sanctuary of Monte

Moro (near ancient Interamna Nahrs/modern Terni) bronze figurines were used alongside anatomical terracottas confirms the hypothesis that worshippers could 'switch' from one object form to the other within the realm of the same ritual practice.

Conclusion

In recent years, scholars have investigated rituals and their material remains and have made significant and novel contributions to the contextualisation of ritual theory. One line of research has attempted to apply posthuman approaches to the archaeology of ritual and has successfully demonstrated that abandoning human agency and giving priority to objects can shed light on the ritual behaviour of ancient populations.

This chapter has shown that by disentangling the study of votive figurines from the centre stage of the human subject, we can better appreciate their ritual meaning and their development across time. The ritual identifiable through the analysis of the votive figurines from Grotta Bella provides a glimpse of cultural continuity, modifications, and reinterpretations as a result of and in response to, Roman expansion. The ritual practised in the shrine at Grotta Bella from the Archaic period onward was likely aimed at securing the wellness of individuals as well as the community. In addition to this, I have suggested that the function of the objects was not decided *a priori* during their making. Through their materiality, by the appropriation of identification data, along with the spatial association with the sacred sphere, votive figurines may have dictated the well-being ritual associated with them.

The presence of anatomical terracottas in the Roman period indicates the continuity of this ritual but also sheds light on the mechanism of adoption and adaptation visible in the material culture after Roman expansion in Umbria. As Wallace-Hadrill demonstrated when he applied the code-switching model to Roman material culture, elements of foreign culture were selectively adopted and adapted in response to active local social mechanisms rather than mere emulation. In the specific case presented in this chapter, the tradition of dedicating anatomical votives, widespread on the Tyrrhenian coasts of Latium and Etruria, was selectively applied in the Roman period to a ritual rooted in the Archaic period, and sometimes used alongside the more traditional Umbrian bronze figurines.

The question arises as to why people dedicated anatomical terracottas instead of the previously ubiquitous bronzes in order to perform a ritual with the same teleological meaning. Several reasons account for this shift. First, in virtue of their capacity to serve as *pars pro toto*, anatomicals may have been considered as a more direct way to represent the votaries' selves as members of a religious community. Second, the wide popularity of anatomical votives in several areas of the Mediterranean indicates that they may have been regarded as fashionable. Additionally, it is possible that terracotta figurines were preferred over bronze or lead because they were easy to produce and cheaper than bronze figurines than bronze. Anatomical votives were generally mould-made – a process of applying clay or plaster to a dried prototype. Compared to bronzes, terracottas are produced using a far simpler process, and the finished work is accomplished with much lower material costs. It is therefore possible that, during the Roman period, a broader range of people was able to buy them, and this could explain their popularity throughout Central Italy. However, the system of production associated with anatomical terracottas does not necessarily assume that these were inexpensive objects or that the practise was strictly limited to poorer classes. 'Ancient eyes,' Glinister holds, 'did not view terracotta as inherently poor quality, cheap, or lower class' (Glinister 2006b: 28). Many anatomical votives exhibit embellishment, which may suggest that the commissioning process would have been more expensive than other forms of votive dedication, such as coins or figurines (Glinister 2006b: 11). It is clear, therefore, that there are several possible explanations for the use of terracotta anatomical votives to perform the ritual of well-being identified in the archaeological data.

The question remains: why did a worshipper dedicate one particular body part instead of another? Glinister proposes that some objects express a request more specific than generalised well-being. For example, a dedication of terracotta genitalia could be seen as a petition for fertility or to mark a rite of passage into puberty, while other parts of the body, such as feet, may represent a journey or pilgrimage, hands a prayer, and so on (Glinister 2006b: 12). Although it is difficult to ascertain the exact meaning of these separate body parts, the variety of anatomical dedicated at Grotta Bella, and more broadly, in Central Italian sanctuaries, seems to suggest that forms were indeed an important factor in the worshipers' decision to make a vow.

Further research is required to validate the interpretation of ritual continuity and change in the Umbrian shrine of Grotta Bella and more broadly in the sacred spaces of the Umbrian region. The lack of textual evidence and of a comprehensive study of votives from the region preclude a definitive account. As a result, it is difficult to conclude that the teleological function of the ritual carried out at Grotta Bella was only to secure well-being. Future studies of ritual practices at Grotta Bella should examine the broader votive categories from the site and explore the possibility that other rituals may be associated with them. A further step in such research should be the analysis of how the votive objects from the cave are, or are not, part of a more universal expression of ritual(s). In order to achieve this goal, it is necessary to study the votive offerings from the other Central Italic Umbrian sanctuaries, in both the Archaic and Roman periods, and to assess whether the ritual(s) identified at Grotta Bella was similarly practised in the rest of the region.

This type of contextual analysis of the archaeological record is advocated by Renfrew (2007) but scarcely put into practice by Roman archaeologists. Attempts to use a contextual analysis of the data from sacred spaces have been made in Greek archaeology, as in the recent publication on the votive materials from the sanctuary at Veste demonstrates (Mastronuzzi-Ciuchini 2011). The study of sanctuaries in Central Italy, however, still tends to be limited to the analysis of monuments or selected categories of finds. As Eleri Cousins has rightly pointed out, this can be seen, in part, as a side effect of the specialist knowledge needed for full publication of classes of artefacts (Cousins 2014: 52). Coins, vessels, terracottas, bronzes, faunal and botanical remains are usually studied by different scholars, rendering synthesis difficult.

Turning once again to the lead and bronze figurines from Grotta Bella, several other questions remain to be addressed. I have argued that their materiality contributed to their function within the ritual carried out at the cave. But how were the votives displayed in the sacred area? Scholars have formulated a hypothesis as to how the votive statuettes were fixed on surfaces, but they have not addressed the religious way of viewing these offerings. By bringing together ancient sources and material artefacts, classical scholarship has only recently started to investigate modes and modalities of Greco-Roman visuality and the existence of a specific religious gaze (Favro 2006; Elsner 2007; Balm 2016). As Julia Kindt rightly remarks with respect to Greek votives (Kindt 2012: 355), an interdisciplinary study that combines votive offerings, literary evidence for religious dedications, and their perception in Greco-Roman Antiquity can illuminate the aesthetic dimension of dedications within their religious context. Although no ancient Roman sources mention the small votive offerings that have been the object of this chapter, the study of literary evidence of religious dedications from other cultural contexts (*e.g.*, Greek) and ethnographic comparisons may provide a way of reconstructing the conceptualisation of the religious visuality in the sanctuaries of ancient Umbria.

To conclude, the study of votive material from Grotta Bella sheds new light on the ritual practices in Central Italy during the Archaic and Middle Republican period. First, it opens a new way to interpret the cultural change that followed Roman expansion into the region. It underscores the continuity of local traditions and their integration within Roman culture. The use of a new medium within a traditional pre-Roman ritual practice seems to suggest that the encounter between the local population and new Roman arrivals happened through cultural negotiation – rather than displacement – and resulted in a cultural mix. Second, it encourages us to apply new material theories to the understanding of ancient rituals. A move beyond the limitations of human exceptionalism allows archaeologists to recognize the vibrancy of matter and the relationships between human and nonhuman from which the agency of the objects emanates.

Interdepartmental Program in Classical Art and Archaeology, University of Michigan

Acknowledgments

I am very grateful to Celia Schultz and Nicola Terrenato for their useful comments on my research, to the Soprintendenza Archeologia Belle Arti e Paesaggio dell'Umbria for allowing me to study the objects stored in the depot and to the staff of the depot, who gave me logistical support during my research. I would also like to thank Gregory Tucker and Alexander Hoer for their insightful suggestions. Finally, a special thanks goes to the editors, who gave me the chance to publish part of my research.

Note

1. Other material found in the cave comprises coins of the Late Imperial level (second to fourth centuries B.C.), glass, pottery and *lucernae* of the first to third centuries AD, and seventy-five coins, black gloss pottery, Italo-Megarian pottery of the Republican period. A preliminary archaeological report of this excavation was published by Arena in 1975–1976 and an overview of its materials has been presented by Monacchi (1988).

Bibliography

Ancient Sources

Iguvine Tables (Translated by J. Poultney). 1959. *The Bronze Tables of Iguvium*. Baltimore: American Philological Association.

Modern Sources

Arena, M.S. 1975–1976. Montecastrilli. *Fasti Archeologici* 30–31: 481.

Balm, R. 2016. *Archaeology's Visual Culture: Digging and Desire*. London: Routledge.

Barrett, J.C. 1994. *Fragments from Antiquity: An Archaeology of Social Life in Britain, 2900–1200 BC*. Oxford: Blackwell.

Barrett, J.C. 2000. A thesis on agency. In M.-A. Dobres and J. Robb (eds) *Agency in Archaeology*. London: Routledge: 61–68.

Barrowclough, D. and Malone, C. (eds) 2007. *Cult in Context: Reconsidering Ritual in Archaeology*. Oxford: Oxbow Books.

Battiloro, I. 2018. *The Archaeology of Lucanian Cult Places: Fourth Century BC to the Early Imperial Age*. London: Routledge.

Bell, C.M. 1997. *Ritual: Perspectives and Dimensions*. Oxford: Oxford University Press.

Bonomi Ponzi, L. 1989. *Cesi: cultura e ambiente di una terra antica*. Todi, PG: Ediart.

Bonomi Ponzi, L. 1991. Gli Umbri: territorio, cultura e società. In F. Roncalli and B. Adembri (eds) *Antichità dall'Umbria a New York*. Perugia: Electa: 53–67

Bourdieu, P. 1977. *Outline of a Theory of Practice.* Cambridge: Cambridge University Press.

Bourdieu, P. 1980. *The Logic of Practice.* Stanford: Stanford University Press.

Bradley, G. 2000. *Ancient Umbria: State, Culture, and Identity in Central Italy from the Iron Age to the Augustan Era.* Oxford: Oxford University Press.

Bradley, G. and Glinister, F. 2013. Italic religion. In L. Bredholt Christensen, O. Hammer and D.A. Warburton (eds) *The Handbook of Religions in Ancient Europe.* Durham: Acumen: 173–191.

Burkert, W. 1987. *Homo Necans: The Anthropology of Ancient Greek Sacrificial Ritual and Myth.* Berkeley: University of California Press.

Cenciaoli, L. 1991. Il Santuario di Monte Acuto di Umbertide. In L. Bonfante (ed.) *Antichità dall'Umbria a New York.* Milano: Electa: 211–226.

Cohen, A.P. 1985. *The Symbolic Construction of Community.* Chichester: E. Horwood.

Colonna, G. 1970. *Bronzi votivi umbro-sabellici a figura umana.* Firenze: Sansoni.

Comella, A. 1981. Complessi votivi in Italia in epoca medio e tardo repubblicana. *Mélanges de l'École française de Rome* 93: 717–803.

Cousins, E.H. 2014. Votive objects and ritual practice at the King's Spring at Bath. In H. Platts, J. Pearce, C. Barron, J. Lundock and J. Yoo (eds) *TRAC 2013: Proceedings of the Twenty-Third Annual Theoretical Roman Archaeology Conference.* London: Oxbow Books: 52–62.

De Cazanove, O. 2000. Some thoughts on the religious romanization of Italy before the Social War. In E. Bisham and C. Smith (eds) *Religion in Archaic and Republican Rome and Italy: Evidence and Experience.* Chicago: Fitzroy Dearborn: 71–76.

De Grummond, N.T and Simon, E. (eds) 2006. *Religion of the Etruscans.* Austin: University of Texas Press.

Devoto, G. 1948. *Le tavole di Gubbio.* Firenze: Sansoni.

Draycott, J. and Graham, E.J. 2017. *Bodies of Evidence: Ancient Anatomical Votives Past, Present and Future.* London: Routledge.

Edlund-Berry, I.E.M. 1988. *The Gods and the Place: The Location and Function of Sanctuaries in the Countryside of Etruria & Magna Graecia (700–400 BC).* Stockholm: Svenska Institutet i Rom (The Swedish Institute in Rome).

Elsner, J. 2007. *Roman Eyes: Visuality and Subjectivity in Art and Text.* Princeton: Princeton University Press.

Faro, E.Z. 2008. *Ritual Activity and Regional Dynamics: Towards a Reinterpretation of Minoan Extra-Urban Ritual Space.* PhD Thesis. University of Michigan.

Favro, D. 2006. In the eyes of the beholder: virtual reality recreations and academia. In L. Haselberger (ed.) *Imaging Ancient Rome: Documentation, Visualization, Imagination.* Portsmouth: Journal of Roman Archaeology: 321–334.

Fowler, C. 2004. *The Archaeology of Personhood: An Anthropological Approach.* London: Routledge.

Gebel, H.G., Dahl Hermansen, B. and Hoffman Jensen, C. (eds) 2002. *Magic Practices and Ritual in the Near Eastern Neolithic: Proceedings of a Workshop held at the 2nd International Congress on the Archaeology of the Ancient Near East (ICAANE), Copenhagen University, May 2000.* Berlin: Ex Oriente.

Gell, A. 1998. *Art and Agency: An Anthropological Theory.* Oxford: Clarendon Press.

Gentili, M. 2005. Riflessioni sul fenomeno storico dei depositi votivi di tipo etrusco-laziale-campano. In A. Comella and S. Mele (eds) *Depositi votivi e culti dell'Italia antica dall'età arcaica a quella tardo-repubblicana.* Bari: Edipuglia: 367–378.

Giddens, A. 1984. *The Constitution of Society: Outline of the Theory of Structuration.* Cambridge: Polity Press.

Gleba, M. and Becker, H. 2009. *Votives, Places and Rituals in Etruscan Religion: Studies in Honor of Jean MacIntosh Turfa.* Leiden: Brill.

Glinister, F. 2006a. Women, colonisation and cult in Hellenistic Central Italy. *Archiv für Religionsgeschichte* 8: 89–104.

Glinister, F. 2006b. Reconsidering 'religious Romanization'. In C. Schultz and P.B. Harvey (eds) *Religion in Republican Italy.* Cambridge: Cambridge University Press: 10–33.

Gosden, C. 2005. What do objects want? *Journal of Archaeological Method and Theory* 12 (3): 193–211.

Graham, E.J. 2017. Partible humans and permeable gods: anatomical votives and personhood in the sanctuaries of central Italy. In J. Draycott and E.J. Graham (eds) *Bodies of Evidence: Ancient Anatomical Votives Past, Present and Future.* London: Routledge: 45–63.

Griffith, A. 2013. Reconstructing religious ritual in Italy. In J. DeRose Evans (ed.) *A Companion to the Archaeology of the Roman Republican Period.* Chichester: Wiley-Blackwell: 392–405.

Harris, O.J.T. 2016. Becoming post-human: identity and the ontological turn. In E. Pierce, A. Russell, A. Maldonado and L. Campbell (eds) *Creating Material Worlds: The Uses of Identity in Archaeology.* Oxford: Oxbow Books: 17–38.

Hawkes, C.F.C. 1954. Archaeological theory and method: some suggestions from the Old World. *American Anthropologist* 56: 155–68.

Hodder, I. 2010. *Religion in the Emergence of Civilization: Çatalhöyük as a Case Study.* Cambridge: Cambridge University Press.

Hodder, I. 2012. *Entangled: An Archaeology of the Relationships between Humans and Things.* Chichester: Wiley-Blackwell.

Hodder, I. 2014. The entanglements of humans and things: a long-term view. *New Literary History*, 45 (1): 19–36.

Hughes, J. 2008. Fragmentation as metaphor in the Classical healing sanctuary. *Social History of Medicine* 21 (2): 217–236.

Hughes, J. 2017. *Votive Body Parts in Greek and Roman Religion.* Cambridge: Cambridge University Press.

Insoll, T. 2004. *Archaeology, Ritual, Religion.* London: Routledge.

Insoll, T. 2012. *The Oxford Handbook of the Archaeology of Ritual and Religion.* Oxford: Oxford University Press.

Jehne, M., Linke, B. and Rüpke, J. (eds) 2013. *Religiöse Vielfalt und soziale Integration: Die Bedeutung der Religion für die kulturelle Identität und politische Stabilität im republikanischen Italien.* Heidelberg: VA, Verlag Antik

Jones, A. 2004. Archaeometry and materiality: materials-based analysis in theory and practice. *Archaeometry* 46 (3), 327–338.

Kindt, J. 2012. *Rethinking Greek Religion*. Cambridge: Cambridge University Press.

Knappett, C. 2005. *Thinking Through Material Culture: An Interdisciplinary Perspective*. University of Pennsylvania Press, Philadelphia.

Kyriakidis, E. (ed.) 2007a. *The Archaeology of Ritual*. Los Angeles: Cotsen Institute of Archaeology, University of California.

Kyriakidis, E. 2007b. In search of ritual. In E. Kyriakidis (ed.) *The Archaeology of Ritual*. Los Angeles: Cotsen Institute of Archaeology, University of California: 1–8.

Kyriakidis, E. 2007c. Finding ritual: calibrating the evidence. In E. Kyriakidis (ed.) *The Archaeology of Ritual*. Los Angeles: Cotsen Institute of Archaeology, University of California: 9–22.

Laneri, N. 2015. *Defining the Sacred: Approaches to the Archaeology of Religion in the Near East*. Oxford: Oxbow Books.

Latour, B. 1990. Technology is society made durable. *Sociological Review* 38 (1): 103–131.

Latour, B. 1999. On recalling ANT. In J. Law and J. Hassard (eds) *Actor Network Theory and After*. Oxford: Blackwell: 15–26.

Latour, B. 2005. *Reassembling the Social: An Introduction to Actor-Network-Theory*. Oxford: Oxford University Press.

Malone, C. and Stoddart, S. (eds) 1994a. *Territory, Time, and State: The Archaeological Development of the Gubbio Basin*. Cambridge: Cambridge University Press.

Malone, C. and Stoddart, S. 1994b. The settlement system of Gubbio in the Later Bronze Age and the early Iron Age. In C. Malone and S. Stoddart (eds) *Territory, Time, and State: The Archaeological Development of the Gubbio Basin*. Cambridge: Cambridge University Press: 127–141.

Mastronuzzi, G. and Ciuchini, P. 2011. Offerings and rituals in a Messapian holy place: Vaste, Piazza Dante (Puglia, Southern Italy). *World Archaeology* 43 (4): 676–701.

Meskell, L. 2004. *Object Worlds in Ancient Egypt: Material Biographies Past and Present*. New York: Berg,

Monacchi, D. 1986. Note sulla Stipe Votiva di Grotta Bella (Terni). *Studi Etruschi* 52 (3): 77–89.

Nijboer, A.J. 2001. *Interpreting Deposits: Linking Ritual with Economy: Papers on Mediterranean Archaeology*. Groeningen: Peeters.

Osborne, R. 2004. Hoards, votives, offerings: the archaeology of the dedicated object. *World Archaeology* 36 (1): 1–10.

Pakkanen, P. and Bocher, S. (eds) 2015. *Cult Material: From Archaeological Deposits to Interpretation of Early Greek Religion*. Helsinki: Suomen Ateenan-Instituutin Säätiö (Foundation of the Finnish Institute at Athens).

Poultney, J.W. 1959. *The Bronze Tables of Iguvium*. Baltimore: American Philological Association.

Prosdocimi, A.L. 1984. *Le tavole iguvine*. Firenze: L.S. Olschki.

Renfrew, C. (ed.) 1985. *The Archaeology of Cult: The Sanctuary at Phylakopi*. London: The British School at Athens/Thames and Hudson.

Renfrew, C. 2007. The archaeology of ritual, of cult, and of religion. In E. Kyriakidis (ed.) *The Archaeology of Ritual*. Los Angeles: Cotsen Institute of Archaeology, University of California: 109–122.

Roncalli, R. (ed.) 1989. *Gens Antiquissima Italiae. Antichità dall'Umbria a Budapest e Cracovia*. Perugia: Electa Editori Umbri.

Rosenzweig, I. 1937. *Ritual and Cults of Pre-Roman Iguvium: With an Appendix Giving the Text of the Iguvine Tablets*. London: Christophers.

Schultz, C.E. 2006. *Women's Religious Activity in the Roman Republic*. Chapel Hill: University of North Carolina Press.

Scopacasa, R. 2015. Moulding cultural change: a contextual approach to anatomical votive terracottas in Central Italy, fourth-second centuries BC. *Papers of the British School at Rome* 83: 1–27.

Sigismondi, G. 1979. *Nuceria in Umbria. Contributo per la sua storia dalle origini all'età feudale*. Foligno: Ediclio.

Sillar, B. 2009. The social agency of things? Animism and materiality in the Andes. *Cambridge Archaeological Journal* 19 (3): 366–377.

Sisani, S. 2013. *Nursia e l'ager Nursinus: un distretto sabino dalla praefectura al municipium*. Roma: Quasar.

Steadman, S. 2009. *Archaeology of Religion. Cultures and their Beliefs in Worldwide Context*. New York: Routledge.

Stek, T.D. 2009. *Cult Places and Cultural Change in Republican Italy: A Contextual Approach to Religious Aspects of Rural Society after the Roman Conquest*. Amsterdam: Amsterdam University Press.

Stek, T.D. and Burgers, G.-J. (eds) 2015. *The Impact of Rome on Cult Places and Religious Practices in Ancient Italy*. London: Institute of Classical Studies, School of Advanced Study, University of London.

Swenson, E. 2015. The archaeology of ritual. *Annual Review of Anthropology* 44: 336–339

Torelli, M. 1999. *Tota Italia: Essays in the Cultural Formation of Roman Italy*. Oxford: Clarendon Press.

Turfa, J. 2006. Votive offerings in Etruscan religion. In N.T. De Grummond and E. Simon (eds) *Religion of the Etruscans*. Austin: University of Texas Press: 90–116.

Van Straten, F. 2000. Votives and votaries in Greek sanctuaries. In R. Buxton (ed.) *Oxford Readings in Greek Religion*. New York: Oxford University Press: 191–223.

Wallace-Hadrill, A. 2008. *Rome's Cultural Revolution*. Cambridge: Cambridge University Press.

Warren, P. 1988. *Minoan Religion as Ritual Action*. Gothenburg: Paul Åströms Förlag.

Whitley, D.S. and Hays-Gilpin, K. 2008. *Belief in the Past: Theoretical Approaches to the Archaeology of Religion*. Walnut Creek: Left Coast Press.

Zapelloni Pavia, A. *forthcoming*. *Cultural Change in the Religious Sphere of Ancient Umbria between the Sixth and the First Centuries BCE*. PhD Thesis. University of Michigan.

5

The Materiality of Divine Agency in Imperial Rome

Kristine Iara

Introduction

This chapter seeks out the reciprocal relationship between the Romans and their religion-related objects. It does so by examining the materialisation (Hicks 2010; Raja and Rüpke 2015a) of divine agency in the city of Rome in the first four centuries AD – sometimes earlier – in order to explore the means and mechanisms through which the divine was rendered material or how it was 'presenced'. The notion of 'presencing the god', as it has been shaped by Pongratz-Leisten and Sonik (2015), offers a wide range of possibilities of understanding and interpretation, inasmuch as it encompasses 'multifarious modes of rendering the immaterial material, accessible, and relatable', as defined by Pongratz-Leisten and Sonik (2015: esp. 10–11) concerning the materiality of divine agency in the Ancient Near East. Their study offers – the spatiotemporal distance of its focus notwithstanding – a valid methodological framework for this chapter.

This chapter is embedded within the framework set by previous studies on Roman religion seen from the point of view of material culture in general (Raja and Rüpke 2015a; 2015b), and on divine imagery in particular (see further below). At the same time, the chapter attempts to engage with some recently developed theoretical approaches, which have been brought into the field of Classical Archaeology in general – namely posthuman approaches in archaeology (overviews in Hicks 2010; Robb 2010; Fahlander 2012; Harris 2016; Harris and Cipolla 2017; on questions of entanglement and human-thing-relations a dense overview on recent scholarly discussion and rich bibliography is provided by Hodder and Lucas 2017) – and on material culture studies in particular (with special regard to Roman archaeology: Versluys 2014 and the related discussion papers; van Eck *et al.* 2015 offer a programmatic framework of how to approach the topic; Moyer 2016 bundles several of these approaches on the crossroad to the study of religion and gives a useful bibliography).

These studies have influenced – even if not traceable in every detail – this chapter and its outcome by setting up the background and framing the approach. Given that these theoretical approaches are mostly applied to the study of past societies without written records, adaptations and modifications are needed for the study of a historical-period society such as the Romans, who produced extensive written records that have to be taken into account together with the material evidence. A further challenge promising new insight is the attempt to refrain from an anthropocentric approach and to rethink the position of humans in their material environment when examining a topic within religious history, for religious discourse is invariably a mental construct by the human mind and imagination. Focusing on the materiality of religion of the society in question allows us to grasp elements of mental constructs that are rendered material in the form of objects. These objects in turn influence by means of their own agency – either inherent or acquired – humans and their imagination. Objects and humans were thus in a perpetual relationship of reciprocity, both as active agents and in undergoing the other's agency.

Scholarly Context

Although scholarly interest in divine imagery or representations of gods in the Greek and Roman worlds – be it within the field of art history or of history of religions – is not new, recent years have seen a great increase of publications in this field. Given the broadness of the topic on the one hand and its ramifications on the other, it has to be stated from the outset which aspects of the whole range of the topic cannot be dealt with, even though the limitation might appear artificial. As the chapter deals specifically with the Roman world (following Ando 2010: 47, 'Roman religion and the intellectual apparatus that developed around it are distinct from Greek religion and religious culture of the same period and must be studied and understood as an autonomous cultural formation'), parallel developments in the study of Greek religion can be mentioned only briefly (beginning with the seminal paper of Gordon 1979; quite recent and comprehensive is the monographic study Scheer 2000, also discussing earlier scholarship and offering convincing conclusions; Scheer 2015; for specific aspects see further below). Recent collective volumes shed light on different aspects of the topic from various points of view (Mylonopoulos 2010a; Bourgeaud and Fabiano 2013; Estienne *et al.* 2015; Belayche and Pirenne-Delforge 2015; Arnhold, Maier, and Rüpke 2018, each with previous bibliography), with some contributions dealing with the Greek world, some with the Roman; others analysing aspects of art history, the religious or philosophical discourse, or the involvement of divine images in cult practice (see further below); and yet others examining representations of gods or their statuary representation on objects of everyday use (*e.g.* lamps: Stewart 2000; Bielfeldt 2014; weaponry: Fischer 2015; coins: Williams 2007; objects within the domestic context, such as ceramics, silverware, etc.: Kaufmann-Heinimann 2007). Further studies examined how the Romans dealt with Greek sculpture of the gods (Anguissola 2007 on 'sacred copies'; Bumke 2008; Auffarth 2009). As regards Late Antiquity, the question arises how the Christians dealt with 'pagan' gods and their images (*e.g.* most recent, Lavan 2011; Kristensen 2013; Bremmer 2015 with previous bibliography; Selsvold 2019; on issues of iconoclasm seen through a broad horizon Elsner 2012). Studies on objects used for religious purpose or in ritual practice – such as cultic utensils or votive objects – have furthered the understanding of the materiality and the agency proper of these objects (*e.g.* contributions in Blakely 2017; Moser and Knust 2017).

A crucial aspect within the topic's full range – but not dealt with in this chapter – is that of divine epiphanies (most important: Platt 2011; 2015; Petridou 2016; Petridou and Platt 2018; see also Ando 2010; 2011; 2015). Two further topics that remain too fathomless and complex to be dealt with here – although they are tightly related to many of the issues discussed in the following – are, first, aniconism proper (Wissowa 1904; Taylor 1931; Metzler 1985–1986; Ando 2010; 2011; 2015; Blume 2016; Gaifman 2017; further Pongratz-Leisten and Sonik 2015: 22–23, with reference to Gell 1998), and second, non-anthropomorphic Roman gods. The latter also embraces the question whether the Roman gods, or some Roman gods, were – rather than anthropomorphised beings with proper biographies – to be understood as conceptions, divine powers of assent (or dissent), specific properties, or divine agencies, implying even that god and divine agency would be one and the same (such as Jupiter Fulgur, Terminus, or Tellus, see Wissowa 1904), which does not necessarily mean that they were imagined as non-anthropomorphic but in a different, specific form. It may not have mattered, or they would not have been imagined in a specific form at all.

Thus, the chapter quite narrowly focuses on the issue within Roman religion, within the Roman world, and on those gods which were usually imagined as anthropomorphic, or, at least, that were not specifically thought of as being non-anthropomorphic (most recent and important, alongside the abovementioned collective volumes: Ando 2008; 2010; Estienne 2010; Mylonopoulos 2010b; Rüpke 2010; Ando 2011; 2015; Estienne 2015; on the available material evidence from the city of Rome and the Roman Empire respectively, see Martin 1987; Vermeule 1987). Equally important for the study of the issue within the Roman world, especially in the city of Rome, are the studies on the Romans' attitudes towards these images – as it becomes evident through their writings (McMullen 1981: esp. 44–45; Ando 2008; Jenkyns 2013: 235–240) – and the study of divine images embedded in the larger context of art history and cultural history, including issues such as theories of visuality, perception, and reception (esp. Elsner 2007; comprehensively Trimble 2015 with previous bibliography).

These pictorial representations of the gods in anthropomorphic form, both two and three-dimensional, were virtually ubiquitous in the Roman world (Clarke 2003: 73–94; Rives 2007: esp. 35–36), in public spaces and in the domestic realm alike, both in places used primarily for religious purposes and in those dedicated to any non-religious activity. However, statuary representations of gods were only one of many possible material forms of 'presencing' the divine. This chapter argues not only that the anthropomorphic representation of a god was not indispensable for religious or cultic purposes (independently of whether the god her/himself was imagined as anthropomorphic or not), but it states, even more, that *any* kind of non-anthropomorphic, and even initially unspecific object, was a suitable material means to show divine agency or to presence the gods. It was unnecessary to depict the gods themselves.

It is argued here that anthropomorphic statuary of the divine and other non-anthropomorphic objects – be it monumental architecture, altars, stones, or other – can be examined together as there is not much difference between them regarding their capacity to materialise or represent divine agency or to presence the gods. In the same manner, it seems irrelevant whether the Romans considered some representations of gods in anthropomorphic shape as a distinct category – namely the 'cult images' – as opposed to 'images of the gods' or not (comprehensively Mylonopoulos 2010b: esp. 4–6). Any representation of a god had the potential to hold a role in cultic activity or to facilitate cultic attention towards the god and be, therefore, either for only a limited time span or permanently, the 'cult image'. Inside the temples and in the cases of multiple divine statues, the statue of the 'main' god – that is, the owner of the temple and the addressee of cultic attention – was usually the central statue.

However, 'between such a cult statue and others that were merely dedications there was no difference in sacral quality' (Rüpke 2006: 221); above all, there was no difference in their potential to presence the gods.

Focusing thus on those Roman gods who were imagined by the Romans as anthropomorphic beings, the chapter argues that both anthropomorphic statues and non-anthropomorphic objects could, with the same effectiveness, materially represent divine agency and allude to its effectiveness and presence the gods. Without denying the importance of the aesthetics of religious art or objects used in cult practices, the chapter states that the essential criteria for an object to be capable of representing or embodying divine agency or to presence the god was not its physical appearance, material value, or the quality of the artistic handicraft alone.

Rather – as will be seen – context, knowledge (collective as well as individual), and empiricism were the factors that rendered objects effective means of making divine agency material or presencing the gods. All of these objects served the same ultimate purpose – namely to facilitate communication between humans and gods and to make deities accessible to humans. In this very need to enable and to facilitate communication between men and gods lies, at the same time, the explanation for the exceedingly superior number of objects to the purpose that showed anthropomorphic features. Objects with anthropomorphic features do – as has been pointed out within the context of the Ancient Near East and which seems valid also for the Roman world – 'emphasize particular communicative potentials in a way that objects adopting other forms do not – a point that *may* contribute [...] to the privileging of the anthropomorphic form for the presenting of the divine [...]' (Pongratz-Leisten and Sonik 2015: 23–24). Through physical likeness, the anthropomorphism suggested a 'common ground' for communication between humans and divine beings (Pongratz-Leisten and Sonik 2015: 51; see also Rüpke 2016: 75, who states that the anthropomorphic images were essential for the differentiation of the increasing number of deities within the city; in general: Krech 2015). The anthropomorphisation of the gods beyond rendering them material in the form of a statue is further attested to by evidence for a wide range of interaction with the gods, or rather, with the divine statues standing in for the gods, such as talking to, feeding, dressing, giving gifts, touching and more – activities for which the Roman world is full of evidence (Boschung 2007; Weddle 2010; Perry 2015). These interactions were needed and sought-after; they fulfilled the desire for intimate contact with the gods.

Evidence

The abovementioned statement – any object could be a suitable material means to presence the divine – will be exemplified through some evidence from the city of Rome, in particular, evidence available from the Forum Romanum and Capitoline Hill. Occasionally, evidence deriving from other areas of Rome will be brought in, too.

The area of the Forum Romanum and Capitolium lends itself particularly to this exercise mainly for two reasons. Firstly, because of its centrality both in topographical and political terms, which resulted in its exceeding significance for Rome's civic, public, and religious life. Secondly, the area is suitable for this kind of examination for practical reasons. In this part of the city, there is an unparalleled accumulation of aforementioned objects that either emanated divine agency or presenced the gods. This allows for a focused examination of a large spectrum of different phenomena condensed in one single spot in the city of Rome and an identification of the manifold possibilities of how the divine was rendered material, relatable and perceivable, or how it was presenced.

The Capitoline Hill has always been, in terms of politics and religion, of the highest importance for Rome – both for Rome the city and the Empire (Reusser 1993; Hölkeskamp 2001; Scheid 2005; Grig 2009; Arata 2010a; 2010b; Moralee 2018). The Capitoline Hill housed, most prominently, the Temple of Jupiter Optimus Maximus (De Angeli 1996; Grig 2009; Arata 2010b; Perry 2012), who, with Juno and Minerva, formed the Capitoline Trias (Triad); nevertheless, the temple on the Capitoline was always referred to as Jupiter's. Additionally, the Capitoline Hill has attracted other cults. Further, the Area Capitolina housed numerous other gods and their cult places (Reusser 1993; Scheid 2005). Many of these divinities were connected to Jupiter and his spheres of action, while some were even extensions of aspects of his divine agency or his divine properties.

The Forum Romanum (Coarelli 1983; 1985; Purcell 1995; Giuliani and Verduchi 1995; Tagliamonte 1995; Bauer 1996; Köb 2000; Freyberger 2012; Muth 2012; Kalas 2015) remained Rome's public space *par excellence* and it represented, to a particular extent, common history and common memory whilst generating collective identity (Hölkeskamp 2001; 2014; Hölscher 2006; Wiseman 2014). At the same time, the Forum showed in its quality as public space – peerless in the city of Rome – a high degree of sacredness, as it was exposed to perpetual sacralisation through the agency of countless and different objects bearing sacralising potential or imbued with divine agency.

In the Forum there are – among many other buildings of religious, or primarily administrative, political, civic or other purposes – seven monumental temples, as well as numerous *sacella* – chapels or smaller buildings of cultic purpose – dedicated to different gods. The edges of the Forum square were lined with smaller cultic spots, such as, among others, the *sacellum* of Venus Cloacina and the Puteal Libonis. These buildings and cult places usually housed statues or were additionally decorated with sculptural work. There were also freestanding statues and other objects, such as the Lapis Niger (the Black Stone) or sacred trees, as well as altars, many of which preceded the temples in terms of old age. All of these sheer numberless objects bore one or another sort of religious significance, and they appeared on the Forum's sacral topography at various times, each contributing to intensely presence the gods and make divine agency perceivable.

In terms of ubiquity and unambiguousness, the anthropomorphic statues of the gods are followed immediately by architectural objects, most conspicuously, the temples. Commonly, the Roman temple was immediately recognisable as such, due to its typical façade consisting of a high podium, columns, and a tympanum. This applies to virtually all major temples as well as to the smaller *sacella*, which often also had this characteristic form. Thus, a temple was usually immediately recognisable as 'temple', as cult building, and in a generic sense, as an object resulting from architectural construction which presenced the divine. In the following, the temples are not so much considered in their role as the place of cultic activities, or the dwelling of the divinity. In fact, although temples had a fundamental role as places for ritual communication, they were not the only places for such activities, only the preferred ones (Rüpke 2006: 221). Rather, the temples – architectural objects – will be considered as objects capable of presencing the god: in the same way as a divine statue, any temple communicated, first and foremost, the presence of the divinity and thus the possibility to interact with him or her. The temple is 'not just a building, but a representation and a perpetuation of a specific religious communication aimed at higher powers' (Rüpke 2018: 129–130). The temples' capacity to actively presence the gods is also illustrated by Cicero (*Cat.* 1.33), who reminds his fellow citizens of the gods' presence by pointing to the temples in the Forum. By briefly analysing some examples, it will be clear how the objects of different types added to the complexity of presencing the gods.

The Temple of Saturn was one of the most ancient cult buildings in the Forum Romanum, and even, in the city of Rome. It was erected at the turn of the sixth to the fifth century BC and still stood upright in Late Antiquity (Pensabene 1984; Coarelli 1999a; Köb 2000: 70–83). This temple served as the public treasury (the *aerarium*) as well as for receiving ambassadors and other political and administrative activities (see further Versnel 1994; Köb 2000: 78–79 with notes). Saturn's nearby altar (Coarelli 1999b), preceding chronologically the temple building, was believed by the Romans to exist since time immemorial. In addition to the temple and altar, Saturn's statue substantially contributed to presencing the god: Saturn's presence guaranteed that the political and administrative activities and procedures of highest importance carried out in or around this temple worked smoothly and properly, and it saw to the wellbeing of the Roman state. Thus, the god was believed to be present at such activities and his statue contributed to presencing him. The statue had another unique property as it was also believed to have the capacity to move on its own. Saturn's legs (or the statue's legs) were bound with woollen threads and he was released only during one period of the year on the occasion of his festival, the Saturnalia (Versnel 1994: esp. 154; Köb 2000: 80–81 with notes).

The Temple of the Castores and their cult in the Forum Romanum were similarly long-established as the cult and the Temple of Saturn. The temple was vowed in 484 BC and its use is attested well into Late Antiquity (Nielsen and Poulsen 1992–2008; Nielsen 1993). The Castores, the twin-gods Castor and Pollux, were presenced intensively in the Forum Romanum. In addition to their temple, the nearby Lacus Iuturnae (the Spring of Juturna) – the place where the visual apparition of the twin-gods took place after the battle at Lake Regillus in 495 BC – recalled the memory of the gods' favourable intervention in this battle. Further, the twin-gods were presenced by means of statuary: they were not only represented once, within the temple, but again outside. This double setup begs the assumption that the statues themselves were not 'manifestations' of the gods or their representations, their deputies, or their proxies, but, rather, intensified means to presence the gods, to remind the humans of their existence, and assure of their benevolence. Albeit remote both topographically and chronologically, a Greek relief (relief of Argenidas, second century BC, Verona, Museo Lapidario Maffeiano; Estienne 2015: 380–381, fig. 28:1) might be brought in merely to further illustrate this notion. On this relief, the twin-gods are being presenced three times, each time by different means – once in the form of anthropomorphic statues, and twice by means of non-anthropomorphic objects relatable to these gods (for further discussion see Estienne 2015: 380–381; on doubleness as *leitmotif* in representing Castor and Pollux, see Platt 2018), all objects acting jointly in the same pictorial setting.

The Temple of Concordia had been erected *ex novo* upon specific political occasions underlining the strong link between religion and politics in the Roman world. The Temple of Concordia was first built in 121 BC and was then replaced by a new building erected by Tiberius in AD 10 dedicated to Concordia Augusta. Each building conveyed political messages beyond the religious (Gasparri 1979; Ferroni 1993; Köb 2000: 56–70). The sculptural decoration of the Temple of Concordia showed the images of Concordia, Salus and Pax, Ceres, Diana and Victories in relief, and Hercules and Mercury in the round. Mercury was further presenced by a *caduceus* – his wand and most characteristic attribute – that was inlaid on the threshold of the temple – subtle, but nevertheless enough to presence this god. But this accumulation of divine statues is not all. The Temple of Concordia served as a sort of treasury for famous statues, most of them representing divinities (Köb 2000: 66–67; Bravi 2014: 185–201). It is noteworthy in this context that political activities were often performed in temples, as seen above in the case of Saturn's temple, and that some institutions essential to the state were housed within temples, near the divinity. For example, the Temple of Concordia often housed meetings of the Senate. It seems that the goddess's presence was, most of all, felt by the people, which implies that the material means that presenced her were effective. Even more, her presence was sought after, especially in times of political or social tension (see further Ferroni 1993: 319; Köb 2000: 64 with notes). Similarly, Victory, who was presenced in the meeting place of the Senate, the Curia, by means of an altar and a statue (Tortorici 1999), validated oaths and gave sanction for political procedures of the Senate.

Some temples had a very specific characteristic that could refer to only one specific god or at least to a limited number of gods. For example, there were only a few round temples in Rome (seven in total; see comprehensively Bratengeier 2010). One of the most prominent examples is the temple of Vesta in the Forum Romanum (Scott 1999; Caprioli 2007; DiLuzio 2016: 119–239). It was of very ancient origins: mytho-historical accounts ascribe its foundation to Numa Pompilius in the second half of the eighth century BC. The temple, cult, and priestesses continued to exist until Late Antiquity. The cult of Vesta and the temple had a very prominent place both topographically and in terms of state religion. The temple was, because of its physical appearance and additional elements, immediately recognisable as Vesta's and relatable to this very goddess. Both the building itself and its depictions on coins and other media evidenced its distinctive roundness – a specific architectural feature which in and of itself was enough to presence the goddess, along with her image that stood on the apex of the building's roof (Cody 1973: 34; Caprioli 2007: 61, 63). The representations on coins usually show additionally other objects related to Vesta: the statue on the apex of the building is often depicted holding a *patera* or the goddess is shown with the Palladium, a statuette of small scale tightly associated with Vesta, which was significant both for Rome's grand past and as a pledge for her glorious future. Pontifical instruments in depictions can allude to the priesthood close to the cult and the Vestals (see further, also for the discussion of other elements, Cody 1973; Caprioli 2007: 51–67).

As seen with the numismatic representations, the frieze of the temple shows how the context and specific features put objects and representations in an unambiguous relationship with the goddess. Her temple's frieze was adorned with cultic instruments, as were the lateral friezes of the Temple of Divus Vespasianus at the north-west end of the Forum. Objects of this kind or their depicted representations could, at first glance, indicate ownership and thus refer to the specific god who dwelled in the temple. They were, at the same time, very much a constant and everlasting reminder of the ephemeral activities in honour of the gods and thus very powerful means of presencing the divine and reminding the humans of the communication between gods and humans that took place by means of the ritual activities in which these instruments played an important role.

Often objects of this kind are generic and refer to the possibility of communication between gods and humans. However, in combination with particular objects or in specific contexts, the depictions gain (further) relatability to specific gods. For example, on the frieze of the Temple of Vesta, additional and specific elements underline the tight connection of the depicted objects to this goddess and her cult (DiLuzio 2017 with reference to La Folette 2011–2012). Similarly, the frieze of the Temple of Divus Vespasianus also reveals elements for an interpretation beyond the generic religious meaning (De Angeli 1992; Blevins 2017 for a new reading of the frieze). Here, too, it has been stated that 'the repetition of object sequences on the frieze implied potentially limitless ritual repetition reenacting the timeless Roman religious order by recalling past sacrifices that reminded viewers of present and future cultic obligations' (Blevins 2017: 250), in short, the possibility for the continuing communication between gods and humans.

Another example that illustrates how specific characteristics could render initially unspecific objects specific is the Temple of Jupiter Optimus Maximus on the Capitoline Hill. This temple – in other respects a Roman temple of standard form – had three *cellae* and therefore three doors, and it could thus only belong to Jupiter together with Juno and Minerva. This was the one and only temple with a triple *cella*, and this was known. Jupiter's temple on the Capitoline Hill is often depicted on coins and in other media. Whereas on imperial coins the temple of Jupiter was rendered relatable by means of three divine statues (those of Jupiter, Juno, and Minerva), on earlier coins the same recognisability was ensured by depicting a temple with three closed *cella* doors (*e.g.* Hill 1989; Grunow 2002: 30). Collectively, the three *cellae*, or even their doors as a short-cut, were a clear visual metonym that was sufficient to refer unequivocally to who dwelled in the temple.

Again, the triple *cella* doors are shown, closed and slightly ajar respectively, on two imperial reliefs representing the Temple of Jupiter Optimus Maximus. One of these shows a ceremony in front of the temple (Extispicium relief, Paris, Louvre; Arata 2010b with notes: 593 fig. 7; Perry 2012: 185 fig. 6.3). The other represents the emperor Marcus Aurelius sacrificing before Jupiter's temple (Rome, Palazzo dei Conservatori; Arata 2010b: 592 with notes, fig. 6; Perry 2012: 186 fig. 6.4). In both reliefs, the image of the god is not depicted. Even so, it was obvious to which temple, and therefore, to which god the depiction related to. The temple as such, as an unambiguous building, was enough to refer to the religious content of the depiction. Beyond the general religious content, it was the concrete *number* of the doors, a numeric feature, which was so specific that it sufficed to presence this very god, Jupiter Optimus Maximus. Number, as such (of gods, of statues, of objects), serving as an 'identifying feature to the viewer-worshipper', also works in other cases as seen in the case of the Castores. It was the doubleness both of anthropomorphic representations and objects – secondary agents (on these see further below) – related to these gods that were an unambiguous hint to the divine twins (Platt 2018).

Thus, the perceptibility of Jupiter's presence and his agency was achieved by means of a numeric feature – three doors – and the door as an object, which in itself is, initially, unspecific. It becomes specific and relatable in this context. An initially unspecific object, rendered specific, presenced Jupiter Optimus Maximus with the same unambiguousness and efficacy as any anthropomorphic statue (on the anthropomorphic representations of Jupiter, immediately relatable: Martin 1987: 143; Vermeule 1987: 53–54; Perry 2012: 190–194; Vlizos 2015). We will see further below, though, how the door as an initially unspecific object becomes, in a different context, relatable to another god, Janus. This object – the door – illustrates very well how much the relatability of unspecific objects is dependent on the context.

Hence, context and knowledge were the main factors that determined the relatability of objects to gods and made unspecific objects specific, enabling these to unambiguously presence a god. This combination of object, context, and knowledge saw to the smooth rendering of the comprehensibility of the material means that presenced the gods. 'Knowledge', of course, is an enormous field of research. Its ramifications and implications, such as religious knowledge, the production, distribution or dissemination of knowledge, or the withholding thereof cannot be dealt with in this chapter (see Keane 2008; Rüpke 2010: esp. 183–186; Ando 2010; 2015; Rüpke 2015: esp. 87–90; see also Pongratz-Leisten and Sonik 2015: 32, 35). Particularly important in this context seems to be the notion of 'empiricist epistemology' (Ando 2008: xiii–xvii, 1–18 in the context of religious knowledge in Rome). We will return to this at the end of the chapter.

In the case of Jupiter, knowledge and, consequently, the comprehension and relatability of the material means presencing this god was not limited to the inhabitants of Rome. Virtually everywhere in the Roman Empire, the Capitoline Trias and the triple *cella* were understood immediately. Knowledge accompanied, apparently, the spread of material representation or iconography. This can be observed to a particular extent regarding the representations of Jupiter spread or disseminated throughout the Roman Empire (Martin 1987: 143; regarding the mechanisms of spread and dissemination see Rieger 2007 in case of Magna Mater: knowledge accompanied divine beings). Although, these mechanisms or strategies do not work or were not intended in the case of every deity (see, *e.g.* Ando 2008: 43–58).

Turning again to the Forum, we see another example for how the divine is presenced by means of architectural objects and how these were rendered specific: the cult place of Janus or, in Latin, *Ianus Geminus* (Coarelli 1983: 89–97; Simon 1986; Tortorici 1996; Taylor 2000). It was one of the oldest cult places in the Forum, going back into the sixth century BC. Literary evidence attests to its existence in Late Antiquity (Procop. *Goth.* 1.25.19–25; Bauer 1996: 37–38). It seems that, at least until imperial times, or even until the end of its use, the architecture consisted of a double gate, an *ianus* (Tortorici 1996: 92 with evidence). Independently of whether the structure was transformed into a *sacellum* proper in imperial times or remained a double *ianus*, the doors were undoubtedly the main feature of the structure and determined its appearance.

The gate as object – be it as a stand-alone or main feature of a *sacellum* – was indeed the most suitable architectural element to presence this god, the guardian of gateways, passages, and doors, both literal and symbolic. The building's strategy in order to presence Janus was not by means of the standard forms of a temple, but simply by being and materially embodying Janus' sphere of action: the gate, the passage, the doorway. It was an unambiguously relatable and powerful means to presence this particular god. It was, though, unambiguous and understandable only with the precondition of shared knowledge, religious and linguistic knowledge alike: the constructed *ianus*, in Latin, the gate or passage, referred directly and immediately to this god himself – in Latin the very same word, Ianus. In a certain sense, the object not only represented the god but could even seem to *be* the god. This notion is further confirmed by Ovid (*e.g. Fast.* 1.63–293; 2.51), who, when referring to the god or the building, slips between the two: the god and the gate, both, actually, *Ianus* or *ianus*. In literature, this slippage between god on the one hand and material means presencing the god on the other, is usually found in the case of statues (Weddle 2010: 15–16), but rarely in the case of architectural structures.

There are more objects or material means that can be brought in that presenced, in one way or another, the divine. They are peculiar and somehow related to the gods or their sphere of action, as seen in the previous example. These objects are sometimes congruent with the category of aniconic objects (on aniconism see references above). In a certain sense they represent the god, often blurring the distinction between representing and being. This was the case in the last example, Janus/Ianus the god and *ianus* the gate. Although peculiar, these objects – the gate included – are, or become, usually specific and unique to such an extent that they are relatable unambiguously and they presence in an immediate and clearly understandable way the god in question. In addition to the architectural object in the Forum Romanum, there was another object that presenced Janus in a straightforward and unambiguous way. The Tigillum Sororium, situated not in the Forum, but not far away, was of very ancient origins. Literary evidence tracks it back into mytho-historical times but also testifies to its existence in the fourth century AD (Holland 1961: 77–91; Coarelli 1999c). This object consisted of a sort of wooden architrave, or a door bolt, spanning the street. At its left and right there were two altars dedicated to Juno Sororia and Janus Curiatius, respectively. Here again, an initially unspecific object, an architrave, becomes in the particular context of its action – spanning a street – and together with an altar, a very specific and effective material means to presence this particular god of doorways, gates, and passages of any kind. We have seen above how in a different context and with different mechanisms – by multiplication and by the specific numeric feature, the triple – the door became unambiguously relatable to another god, Jupiter.

Similar to the equation of god Ianus = *ianus* the gate, the god or the divine being Terminus (who held *numen* and was *deus* at the same time: Piccaluga 1974: 287) was referred to by the very object he was the guardian of: a boundary stone, in Latin *terminus*. The boundary stone, the *terminus*, was kept – or one could also say that Terminus dwelled – in the temple of Jupiter Optimus Maximus on the Capitoline Hill. God and object shared not only the name and the place but also features of behaviour. It was said that when the temple of Jupiter was to be erected, Terminus was already there, and he could not be moved, or rather, he did not want to be moved, so he – or it – was incorporated into the new temple (Piccaluga 1974; Tagliamonte 1999). This is a shared feature between Terminus the god and *terminus* the boundary stone: neither can be moved, or at least, not easily.

Further, we can see the fluid boundaries between the conceptual notions of things, deities, divine representations, animated objects, and the materialised imaginations of gods on the one hand, and primary and secondary divine agents on the other, along with materialised divine agency. The case of Terminus also touches on the question of aniconic images or imaginations of the gods. However, it is not exactly the case, because more than being an aniconic image, this object is – beyond being a sort of prototype of all boundary stones – also the embodiment of an abstract divine feature, a characteristic, a property of divine action: the immovability and the steadiness of the boundary stone.

This example leads to two other cases, not from our topographical area of study, the Forum Romanum and Capitoline Hill, but worthy of mention in order to show the spectrum of possibilities of how the divine could be presenced or how divine agency was materialised by various objects. Asclepius arrived in 293 BC to the city of Rome (Livy *Per*. 11; further literary sources listed in Degrassi 1993) – or rather, the god's cult was imported to Rome. What travelled with the Romans on the sea and went later offshore was a snake. The snake explicitly declared Asclepius' choice for the place of a sanctuary to be built on the Tiber Island. The snake not only presenced the god in the city of Rome for the centuries to come but, even more, it embodied as well as manifested materially Asclepius' divine agency. The relationship between god and snake – the snake being simultaneously the god's materialised agency and its attribute alike – poses interesting questions. Furthermore, many newly founded sanctuaries, branches of the Epidaurian main sanctuary, imported the god, the cult, or the god's divine agency, in serpentine form (Degrassi 1986: 145; van der Ploeg 2018: 65). How does the multiplicity of snakes relate to the god? Is the snake, or are the snakes, subsidiary beings, as seen with the sanctuaries being subsidiarily related to the main sanctuary? Are they infinitely multipliable? How does the partitioning of the materiality of divine agency impact its efficacy? Do the sacred snakes that are known to have lived in the sanctuary grounds have the same or similar divine qualities as the snakes that arrived in the new places as the god's proxy? It seems that the Romans did not address these questions.

Several more objects can be regarded, as the snake in Asclepius' case, as 'secondary agents'. These secondary agents are related either to a specific god as an object used by this god – for example, an attribute or tool – or the objects, usually man-made, served as utensils, used for the cult activities in honour of a god. In the case of the former, these objects are unambiguous and unequivocally relatable, such as Asclepius' snake, or, similarly, Mercury's *caduceus* and Jupiter's thunderbolt. And in the case of the latter, they can either be generic, used in cult activities related to not only one god, such as vessels or incense, or they can be unambiguous and specific, used only in the cult of one specific god, such as the *sistrum* in the cult of Isis. As mentioned above, most objects can reveal more than one mechanism of effectively presencing the divine as in the case of the snake. It provides an example of one and the same object that fluctuates between an object presencing the divine, the embodiment of this god's divine agency (Livy calls it '*numen*', within the snake but not being the snake itself, Livy *Per*. 11) and an attribute of the very same divinity, being primary agent and secondary agent for the divinity at the same time (on this terminology and further reference see Pongratz-Leisten and Sonik 2015, esp. 20–21).

As in the case of Asclepius, Magna Mater arrived to Rome from far away. According to literary sources (Livy 29.11.7; 29.14.10–14), she was brought to Rome in 204 BC in the form of a black stone. Yet, in pictorial representations, she appears mostly in an anthropomorphic form (Ando 2008: 22–42; most recently Vollmer 2014: 226–235). We learn from two literary accounts (Arn. *Adv. nat*. 6.11, 7.49; Prudent. *Perist*. 10.156) that the stone was subsequently embedded in the face of the anthropomorphic image of the goddess. Given that these two texts are firstly late, and secondly Christian accounts aiming to discredit the Roman gods and the practices of the 'pagans', we might have some doubt about their informative value. It seems, rather, that the image of the goddess, be it the statue in the temple on the Palatine Hill or in other representations, usually took the form of an anthropomorphic statue, and that it co-existed, in material forms as well as in the Romans' imagination, with the black stone – the anthropomorphic statue and the stone being equally efficient objects to presence this goddess. Worth mentioning here to further illustrate the question is a group of altars set up in honour of Magna Mater that are decorated with cymbals, pine cones, bulls, and rams (Vermaseren 1977: 49–61, no. 226–245a). These objects are unambiguous and specific and therefore relatable to this goddess. They are all instruments that have been used in cultic activities in her honour. In their role as secondary agents they are capable of unequivocally presencing this divinity and recalling her presence, again, with some knowledge of the onlooker presupposed. Note also that the goddess herself is never represented on these altars.

Synopsis

Whereas the overall image obtained from the evidence deriving from the Capitoline Hill and Forum Romanum is very heterogeneous regarding the physical appearance of the objects examined here, it is, at the same time, very homogeneous. The objects were, in regards to their potential to efficiently presence the gods, equally suitable.

The Forum Romanum and Capitoline Hill form together one of Rome's areas with the highest density of sacral buildings, cultic spots, altars, and divine representations and, therefore, holds the highest intensity of significance in terms of sacredness on the one hand and a particular accumulation of objects of various kinds that materially presenced the gods on the other. The gods and divine agency were presenced by means of all media available, monumental and subtle alike. All of these objects worked in neat interrelation with one another. Most of the objects, despite being unequivocal in regards to the deity they related to and which they presenced, reveal more than one mechanism of how they worked and through which means they acted to relate with humans.

The strikingly visible physical presence of temples, repeating the same architectural scheme, and the sheer ubiquity of very ancient cultic spots were, together with the anthropomorphic statues, the most conspicuous and most straightforward and easily understandable objects that presenced the gods. This high density of conspicuous objects was, furthermore, intensified by additional elements, which emphasised both the meaning of the buildings and cult places and their intention as how they ought to be understood. These objects evoked, in tight collaboration and interaction with one another, by mere sight, and by then triggering imagination, association, and memory, the gods and the ritual actions carried out in their honour. All of these objects worked equally effectively and affected the minds of the humans inasmuch as they reconnected with them and coalesced into a reciprocal relationship.

In an attempt to actively presence the gods, these objects of various kinds not only interacted one with the other through their own agency, but they also interacted with (and even more so, their function and effectiveness depended on) the tight synergy of context, knowledge, and imagination, unfurling their effectiveness in a framework of the mutual and symmetrical relationships of humans and objects. For these objects to be compatible with each other and for them to be understandable by the audience on the one hand, and relatable to specific gods on the other, two additional factors are essential: first, their context, both the larger cultural framework and the temporary, 'ephemeral' context of a specific occasion; and second, and equally essential, the knowledge of the audience. There was knowledge shared by everyone and knowledge shared by few. There was also knowledge held exclusively by distinct groups, and even intentionally withheld knowledge. Surely the objects were understood, and, even more so, one and the same object could be understood on different levels and with different nuances of personal meaning by the individual.

Hence, within the cultural context of the Roman world, or, more specifically, the city of Rome in imperial times, and then depending on the situation, occasion, and audience, one object or the other needed some additional information in order to be understood. This additional information could consist of an inscription, oral exegesis, or more elaborate depictions or added attributes. One and the same object could relate to different deities subject to different contexts as we have seen in the case of the door, relatable to Jupiter in one context, and to Janus in another. One and the same object could work more or less effectively in two different contexts, or, as summarised by Clifford Ando contrasting the image of Cybele (Magna Mater) in the performed procession and the image of Cybele within a procession depicted on a fresco in Pompeii:

> [...] the epistemics of the viewing community of representations were simply altogether different than the epistemics of the community of performance. For the audience of the image, an empty *ferculum* would clearly be a *signum* of some god – but which one? Some further information was necessary [...] but that information would, in the context of performance, have been wholly in surfeit of need (Ando 2015: 72; see also Clarke 2012: esp. 15–18).

Thus, we can see that within this framework that allowed general intelligibility, there was a certain flexibility of interpretation and pliability of meaning that could further, even significantly, change in different spatiotemporal settings (see similar notions in Pongratz-Leisten and Sonik 2015: 11, stressing further the importance of the individual's experience and cultural memory for the construction of meaning and the identification thereof; Blevins 2017: 256). The precondition for all of this to work was that the material manifestations' audience belonged to the same 'epistemic, linguistic and interpretive community' (Ando 2015: 71; or 'cultural learning and experience' in Pongratz-Leisten and Sonik 2015: 32–33, 35), in this case, the community of Imperial Rome's inhabitants as a whole, or the smaller community of those people who were engaged in the cult of Magna Mater, Isis, or any other god. What all these different objects had in common was their ownership of agency through their materiality: they presenced, explicitly and directly or more subtly, the gods and thus the possibility of communication with them, both reminding the people retrospectively that it had taken place in the past and giving them the assurance that it would also take place in the future.

Conclusions

This chapter, dealing with material produced by a historical-period society – the Romans – argued along the lines of and confirms the notion of the importance, the indispensability even, of cultural knowledge and cultural memory of any given society as the context in which the material objects, produced by this society, have to be discussed and attempted to be understood (Pongratz-Leisten and Sonik 2015: 6). The application of the theoretical approaches as outlined in the first part of the chapter on the examination of the materiality of Roman religion benefitted the analysis of the micro-fields within the topic on the one hand, and the development of different points of view on well-known objects on the other – in particular regarding the agency of objects. The gap between humans and non-humans in Roman culture and society – in this case between humans and objects as well as between humans and gods – could be bridged through a focus on their mutual relationship. Of particular importance is the consideration of boundaries between categories as fluid, such as boundaries of and between matter and imagination, representation and being, or primary and secondary agency.

The chapter's real contribution, though, to posthuman theoretical approaches is an indirect one: it argues strongly for a downgrading of the importance of the 'statue', or rather, of the overvaluation of the anthropomorphic representation of Roman divinities in the study of Roman religion. Simultaneously, it claims to acknowledge the equally significant role of non-anthropomorphic objects presencing gods and divine agency, or to extend our view on objects instead of limiting the focus to (divine) images.

American Academy in Rome/
Ludwig-Maximilians-Universität München

Acknowledgements

I am grateful to the editors, Irene Selsvold and Lewis Webb, for their invitation to me to participate in this book, for their valuable input and for opening new horizons to me, and to my colleagues Constanze Graml and Csaba Szabó who read and criticised the chapter, and to the anonymous reviewers for their invaluable input. All shortcomings are my own.

Bibliography

Ancient Sources

Arnobius, *Adversus nationes*.
Cicero, *In Catilinam*.
Livy, *Ab Urbe Condita*.
Livy, *Periochae*.
Ovid, *Fasti*.
Procopius, *De bello Gothico*.
Prudentius, *Peristephanon*.
Varro, *De lingua Latina*.
Varro, *De re rustica*.

Modern Sources

Ando, C. 2008. *The Matter of the Gods: Religion and the Roman Empire*. Berkeley: University of California Press.

Ando, C. 2010. Praesentia numinis 1: the visibility of Roman gods. *ASDIWAL. Revue genevoise d'anthropologie et d'histoire des religions* 5: 45–73.

Ando, C. 2011. Praesentia numinis 2: objects in Roman cult. *ASDIWAL. Revue genevoise d'anthropologie et d'histoire des religions* 6: 57–69.

Ando, C. 2015. Praesentia numinis 3: idols in context (of use). *ASDIWAL. Revue genevoise d'anthropologie et d'histoire des religions* 10: 61–76.

Anguissola, A. 2007. Retaining the function: sacred copies in Greek and Roman art. *RES: Anthropology and Aesthetics* 51: 98–107.

Arata, F.P. 2010a. Osservazioni sulla topografia sacra dell'arx Capitolina. *Mélanges de l'Ecole française de Rome, Antiquité* 122: 117–146.

Arata, F.P. 2010b. Nuove considerazioni a proposito del tempio di Giove Capitolino. *Mélanges de l'Ecole française de Rome, Antiquité* 122: 585–624.

Arnhold, M., Maier, H.O. and Rüpke, J. (eds) 2018. *Seeing the God. Image, Space, Performance and Vision in the Religion of the Roman Empire*. Tübingen: Mohr Siebeck.

Auffarth, C. 2009. Götterbilder im römischen Griechenland, vom Tempel zum Museum? In O.J. Hekster, S. Schmidt-Hofner and C. Witschel (eds) *Ritual Dynamics and Religious Change in the Roman Empire: Proceedings of the 8th Workshop of the International Network Impact of Empire (Heidelberg, July 5–7, 2007)*. Leiden: Brill: 307–325.

Bauer, F.A. 1996. *Stadt, Platz und Denkmal in der Spätantike. Untersuchungen zur Ausstattung des öffentlichen Raums in den spätantiken Städten Rom, Konstantinopel und Ephesos*. Mainz: Philipp von Zabern.

Belayche, N. and Pirenne-Delforge, V. (eds) 2015. *Fabriquer du divin. Constructions et ajustements de la représentation des dieux dans l'antiquité*. Liège: Presses universitaires de Liège.

Bielfeldt, R. 2014. Lichtblicke: Sehstrahlen. In R. Bielfeldt (ed.) *Ding und Mensch in der Antike. Gegenwart und Vergegenwärtigung*. Heidelberg: Winter: 195–238.

Blakely, S. (ed.) 2017. *Gods, Objects, and Ritual Practice*. Atlanta: Lockwood Press.

Blevins, S.L. 2017. Rhetoric, repetition and identity in the frieze of sacred objects on the Temple of Divus Vespasianus and Divus Titus. In S. Blakely (ed.) *Gods, Objects, and Ritual Practice*. Atlanta: Lockwood Press: 233–258.

Blume, H.S. 2016. The furniture of gods: the problem with the importation of 'empty space and material aniconism' into Greek religion. *Archiv für Religionsgeschichte* 17: 55–68.

Boschung, D. 2007. Kultbilder als Vermittler religiöser Vorstellungen. In C. Frevel and H. von Hesberg (eds) *Kult und Kommunikation: Medien in Heiligtümern der Antike*. Wiesbaden: Reichert: 63–87.

Bourgeaud, P. and Fabiano, D. (eds) 2013. *Perception et construction du divin dans l'Antiquité*. Geneva: Droz.

Bravi, A. 2014. *Griechische Kunstwerke im politischen Leben Roms und Konstantinopels*. Berlin: Walter de Gruyter.

Bratengeier, A. 2010. *Die peripterale Tholos in der Geschichte der römischen Architektur*. Hamburg: Kovač.

Bremmer, J.N. 2015. God against the gods. Early Christians and the worship of statues. In D. Boschung and A. Schäfer (eds) *Römische Götterbilder der mittleren und späten Kaiserzeit*. Paderborn: Fink: 139–158.

Bumke, H. 2008. Vom Verhältnis der Römer zu den Kultbildern der Griechen. In K. Junker and A. Stähli (eds) *Original und Kopie. Formen und Konzepte der Nachahmung in der antiken Kunst. Akten des Kolloquiums in Berlin, 17.–19. Februar 2005*. Wiesbaden: Reichert: 109–133.

Caprioli, F. 2007. *Vesta aeterna: L'Aedes Vestae e la sua decorazione architettonica*. Rome: L'Erma di Bretschneider.

Clarke, J.R. 2003. *Art in the Lives of Ordinary Romans. Visual Representation and Non-Elite Viewers in Italy, 100 BC–AD 315*. Berkeley: University of California Press.

Clarke, J.R. 2012. Representations of worship at Rome, Pompeii, Herculaneum, and Ostia in the Imperial period. A model of production and consumption. In D.L. Balch and A. Weissenrieder (eds) *Contested Spaces. Houses and Temples in Roman Antiquity and the New Testament*. Tübingen: Mohr Siebeck: 3–20.

Coarelli, F. 1983. *Il Foro Romano. Periodo arcaico*. Rome: Quasar.

Coarelli, F. 1985. *Il Foro Romano. Periodo repubblicano e augusteo*. Rome: Quasar.

Coarelli, F. 1999a. Saturnus, aedes. In *LTUR IV*: 234–236.

Coarelli, F. 1999b. Saturnus, ara. In *LTUR IV*: 236.

Coarelli, F. 1999c. Tigillum Sororium. In *LTUR V*: 74–75.

Cody, J. 1973. New evidence for the Republican Aedes Vestae. *American Journal of Archaeology* 77: 43–50.

De Angeli, S. 1992. *Templum Divi Vespasiani*. Rome: De Luca.

De Angeli, S. 1996. Iuppiter Optimus Maximus Capitolinus, aedes (fasi tardo-repubblicane e di età imperiale). In *LTUR III*: 148–153.

Degrassi, A. 1986. Il culto di Esculapio in Italia centrale durante il periodo repubblicano. In F. Coarelli (ed.) *Fregellae 2: Il santuario di Esculapio*. Rome: Quasar: 145–152.

Degrassi, A. 1993. Aesculapius, aedes, templum (Isola Tiberina). In *LTUR I*: 21–22.

DiLuzio, M. 2016. *A Place at the Altar: Priestesses in Republican Rome*. Princeton: Princeton University Press.

DiLuzio, M. 2017. Priestesses in action. Ritual instruments employed by Roman women. In S. Blakely (ed.) *Gods, Objects, and Ritual Practice*. Atlanta: Lockwood Press: 215–232.

Elsner, J. 2007. *Roman Eyes: Visuality and Subjectivity in Art and Text*. Princeton: Princeton University Press.

Elsner, J. 2012. Iconoclasm as discourse: From antiquity to Byzantium. *Art Bulletin* 94 (3): 368–394.

Estienne, S. 2010. *Simulacra deorum* versus *ornamenta aedium*: the status of divine images in the temples of Rome. In J. Mylonopoulos (ed.) *Divine Images and Human Imaginations in Ancient Greece and Rome*. Leiden: Brill: 257–271.

Estienne, S. 2015. Images. In R. Raja and J. Rüpke (eds) *A Companion to the Archaeology of Religion in the Ancient World*. Malden: Wiley Blackwell: 379–387.

Estienne, S., Huet, V., Lissarague, F. and Prost, F. (eds) 2015. *Figures de dieux. Construire le divin en images*. Rennes: Presses universitaires de Rennes.

Fahlander, F. 2012. Ontology matters in archaeology and anthropology: people, things and posthumanism. In J.D. Englehardt and I.A. Rieger (eds) *Thin Partition. Bridging the Growing Divide between Cultural Anthropology and Archaeology*. Louisville, Colorado: University Press of Colorado: 69–86.

Ferroni, A.M. 1993. Concordiae, aedes. In *LTUR I*: 316–320.

Fischer, T. 2015. Götterbilder auf römischen Waffen. In D. Boschung and A. Schäfer (eds) *Römische Götterbilder in der mittleren und späten Kaiserzeit*. Paderborn: Fink: 343–369.

Freyberger, K.S. 2012. Sakrale Kommunikationsräume auf dem Forum Romanum. In F. Mundt (ed.) *Kommunikationsräume im kaiserzeitlichen Rom*. Berlin: Walter de Gruyter: 49–76.

Gaifman, M. 2017. Aniconism: definitions, examples and comparative perspectives. *Religion* 47 (3): 335–352.

Gasparri, C. 1979. *Aedes Concordiae Augustae*. Rome: Istituto di Studi Romani.

Gell, A. 1998. *Art and Agency: An Anthropological Theory*. Oxford: Clarendon Press.

Giuliani, C.F. and Verduchi, P. 1995. Forum Romanum (età tarda). In *LTUR II*: 342–343.

Gordon, R. 1979. The real and the imaginary: production and religion in the Greco-Roman world. *Art History* 2: 5–34.

Grig, L. 2009. Imagining the Capitolium in Late Antiquity. In A. Cain and N. Lenski (eds) *The Power of Religion in Late Antiquity*. Farnham: Ashgate: 279–291.

Grunow, M.D. 2002. *Architectural Images in Roman State Reliefs, Coins, and Medallions: Imperial Ritual, Ideology, and the Topography of Rome*. PhD Thesis. University of Michigan.

Harris, O.J.T. 2016. Becoming post-human: identity and the ontological turn. In E. Pierce, A. Russell, A. Maldonado and L. Campbell (eds) *Creating Material Worlds: The Uses of Identity in Archaeology*. Oxford: Oxbow Books: 19–37.

Harris, O.J.T. and Cipolla, C.N. 2017. *Archaeological Theory in the New Millennium: Introducing Current Perspectives*. Abingdon/New York: Routledge.

Hicks, D. 2010. The material-cultural turn: event and effect. In D. Hicks and M.C. Beaudry (eds) *The Oxford Handbook of Material Culture Studies*. Oxford: Oxford University Press: 25–98.

Hill, P. 1989. *The Monuments of Ancient Rome as Coin Types*. London: Seaby.

Hodder, I. and Lucas, G. 2017. The symmetries and asymmetries of human-thing relations. A dialogue. *Archaeological Dialogues* 24 (2): 119–137.

Hölkeskamp, K.J. 2001. Capitol, Comitium und Forum: Öffentliche Räume, sakrale Topographie und Erinnerungslandschaften der römischen Republik. In S. Faller (ed.) *Studien zu antiken Identitäten*. Würzburg: Ergon: 97–132.

Hölkeskamp, K.J. 2014. In defense of concepts, categories and other abstractions: remarks on a theory of memory (in the making). In K. Galinsky (ed.) Memoria Romana*: Memory in Rome and Rome in Memory*. Ann Arbor: University of Michigan Press: 63–70.

Holland, L.A. 1961. *Janus and the Bridge*. Rome: American Academy in Rome.

Hölscher, T. 2006. Das Forum Romanum: die monumentale Geschichte Roms. In K.J. Hölkeskamp and E. Stein-Hölkeskamp (eds) *Erinnerungsorte der Antike: Die römische Welt*. Munich: Beck: 100–122.

Jenkyns, R. 2013. *God, Space, and City in the Roman Imagination*. Oxford: Oxford University Press.

Kalas, G. 2015. *The Restoration of the Forum Romanum in Late Antiquity: Transforming Public Space*. Austin: University of Texas Press.

Kaufmann-Heinimann, A. 2007. Religion in the house. In J. Rüpke (ed.) *A Companion to Roman Religion*. Malden, MA: Blackwell: 188–201.

Keane, W. 2008. The evidence of the senses and the materiality of religion. *The Journal of the Royal Anthropological Institute* 14: 110–127.

Köb, I. 2000. *Rom, ein Stadtzentrum im Wandel: Untersuchungen zur Funktion und Nutzung des Forum Romanum und der Kaiserfora in der Kaiserzeit*. Hamburg: Kovač.

Krech, V. 2015. Communication. In R.A. Segal and K. von Stuckrad (eds) *Vocabulary for the Study of Religion, Volume 1: A–E*. Leiden: Brill: 285–294.

Kristensen, T.M. 2013. *Making and Breaking the Gods. Christian Responses to Pagan Sculptures in Late Antiquity*. Aarhus: Aarhus University Press.

La Follette, L. 2011–2012. Parsing piety. The sacred still life in Roman relief sculpture. *Memoirs of the American Academy in Rome* 56–57: 15–35.

Lavan, L. 2011. Political talismans? Residual 'pagan' statues in late antique public space. In L. Lavan and M. Mulryan (eds) *The Archaeology of Late Antique Paganism*. Leiden: Brill: 439–477.

MacMullen R. 1981. *Paganism in the Roman Empire*. New Haven: Yale University Press.

Martin, H.G. 1987. *Römische Tempelkultbilder*. Rome: L'Erma di Bretschneider.

Metzler, D. 1985–86. Anikonische Darstellungen. *Visible Religion* IV–V: 97–113.

Moralee, J. 2018. *Rome's Holy Mountain: The Capitoline Hill in Late Antiquity*. Oxford: Oxford University Press.

Moser, C. and Knust, J. (eds) 2017. *Ritual Matters. Material Remains and Ancient Religion*. Ann Arbor: University of Michigan Press.

Moyer, I.S. 2016. Introduction: the religious life of things. *Archiv für Religionsgeschichte* 17: 3–9.

Muth, S. 2012. Der Dialog von Gegenwart und Vergangenheit am Forum Romanum oder: Wie spätantik ist das Forum? In T. Fuhrer (ed.) *Rom und Mailand in der Spätantike: Repräsentationen städtischer Räume in Literatur, Architektur und Kunst*. Berlin: Walter de Gruyter: 263–282.

Mylonopoulos, J. 2010a. Divine images versus cult images: an endless story about theories, methods and terminologies. In J. Mylonopoulos (ed.) *Divine Images and Human Imaginations in Ancient Greece and Rome*. Leiden: Brill: 1–19.

Mylonopoulos, J. 2010b (ed.). *Divine Images and Human Imaginations in Ancient Greece and Rome*. Leiden: Brill.

Nielsen, I. 1993. Castor, aedes, templum. In *LTUR I*: 242–245.

Nielsen, I. and Poulsen, B. (eds) 1992–2008. *The Temple of Castor and Pollux*. Rome: De Luca.

Pensabene, P. 1984. *Tempio di Saturno: Architettura e decorazione*. Rome: De Luca.

Perry, E. 2012. The same but different: the Temple of Jupiter Optimus Maximus through time. In B.D. Wescoat and R.G. Osterhout (eds) *Architecture of the Sacred: Space, Ritual, and Experience from Classical Greece to Byzantium*. Cambridge: Cambridge University Press: 175–200.

Perry, E. 2015. Human interaction with statues. In E.A. Friedland, M. Grunow Sobocinski and E.K. Gazda (eds) *The Oxford Handbook of Roman Sculpture*. Oxford: Oxford University Press: 653–666.

Petridou, G. 2016. *Divine Epiphany in Greek Literature and Culture*. Oxford: Oxford University Press.

Petridou, G. and Platt, V. 2018. Introduction. *Archiv für Religionsgeschichte* 20: 185–272.

Piccaluga, G. 1974. *Terminus. I segni di confine nella religione romana*. Rome: Edizioni dell'Ateneo.

Platt, V. 2011. *Facing the Gods. Epiphany and Representation in Graeco-Roman Art, Literature, and Religion*. Cambridge: Cambridge University Press.

Platt, V. 2015. Epiphany. In E. Eidinow and J. Kindt (eds) *The Oxford Handbook of Ancient Greek Religion*. Oxford: Oxford University Press: 491–502.

Platt, V. 2018. Double vision. Epiphanies of the Dioscuri in Classical Antiquity. *Archiv für Religionsgeschichte* 20: 229–256.

Pongratz-Leisten, B. and Sonik, K. 2015. Between cognition and culture: theorizing the materiality of divine agency in cross-cultural perspective. In B. Pongratz-Leisten and K. Sonik (eds) *The Materiality of Divine Agency*. Berlin: Walter de Gruyter: 3–69.

Purcell, N. 1995. Forum Romanum (the republican period). In *LTUR II*: 325–336.

Raja, R. and Rüpke, J. 2015a. Archaeology of religion, material religion, and the ancient world. In R. Raja and J. Rüpke (eds) *A Companion to the Archaeology of Religion in the Ancient World*. Malden, MA: Wiley Blackwell: 1–26.

Raja, R. and Rüpke, J. (eds) 2015b. *A Companion to the Archaeology of Religion in the Ancient World*. Malden, MA: Wiley Blackwell.

Reusser, C. 1993. Area Capitolina. In *LTUR I*: 114–117.

Rieger, A.-K. 2007. Lokale Tradition versus überregionale Einheit: der Kult der Magna Mater. *Mediterranea* 4: 89–120.

Rives, J.B. 2007. *Religion in the Roman Empire*. Malden, MA: Blackwell 2007.

Robb, J. 2010. Beyond agency. *World Archaeology* 42 (4): 493–520.

Rüpke, J. 2006. Communicating with the gods. In N. Rosenstein and R. Morstein-Marx (eds) *A Companion to the Roman Republic*. Malden, MA: Blackwell: 215–235.

Rüpke, J. 2010. Representation or presence? Picturing the divine in ancient Rome. *Archiv für Religionsgeschichte* 12: 181–196.

Rüpke, J. 2015. The role of priests in constructing the divine in ancient Rome. In N. Belayche and V. Pirenne-Delforge (eds) *Fabriquer du divin. Constructions et ajustements de la représentation des dieux dans l'antiquité*. Liège: Presses universitaires de Liège: 79–92.

Rüpke, J. 2016. Individual appropriation of sacred space. In Y. Lafond and V. Michel (eds) *Espaces sacrés dans la Méditerranée antique. Actes du colloque des 13 et 14 octobre 2011*, Université de Poitiers. Rennes: Presses universitaires de Rennes: 69–80.

Rüpke, J. 2018. *Pantheon. A New History of Roman Religion.* Princeton: Princeton University Press.

Scheer, T.S. 2000. *Die Gottheit und ihr Bild. Untersuchungen zur Funktion griechischer Kultbilder in Religion und Politik.* Munich: Beck.

Scheer, T. 2015. Art and imagery. In E. Eidinow and J. Kindt (eds) *The Oxford Handbook of Ancient Greek Religion.* Oxford: Oxford University Press: 165–178.

Scheid, J. 2005. Les dieux du Capitole: un exemple des structures théologiques des sanctuaires romains. In X. Lafon and G. Sauron (eds) *Théorie et pratique de l'architecture romaine. La norme et l'experimentation. Études offertes à Pierre Gros.* Aix-en-Provence: Publications de l'Université de Provence: 93–100.

Scott, R.T. 1999. Vesta, aedes. In *LTUR V*: 125–128.

Selsvold, I. 2019. *Pagan Pasts, Christian Futures: Memory Manipulation and Christianisation in the Cities of Western Asia Minor.* PhD Thesis. University of Gothenburg.

Simon, E. 1986. Ianus Curiatius und Ianus Geminus im frühen Rom. In R. Altheim-Stiehl and M. Rosenbach (eds) *Beiträge zur altitalischen Geistesgeschichte. Festschrift für Gerhard Radke zum 18. Februar 1984.* Münster: Aschendorff: 257–268.

Stewart, P. 2000. Cult images on Roman lamps. *Hephaistos* 18: 7–28.

Tagliamonte, G. 1995. Forum Romanum (fino alla prima età repubblica). In *LTUR II*: 313–325.

Tagliamonte, G. 1999. Terminus, fanum, sacellum, ara. In *LTUR V*: 27–28.

Taylor, L.R. 1931. Aniconic worship among the early Romans. In G.D. Hadzsits (ed.) *Classical Studies in Honor of John C. Rolfe.* Philadelphia: University of Philadelphia Press: 305–319.

Taylor, R. 2000. Watching the skies: Janus, auspication and the shrine in the Roman Forum. *Memoirs of the American Academy in Rome* 45: 1–40.

Tortorici, E. 1996. Ianus Geminus, aedes. In *LTUR IV*: 92–93.

Tortorici, E. 1999. Victoria, ara. In *LTUR V*: 150.

Trimble, J. 2015. Reception theory. In E.A. Friedland, M.G. Sobocinski and E.K. Gazda (eds) *The Oxford Handbook of Roman Sculpture.* Oxford: Oxford University Press: 606–621.

Vermeule, C. 1987. *The Cult Images of Imperial Rome.* Rome: Giorgio Bretschneider.

van der Ploeg, G.E. 2018. *The Impact of the Roman Empire on the Cult of Asclepius.* Leiden: Brill.

van Eck, C., Versluys, M.J. and ter Keurs, P. 2015. The biography of cultures: style, objects and agency. Proposal for an interdisciplinary approach. *Cahiers de l'École du Louvre* 7: 2–22.

Vermaseren, M.J. 1977. *Corpus Cultus Cybelae Attidisque, Volume 3: Italia. Latium.* Leiden: Brill.

Versluys, J.M. 2014. Understanding objects in motion. An archaeological dialogue on Romanization. *Archaeological Dialogues* 21.1: 1–20.

Versnel, H. 1994. *Inconsistencies in Greek and Roman Religion, II. Transition and Reversal in Myths and Ritual.* Leiden: Brill.

Vlizos, S. 2015. Das Vorbild des Zeus aus Olympia. In D. Boschung and A. Schäfer (eds) *Römische Götterbilder der mittleren und späten Kaiserzeit.* Paderborn: Fink: 41–70.

Vollmer, C. 2014. *Im Anfang war der Thron. Studien zum leeren Thron in der griechischen, römischen und frühchristlichen Ikonographie.* Rahden/Westfalen: Leidorf.

Weddle, P. 2010. *Touching the Gods: Physical Interaction with Cult Statues in the Roman World.* PhD Thesis. Durham University.

Williams, J. 2007. Religion and Roman coins. In J. Rüpke (ed.) *A Companion to Roman Religion.* Malden, MA: Blackwell: 143–63.

Wiseman, T.P. 2014. Popular memory. In K. Galinsky (ed.) *Memoria Romana. Memory in Rome and Rome in Memory.* Ann Arbour: University of Michigan Press: 43–62.

Wissowa, G. 1904. Römische Götterbilder. In *Gesammelte Abhandlungen zur römischen Religions- und Stadtgeschichte.* Ergänzungsband zu des Verfassers Religion und Kultus der Römer. Munich: Beck: 280–298.

Abbreviations

LTUR I	Steinby, E.M. (ed.) 1993. *Lexicon Topographicum urbis Romae, volume primo, A–C.* Rome: Edizioni Quasar.
LTUR II	Steinby, E.M. (ed.) 1995. *Lexicon Topographicum urbis Romae, volume secondo, D–G.* Rome: Edizioni Quasar.
LTUR III	Steinby, E.M. (ed.) 1996. *Lexicon Topographicum urbis Romae, volume terzo, H–O.* Rome: Edizioni Quasar.
LTUR IV	Steinby, E.M. (ed.) 1999. *Lexicon Topographicum urbis Romae, volume quarto, P–S.* Rome: Edizioni Quasar.
LTUR V	Steinby, E.M. (ed.) 1999. *Lexicon Topographicum urbis Romae, volume quinto, T–Z, addenda et corrigenda.* Rome: Edizioni Quasar.

6

Chicken Hybrid Imagery on Late Iron Age Coinage in Northern Gaul and Southern England during the Iron Age–Roman Transition

Mike P. Feider, Ellen Hambleton, and Mark Maltby

Introduction

Many zooarchaeological studies have principally focused on the economic exploitation of animals at the expense of examining the social relationships between humans and animals. Gradually, however, social zooarchaeology is increasingly using evidence from other disciplines, particularly anthropology, to furnish deeper discussions of these relationships (*e.g.* Morris and Maltby 2010; Russell 2014; Sykes 2014). Naomi Sykes has championed the adoption of social zooarchaeology to address 'the most fundamental issues concerning past societies: how people behaved and how they thought' (Sykes 2014: 1). Importantly, social zooarchaeology frameworks (*e.g.* Overton and Hamilakis 2013; Sykes 2014) place animals at the centre of this discourse, recognising that animals and their autonomous actions, inherent behaviours, appearance, physical and vocal presence, and indeed their individual quirks, are integral to the negotiation and mutual construction of human-animal (or animal-human!) relationships. The concept that animals have agency is an important aspect in this approach and the social contract, as defined by Kristin Armstrong Oma (2010), is more likely to be reflected in imagery rather than bones. Concepts of human and animal are constantly evolving and have to be examined in this context (Braidotti 2019: 36–37). Some of the images discussed in this chapter reflect hybridisation between humans and non-humans, which has relevance to the focus of this volume. This is a posthuman, non-anthropocentric 'multispecies' approach, and we adopt it here in our exploration of the imagery of chickens and chicken-human hybrids on later Iron Age coinage.

Zooarchaeologists have also increasingly realised that human-animal relationships can be explored through other media rather than the bones themselves. Chickens were introduced into western Europe during the Iron Age and possible reasons for, and impact of, their introduction has recently been considered (Sykes 2012; Maltby *et al.* 2018; Pitt *et al.* 2019). However, most of the discussion has been based primarily on zooarchaeological data. The relationship between chickens and humans is also reflected in the material culture of this period and region, and it is the investigation of material culture, specifically locally distinct groups of late Iron Age coins depicting chicken-human hybrids, which forms the basis of this chapter. We take a posthuman approach, drawing on aspects of 'new materialism', recognising that material objects can act as surrogate people (Harris and Cipolla 2017: 76). It is this aspect of the coins discussed in this chapter that is considered in relation to their role in Belgic Gaul, where the chicken and chicken-human images on the coins may have provoked responses that served the ideological purpose of their makers. Importantly, we recognise that objects themselves have agency, often divorced from the original intent of their human makers (Harris and Cipolla 2017: 73), and it is this aspect that we consider in relation to the chicken and chicken-human imagery on coins from Britain. This chapter emphasises the importance of contextual archaeology as well as the 'post-anthropocentric' (Ferrando 2013: 29) interpretation of non-human animals, images, and objects and their interactions; we explore how these manifest in the context of the early Roman world – especially at the periphery of the empire.

During the Late Iron Age, a series of images depicting an unusual hybrid of a chicken with a human face on its belly became the earliest native chicken imagery produced in northwest Europe. These images appear on a very geographically and temporally restricted set of coins from Belgic Gaul and south-east England, and represent the earliest native chicken imagery in that part of the world. Other coins from the period include images of animals such as horses and boars (de Jersey 2006: 119); strong, powerful creatures whose inclusion is fairly understandable. The use of a chicken is less explicable and becomes even more complicated by the human face on the stomach of the bird. Miranda Aldhouse-Green (2004: 150) has noted that most of the human-animal hybrids from Late Iron Age north-west Europe are animals that share a close relationship with humans, and chickens possibly share an intimacy with humans greater than any other domestic species apart from pets. While this tradition of hybridisation goes some distance towards an explanation of this unusual image, the extremely limited geographical and temporal distribution of these coins permits a more focused exploration, and it is on this particular case study that this chapter will concentrate. Why is the image that appears on some of the earliest base metal coins in this part of the world not just a chicken, but a chicken with a human face?

Gaul

The earliest coins of this type appear in Belgic Gaul in Colin Haselgrove's Western zone, which includes the territories of the Ambiani, Atrebates, Bellovaci, and Veliocasses (Haselgrove 1999: 119). Using the typologies of Louis-Pol Delestrée and Marcel Tache (2002), these coins are types DT 509 through DT 521.

Delestrée described these chicken-themed coins and their possible evolution over thirty years ago (Delestrée 1980), and has further clarified the typologies since (Delestrée and Tache 2002). For this investigation a detailed discussion of how they interrelate is not important, and a short summary of the earliest one and its variations will suffice.

Type DT 511 (Fig. 6.1), sometimes called the Bracquemont type, appears to be the earliest of this series. It is less stylised than the others, featuring a helmeted, female head on the obverse. The reverse image is of a cockerel, clearly recognisable by its wattles, comb, and tail feathers. Its wings are spread, which is unusual for depictions of chickens, but most bizarre is the human face placed on its belly.

It is thought that this coin was inspired by Central Italian coins dating back to the late third century BC (Delestrée 1980: 55), but the themes of Classical art would have been readapted for use by these communities, not simply copied (MacDonald 2007: 493). The decision to produce this image and hybridise it with a human would certainly have been influenced by local interpretations of what a chicken is, resulting in a new image with a unique set of meanings attached to it (Aldhouse-Green 2004: 178). At least two coins of this type have been found by metal detectorists in Britain (Portable Antiquities Scheme numbers KENT12 and HAMP-B15408), and while it is impossible to be sure that they were deposited in Antiquity, it does suggest that Mediterranean coins occasionally made their way to the far northern edge of the empire. Such copying is not an unusual concept, with the earliest gold coins from this part of Gaul thought to have ultimately taken their imagery from far-flung Macedonia and the coins of Philip II (Creighton 2000: 26).

A comparison of the Gaulish coin to one of the above Central Italian coins does show some similarities. Both have a helmeted, possibly female, head on the obverse and a chicken on the reverse. The Gaulish coin has round shapes corresponding to the locations of a starburst while the Italian example has a crescent. However, the chicken on the Campanian coin is more erect in the manner of modern breeds of gamecock like the Shamo and its wings are folded. The Gaulish coin's chicken, apart from the addition of a human face, has spread its wings and holds its head back. While the design of the later coin may have been influenced by the earlier one, it was not a slavish copy.

Delestrée suggested that the plump crop shown on some of the Campanian coins inspired the Belgic coin makers to fill in the space with a human face (Delestrée 1980: 56), but it is unlikely that such an unusual image would be created on a whim. It must have been born out of some aspect of Belgic culture, creating a local icon out of an imported image.

Accepting type DT 511 as the first of the Belgic cockerel coins, it is easy to see the other types as either derivatives or otherwise inspired by the same sources. While the imagery of the DT 511 coin is relatively naturalistic, some of the others become quite stylised and abstract, with DT 509 being perhaps the most extreme example.

The hybrid image is by no means universal, with types DT 510, DT 517, DT 518, and DT 521 having the bird without the face. Type DT 515 is unusual in having the human face at the edge of the coin, facing the non-hybridised chicken. Types DT 519 and DT 520 have two hybrid birds facing each other. Type DT 521 is the most deviant of the cockerel coins, not only having a significantly different form of chicken on the reverse, but also featuring a boar instead of a human face on the obverse.

Nearly all of the coins in Gaul were recovered from Late Iron Age religious sites in Picardy and Normandy (Fig. 6.2). The most significant were Digeon, Fesques, Bois-l'Abbé, Camp Rouge, and Vendeuil-Caply, all of which had later Gallo-Roman religious activity. The vast majority of coins from these sites were recovered by metal detectorists, with the exception of Fesques, which limits contextual interpretation to the site level.

Known in the nineteenth century as the *terre d'argent* (land of money/silver, Delplace *et al.* 1986: 83), the temple site at Digeon (Somme) has the highest concentration of coins in Belgic Gaul (Delestrée and Delplace 1986: 19). Nearly 1,200 identifiable coins from this site, largely from museum collections and metal detectorists, were examined in one study (Delestrée and Delplace 1986). Coins with chickens on them were the most abundant type of bronze coin recorded there, especially the Bracquemont type, DT 511 (Table 6.1). Smaller numbers of other chicken coins were present, all of them minted locally, and all of them seem to be of a similar date, making for a remarkably homogeneous assemblage (Delestrée and Delplace 1986: 18–19). From Digeon, it is thought that chicken imagery spread to the other religious sites (Delestrée 1994: 27). One of these sites was Fesques, a large temple complex in use from the third century BC to the second

Figure 6.1: Belgic coins. Top: type DT 511, the so-called 'Bracquemont' type (www.cgb.fr, Lot 531625, June 2019). Bottom: type DT 516 (www.cgb.fr, Lot 423755, March 2017). (Courtesy of CGB Numismatic Paris – www.cgb.fr. Photo credit and copyright: CGB Numismatic Paris – www.cgb.fr).

century AD (Mantel 1997: 7). Many of the coins from this site were, fortunately, recovered during controlled excavations and therefore come from known contexts, most of which were within the main three structures on site (Delestrée 1997: 283). Most of these contexts were pits and ditches, and it is possible that the coins were redeposited within these features during later renovations to the site (Haselgrove 1999: 115), but it is also possible the coins may have been primary deposits of votive offerings. As with Digeon, the coins are mostly local and form a homogeneous group (Delestrée 1997: 285). Type DT 511 is likewise the most common type, followed by DT 512, which is a smaller variation of the Bracquemont type (Table 1).

The site of Bois l'Abbé, near Eu (Seine-Maritime), is another large sanctuary with a high concentration of chicken coins (Delestrée 2008). The numbers are smaller than the previous two sites, but DT 511 still dominates (Table 1). Here, however, type DT 517, which otherwise was only represented by a single example at Fesques, is the second most common. This coin lacks the human face on the

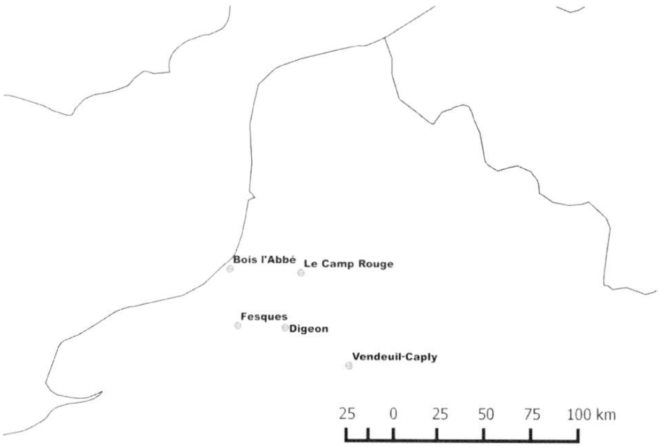

Figure 6.2: Locations of Late Iron Age temples where these coins were recovered.

Table 6.1: Iron Age religious sites and the number of the coin types found there.

Coin type	*Digeon*	*Fesques*	*Bois-l'Abbé*	*Camp Rouge*	*Vendeuil-Caply*
DT 509	14	1			6
DT 510	1				
DT 511	443	169	49	12	
DT 512	2	57	3		
DT 514				2	
DT 515				1	
DT 516	19	1		12	
DT 517		1	34		
DT 519	13	1		3	
DT 521	1				

chicken and appears less stylised than most of the others. Whether these differences indicate an earlier coin type or merely a different artistic tradition is unknown.

Le Camp Rouge near the town of Fontaine-sur-Somme (Somme) had a smaller, but more diverse, collection of coins (Delestrée 1987). Type DT 511 was still one of the two most common types, in equal abundance with type DT 516. Type DT 516 was found in small numbers at Digeon and Fesques, but the relative proportions suggest a local prominence at this site. The coin bears similarities to both types DT 511 and DT 517, and is unusual in that a small lyre appears in front of the face on the obverse side. Although they appear in smaller numbers, this site also possessed the only examples of types DT 514 and DT 515 (Table 1).

The temple complex at Vendeuil-Caply is quite different from the others, having only six chicken coins in its assemblage and lacking type DT 511 entirely (Delestrée 1985). Here only type DT 509 was found, which only appears in small numbers at Digeon and Fesques. This type is perhaps the most stylised and abstract of the coins discussed here, with the shapes being made up of simple lines and dots. This site is the most peripheral of the group, and so may be located on the edge of the 'chicken zone', with different influences at play.

It has been suggested that during the Late Iron Age, religious sites such as these were where coins were minted (Delestrée and Delplace 1986: 19; Haselgrove 2007: 501). For 'tribal states', defining themselves around a group rather than a geographic point, such as a city, such sites would be ideal for this sort of centralised activity, and would have served as a geographic anchor for such a group (Collis 2007: 524–525). This would explain the high volume of coins and some of the variation between the sites. A site might be expected to have a large proportion of the coins minted there, including coins from the more important sites with which it was associated. The huge number of coins from Digeon may reflect a recovery/reporting bias rather than the status of the site, but it does appear to be a site of great importance for the chicken coins. The dominance of the possibly prototypical version (type DT 511) of these coins, suggests that it may have been where they were minted, and possibly the original local source of this image.

A look at the list of types in Table 1 suggests possible local issues at the other sites and highlights the importance of type DT 511, even if it was not the earliest type. Fesques lacks any strong contender, with the possible exception of type DT 512, a smaller variation of type DT 511. That both are often listed generically as 'Bracquemont type' makes it difficult to explore this particular deviation further.

Bois l'Abbé would appear to be the home of type DT 517, with only the Bracquemont types making an appearance alongside it. Le Camp Rouge is likely to have been where type DT 516 was minted, and possibly types DT 514 and DT 515, although they may represent coin types from other religious sites not included here. The coin catalogues of Vendeuil-Caply contained only type DT 509, so of these sites, it is the only likely mint. It appears that there may be a difference based on the river valleys, with Digeon, Fesques, and Bois l'Abbe all being along the Bresle River, and le Camp Rouge and Vendeuil-Caply being along the Somme's tributaries. This explains where the coins were found and their potential minting sites, but the question of when they were minted remains. Unfortunately, the Western zone coinage is difficult to date (Haselgrove 1999: 160). They appear to fall into Haselgrove's Stage 3 (125–60 BC) or Stage 4 (60–20 BC), with Stage 4 being the most likely. Delestrée has dated them to after the Gallic War (Delestrée 1980: 47), with the provenanced coins from Fesques coming from buildings dating to the second half of the first century BC (Delestrée 1997: 285), but he has at least once suggested they may have been in circulation before the Roman conflict was resolved (Delestrée and Delplace 1986: 19). Haselgrove has noted that it is particularly difficult to determine which changes in this region were due to the social changes during the war versus those that came after (Haselgrove 1999: 149). A mid to late first century BC date for these coins appears to be as close as it is possible to estimate for now.

Britain

The situation in Britain is quite different, with only a single chicken-human hybrid coin type, type ABC 737, the Chichester 'cock bronze'. It has been examined in the most detail by G.L. Cottam (1999), who determined that minor variations among coins of type ABC 737 suggested at least three distinct minting events potentially resulting in the creation of hundreds of thousands of coins. They are thought to have been copied from the Gaulish coins, possibly more than once, with early examples being influenced by types DT 511 and DT 509 (Cottam 1999: 10) and some later ones seemingly copying elements of types DT 517 and DT 518 (Cottam 1999: 12).

The images on the coin are more stylised and abstract than many of the Gaulish examples (Fig. 6.3), with a human head wearing some kind of helmet or headdress on the obverse and a chicken with a human face on its stomach

Figure 6.3: Chichester 'cock bronze', type ABC 737. SUSS-969FEE (Courtesy of the Portable Antiquities Scheme [CC-BY]).

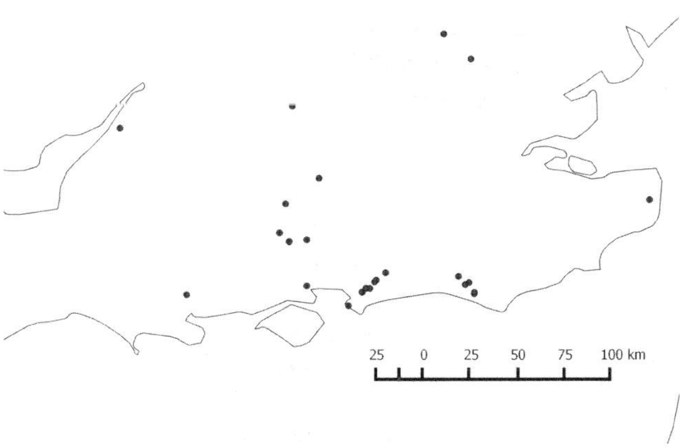

Figure 6.4: Find spots of British cock bronzes.

on the reverse. Here the face appears to be bearded, with the line of feathers merging into a beard towards the front of the bird.

The exact ancestry of the British coin is difficult to determine, but it is clearly related to the Gaulish examples and can be ultimately traced back to the theoretical prototype DT 511. Without the intervention of the British Channel, it would most likely have been classified as another, more stylised Bracquemont derivative.

The distribution pattern of the Chichester cock bronzes is very different from the Gaulish coins, however. It is made up of approximately 65 individual coins found across south-east Britain, albeit with a heavier concentration around Chichester, rather than a few sites with large deposits (Fig. 6.4). None of the known examples came from a secure context, and so it is difficult to discuss their locational context as anything but points on a map.

Despite the presence of a number of religious sites near Chichester, including Hayling Island (Briggs *et al.* 1993) and Westhamptnett (Fitzpatrick 1997), both in the area of highest concentration of these finds, none of the coins have been unambiguously recovered from within their confines, and certainly not in high numbers. While the primary structures on these sites tend to be poor in finds, they have produced some artefacts in the surrounding features (Hamilton 2007: 94). Although the images on the coins are similar, it appears that they were not used and deposited in the same way as they were in Belgic Gaul.

As with the Gaulish coins, it is difficult to determine an exact date for the British examples. If they are derived from Gaulish coins, as seems likely, then they will naturally post-date them, but this is of little help due to the limited chronology available. A date of the late first century BC seems most likely, but Haselgrove (1999: 165) has noted that with the early use of struck bronze in that part of Gaul it may be necessary to consider an earlier date for these coins as well.

The lack of coins at Hayling Island could help in this respect. The coin evidence from the temple suggests it was initially in use around 30–25 BC, followed by a gap until the appearance of coins from just before the Claudian invasion (Creighton 2000: 195). It seems reasonable to suggest that the Chichester coins went out of use either before the temple was established or that they were minted and circulated between these periods of use.

Discussion

Having addressed the background of coins as objects, we can now discuss the iconography of the hybrid chicken and what it means. While there may be more to be learned from a purely numismatic perspective, such an approach is beyond the scope of this study. The question being asked here is, why a chicken, and why add a human face to it? While recent studies have shown that interest in chickens in Iron Age Europe was greater than previously thought (Maltby *et al.* 2018), Late Iron Age faunal assemblages from this particular region of England usually have, at best, only a small percentage of chicken bones (Hambleton 2008: 27), and so can offer little in the way of answers. It is important to note that these coins represent the earliest depictions of chickens created in northern Gaul and Britain. While the foreign coins discussed above may have been known to the people in the areas where these coins were minted, they were all products of another culture. If they influenced the art of native craftspeople, it would have built upon pre-existing notions of what a chicken was and not simply replaced it with that of the original creators.

These images were created during a time of great change, with a new and relatively sudden pressure from a powerful, expanding empire leading to war and eventual conquest, but there is also an introduction of new goods and ideas, which, it must be said, may not all have been viewed as 'Roman', but merely exotic (Haselgrove 2007: 512). Without accurate dating, it is difficult to determine exactly where these coins fit into this picture. If they were minted prior to Caesar's victory over the Belgic tribes, their meaning might be quite different than if this happened afterwards, or even during the later uprisings. And what of the British examples, which pre-date the arrival of Roman bureaucracy? What effect did this difference in Roman relations have on how these images were viewed?

Philip MacDonald has argued that 'exploring the potential artistic nexus provides a useful way of thinking about the possible roles of art within the social relations of Iron Age societies' (MacDonald 2007: 494). Here, consideration of different agents and forms of agency and how they inter-relate (the agencies of animals, coins, images, humans, and the location and social context of object manufacture, circulation, and use) has helped to develop routes for understanding and explaining the chicken-human imagery. Consideration of the relationships between different agents, has enabled exploration of the impact that the use of the chicken-human image on coinage may have had on two different local groups of people as they negotiated their place and identity within the Roman empire.

As Gaul appears to be the birthplace of this image, any investigation should begin there. This region does not appear to have any unusual relationship with chickens. The known animal bone assemblages are unremarkable, containing neither high numbers nor unusual specimens (Méniel 1986; 1997; 2008). They appear on no other iconography from this period, and the representation of chicken-related artefacts in this particular area during the Roman period is unremarkable (Feider 2017). Whatever the source of the hybrid chicken, it does not appear to have left any sign of great affinity in the faunal record or subsequent material culture. However, these images are a fantastic way to examine the influence animals have on the people who keep them that might not be visible in the faunal remains. It is impossible to interact with an animal at any meaningful level and not be changed by that experience (Armstrong Oma 2010; Sykes 2014: 5). Something of the animal seeps into the social consciousness.

Exploring the agency of objects, and indeed the agency of animals, in the past can be difficult, especially if it is not clear how the objects or animals were used or perceived, or how their use and perception may have changed over time or in different circumstances (Harris and Cipolla 2017: 78–80). During the Late Iron Age and Early Roman period, there were changes in how coins were used as these cultures became more integrated with Roman trade networks (Haselgrove and Krmnicek 2012: 241), and those changes may have occurred during the time these coins were in use. In this case, if we consider the coins as 'secondary agents' (Gell 1998: 20) the uncertainty of how the coin-makers intended the coins to be used and their imagery understood is a limiting factor, but it is still possible to tease out some of their meaning or purpose.

If these coins were being minted at religious sites, as discussed above, then an additional question is whether these objects took on a religious significance. As a geographic focus, a sanctuary may have played many roles, minting among them, which may not have been seen as religious in nature. The large deposits of coins on these sites are certainly suggestive of the objects' nature as a votive offering, but to what extent were they seen as religious themselves? It is also possible that these were undistributed coins, deposited either as waste, possibly as secondary deposits, but given such large numbers across a site this seems unlikely. At later Mithraic sites, such as Tienen, Belgium, large deposits of animal bones and associated feasting material have been interpreted as a sort of ritual memory of the act, and with processions of worshippers all making their own deposit (Martens 2004: 44–45). Possibly some coins from each batch created were buried to commemorate the act of creation, collection, or pilgrimage. The lack of this type of deposit on British temple sites suggests that either coins were not minted there or that there was a difference in their use as votive objects at the time they were made. The nature of the coins as an offering could have more than one explanation, as well. While they may have been of a propitiatory nature, sacrificing an object with a value attached to it in return for some blessing, even this could have variations. Pilgrims to one of these sites may have obtained a coin to use as an offering for a safe journey, or the coins may have served as a sort of token in lieu of another, more traditional offering. On a less individual scale, if the coins were collected from this site for use or redistribution elsewhere, perhaps one or two were left behind from each batch as a form of offering or to create a symbolic link back to an important site.

Regardless of why coins were deposited on these sites, the presence of many different types of coins suggests that the images they contained were of less importance than the objects as a whole. If so, they were not deposited because they were chickens, but because they were coins, and the search for insight into the chicken imagery will have to move elsewhere.

The coin assemblages from these sites and across the region suggest a relatively insular community, with few of these types travelling very far and few coins from other groups making their way in (Delestrée 1997: 285; Haselgrove 1999: 160–161). Whether this was because these people turned inwards during or after the events relating to the coming of Julius Caesar, or because they had an underdeveloped trading network making little use of coins between territories is uncertain. It does bring to mind Caesar's statement that some groups in this region refused to trade (Caes. *BGall.* 2.15), but those groups, namely the Nervii, were found further north than this region.

With the coins as a whole having a strong local focus, it must be asked whether their iconography shares a similar introspection, with images selected because of some strong local cultural connection. It is time to take a closer look at the images themselves and see if they can reveal their meaning.

The use of the chicken, regardless of its hybridisation, is immediately striking, as it is not an animal commonly depicted on coins. While the inspiration may have come from Mediterranean coins, there must have been some attribute associated with the bird to make it worth selecting for duplication. Humans and animals cannot coexist without both influencing the other (Armstrong Oma 2010), and the people who created these images would have made space in their cultural lexicon for chickens and subsequently expressed it, in some fashion, through depictions such as these. The difficulty is in interpreting them in their context.

The chicken, which is most commonly assumed to be a male because of its physical features, is reared back with its wings spread. While often unclear, on some coins it appears that its beak could be open, although the wattles and lower beak can be hard to differentiate (*e.g.* types DT 516, Fig. 6.1, and DT 517). Could it be an image of a cockerel stretching its wings and crowing? Although the designs on the coins reflect a conscious decision on the part of the coin-maker, from a posthuman perspective the bird has agency to influence the choice of image by the human artist; the final image communicates the artists' perception of chickens, as influenced by their experience of the bird. The cock's crow would certainly have been a strong mental association amongst people familiar with the bird. The depiction of wings on a chicken is unusual, therefore, is the presence of wings important, with them spread to ensure their visibility?

If the bird is crowing, it could indicate an association with dawn, the sun, or light in general. As some of the earliest literary records of chickens relate to crowing (Arnott 2007: 10) and solar imagery is fairly common on coins from this period (Creighton 2000: 42), an early depiction doing the same would not be unexpected. Suns or starburst symbols are quite common on coins of this era, and the addition of another solar symbol might not be implausible. Whether a solar connection is intended or not, a closer look at some of the coin types adds weight to the idea of sound being an important component of this image. Some of the coins have unusual curvilinear shapes in front of the chicken. This shape appears on type DT 511 (Fig 6.1), but is often at or just off the edge of the coin. It is more pronounced on types DT 510, DT 516 (Fig. 6.1), and DT 517.

On the obverse side of these coins, the human head also has an unusual set of curves in front of it, appearing to emerge from the person's mouth. On type DT 516 this shape is less abstract and takes the form of a lyre. Could the shape be a depiction of speech or song? If so, are the lines on the other coin types a more abstract representation, perhaps the breath that carries the sound or the sound itself? Similar symbols in front of a cockerel are suggestive of a shared importance of sound. Of course, these birds do not only crow at first light, and the sound may not suggest the arrival of dawn, but another event that makes them vocal; being victorious.

Images of cockerels are often associated with combativeness and victory, particularly in older works (for example, Bruneau 1965). The stance of the figure in these images is not particularly evocative of a bird in combat, however, although type DT 510, where the chicken appears to be leaping with its feet extended in front of it, is an exception. Even if the image is not one of combat, it may still be meant to invoke images of it. Although organised cockfighting is almost impossible to detect archaeologically, people would still have been aware of the cockerel's natural behaviour and could have incorporated that into their cultural concept of what a chicken is. It could be the cockerel is not crowing for the dawn, but for combat. Against the background of the Gallic War this association becomes quite interesting, but its exact interpretation could vary depending on when exactly these coins were in use. The use of the cockerel as a martial symbol during a conflict needs little explanation, but how could it still be used in defeat?

Up to this point, the use of tribal names has been largely avoided because of the issues surrounding their use (Haselgrove 1999: 119; Isayev 2010: 224). However, it could now be informative to bring in one particular group to explore this association further. This region includes the land of the Bellovaci tribe, who fought against Caesar and later rebelled against Roman rule. They are often associated with these coins and probably produced the original, type DT 511.

The lack of precise dating or a deep understanding of the history of this region on such a small timescale limits interpretation, but enough of a general history is known to examine one possibility. The insular nature of the assemblages containing these coins could indicate a society under pressure from external forces. During the initial war with Caesar or during an anti-Roman uprising this makes sense, and the selection of an animal associated with combat is also appropriate. However, if the coins were minted after the Gallic War, as seems likely, then the image offers an intriguing new meaning.

Miranda Aldhouse-Green (2004: 15) has suggested that animal behaviour may be one route to understanding the human-animal hybrid symbolism. In some modern cockfighting cultures, such as that of the Canary Islands, the way a bird loses is as important as if it wins (Ontillera 2016). A cockerel that loses well is more deserving of respect than one that 'turns chicken'. In the case of the Gallo-Roman chicken-man hybrids this 'plucky chicken' behaviour in defeat is a rather more subtle and subversive message than the overtly aggressive fighting cock. If the Bellovaci, or whatever group was responsible for minting these coins, shared that belief, then the image may be a proud symbol of a noble defeat. They may have been conquered by the Romans, but they went down fighting and could still raise their heads high. Such a sentiment could have formed a central conceit of this group's post-conquest identity and helped fuel later revolts.

Animal-human hybrid imagery occurs in other examples of Gallo-Roman art. Aldhouse-Green (2004: 15, 79) has discussed two antlered human female bronze figurines from Roman Gaul, considering both the transgression of species and (especially) gender boundaries. As with the interpretation of the merged chicken-human depicted on the coins, she highlights the importance of seeking meaning within the image form itself, but also stresses the need to consider meaning in relation to both the producers and consumers of such images. This aspect of the coinage can be appreciated through Gell's (1998: 6) discussion of the agency of objects whereby art (or images) can be seen as a 'system of action, intended to change the world rather than encode symbolic propositions about it'. As such, we should perhaps be less concerned with what the chicken images *mean* or *symbolise* and more concerned with their secondary agency and what these coins were intended to *do*. In the context of the Bellovaci, what reactions, or more importantly, what actions, might these coins have helped provoke? Did they instil a sense of pride and fortify the defeated into further acts of defiance and revolution? What of the effect on other groups coming into contact with these coins? Did the images on the coins communicate insult or challenge to this group? Of course, it is impossible to know for sure if this is what happened, but it is an intriguing possibility.

While this may explain why a chicken was used, it does not address why the human face appears on so many of these coins. It has been suggested that hybrid images themselves hint at instability and violence (Aldhouse-Green 2004: 149), but the image must have some deeper meaning. Such hybrids can be gods, spirits, or magicians (Aldhouse-Green 2004: 150; Kristoffersen 2010: 264–265), which may be the case here. While the image may not necessarily be a true hybrid creature, perhaps representing a person wearing a headdress of some sort, the ultimate result is a human and chicken being linked together on a symbolic level. Beyond even a normal depiction of an animal, this blurring of the boundaries between human and animal demonstrates a deeper cultural understanding between chickens and humans.

John Creighton (2000: 42–47) has suggested that some of the more abstract and unusual images and shapes on Iron Age coins were meant to capture the visual aspects of a trance state. While he only mentioned these coins in passing, he did discuss coins from the same region that feature a human-headed horse as possibly trying to capture the same imagery, which Aldhouse-Green has discussed elsewhere as a response to the Gallic War (Aldhouse-Green 2004: 163). This raises the possibility that the chicken-man may be linked to some form of shamanistic practice, perhaps reinforcing a cultural connection to some aspect of the bird. Some people have reported synaesthesia, or seeing sounds, while under the effect of psychotropic drugs (Abel 1985: 111), which adds weight to the idea of sounds being depicted.

Even if it did have psychotropic influences, such a hallucinogenic component is not necessary, and the image could also have had a more mundane source. Perhaps it represents an individual with some intimate connection with chickens. Maybe it references a similarity of name, or even a nickname, and naming can be a complex issue, conveying behaviours, histories, and stories, sometimes even in riddle form (Ingold 2011: 165–176). If so, then the meaning is lost to time. It may also represent a previously aniconic deity, taking on a more visible form in this new medium, who might later evolve into a local version of a god like Mercury. Whatever the case, too much of the cosmological context of the image is lost to be sure. If the curvilinear lines are meant to evoke sounds, then perhaps it is a reference to a famous oration or song. One can imagine a leader during this period speaking of a new dawn for his or her people, with images being created to evoke the same response.

In Britain, the image on the coin is too similar to have developed independently. This region is known to have had close contacts with the Belgic people, with even earlier gold coins making their way back and forth between them (Haselgrove 1999: 119; de Jersey 2006: 126–127). The image was adopted by people living in and around Chichester and the coins spread across much of south-east England, but with none of the large temple deposits seen in Gaul. This wider distribution and lack of highly concentrated deposits at religious sites show the coins' agency was not the same as it was across the Channel and suggests a difference in culture, and possibly in meaning. It also demonstrates that despite their similar appearance, the agency of the British coins and the impact of their imagery on people interacting with them in this context is independent from the original intent of their Belgic counterparts.

Without the pressure of the Romans, perhaps the British tribes were less insular, with base metal coinage taking a greater role in long distance trade. If coins were being minted at other, non-religious, sites then they may have been less convenient to use as votive offerings. It is intriguing that none of these coins have yet been found at the Hayling Island temple, which is otherwise quite similar to the Belgic examples (Briggs *et al.* 1993: 41).

The image on the Chichester coin is more simplified than many of the Gaulish types, but it is still recognisably the same image. This could indicate a shared deity, mythical figure, or culture hero; perhaps even a ruler associated with the chicken. However, if it was tied into a post-Caesar identity, then surely some of that would be lost amongst people who had had only minimal contact with these southern people. It is possible that there was a fundamentally different dialogue between humans and chickens in Britain that changed the meaning altogether.

The role of an object can change over time, especially as it moves between different cultures (Harris and Cipolla 2017: 80–84). Just as the chicken itself took on a new role when it was introduced to these regions, so did the hybrid chicken that appeared on these coins. As mentioned above, the difference in deposition practices suggests coins themselves may have behaved differently.

While any number of Belgic elites may have crossed to Britain during this period, bringing their iconography with them, one figure in particular presents an intriguing possibility. Commius is famously linked with both of these regions on the assumption that the 'Commios' appearing in inscriptions on British coins is either the same person or a relative. His personal history fits the ideas behind the source of the image quite well. He was familiar with the Roman world and later allied with the Bellovaci to fight against the Romans. Then, possibly to put a still useful but dangerous figure out of the way, he may have been set up as a client-king in the region of southern Britain where these coins were made (Creighton 2000: 60–64). If the Hayling Island temple does, in fact, represent a Commian dynastic cult, built either late in, or soon after, his reign (Creighton 2000: 192), then could the Chichester coins be an issue from earlier in his career, perhaps soon after his arrival from Gaul and minted in large numbers as a form of propaganda?

Regardless of how it arrived, it is not clear how much the meaning behind the Gaulish image was carried over. This region of England appears to have casually adopted objects and traditions from across northern Gaul (Hamilton 2007: 98). While the meaning may have remained intact, it could also have been adopted as a sign of kinship with the groups that invested more of their own culture into it. Whatever the case, it would surely have carried a positive association in order for it to be adopted.

Conclusion

With the arrival of Julius Caesar and the first steps in becoming a part of an increasingly multicultural Roman world, this was a time of great social and political change, with war, defeat, revolt, and eventual acceptance. Without being able to pinpoint exactly when the coins were created in this process, it is difficult to extract the history of the iconography. However, although they may have been influenced by coins from the far-flung south, these images were forged out of a sense of local identity, possibly after the initial defeat of these groups by Caesar's legions. It is the connection between these people and the chicken, which otherwise appears to have held little importance on the sites where these coins were found and produced, that lies behind this image, but without further evidence, it is difficult to say what meaning the hybrid chicken had. It could intentionally or inadvertently have encouraged cohesion within a community and revolt against those outside the community. It could have been an image of nobility in defeat, a representation of a god from a dream state, a reference to a local hero, or intended to recall a speech or song. This latter option is particularly intriguing and could tie into any of the others, and these coins may represent an early depiction of sound in a visual medium. Whatever the reason, 'chicken' would have come with a package of images, meanings, myths, memories, and sounds. By creating this image, these people forged a connection between this concept of a chicken and 'us', creating a new symbol which would then begin accreting meanings as its own entity.

The relationship between the coins of Belgic Gaul and Britain is also obscured, but they share an obvious ancestry. Lacking the pressures of northern Gaul, the image may have taken on another meaning in Britain, and there are certainly differences in where they have been recovered. How much these distributions reflect underlying cultural variation or merely differences in metal detecting legality and reporting and excavation is unclear, but the lack of large temple deposits in Britain seems to be genuine.

Until recently, the chicken was often the forgotten domesticate, although over the last few years research has shown their importance as both a source of food and as a symbol (Sykes 2012; Gordon *et al.* 2015; Fothergill 2016; Colonese *et al.* 2017; Feider 2017; Bennett *et al.* 2018; Maltby *et al.* 2018). They scratch away in the dust while the larger mammals dominate archaeology's bone assemblages and thoughts. They occupy a strange space in the world of humans, solely occupying the domestic sphere while cows, sheep, pigs, and horses venture out into the wilder stretches of human settlement. This gives them a strong connection to their human keepers, one that will have inserted the species into the cultural cosmology of any people who keep them. By close study of artefacts like these, it is possible to get a glimpse into that abstract world of meaning.

Something drove the people of Belgic Gaul and Britain to celebrate the chicken in the form of the hybrid chicken-man on these coins. It is poetic that after over two millennia, the Gallic Rooster still appears on coins in this region.

Department of Archaeology and Anthropology,
Bournemouth University

Bibliography

Ancient Sources

Caesar (Translated by C. Hammond). 1996. *Seven Commentaries on the Gallic War, with an Eighth Commentary by Aulus Hirtius*. Oxford: Oxford University Press.

Modern Sources

Abel, E.L. 1985. Hallucinogens. In E.L. Abel (ed.) *Psychoactive Drugs and Sex*. New York: Springer.

Aldhouse-Green, M.J. 2004. *An Archaeology of Images: Iconography and Cosmology in Iron Age and Roman Europe*. London: Routledge.

Armstrong Oma, K. 2010. Between trust and domination: social contracts between humans and animals. *World Archaeology* 42: 175–187.

Arnott, W.G. 2007. *Birds in the Ancient World from A to Z*. London: Routledge.

Bennett, C., Thomas, R., Zalasiewicz, J., Edgeworth, M., Williams, M., Miller, H., Coles, B., Foster, A., Burton, E.J. and Marume, U. 2018. The broiler chicken as a signal of a human reconfigured biosphere. *Royal Society Open Science* 5 (12): 1–11.

Braidotti, R. 2019. A Theoretical Framework for the Critical Posthumanities. *Theory, Culture & Society (Special Issue: Transversal Posthumanities)* 36 (6): 31–61.

Briggs, D., Haselgrove, C. and King, A.C. 1993. Iron Age and Roman coins from Hayling Island temple. *British Numismatic Journal* 62: 1–62.

Bruneau, P. 1965. Illustrations antiques du coq et de l'ane de Lucien. *Bulletin de Correspondance Hellénique* 89 (2): 349–357.

Collis, J. 2007. The polities of Gaul, Britain, and Ireland in the Late Iron Age. In C. Haselgrove and T. Moore (eds) *The Later Iron Age in Britain and Beyond*. Oxford: Oxbow Books: 523–528.

Colonese A.C., Lucquin, A., Guedes, E.P., Thomas, R., Best, J., Fothergill, B.T., Sykes, N., Foster, A., Miller, H., Poole, K., Maltby, M., Von Tesch, M. and Craig, O. 2017. The identification of poultry processing in archaeological ceramic vessels using in-situ isotope references for organic residue analysis. *Journal of Archaeological Science* 78: 179–192.

Cottam, G.L. 1999. The 'cock bronzes' and other related Iron Age bronze coins found predominantly in West Sussex and Hampshire. *British Numismatic Journal* 69: 1–18.

Creighton, J. 2000. *Coins and Power in Late Iron Age Britain*. Cambridge: Cambridge University Press.

de Jersey, P. 2006. Belgic coins in Britain. In P. de Jersey (ed.) *Celtic Coinage: new discoveries, new discussion*. Oxford: British Archaeological Reports: 117–137.

Delestrée, L.-P. 1980. Les monnaies «au coq» frappées en Gaule belgique. *Revue Numismatique* 22: 33–62.

Delestrée, L.-P. 1985. Les monnaies gauloises du temple des «châtelets» à Vendeuil-Caply (Oise). *Revue Archéologique de Picardie* 1/2: 51–64.

Delestrée, L.-P. 1987. Les monnaies gauloises du Camp Rouge (Hallencourt-Fontaine-sur-Somme, département de la Somme). *Revue Archéologique de Picardie* 3/4: 51–60.

Delestrée, L.-P. 1994. La numismatique gauloise en Gaule Belgique. Problématique et axes de recherche. *Revue Archéologique de Picardie* 3/4: 19–30.

Delestrée, L.-P. 1997. Les monnaies gauloises en contexte du sanctuaire de Fesques. In E. Mantel (ed.) *Le sanctuaire de Fesques «Le Mont du Val aux Moines» (Seine Maritime)*. Berck-Sur-Mer: CRADC: 283–294.

Delestrée, L.-P. 2008. Inventaire raisonné des monnaies gauloises. In M. Mangard (ed.) *Le Sanctuaire Gallo-Romain du Bois l'Abbé à Eu (Seine-Maritime)*. Lille: Revue du Nord: 209–233.

Delestrée, L.-P. and Delplace, C. 1986. Les monnaies gauloises de Digeon (Somme). Les ramassages de surface: première approche statistique. *Revue Archéologique de Picardie* 1/2: 13–22.

Delestrée, L.-P. and Tache, M. 2002. *Nouvel Atlas des Monnaies Gauloises, I: De la Seine au Rhin*. Saint-Germain-en-Laye: Éditions Commios.

Delplace, C., Jobic, F., Méniel, P. and Rapin, A. 1986. Le sanctuaire de Digeon, commune de Morvillers- Saint-Saturnin (Somme): relation préliminaire aux fouilles de 1983 à 1985. *Revue Archéologique de Picardie* 3/4: 83–98.

Feider, M.P. 2017. *Chickens in the Archaeological Material Culture of Roman Britain, France, and Belgium*. PhD Thesis. Bournemouth University.

Ferrando, F. 2013. Posthumanism, transhumanism, antihumanism, metahumanism and new materialisms: differences and relations. *Existenz* 8 (2): 26–32.

Fitzpatrick, A.P. 1997. *Archaeological Excavations on the Route of the A27 Westhampnett Bypass, West Sussex, 1992, Volume 2: The Late Iron Age, Romano-British, and Anglo-Saxon Cemeteries*. Salisbury: Trust for Wessex Archaeology Report 12.

Fothergill, B.T. 2016. Urban animals: human-poultry relationships in Later Post-Medieval Belfast. *International Journal of Historical Archaeology*: 1–27.

Gell, A. 1998. *Art and Agency: An Anthropological Theory*. Oxford: Clarendon Press.

Gordon, R., Thomas, R. and Foster, A. 2015. The health impact of selective breeding in poultry: a probable case of 'creeper' chicken (*Gallus gallus*) from 16th-century Chester, England. *International Journal of Paleopathology* 9: 1–7.

Hambleton, E. 2008. *Review of Middle Bronze Age – Late Iron Age Faunal Assemblages from Southern Britain*. Portsmouth: English Heritage.

Hamilton, S. 2007. Cultural choices in the 'British Eastern Channel Area' in the Late Pre-Roman Iron Age. In C. Haselgrove and T. Moore (eds) *The Later Iron Age in Britain and Beyond*. Oxford: Oxbow Books: 81–106.

Harris, O.J.T. and Cipolla, C. 2017. *Archaeological Theory in the New Millennium: Introducing Current Perspectives*. Abingdon/New York: Routledge.

Haselgrove, C. 1999. The development of Iron Age coinage in Belgic Gaul. *The Numismatic Chronicle* 159: 111–168.

Haselgrove, C. 2007. The age of enclosure: Later Iron Age settlement and society in northern France. In C. Haselgrove and T. Moore (eds) *The Later Iron Age in Britain and Beyond*. Oxford: Oxbow Books: 492–522.

Haselgrove, C. and Krmnicek, S. 2012. The archaeology of money. *Annual Review of Anthropology* 41: 235–250.

Ingold, T. 2011. *Being Alive: Essays on Movement, Knowledge and Description*. Routledge: Abingdon/New York.

Isayev, E. 2010. Unintentionally being Lucanian. In S. Hales and T. Hodos (eds) *Material Culture and Social Identities in the Ancient World*. Cambridge: Cambridge University Press: 201–226.

Kristoffersen, S. 2010. Half beast-half man: hybrid figures in animal art. *World Archaeology* 42 (2): 261–272.

MacDonald, P. 2007. Perspectives on insular La Tène art. In C. Haselgrove and T. Moore (eds) *The Later Iron Age in Britain and Beyond*. Oxford: Oxbow Books: 329–338.

Maltby, M., Allen, M., Best, J., Fothergill, T. and Demarchi, B. 2018. Counting Roman chickens: multidisciplinary approaches to human-chicken interactions in Roman Britain. *Journal of Archaeological Science* 19: 1003–1015.

Mantel, E. 1997. *Le Sanctuaire de Fesques «Le Mont du Val aux Moines» (Seine Maritime)*. Berck-Sur-Mer: CRADC.

Martens, M. 2004. The Mithraeum in Tienen (Belgium): the small finds and what they can tell us. In M. Martens and G. De Boe (eds) *Roman Mithraism: The Evidence of the Small Finds*. Brussels: Instituut voor het Archeologisch Patrimonium: 25–56.

Méniel, P. 1986. Les restes animaux du sanctuaire de Digeon. *Revue Archéologique de Picardie* 3–4: 109–113.

Méniel, P. 1997. La faune du sanctuaire de Fesques «le mont du Val-Aux-Moines». In E. Mantel (ed.) *Le Sanctuaire de Fesques «Le Mont du Val aux Moines» (Seine Maritime)*. Berck-Sur-Mer: CRADC: 283–294.

Méniel, P. 2008. Les restes animaux du sanctuaire du Bois l'Abbé. In M. Mangard (ed.) *Le Sanctuaire Gallo-Romain du Bois l'Abbé à Eu (Seine-Maritime)*. Lille: Revue du Nord: 291–294.

Morris, J. and Maltby, M. 2010. *Integrating Social and Environmental Archaeologies: Reconsidering Deposition*. Oxford: Archaeopress.

Ontillera, R. 2016. Chicken cultures and male identities in the Canary Islands. Unpublished conference paper. University of Roehampton Research Seminars. Roehampton University: Centre for Research in Evolutionary, Social and Inter-Disciplinary Anthropology (CRESIDA).

Overton, N. and Hamilakis, Y. 2013. A manifesto for a social zooarchaeology: swans and other beings in the Mesolithic. *Archaeological Dialogues* 20 (2): 111–136.

Pitt, J., Gillingham, P., Maltby, M., Stafford, R. and Stewart, J. 2019. Changing cultures, changing environments: a novel means of investigating the effects of introducing non-native species into past ecosystems. *Journal of Archaeological Science: Reports* 23: 1066–1075.

Russell, N. 2014. Social zooarchaeology. In C. Smith (ed.) *Encyclopedia of Global Archaeology*. New York: Springer: 6761–6765.

Sykes, N. 2012. A social perspective on the introduction of exotic animals: the case of the chicken. *World Archaeology* 44 (1): 158–169.

Sykes, N. 2014. *Beastly Questions: Animal Answers to Archaeological Issues*. London: Bloomsbury.

7

Weeds in the Field, Weeds in the City: Posthuman Approaches to Plants in the Roman World

Lisa Lodwick

Introduction

In seeking to de-centre humans from the study of the Roman world, a productive life form to consider would be weeds – plants which succeed in living in a range of ecological conditions against the desires of humans. Weeds sit within the broader category of plants, a life form rarely given a primary analytical position in current approaches to the Roman world. This chapter takes inspiration from more-than-human geographies to explore the effect of recently introduced weeds (alien species) on daily experience within the arable fields and the new urban foundations of Roman Britain, where the unintended biological by-products of Roman imperialism entangled with daily activities.

Whilst a plant-centred study, taking into account plant agency, could be seen as a dehumanising approach to the Roman past, alien weeds are taken as the primary focus here in order to consider the social effects of changing human-weed relationships in a period of climatic amelioration and rapid urbanisation. The spread of invasive species is a major economic, ecological, and social challenge in the contemporary world (Head 2017). Research within human geography has shown that taking a relational approach to human-plant interaction also informs upon the impacts of invasive plants on contemporary human social experience (Head *et al.* 2015). The Roman empire provides a comparative picture of an increasingly connected society in a period of climatic warming. The effects of late Republic and early Imperial period expansion on global environmental systems is clear, from lead pollution records (McConnell *et al.* 2018) to impacts upon biodiversity (Hughes 2003). Recent scholarship has also drawn attention to the agency of non-human forces in the Roman world (rats, volcanoes, microbes), and their impacts upon the major socio-economic changes during the Late Roman empire (Harper 2017). The homogenous and connected Roman cereal-based agricultural system of the north-western provinces (Lodwick 2017a; Lepetz and Zech-Matterne 2018) enabled a number of non-native weeds to spread into this region, an unintended side-effect of Roman expansion. Whilst the impact of new weeds is less marked than other organisms on the Roman empire, their spread did impact upon the daily lives of rural workers and urban dwellers.

This chapter explores the impacts of the introduction of new weeds by starting from the plant, by considering the effects of plant characteristics upon humans within a relational plant agency framework. The impacts of relational archaeology have been felt within Roman archaeology over the last decade, especially through the material-culture turn (Van Oyen and Pitts 2017). More recently, the animal turn has also been felt in Roman archaeology, through studies of cattle, chickens, and deer in the north-western provinces (Sykes 2012; Chadwick 2016; *cf.* Feider *et al.* in this volume). A general move towards studying plant life can also be detected in Roman archaeology. Plants, considered here as all members of the plant kingdom, permeated all areas of the Roman world with studies ranging from religion to food and agriculture (Van der Veen 2018), although plants tend to be studied from an anthropocentric perspective, through their exploitation as economic resources such as fuel and crops (Hughes 2011; Harris 2017; Veal 2017). Work has also begun to explore the affective agency of plants – considering the impact of plant agency on the temporality of place within Roman cemeteries (Graham 2018), the sensory experience of Roman gardens (Baker 2018), and the planty agency of introduced ornamental species (Lodwick 2017b). These studies call attention to the colour, growth habit, and smell of plants, and this line of research will be explored further here. Occasionally, as at Pompeii, a wide range of evidence types from wall paintings and mosaics, to graffiti, inscriptions, and literary evidence, to archaeobotanical evidence provide information on floral life (Jashemski *et al.* 2002; Murphy *et al.* 2013). However, in most regions of the Roman world the reconstruction of human-plant relationships is much more heavily reliant on archaeobotanical evidence – that is, seeds, grains, nuts, and vegetative plant parts preserved as charred, mineralised, and waterlogged plant remains (Van der Veen 2008), and it is this form of evidence that is utilised here.

This chapter seeks to build upon previous plant agency inspired studies (Lodwick 2017b; 2019, Graham 2018) to consider plant species in their own rights in terms of their biological and ecological attributes, such as growth habit, growth cycle, toxicity, and seed characteristics, rather than as a homogenous category of 'plants' to extend such studies to a group of plants that are often ignored – weeds. Weeds are at the edge of human society, which are distributed and cultivated unintentionally by humans, thus providing an interesting case study for plant agency.

The daily lives of agricultural labourers in Roman Britain are often overlooked (Taylor 2013), despite them representing a substantial proportion of the population. However, their daily lives are poorly represented in the material culture and architectural record of farmsteads (see, *e.g.* Smith *et al.* 2016). Much of their daily lives was spent tending to crop plants, and without considering these plants as beings, such activities are hard to explore (Lodwick 2019). Through applying a planty agency approach to the study of weed seeds, the first case study seeks to illuminate aspects of the daily lives of farmers in Roman Britain. The second case study turns to weeds in the city, where daily encounters with plants are rarely visible. Recent approaches have explored the multi-sensory character of urban experience, mainly focusing on built environments (Betts 2017). Building upon previous usages of environmental evidence (Derrick 2017), this chapter will explore the effects of weeds on daily life within Roman cities.

The dispersal of weeds alongside domesticated crops is widely recognised (Boivin *et al.* 2016: 6390) and the spread of further weed species in the Roman period has been recently acknowledged (Van der Veen 2018: 61), but the posthuman inspired approach taken here seeks to study individual weed species in detail to explore their effect upon human experience. A starting point is taken from several weed species which were success stories of the Roman world – *Agrostemma githago* (corncockle) and *Atropa belladonna* (deadly nightshade) (Fig. 7.1) – in the province of Roman Britain where a wealth of archaeobotanical data is available.

Figure 7.1: Agrostemma githago *(Photo by Stefan Lefnaer [CC BY-SA 3.0]) and* Atropa belladonna *(Photo by H. Zell [CC BY-SA 3.0]).*

Posthuman Inspired Approaches to Plants

Posthumanist thought is a broad group of theoretical approaches which seek to decentre human life and deny human exceptionalism. A working definition presented by Christina Fredengren is 'the questioning of anthropocentrism and the ontological divide between humans and nonhuman others with a focus on the interrelation between different species and the surroundings, arguing for a nature: culture continuum' (Fredengren 2013: 55). The impact of posthumanist and new materialist thought on the study of animals in the past has been sizable over the last decade, including studies of Mesolithic deer and swans, Bronze Age horses and Roman cattle (Boyd 2017). The success of animal studies across the social sciences has, however, led to the problem that human-animal studies have left out plants and microorganisms (Smart 2014). The prioritisation of animal over other non-human life in the Roman period is well-demonstrated by a recent piece entitled '*Multi-species dynamics and the ecology of urban spaces in Roman antiquity*' which focused on animals as livestock, pack-animals, pets, and commensals (MacKinnon 2018), with no mention of the many other species present in urban spaces. Plants have also received limited attention so far within new materialist or relational archaeology (Harris and Cippolla 2017: 163–165).

Exploring the relational agency of plants has been described as both 'methodologically and conceptually challenging', despite ethnographic evidence showing the perception of plants as agentic (Overton and Taylor 2018: 399). An initial difficulty in advocating for exploring plants through a relational or posthumanist framework is that plants tend to be marginalised in western worldviews. Matthew Hall has traced this tendency through post-enlightenment thought back to Aristotle and Plato, whereby plants were placed in a lower category of being than humans and animals (Hall 2011). Within daily life, the concept of 'plant blindness' encapsulates these philosophical considerations, by describing how many people in the western world have an inability to appreciate the aesthetic and unique biological features of plants (Wandersee and Schussler 2001). Plant movements are often imperceptible to humans, and the duration of plant life can range from a few days or weeks for annual weeds, through to centuries for trees. Despite these tendencies, a range of scientific work has shown the advanced capabilities of plants as sensing, knowledgeable life forms (Head *et al.* 2015). The ability of plants to affect humans has been traced through multi-species ethnography and participant observation in a range of locales, from gardens (Hitchings 2003) to vineyards (Brice 2014).

A second challenge is deciding how to address the study of plants. One option is to consider plants as one other type of 'thing'; as Greg Woolf has recently suggested us to 'include humans and animals and plants within our super-category of Roman period artefacts' (Woolf 2017: 215). Many aspects of objects which would be considered within new materialist approaches (colour, texture, sensory affordances) can be equally considered for plants. For instance, the shrub Box (*Buxus sempervirens*) can be considered in terms of its dark green glossy colour, specific smellscape, and the ways in which these contrast with native flora of Roman Britain (Lodwick 2017b). However, applying relational thought to plants loses the specific and unique properties of plants (Jones and Cloke 2002). Instead, Jones and Cloke call for a consideration of non-human agency 'within its own ecological time-scales as well as in its own places' (2008: 82). Barry Taylor has taken such an approach to Mesolithic Yorkshire, by considering the annual rhythms of plants evidenced in palaeoenvironmental studies around Lake Flixton, and by considering the spatial distribution of different plant communities and the impact of this upon the structuring of human activities (Taylor 2018). Advancement of the study of 'plant materiality' has also pointed to the temporal cycles of agricultural labour, for instance, the effects of the introduction of summer crops to areas around the Mediterranean in the Islamic period (Van der Veen 2014). The change in form of vegetative crops in south-east Asia, such as taro, sago, and banana, was crucial for showing links between the reproduction of social and plant life (Barton and Denham 2018), and the exploration of the ecological temporalities of cultivated plants and wild vegetation in Late Iron Britain has provided insights into the annual nature of labour and the social organisation of the community (Lodwick 2019). Emma-Jayne Graham has considered how the seasonally specific appearance and smells of flowering plants created temporally specific senses of place within cemeteries at Pompeii (Graham 2018). These approaches have all considered the physical characteristics (colour, growth habit) of plants within the temporal context of the plant itself, and in doing so, illuminated the ways in which plants affect humans through routine activities.

A further step in the consideration of plant agency is that of distinctive plant capacities, grounded in biological realities rather than just the effect of plants on humans. Drawing upon a range of studies, Lesley Head *et al.* (2015) have described four distinct capacities within which to frame considerations of plant-life on the basis of biological research; distinctive materialities (photosynthesising, cellulose cell walls, sporic meisosis), moving without humans (seed dispersal, circumnutating, tropic responses, nastic responses), sensing and communication (chemical signalling), and flexible bodies (reconfiguration of cell confederations). They use these headings to explore the invasive plant rubber vine in northern Australia, presenting its biogeographical history, along with details on its reproduction, growth habit, and wider ecological relationships. Ethnographic work with those responsible for controlling the invasive weed builds upon reflections on visibility due to the plants distinctive materialities, its growth cycle, and its relations with cattle, humans, pigs, and wallabies, providing new insights into the effect of vines on biosecurity strategies employed to destroy it (Head *et al.* 2015).

In essence, this approach requires us to take plants seriously by paying attention to specific species-level capacities (Head *et al.* 2015). Such an approach, bridging botanical and ecological detail in a theoretical framework is currently lacking in the study of weeds in the past. The archaeobotanical record may at first appear an intractable source of similar information to explore human-plant relations. Importantly, we do not recover plant bodies, but dead seeds – the propagule of one plant, and the potential beginnings of a new plant. Archaeobotanical identification techniques can usually identify a seed to either a species, genus, or family, and botanical and ecological information on the particular taxa can provide a wealth of information on growth habit, growth cycle, and ecological relationships. What archaeobotanical data lacks in being able to identify the location where the past or future plant grew (seeds can be deposited at long distances from the site of production) it gains from providing temporal and social insights into the relations between weeds and humans.

What is a 'Weed'?

The definitions of a weed range from human-centred classifications of unwanted and unvalued plants, to ecological definitions of plants which grow in areas of ground disturbed by humans (DeWet and Harlan 1975). Richard Mabey provides a more favourable definition to weeds, of 'a plant in the wrong place' (Mabey 2012: 5). However, attitudes towards weeds are culturally specific, with behaviour towards plants varying within one community on the basis of food security (Jones 1988), and more widely on the basis of crop husbandry practices. For instance, ethnographic studies in Greece have shown that similar weed plants were abandoned in northern Greece and collected in southern Greece for food or fodder (Halstead 2014: 237–238).

In the arable field, different plants undertake various strategies to compete with crops (Baker 1974). Amy Bogaard and others characterise weeds into 'opportunists' and 'mimics' (Bogaard *et al.* 2018). Opportunists tend to have seasonal growth habits and seasonality distinctive from the crop, providing a source of food and fodder throughout the crop-growing season. In contrast, the growth habit and physical appearance of 'mimics' are comparable to the crop, against which these weeds compete (Bogaard *et al.* 2018).

Arable weeds are known to have co-evolved with crops. Dorian Fuller and Chris Stevens have recently characterised arable weeds as parasitic domesticoids–parasitic, due to the acquirement of nutrients at the expense of human food production, and domesticoid as the species have undergone some aspects of parallel domestication alongside domesticated crop plants (Fuller and Stevens 2017). It is this status, of directly affecting human action throughout the stages of cereal farming, which makes weeds a fruitful, if overlooked, area of study for a posthuman Roman archaeology.

Beyond the specific context of the arable field, weeds can include plants growing in a range of ruderal and disturbed habitats. Within Britain, many of these plants are often later introductions to the original 'native' flora and can be considered as alien plants, of which archaeophytes were present in a wild state before AD 1500, and neophytes after (Stace and Crawley 2015: 4). Within alien plants, invasive weeds are unwanted plants which are non-native to a region and cause harm to humans (Head 2017).

In contrast to the often negative connotations that go with alien species, archaeophytes often occur on lists of at-risk plants which require protecting, with many previous corn-field weeds in Britain now listed on the Botanical Society for Britain and Ireland's Red List (Stroh *et al.* 2014). Indeed, many previous arable weeds are now valued as 'crowd-pleasing archaeophytes' included in corn-field wildflower seed mixtures (Stace and Crawley 2015: 179).

Currently, the study of weeds in archaeobotany has been limited to two main approaches. First, the analysis of arable weeds in order to reconstruct past farming practice, through a range of autecological (characteristics of individual species) and phytosociological (characteristics of weed communities) approaches (see Van der Veen 2018, for a review). These essentially utilise a western palaeoecological mindset to categorise plant communities into human-orientated groups (weeds of winter-sown crops, weeds of summer-sown crops). In this way, conclusions have been drawn about crop husbandry practices in the Roman world. For instance, arable farming in Roman Britain is considered to have involved the autumn-sowing of wheat and barley in fields of intermediate soil fertility (Lodwick 2017a). Second, weeds are seen as indicators of the provenance of crops, indicating trade in cereals (Lodwick 2018).

Archaeobotanical evidence for the presence of weeds can be complemented with references to weeds in the written Roman sources, providing insight into human-plant relations. The Latin term for weeds, *viriditas*, meaning 'a green thing', provides a relatively neutral categorisation (Edwards 2015). The Roman agronomists provide a more combative approach to weeds. Cato lists several instructions to remove weeds, such as 'Hoe often, and clear off the weeds as soon as they begin to grow' (*Crebro runcato. Simul herbae inceperint nasci, eximito,* Cato, *Agr.* 48.2), and 'Clean them [seed-beds] when the weeds are very young, and as often as is necessary' (*Quam tenerrimis herbis, et quotiens opus erit, purge*, Cato, *Agr.* 151.4). Pliny the Elder suggests several ways for dealing with weeds, including burning and slicing (Plin. *HN* 18, 153–156), whilst weeds were also uprooted by hand, such as in Campania (Spurr 1986: 85–64). The importance of weeding is highlighted by the legal role of the censors in punishing bad cultivation which included weeding in Republican Rome (Jakab 2015: 121). These references indicate an awareness of the importance of weeding amongst estate owners, which extends to the specific characteristics of weeds. Whilst Varro uses the collective term *herba* for weeds (Varro, *Rust.* 1.30), Virgil lists a range of weeds including *Carduus*, *Lappae*, *Triboli*, *Lolium* and *Avena* (Verg. *G.* 1.150–5), and *Galium* is noted for its stickiness (Jashemski *et al.* 2002: 112). Spurr also highlights the secondary uses of weeds, as fencing, animal litter, and fodder (Spurr 1986: 62). Theophrastus had a detailed understanding of plant anatomy and plant reproduction (Hall 2011: 28–35), but had misconceptions, describing how wheat and barley turned into darnel after heavy rain (Theophr. *Hist. pl.* VIII, 183).

Modern perceptions of biodiversity change in the Roman world range from a continuation of major animal and plant species (Woolf 2017: 215), a loss of biodiversity in some regions (Hughes 2003), and the introduction of new species from areas beyond the Roman world (Boivin *et al.* 2016). This increase in new species has been principally studied through the trade in cultivated plant foods and the cultivation of food plants in new regions, such as coriander, grape, fig, and olive (Van der Veen 2018), and is often seen as a positive change and beneficial contribution (Witcher 2013). Alongside these cultivated plant foods, many weeds were introduced to new regions, but less attention has been paid to these within archaeological and historical accounts (Witcher 2013: 15). The pervasive concept of the 'Roman introduction' explains the introduction of new species as a purposeful action. The stories of the introduction of *Urtica romana* or *pilulifera* (Roman nettle) place agency with Roman soldiers introducing the weed, whose stings were used to guard against the cold (Witcher 2013: 19). The key discussions of the environmental impact of the Roman world have given no attention to introduced weeds (Hughes 2003; Sallares 2007; Hughes 2014: 101; Thommen 2012). However, the growing number of archaeobotanical studies, especially within the north-western provinces, have enabled the identification of numerous weed introductions during the Roman period. For instance, in the Upper Rhine and south-west Germany, numerous new weeds have been recorded in archaeobotanical samples, included *Caucalis platycarpos*, *Orlaya grandiflora*, *Vaccaria hispanica*, *Adonis aestivalis*, *Bupleurum rotundifolium*, *Legousia speculum-veneris*, *Nigella arvensis*, *Ranunculus arvensis* and *Myagrum perfoliatum* (Jacomet and Vandorpe 2011; for further examples, see Van der Veen 2018: 61).

Agricultural tools from Roman sites have been associated with weeding activities, such as the *sarcula*, a single-bladed digging hoe considered to have been used for a range of crop management activities including weed suppression, soil aeration, and incorporating manure (Jashemski 2018). Information on human-weed relationships from Roman literary sources also showed an awareness of weeds and weeding activities in the Roman world. I now turn to a weed-centred approach to everyday life, taking into account the specific plant capacities (Head *et al.* 2015) in order to explore the embodied experience of arable farming and urban dwelling in Roman Britain.

Weeds are ubiquitous presences within crop fields and human settlements, and provide an insightful case study in the way that non-cultivated plants exhibit independence – as weeds 'act autonomously in seeding themselves and growing in unexpected places and in an unexpected forms' (Jones and Cloke 2008: 81). Whilst there are a wide range of plants that can be categorised as weeds, alien weeds, and in their starkest forms as invasive species, provide a particularly interesting case study as they are a key challenge in today's changing environment (Head 2017; Shackleton *et al.* 2019). Major examples of damaging invasive plants include cultivated crops (rubber plant) or ornamental species (rhododendrons) which escaped after original introduction to enter unmanaged environments, becoming dominant within ecosystems and suppressing biodiversity (Head *et al.* 2015). In terms of the arable environment, fields are especially vulnerable to alien plants due to the combination of highly fertile and disturbed soils, a homogenous environment, and the globalised trade in agricultural products. In combination with pests and pathogens, weeds cause annual losses of US$248 billion to global agriculture (Fried *et al.* 2017). Over half of the annual £1.67 billion impact of non-native species is due to losses to agricultural production in the UK (Williams *et al.* 2010). Weeds have significant social and environmental impacts, and can be studied within frameworks of plant agency.

The extension of agency to plants, after first objects, and then animals, could however be open to critiques of further removing human agency from the past (Barrett 2016). However, the survival of humanity is reliant upon the integrity of the global environment, in terms of biodiversity, atmosphere, and soils (Ferrando 2016). To take a plant-centred approach is not to deny the central place of humanity within archaeology, but rather to draw attention to the ecological and social implications of changes in biodiversity upon humans in times of increased connectivity and environmental change. Countenancing some space to plants, within a specific historical context of the Roman world, informs upon the social lives of people in Roman Britain within the context of agricultural labourers and urban dwellers.

Weeds in the Field

The range of weed flora in Britain had remained relatively static since a range of taxa were introduced in the Mid Bronze Age – Early Iron Age, but at the end of the first millennium BC, several new weeds began to appear (Stevens and Fuller 2018). The precise chronology for their introduction requires direct dating, but it is clear that very few people had come into contact with *Agrostemma githago* (corncockle) before the last century BC (Lodwick 2018) – it was an alien species in Roman Britain.

Agrostemma githago is an annual weed of cornfields. A member of the Caryophyllaceae family, corncockle was previously a common weed in Britain, before becoming rare from the 1950s due to improvements in seed cleaning (Firbank 1988). Corncockle plants are upright annual plants, growing up to 1.4 m high with several reddish-purple flowers (Firbank 1988: 1232). Corncockle is a type 1 weed – germinating soon after sowing and growing into a large herbaceous plant (Thompson and Grime 1979; Fuller and Stevens 2017). Corncockle seeds measure 3–3.5 cm (Firbank 1988), comparable to the size of cereal grains. For this reason, corncockle seeds remain alongside cereal grains (wheat, barley, rye) until the final stage of crop-processing of hand-sorting (Hillman 1981: 136). Corncockle's success as an arable weed is due to its behaviour as a seed mimic. Seed capsules do not release their seeds until after threshing of cereals (Percival 1900: 600), and each capsule can contain up to 60 seeds (Firbank 1988: 1240). Cereal sieve sizes would have applied the selective pressure whereby larger seeds of corncockle would be retained with the cereal grains and re-sown as seed corn (Hillman 1984). Beyond their size, corncockle seeds also have no chilling requirement before germination, and a short after-ripening period, meaning seeds can germinate at any time of the year (Firbank and Watkinson 1986), but also that corncockle plants are likely to grow when seeds are sown alongside seed corn into a prepared field (Stevens and Fuller 2018: 24). Corncockle also behaves as a crop mimic, whereby plants appear similar to cereal crops, hence evading weeding. Size, colour, and leaf direction of growth are observed as being similar to cereals (Firbank 1988: 1237).

The concept of co-evolution considers that plants (and animals) may self-transform to take advantage of new husbandry conditions, including weeds in arable fields (Rindos 1984: 120–127). Variations in corncockle seeds hint at how it may have co-evolved alongside crops. A seed size increase has been observed from the Neolithic to the Middle Ages (Hellmund 2008) and several varieties of *A. githago* have been recorded – ranging from the large-seeded *A. macrospermum* found growing amongst wheat in southern Europe, to small seeded *A. linicola* growing alongside flax in Russia (Hammer *et al.* 1982). The combination of the characteristics of fast-growing annuals, with the ability to self-fertilise, with non-shattering heads, and a high harvest-index, would indicate that *Agrostemma githago* is itself a product of the domestication syndrome. This concept is usually applied to cereals (Allaby *et al.* 2008) but has also been applied to the weed *Lolium temulentum* (darnel) (Thomas *et al.* 2016) and it would seem appropriate to also apply it to corncockle.

Most accounts of *A. githago* suggest an origin in the eastern Mediterranean, perhaps originating from *A. gracilis* (Firbank 1988: 1243; Hellmund 2008: 126), and more specifically from Greece (Greuter 1995; Coward *et al.* 2008). Corncockle has been recorded in the early Neolithic phases of north-west Greece and Italy (Coward *et al.* 2008) and becomes frequent in the mid and late Neolithic period in central Europe, with many finds recorded in central Europe from the late Bronze Age and Iron Age periods (Hellmund 2008).

In the regions which became the north-western Roman provinces, corncockle appears largely absent. In Late Iron Age northern Gaul and Southern Britain, corncockle was present at a small number of sites, before spreading after the Roman conquest (Derreumaux and Lepetz 2008; Lodwick 2018). In Scotland, corncockle was first recorded in the Roman period at the forts Bearsden, Birrens, and Newstead (Dickson and Dickson 2000: 245). Beyond the Roman frontiers, corncockle was not recorded in Ireland until the early Medieval period (McCormick *et al.* 2011). In Germany, corncockle only spread beyond the Limes after the Roman period (Kreuz 2004) and in Sweden, the first records are Later Iron Age (Grabowski 2011). Hence there is clear evidence for the advancement of this weed with the Roman world (Bakels 2010). Due to improvements in seed cleaning methods corncockle is now regarded as an extinct weed in arable fields, although is still wildly present due to wildflower seed mix and it remains on the waiting list for the Red List (Cheffings and Farrell 2005: 99).

Corncockle is described as a pernicious weed, both suppressing crop yield and being poisonous to humans and animals (Henslow 1901). Corncockle plants, including the seeds, contain a saponin called githagenin, which damages cell walls, and also contain type I ribosome-inactivity protein agrostin, which has cytotoxic effects (Böttger and Melzig 2011). Githagenin causes poisoning, with symptoms such as gastrointestinal problems, salivation, paralysis, and ultimately death (Cooper and Johnson 1984). The quantities of seeds which can cause ill-health vary depending on age and species. 2.5 seeds per 1000 cereal grains by weight is sufficient to kill calves and fowl (Henslow 1901). With regard to humans, the Russian army allowed a maximum proportion of corncockle seeds 0.5% out of the total amount of seed grain at the end of the nineteenth century (Pals and Hakbijl 1992).

The first written evidence for the toxicity of corncockle seeds is that of John Gerard writing in the sixteenth century – 'Cockle is a common and hurtful weede in our corne – what hurt it doth among corn, the spoile unto bread, as well in colour, taste, and unholsomnes, is better known than desired' (Gerard 1597). It is unclear whether the harmful effects of corncockle were recognised in the Roman world. Corncockle has not been securely identified in any written sources, but the possibility has been raised that the 'melanthion' in Hippocratic texts may refer to corncockle rather than *Nigella arvensis* or black cumin (Heiss *et al.* 2012).

Corncockle seeds would have affected the colour and taste of bread (Hall and Kenward 2016), and poisoning symptoms would have been noticeable. Corncockle was abundant in a second century AD shipment of clean grain transported to the fort at Laurium, the Netherlands, possibly from northern Gaul (Pals and Hakbijl 1992). Corncockle seeds are common occurrences in stores of cereal grain, for instance at South Shields (Van der Veen 1988), the Roman Forum in London (Straker 1987), York (Hall and Kenward 1990), and Colchester (Murphy 1984). Some of these derive from Boudican destruction (*c.* AD 60/61) deposits, for instance the London Forum, indicating that the spread of an invasive weed was intimately associated with Roman colonisation. Stores of cereals in Trier, Maastrict, Woerden, Xanten, and Valkenburg also all contained corncockle seeds (Bakels 2009: 170–171). This shows that corncockle infested grain would have been eaten regularly, and provides the mechanism by which corncockle spread, as seed corn from these stores could have been sown into arable fields. Furthermore, assemblages of cereals and weeds generated in rural settlements had the capacity to affect the health of urban residents.

In a few instances, there are indications that corncockle was purposefully removed from a crop. At Southshields fort in northern Britain, several mineralised corncockle seeds found near the entrance to the granary were tentatively interpreted as evidence for soldiers hand-cleaning their grain upon collection (Van der Veen 1988: 363); and at Roman Winchester, charred capsule fragments but not seeds were identified, interpreted as showing the purposeful removal of any corncockle seeds (Carruthers 2011: 12). Calcium-phosphate mineralised plant remains from latrine pits provide firm evidence for a range of plant foods such as a cesspit from mid-Roman Silchester from which corncockle was identified (Robinson 2011). At Bearsden Roman fort, numerous seeds of corncockle were found amongst a deposit of Roman sewage (Dickson and Dickson 2016), as at York (Hall and Kenward 2016), indicating that they may have passed through the human digestive system. Not only are these seeds common occurrences, but they are also often fragmented, implying that they were milled alongside cereal grains and consumed. Mineralised corncockle seeds have also been recorded from Pompeii Regio VI, Insula I (Murphy *et al.* 2013). Despite the lack of firm literary evidence (Heiss *et al.* 2012), the widespread presence of corncockle, combined with its distinctive materialities of colour and toxicity, makes it highly unlikely that corncockle went unnoticed, and even so, it retained its capacity to affect humans working in cereal fields, during crop processing and during consumption. As a comparison, over 20 names are known of in British dialect for corncockle, highlighting the importance of the weed amongst recent agricultural communities (Stace and Crawley 2015: 44).

Now that the distinctive capacities of corncockle have been considered, it is possible to consider its role in the Roman world through the terms proposed by Head *et al.* (2015). Its *distinctive materialities* of form of seed and plant account for its success as a crop mimic, and would have forced human action to remove the weed in the field and remove the seeds during processing after the capsules had dehisced. The physical and germination characteristics of corncockle seeds inform upon its movement. Only surviving through being sown with seed-corn, corncockle was able to *move* through human agency of grain exchange but only due to its own characteristics. The toxicity of corncockle seeds enabled it to *communicate* with humans, whilst the ecological *flexibility* of its seeds, that is their flexibility to germinate in a wide range of soil conditions and times of the year, ensured it was able to establish itself across much of the north-western Roman world. The combination of these actions meant it forced human labour throughout the annual crop-growing and processing period. The evolution of corncockle within the arable field ensured its survival, but now seed-cleaning processes have changed, *Agrostemma* survives due to the distinctive materialities of its colourful pink flowers and ease with which it can be grown as an ornamental plant. The entanglement of corncockle and cereal cultivation was ultimately underway long before the expansion of the Roman world, but corncockle was able to take advantage of the increased connectivity and exchange of cereals to spread into new areas. Although it is not possible to definitely identify the health-impacts of corncockle, the widespread occurrence in both storage and cesspits makes it highly likely that its presence was noted in the Roman world, as in later periods.

Human motivations have been given primacy for the spread of plants throughout the Roman world (Boivin 2017; Van der Veen 2018: 61). A consideration of corncockle highlights that undesirable weeds were also spread unconsciously, largely due to their previous evolution. A reliance on large-scale cereal cultivation in the north-western provinces meant the annual sowing of seed corn infested with corncockle proliferated the distribution of corncockle, whilst the flows of cereals between rural producers and large-scale storage facilities at military and urban sites facilitated this spread. It is currently unclear when this specific weed made it into the field, but it is clear that the Roman period saw a wider distribution. In essence, corncockle was able to take advantage of the large-scale flow of cereals to increase their distribution beyond the control of humans, forcing the actions of farmers and having a negative impact upon human labour and health.

In contrast to recent considerations of architectural and material culture evidence, which have shown the low-level impact of the Roman empire on life for many of the residents of the countryside of Roman Britain (Smith *et al.* 2016) by paying attention to plants, the impacts of new species did have an enduring impact on the labour scheduling and health of agricultural labourers, showing the impact of a by-product of imperialism on all aspects of life (*cf.* Gardner 2012). Extra labour would have been required throughout the growing cycle to detect the presence of corncockle, and especially at harvest time to remove the seeds from grain. The standardisation of large-scale cereal agriculture has many benefits in terms of ease for taxation and increased production, but it also unleashed unintended by-products in the spread of noxious weed seeds.

Weeds in the City

Whilst some unwanted plants found their way into arable fields and cereal stores across the Roman world, others took advantage of the environments provided by new urban settlements. Following definitions of weeds as undesired or unwanted plants, weeds can also be considered as the plants growing within backyards and paths within settlements. Considerations of vegetation within Roman towns has previously focused on managed landscapes of parks and gardens (Jashemski *et al.* 2018), but as Manuel DeLanda brings to the attention for medieval towns, we can also consider urban centres as alien ecosystems, whereby the flow of matter results in the establishment of new weed communities (DeLanda 1997: 149, 154). Urban vegetation is constantly in flux, affected by local geology, building materials, animal life, and human activities, ensuring towns provide distinctive environments for plants (Gilbert 1989). A range of animals and insects which dwell within towns have been considered (MacKinnon 2018), though not plants.

Identifying plant bodies within towns is sometimes possible through textual sources, for instance the lotus trees grown in the garden of Licinus Crassus on the Palatine Hill in Rome (Marzano 2014), or the interpretation of plane trees in the Portico of Pompey from the Forma Urbis (Gleason 1994). In exceptional circumstances, plant bodies are preserved archaeologically. For instance, a stump of an apple or hawthorn tree was recorded in an area north-west of the Forum in Roman London, perhaps in a back garden (Goodburn 2012). But these are exceptional pieces of historical and archaeological preservation. To follow Michael MacKinnon's example with animals (MacKinnon 2018), we can consider the range of ways in which plants would have been introduced into urban centres. This could be as both dead food substances – ranging from unprocessed grain to milled flour, fresh fruit and vegetables, processed products such as bread, to plant bodies used for decorative or functional substances, such as wooden furniture, building timber, garlands, and swags. As living beings, plants may have existed as pot plants (Macaulay-Lewis 2006), plants tended to in gardens (Lodwick 2017b), and of interest here, weeds which have found their own place amongst the new urban environment.

Urban waterlogged plant assemblages typically contain a wide range of species. Several approaches have been used to reconstruct settlement vegetation, from considerations of individual species to plant communities (Hall 1988). Alternatively, some plants are highlighted for their medical or magical properties in archaeobotanical studies of Roman and medieval settlements in Britain, especially the members of the Solanaceae (nightshade) family (Hall and Kenward 2003: 126). These approaches mask the distinctive characteristics of individual plants. Rather than starting from human ascribed categories, here the distinctive characteristics of one plant are taken as a starting point.

Atropa belladonna is a perennial plant found on disturbed ground, woodland, and scrubland on calcareous soils and in urban settlements (Stace 2010: 573). Some botanical literature classifies *A. belladonna* as a native to Britain in calcareous areas (Butcher 1947; Stace 2010: 573), whilst others state it is an introduction (Eversham and Arnold 1992). *Atropa* is rare prior to the Roman period in Britain but occurs commonly in settlements in the Roman period, including Alchester, Caerwent, Dalton Parlours, and York (Tomlinson and Hall 1996). The location where *Atropa* has been identified tend to have a strong urban distribution – out of 173 site phases around the Roman town of Silchester, *Atropa* occurs only at Silchester, a *civitas* capital (Lodwick 2015). *Atropa* is often recorded alongside a distinct urban flora of *Hyoscyamus niger* (henbane), *Conium maculatum* (hemlock) and *Solanum nigrum* (black nightshade) (Hall 1988), occurring together at Early Roman Silchester (Lodwick 2017c) and Roman York (Hall *et al.* 1980).

The archaeobotanical evidence indicates that *Atropa* was part of plant communities in some urban settlements in Roman Britain. The plant has distinctive characteristics, in that it is a perennial weed growing for several years, hence detectable within the life-span of a human. *Atropa* is also a very persistent plant, able to regenerate and flower in the autumn if cut or grazed earlier in the year (Butcher 1947). Similarly, *Atropa* grows to 0.5–2 m in height, meaning it would be at eye-level with humans. We can imagine *Atropa* growing in nitrogen rich environments within urban settlements – back gardens, side alleys, etc. The berries are shiny black purple berries, similar to blueberries, and tasty. The poisonous berries give *Atropa* the ability to communicate with consumers, but only if ingestion happens.

All parts of the plant contain atropine and hyoscyamine (Lee 2007). The deadly aspect of *Atropa* was known of in the Roman world, with the potential harm to the young and its use as a poison highlighted by Pliny (*HN* 21.177–182). The alkaloids atropine, hyocynamine, and scopolamine cause ill-health by disrupting the binding of a neurotransmitter – acetylcholine – to receptors in the central nervous system and neurones. Ten berries for an adult, or two to three for a child would be toxic. Symptoms include lethargy, slurred speech, and flushing (Berdai *et al.* 2012). Today, the poisonous status of *Atropa* means it is often subject to calls to remove the plants (Brady 2014). By considering the distinctive biological capacities of plants we can take into account the capacity of *Atropa* to act-upon humans.

The subversive nature of *Atropa* on other species within the urban environment is further highlighted by the absence of funghi which grow on the plant, and the observation that 'insects visiting the flowers do not appear to be frequent and have been observed to fly away afterwards as if they did not enjoy they visit' (Butcher 1947: 352). The berries are *Atropa*'s dispersal mechanism, as they are consumed by birds (Butcher 1947). These distinctive materialities would have ensured *Atropa* was noticed, hence entailing that the distinctive characteristics did not have a physical effect. The presence of *Atropa*, with its distinctive capacities, would have characterised the multisensory experience of people moving through specific neighbourhoods of towns and cities in Roman Britain, showing how it is not just constructed ornamental plants which affect the sensory experience of urban place, but also weeds.

In contrast, *Agrostemma githago* would have had a much more substantial impact in terms of human labour, if we take into account its effect upon sowing, harvesting, and crop-processing activities. Here we see a difference between the potential agency of *Atropa* in deterring humans from urban areas in which it grew, and the enacted plant agency of *Agrostemma* affecting agricultural labourers working in the field and processing areas, both of which impacted upon the timing and pattern of human movement. These have only arisen by breaking down the category of 'weed' in to individual species with distinctive capacities. Furthermore, the ways in which the distinctive capacities of plants are enacted upon humans is based upon the archaeological context in which that plant was recorded, from which we can infer the social context in which humans and plants interacted.

Conclusion

Taking inspiration from posthumanist thought, this chapter has sought to de-centre humans by providing an exploration of specific weeds in the Roman world, paying attention to their distinctive capacities in a way that is a more respectful way of thinking with – and about plants. Alien weeds have previously received limited discussion with Roman archaeology, but by considering the distinctive capacities of plants, following Head *et al.* (2015), we can both pay attention to the materialities, movement, and communication of plants on their own ground, and how this affected humans through time. By exploring the distinct capacities of *Agrostema githago* and *Atropa belladonna*, new insights have been gained into the social experiences of the agricultural labourers and urban residents of Roman Britain. The widespread presence of corncockle throughout the north-western Roman provinces, in grain stores, and in cesspits shows how one weed was able to take advantage of the Roman world, and negatively impact upon humans at the same time. *Agrostemma githago* required extra labour during the crop growing season and at harvest time, with the potential to cause illness if it wasn't sufficiently removed. *Atropa belladonna* took advantage of new urban environments, bringing it into contact with people, and probably deterring them from the weedy areas of urban places. To tie these effects into social processes will require more fine-grained analysis of the archaeobotanical patterning.

Whilst work to detect plant agency is underway, it is important to embed the affective characteristics of plants within broader assemblages. For weeds in the field this would mean thinking about assemblages of crops, weeds, soil, winnowing sieves and crop stores. For weeds in the cities this would mean all components of the lived environment. This chapter has aimed to show that it is possible to incorporate plants into posthuman accounts of the Roman world, through being attentive to their distinctive capacities as demonstrated by two case studies. Whilst the daily engagements with soils, plants, and animals rarely come to light from historical and archaeological sources; these can be explored through thinking through the capacities of individual species evidenced in the archaeological record. Given the demonstrated impacts on temporal experience and health, these deserve further attention.

All Souls College, University of Oxford.

Acknowledgements

I am very grateful for the insightful comments of the two peer reviewers for greatly improving this chapter.

Bibliography

Ancient Sources

Cato the Elder (Translated by W.D. Hooper, revised H.B. Ash). 2014. *On Agriculture*. Loeb Classical Library 283. Cambridge, MA: Harvard University Press.

Pliny the Elder (Translated by H. Rackham). 1950. *Natural History, Volume V: Books 17–19*. Loeb Classical Library 371. Cambridge, MA: Harvard University Press.

Pliny the Elder (Translated by W.H.S Jones). 1951. *Natural History, Volume V: Books 20–23*. Loeb Classical Library 392. Cambridge, MA: Harvard University Press.

Theophrastus (Translated by A.F. Hort). *Enquiry into Plants, Volume II: Books 6–9. On Odours. Weather Signs.* Loeb Classical Library 79. Cambridge, MA: Harvard University Press.

Varro (Translated by W.D. Hooper, revised by H.B. Ash). 1935. *On Agriculture.* Loeb Classical Library 283. Cambridge, MA: Harvard University Press.

Virgil (Translated by H. Rushton Fairclough, revised by G.P. Goold). 1916. *Eclogues. Georgics. Aeneid: Books 1–6.* Loeb Classical Library 63. Cambridge, MA: Harvard University Press.

Modern Sources

Allaby, R.G., Fuller, D.Q. and Brown, T.A. 2008. The genetic expectations of a protracted model for the origins of domesticated crops. *Proceedings of the National Academy of Sciences* 105: 13982–13986.

Bakels, C. 2009. *The Western European Loess Belt: Agrarian History, 5300 BC–AD 1000.* London: Springer.

Bakels, C. 2010. The earliest finds of corncockle (*Agrostemma githago* L.) in the Netherlands. In C. Bakels, K. Fennema, W. Out and C. Vermeeren (eds) *Of Plants and Snails. A Collection of Papers Presented to Wim Kuijper in Gratitude for forty Years of Teaching and Identifying.* Leiden: Sidestone Press: 13–20.

Baker, H.G. 1974. The evolution of weeds. *Annual Review of Ecology and Systematics* 5: 1–24.

Baker, P. 2018. Identifying the connection between Roman conceptions of 'Pure Air' and physical and mental health in Pompeian gardens (c. 150 BC–AD 79): a multi-sensory approach to ancient medicine. *World Archaeology* 50 (3): 404–417.

Barrett, J.C. 2016. The new antiquarianism? *Antiquity* 90: 1681–1686.

Barton, H. and Denham, T. 2018. Vegecultures and the social–biological transformations of plants and people. *Quaternary International* 489: 17–25.

Berdai, M.A., Labib, S., Chetouani, K. and Harandou, M. 2012. *Atropa belladonna* intoxication: case report. *Pan African Medical Journal* 11: 72.

Betts, E. (ed.) 2017. *Senses of the Empire: Multisensory Approaches to Roman Culture.* London: Routledge.

Bogaard, A., Ater, M. and Hodgson, J.G. 2018. Arable weeds as a case study in plant-human relationships beyond domestication. In C. Stépanoff and J.-D. Vigne (eds) *Hybrid Communities: Biosocial Approaches to Domestication and Other Trans-Species Relationships.* Abingdon: Routledge: 97–112.

Boivin, N.L. 2017. Proto-globalisation and biotic exchange in the Old World. In N.L. Boivin, R. Crassard, and M.D. Petraglia (eds) *Human Dispersal and Species Movement: From Prehistory to the Present.* Cambridge: Cambridge University Press: 349–410.

Boivin, N.L., Zeder, M.A., Fuller, D.Q., Crowther, A., Larson, G., Erlandson, J.M., Denham, T. and Petraglia, M.D. 2016. Ecological consequences of human niche construction: examining long-term anthropogenic shaping of global species distributions. *Proceedings of the National Academy of Sciences* 113 (23): 6388–6396.

Böttger, S. and Melzig, M.F. 2011. Triterpenoid saponins of the Caryophyllaceae and Illecebraceae family. *Phytochemistry Letters* 4: 59–68.

Boyd, B. 2017. Archaeology and human-animal relations: thinking through anthropocentrism. *Annual Review of Anthropology* 46: 299–316.

Brady, T. 2014. Warning over deadly plant growing in Britain in hot weather… and its poisonous berries which look like blueberries could kill. http://www.dailymail.co.uk/news/article-2704544/Warning-deadly-plant-growing-Britain-hot-weather-poisonous-berries-look-like-blueberries-kill.html [Last Accessed 25/07/2018].

Brice, J. 2014. Attending to grape vines: perceptual practices, planty agencies and multiple temporalities in Australian viticulture. *Social and Cultural Geography* 15: 942–965.

Butcher, R.W. 1947. *Atropa belladonna* L. *Journal of Ecology* 34 (2): 345–353.

Carruthers, W. 2011. Charred and mineralised plant remains. In B. Ford, S. Teague and E. Biddulph (eds) *Winchester – a City in the Making: Archaeological Excavations Between 2002 and 2007 on the Sites of Northgate House, Staple Gardens and the Former Winchester Library, Jewry St.* Oxford: Oxford Archaeology: 363–373.

Chadwick, A.M. 2016. Foot-fall and hoof-hit. Agencies, movements, and materialities; and later prehistoric and Roman-British trackways. *Cambridge Archaeological Journal* 26 (1): 93–120.

Cheffings, C.M. and Farrell, L. (eds) 2005. *Species Status No. 7: The Vascular Plant Red Data List for Great Britain.* Peterborough: JNCC.

Cooper, M.R. and Johnson, A.W. 1984. *Poisonous Plants in Britain and their Effects on Animals and Man.* London: H.M.S.O.

Coward, F., Shennan, S., Colledge, S., Conolly, J. and Collard, M. 2008. The spread of Neolithic plant economies from the Near East to northwest Europe: a phylogenetic analysis. *Journal of Archaeological Science* 35 (1): 42–56.

DeLanda, M. 1997. *A Thousand Years of Nonlinear History.* Brooklyn: Zone Books.

Derreumaux, M. and Lepetz, S. 2008. Food supply at two successive military settlements in Arras (France): an archaeobotanical and archaeozoological approach. In S. Stallibrass and R. Thomas (eds) *Feeding the Roman Army: The Archaeology of Production and Supply in NW Europe.* Oxford: Oxbow Books: 52–68.

Derrick, T.J. 2017. Sensory archaeologies: a Vindolanda smellscape. In S. Betts (ed.) *Senses of the Empire: Multisensory Approaches to Roman Culture.* London/New York: Routledge: 72–87.

DeWet, J.M.J. and Harlan, J.R., 1975. Weeds and domesticates: evolution in the man-made habitat. *Economic Botany* 29: 99–107.

Dickson, C. and Dickson, J. 2000. *Plants and People in Ancient Scotland.* Stroud: Tempus.

Dickson, C. and Dickson, J. 2016. Plant remains. In D. Breeze (ed.) *Bearsden: A Roman Fort on the Antonine Wall.* Edinburgh: Society of Antiquaries of Scotland: 223–280.

Edwards, N. 2015. *Weeds.* London: Reaktion Books.

Eversham, B.C. and Arnold, H.R. 1992. Introductions and their place in British wildlife. In P.T. Harding (ed.) *Biological Recording of Changes in British Wildlife.* London: HMSO: 44–59.

Ferrando, F. 2016. The party of the Anthropocene: post-humanism, environmentalism and the post-anthropocentric paradigm shift. *Relations* 4 (2): 159–173.

Firbank, L.G. 1988. *Agrostemma githago* L. (*Lychnis githago* (L.) Scop.). *Journal of Ecology* 76 (4): 1232–1246.

Firbank, L.G. and Watkinson, A.R. 1986. Modelling the population dynamics of an arable weed and its effects upon crop yield. *Journal of Applied Ecology* 23 (1): 147–159.

Fredengren, C. 2013. Posthumanism, the transcorporeal and biomolecular archaeology. *Current Swedish Archaeology* 21: 53–71.

Fried, G., Bruno C., Philippe R. and Ivan S. 2017. Decreases in crop production by non-native weeds, pests, and pathogens. In V. Montserrat and P.E. Hulme (eds) *Impact of Biological Invasions on Ecosystem Services*. Cham: Springer International Publishing: 83–101.

Fuller, D.Q. and Stevens, C.J. 2017. Open for competition: Domesticates, parasitic domesticoids and the agricultural niche. *Archaeology International* 20: 110–121.

Gardner, A. 2012. Time and empire in the Roman world. *Journal of Social Archaeology* 12 (2): 145–166.

Gerard, J. 1597. *The Herball or Generall Historie of Plantes*. London: Norton.

Gilbert, O.L. 1989. *The Ecology of Urban Habitats*. London: Chapman and Hall.

Gleason, K.L. 1994. Porticus Pompeiana: a new perspective on the first public park of ancient Rome. *Journal of Garden History* 14 (1): 13–27.

Goodburn, D. 2012. Worked wood. In J. Leary and J. Butler (eds) *Roman Archaeology in the Upper Reaches of the Walbrook Valley: Excavations at 6–8 Tokenhouse Yard, London EC2*. London: Pre-Construct Archaeology Limited: 48–56.

Grabowski, R. 2011. Changes in cereal cultivation during the Iron Age in southern Sweden: a compilation and interpretation of the archaeobotanical material. *Vegetation History and Archaeobotany* 20 (5): 479–494.

Graham, E.-J. 2018. 'There buds the laurel': approaching nature and place in the cemeteries of Roman Italy. *Theoretical Roman Archaeology Journal* 1 (1): 3.

Greuter, W. 1995. Studies in Greek *Caryophylloideae*: *Agrostemma*, *Silene*, and *Vaccaria*. *Willdenowia* 25: 105–142.

Hall, A. 1988. Problems of reconstructing past urban floras and vegetation. In M. Jones (ed.) *Archaeology and the Flora of the British Isles*. Oxford: Oxford University Committee for Archaeology: 93–95.

Hall, A. and Kenward, H. 1990. *Environmental Evidence from the Colonia: Tanner Row and Rougier Street*. London: Council for British Archaeology.

Hall, A. and Kenward, H. 2003. Can we identify biological indicator groups for craft, industry and other activities? In P. Murphy and P.E.J. Wiltshire (eds) *The Environmental Archaeology of Industry. Symposia of the Association for Environmental Archaeology 20*. Oxford: Oxbow Books: 114–130.

Hall, A.R. and Kenward, H.K. 2016. Sewers, cesspits and middens: a survey of the evidence for 2000 years of waste disposal in York, UK. In P.D. Mitchell (ed.) *Sanitation, Latrines and Intestinal Parasites in Past Populations*. London/New York: Routledge: 99–120.

Hall, A.R., Kenward, H.K. and Williams, D. 1980. *Environmental Evidence from Roman Deposits in Skeldergate*. London: Council for British Archaeology.

Hall, M. 2011. *Plants as Persons: A Philosophical Botany*. Albany: State University of New York Press.

Halstead, P. 2014. *Two Oxen Ahead: Pre-Mechanized Farming in the Mediterranean*. Chichester: Wiley-Blackwell.

Hammer, K., Hanelt, P. and Knüppfer, H. 1982. Vorarbeiten zur monografischen darstellung von Wildpflanzensortimenten: *Agrostemma* L. *Kulturpflanze* 30: 45–96.

Harper, K. 2017. *The Fate of Rome: Climate, Disease, and the End of an Empire*. Princeton: Princeton University Press.

Harris, O.J.T. and Cipolla, C.N. 2017. *Archaeological Theory in the New Millennium: Introducing Current Perspectives*. Abingdon/New York: Routledge.

Harris, W.V. 2017. The indispensable commodity: notes on the economy of wood in the Roman Mediterranean. In A. Wilson and A.K. Bowman (eds) *Trade, Commerce and the State in the Roman World*. Oxford: Oxford University Press.

Head, L. 2017. The social dimensions of invasive plants. *Nature Plants* 3: 17075.

Head, L., Atchison, J. and Phillips, C. 2015. The distinctive capacities of plants: re-thinking differences via invasive species. *Transactions of the Institute of British Geographers* 40 (3): 399–413.

Heiss, A.G., Stika, H-P., De Zorzi, N. and Jursa, M. 2012. Nigella in the mirror of time: a brief attempt to draw a genus' ethnohistorical portrait. *Offa* 69/70: 147–169.

Hellmund, M. 2008. The Neolithic records of *Onopordum acanthium*, *Agrostemma githago*, *Adonis* cf. *aestivalis* and *Claviceps purpurea*. *Vegetation History and Archaeobotany* 17: 123–130.

Henslow, G. 1901. *Poisonous Plants in Field and Garden*. London: Society for the Promotion of Christian Knowledge.

Hillman, G. 1981. Reconstructing crop husbandry practices from charred remains of crops. In R. Mercer (ed.) *Farming Practice in British Prehistory*. Edinburgh: Edinburgh University Press: 123–162.

Hillman, G. 1984. Interpretation of archaeological plant remains: the application of ethnographic models from Turkey. In W. van Zeist and W.A. Casparie (eds) *Plants and Ancient Man: Studies in Palaeoethnobotany*. Rotterdam: A.A. Balkema: 1–42.

Hitchings, R. 2003. People, plants and performance: on actor network theory and the material pleasures of the private garden. *Social and Cultural Geography* 4 (1): 99–114.

Hughes, J.D. 2003. Europe as consumer of exotic biodiversity: Greek and Roman times. *Landscape Research* 28 (1): 21–32.

Hughes, J.D. 2011. Ancient deforestation revisited. *Journal of the History of Biology* 44 (1): 43–57.

Hughes, J.D. 2014. *Pan's Travail: Environmental Problems of the Greeks and Romans: Ecology in the Ancient Mediterranean*. Baltimore: John Hopkins University Press.

Jacomet, S. and Vandorpe, P. 2011. Plantes anciennes et nouvelles. La région du Rhin supérieur et l'Allemagne du Sud-Ouest. In M. Reddé (ed.) *Aspects de la Romanisation dans l'Est de la Gaule. Volume 1*. Glux-En-Glenne: Centre archéologique européen: 346–360.

Jakab, É. 2015. Property rights in Ancient Rome. In P. Erdkamp, K. Verboven and A. Zuiderhoek (eds) *Ownership and Exploitation of Land and Natural Resources in the Roman World*. Oxford: Oxford University Press: 107–131.

Jashemski, W.F. 2018. Gardening practices and techniques. In W.F. Jashemski, K.L. Gleason, K.J. Hartswick and A.-A. Malek (eds) *Gardens of the Roman Empire*. Cambridge: Cambridge University Press: 121–151.

Jashemski, W.F., Gleason, K.L., Hartswick, K.J. and Malek, A.-A. (eds) 2018. *Gardens of the Roman Empire*. Cambridge: Cambridge University Press.

Jashemski, W.F., Meyer F.G. and Ricciardi, M. 2002. Plants: evidence from wall paintings, mosaics, sculpture, plant remains, graffiti, inscriptions, and ancient authors. In W.F. Jashemski and F.G. Meyer (eds) *The Natural History of Pompeii*. Cambridge: Cambridge University Press: 80–180.

Jones, M. 1988. The arable field: a botanical battleground. In M. Jones (ed.) *Archaeology and the Flora of the British Isles*. Oxford: Oxford University Committee for Archaeology: 86–92.

Jones, O. and Cloke, P. 2002. *Tree Cultures. The Place of Trees and Trees in their Place*. Oxford: Berg.

Jones, O. and Cloke, P. 2008. Non-human agencies: trees in place and time. In C. Knappett and L. Malafouris (eds) *Material Agency: Towards a Non-anthropocentric Approach*. New York/London: Springer: 79–96.

Kreuz, A. 2004. Landwirtschaft im umbruck? Archäobotanische untersuchungen zu den jahrhunderten um christi geburt in Hessen and Mainfranken. *Bericht der Römisch-Germanischen Kommision* 85: 97–292.

Lee, M.R. 2007. Solanaceae IV: *Atropa belladonna*, deadly nightshade. *Journal of the Royal College of Physicians of Edinburgh* 37: 77–84.

Lepetz, S. and Zech-Matterne, Z. 2018. Systèmes agro-pastoraux à l'âge du Fer et à la période romaine. In M. Reddé (ed.) *Gallia Rustica 2. Les campagnes du nord-est de la Gaule, de la fin de l'âge du Fer à l'Antiquité tardive*. Bordeaux: Ausonius: 327–400.

Lodwick, L.A. 2015. *An Archaeobotanical Analysis of Silchester and the Wider Region*. PhD Thesis. University of Oxford.

Lodwick, L.A. 2017a. Arable farming, plant foods, and resources. In M. Allen, L. Lodwick, T. Brindle, M. Fulford and A. Smith (eds) *The Rural Economy of Roman Britain: Farming, Industry, Transport and Markets*. Britannia Monograph Series 30. London: Society for the Promotion of Roman Studies: 11–84.

Lodwick, L.A. 2017b. Evergreen plants in Roman Britain and beyond: movement, meaning and materiality. *Britannia* 48: 135–173.

Lodwick, L.A. 2017c. Agricultural innovations at a Late Iron Age oppidum: archaeobotanical evidence for flax, food and fodder from Calleva Atrebatum, UK. *Quaternary International* 460: 198–219.

Lodwick, L.A. 2018. Arable weed seeds as indicators of regional cereal provenance: a case study from Iron Age and Roman central-southern Britain. *Vegetation History and Archaeobotany* 27 (6): 801–815.

Lodwick, L.A. 2019. Farming practice, ecological temporality, and urban communities at a late Iron Age oppidum. *Journal of Social Archaeology* 19 (2): 206–228.

Mabey, R. 2012. *Weeds: The Story of Outlaw Plants*. London: Profile Books.

Macaulay-Lewis, E. 2006. The role of *ollae perforatae* in understanding horticulture, planting techniques, garden design, and plant trade in the Roman World. In J. Morel, J. Juan and J. Matamala (eds) *The Archaeology of Crop Fields and Gardens: Proceedings of the 1st Conference on Crop Fields and Gardens Archaeology*. Bari: EdiPuglia: 207–220.

MacKinnon, M. 2018. Multi-species dynamics and the ecology of urban spaces in Roman Antiquity. In S.E. Pilaar Birch (ed.) *Multispecies Archaeology*. London: Routledge: 170–182.

Marzano, A. 2014. Roman gardens, military conquests, and elite self-representation. In K. Coleman (ed.) *Le jardin dans l'Antiquité. Entretiens sur l'antiquité classique (LX)*. Geneva: Fondation Hardt: 195–244.

McConnell, J.R., Wilson, A.I., Stohl, A., Arienzo, M.M., Chellman, N.J., Eckhardt, S., Thompson, E.M., Pollard, A.M. and Steffensen, J.P. 2018. Lead pollution recorded in Greenland ice indicates European emissions tracked plagues, wars, and imperial expansion during Antiquity. *Proceedings of the National Academy of Sciences* 115 (22): 5726–5731.

McCormick, F., Kerr, T., McClatchie, M. and O'Sullivan, A. 2011. *The Archaeology of Livestock and Cereal Production in Early Medieval Ireland, AD 400–1100*. Reconstructing the Early Medieval Irish Economy EMAP Report 5.1. Belfast.

Murphy, C., Thompson, G. and Fuller, D. 2013. Roman food refuse: urban archaeobotany in Pompeii, Regio VI, Insula 1. *Vegetation History and Archaeobotany* 22 (5): 409–419.

Murphy, P. 1984. The charred cereals from Building 41. In P. Crummy (ed.) *Colchester Archaeological Report 3: Excavations at Lion Walk, Balkerne Lane and Middleborough, Colchester, Essex*. Colchester: Colchester Archaeological Trust: 105.

Overton, N.J. and Taylor, B. 2018. Humans in the environment: plants, animals and landscapes in Mesolithic Britain and Ireland. *Journal of World Prehistory* 31 (3): 385–402.

Pals, J.-P. and Hakbijl, T. 1992. Weed and insect infestation of a grain cargo in a ship at the Roman fort of Laurium in Woerden (Province of Zuid-Holland). *Review of Palaeobotany and Palynology* 73: 287–300.

Percival, J. 1900. *Agricultural Botany: Theoretical and Practical*. London: Duckworth.

Rindos, D. 1984. *The Origins of Agriculture: An Evolutionary Perspective*. New York: Academic Press.

Robinson, M., 2011. The macroscopic plant and invertebrate remains. In M. Fulford and A. Clarke *Silchester: City in Transition: The Mid-Roman Occupation of Insula IX c. AD 125–250/300: A Report on Excavations Undertaken Since 1997*. London: Society for the Promotion of Roman Studies: 281–293.

Sallares, R. 2007. Ecology. In W. Scheidel, I. Morris and R. Saller (eds) *The Cambridge Economic History of the Greco-Roman World*. Cambridge: Cambridge University Press: 15–37.

Shackleton, R.T., Larson, B.M.H., Novoa, A., Richardson, D.M. and Kull, C.A. 2019. The human and social dimensions of invasion science and management. *Journal of Environmental Management* 229: 1–9.

Smart, A. 2014. Critical perspectives on multispecies ethnography. *Critical Anthropology* 34 (1): 3–7.

Smith, A., Allen, M., Brindle, T. and Fulford, M. 2016. *The Rural Settlement of Roman Britain*. London: Society for the Promotion of Roman Studies.

Spurr, S. 1986. *Arable Cultivation in Roman Italy*. London: Society for the Promotion of Roman Studies.

Stace, C. 2010. *New Flora of the British Isles*. 3rd edition. Cambridge: Cambridge University Press.

Stace, C. and Crawley, M.J. 2015. *Alien Plants*. London: William Collins.

Stevens, C.J. and Fuller, D.Q. 2018. The fighting flora: an examination of the origins and changing composition of the weed flora of the British Isles. In E. Lightfoot, X. Liu and D.Q. Fuller (eds) *Far from the Hearth: Essays in Honour of Martin K. Jones*. Cambridge: McDonald Institute Conversations: 23–36.

Straker, V. 1987. Carbonized cereal grain from first-century London: a summary of the evidence for importation and crop processing. In P. Marsden (ed.) *The Roman Forum Site in London*. London: H.M.S.O.: 151–155.

Stroh, P.A., Leach, S.J., August, T.A., Walker, K.J., Pearman, D.A., Rumsey, F.J., Harrower, C.A., Fay, M.F., Martin, J.P., Pankhurst, T., Preston, C.D. and Taylor, I. 2014. *A Vascular Plant Red List for England*. Bristol: Botanical Society of Britain and Ireland.

Sykes, N. 2012. A social perspective on the introduction of exotic animals: the case of the chicken. *World Archaeology* 44 (1): 158–169.

Taylor, B. 2018. Subsistence, environment and Mesolithic landscape archaeology. *Cambridge Archaeological Journal* 28 (3): 493–510.

Taylor, J. 2013. Encountering Romanitas: characterising the role of agricultural communities in Roman Britain. *Britannia* 44: 171–90.

Thomas, H., Archer, J.E. and Turley, R.M. 2016. Remembering darnel, a forgotten plant of literary, religious, and evolutionary significance. *Journal of Ethnobiology* 36 (1): 29–44.

Thommen, L. 2012. *An Environmental History of Ancient Greece and Rome*. Cambridge: Cambridge University Press.

Thompson, K. and Grime, J. 1979. Seasonal variation in the seed banks of herbaceous species in ten contrasting habitats. *Journal of Ecology* 67 (3): 893–921.

Tomlinson, P. and Hall, A. 1996. A review of archaeological evidence for food plants from the British Isles: an example of the use of the Archaeobotanical Computer Database (ABCD). *Internet Archaeology* 1.

Van der Veen, M. 1988. Carbonised grain from the granary at South Shields North East England. In H. Küster (ed.) *Der Prähistorische Mensch und seine Umwelt. Festchrift für Udelgard Körber Grohne zum 65. Geburtstag*. Stuttgart: Konrad Theiss Verlag: 353–365.

Van der Veen, M. 2008. Food as embodied material culture: diversity and change in plant food consumption in Roman Britain. *Journal of Roman Archaeology* 21: 83–109.

Van der Veen, M. 2014. The materiality of plants: plant-people entanglements. *World Archaeology* 46 (5): 799–812.

Van der Veen, M. 2018. Archaeobotany: the archaeology of human-plant interactions. In W. Scheidel (ed.) *The Science of Roman History: Biology, Climate, and the Future of the Past*. Princeton: Princeton University Press: 53–95.

Van Oyen, A. and Pitts, N. (eds) 2017. *Materialising Roman Histories: Beyond Instrumentalism and Representation*. Oxford: Oxbow Books.

Veal, R. 2017. The politics and economics of Ancient forests: timber and fuel as levers of Greco-Roman control. In P. Derron (ed.) *Economie et inégalité: Resources, échanges et pouvoir dans l'Antiquité classique*. Vandœuvres: Hardt Foundation: 317–367.

Wandersee, J.H. and Schussler, E. 2001. Towards a theory of plant blindness. *Plant Science Bulletin* 47 (1): 2–9.

Williams, F., Eschen, R., Harris, A., Djeddour, D., Pratt, C., Shaw, R.S., Varia, S., Lamontagne-Godwin, J., Thomas, S.E. and Murphy, S.T. 2010. *The Economic Cost of Invasive Non-Native Species on Great Britain*. Wallingford: CABI.

Witcher, R. 2013. On Rome's ecological contribution to British flora and fauna: landscape, legacy and identity. *Landscape History* 34 (2): 5–26.

Woolf, G. 2017. Roman things and Roman people. A cultural ecology of the Roman world. In A. Van Oyen and M. Pitts (eds) *Materialising Roman Histories: Beyond Instrumentalism and Representation*. Oxford: Oxbow Books: 211–216.

8

Two Parts Hydrogen, Oxygen One? Re-evaluating the Nature of Roman Urban Water Infrastructure

Jay Ingate

Introduction

The chemical compound of water is two hydrogen atoms and one oxygen. Indeed, along with CO_2, it is a scientific abbreviation that has managed to pierce the popular consciousness. H_2O is an understanding of water in its most absolute terms. It is a pure and uniform substance that represents a 'peak humanisation' of an element that underpins all life on the planet. We are happy to talk about it in generalised terms and impose meaning upon it. In fact, the modern city of the West is often presented as an ultimate victory over water, marginalising its visible presence, and bending its will to human goals. The problem with this sort of attitude towards water is that it belies its complexity and has had a major impact on the way we interpret it in the past. We have endorsed a sense of binary to describe interactions with natural contexts – human-made vs natural, civilised vs barbaric, and consumer vs resource. All these different definitions can be found in the analysis of water, particularly when we are considering changes during the Roman period in provincial settings like Britain. The establishment of Roman cities in marginal parts of the empire has long been entrenched in ideas of human consumption and civilisation, both of which are recurring themes in the topic of water infrastructure.

This chapter proposes that these types of discussions are indebted to modern thinking, rather than Roman attitudes, or an accurate understanding of water over time. When dealing with the classical world, we have a penchant for seeking the familiar in our interpretations of evidence (see Mount 2010). However, in the case of water, this has led to an unfair presentation of our own bias. As we move into a very different relationship with nature, necessitated by the pressures of climate change, we must come to realise that our historical connections to water are far more complicated and diverse. By looking at the work of human geographers, the classical sources, and archaeological evidence from Roman Britain, this chapter will attempt to approach the developments of Roman urbanism by 'thinking through water' (see Krause and Strang 2016). By understanding the complex agency of water in the past, we can start to move away from overbearing dialogues of human domination and acknowledge the need for new approaches to water infrastructure in the future of our cities.

The Modern Abstraction of Water and its Legacy

Writers like Maria Kaika and Erik Swyngedouw note how we have become detached from the source of water in nature (Kaika and Swyngedouw 2000; Kaika 2005). The modern city dweller has relatively little knowledge about where their water comes from, what processes it has been subjected to, and where it goes after their brief encounter with it (Sedlak 2015). Without these connections, external factors can manipulate its meaning. Urban spaces, for instance, imprint particular functions or values upon water in our everyday lives. An example of this is that water in the bathroom is principally reserved for personal hygiene, whereas water in the kitchen is deemed more suitable for human consumption. Despite the same supply flowing from the bathroom faucet, people are often reticent about using it as a drinking source. We also have a great fear of water in the bathroom coming into contact with electricity, but this is not replicated in the kitchen – where it mingles quite happily with almost all of our utilities.

This simplification of water, defining its meaning through human control, is at the heart of our modern urbanism. The process is implicit in the dividing line we draw when discussing the provision of 'running water'; it is the difference between prosperity and poverty. We are regularly reminded, for example, that a lack of water in the developing world is a prime reason for disease. We are shown how the addition of a 'simple' water pump can revolutionise life in these communities – the current 'Ripple Effects' campaign on www.wateraid.org is a clear example of this type of message. Such initiatives provide access to the safe homogenous water of the West, rather than the disease-ridden natural water which we are told proliferates in these areas. While no one doubts the noble aims of charities like Water Aid, their promotions do subtly reinforce our biases concerning water. In this context, natural water is not 'running water', it is uncivilised and unwanted. Indeed, the definition of 'running water' is not described fully by the characteristic of physical movement, something water is doing constantly at a molecular level. The additional ingredient required is the imposition of human agency, which forces water towards 'productive' human goals. As such, we only view water as something positive when it has been suitably humanised and homogenised.

This sentiment is a product of modernity and the historical development of our cities. In London, for instance, water became associated directly with disease and poverty. In 1732, inmates of the Fleet Prison even petitioned against the disease and mortality caused by the vapours emanating from the Fleet River (Ackroyd 2008: 49). In the nineteenth century, an increased understanding of bacteria also led to the connection between water and rampant urban diseases like Cholera (Sedlak 2015: 31). Great intervention programs took place that forced much of the local waterscape underground, and out of contact with the populace of the city. Today, historically prominent rivers such as the Walbrook and the Fleet are hidden and run beneath various buildings in central London (Myers 2011). London was not alone in such a push to banish water, most of Europe also engaged in similar practices. In Germany, for instance, there was an extensive program of reclamation, transforming marshes and riverine zones into habitable land using extensive dyke systems (Blackbourn 2007). In his analysis of the work of the German writer Ludwig Starklof, David Blackbourn (2007: 142) notes that in 1847 such programs in Eastern Friesland were seen as being responsible for communities with neater houses, increased productivity, and even women with more teeth! This human 'improvement' of nature lies at the heart of modern urbanism and our idea of civilised living.

Many would argue that the Roman period drainage of marshes and other large-scale manipulations of water would appear to share similar motivations with these later interventions. The explanations of Roman urban water infrastructure are firmly entrenched within such a framework of human dominance. Much of this relies on the very modern idea that there is a definitive separation between the human and natural world. In this line of thinking, the 'living water' of springs and rivers could have far-reaching significance, but as soon as it was brought into the human/urban sphere, this special nature was eroded (see Wissowa 1912: 180). It is an approach that feels very in tune with modernity, where we emphasise the purity of abstract natural water sources, placing them above our own local piped water supply.

This theoretical abstraction of water from its contextual meaning has led to discussions of Roman urban water features that focus on issues of architectural scale. If people see water as merely a homogenous resource for a 'consumer city', then the only real areas of interest lie in how much of this resource is being extracted and used. This way of thinking ends up being far more concerned with the structures bearing water, rather than with the water itself. Gerda de Kleijn's (2001) work on the water supply of Rome is a clear example. Here the author attempts to use the relative size of the aqueducts that led into Rome to make population estimates. It is an engaging account which has contributed to our understanding of the technological sophistication of such engineering in the capital, but it also overemphasised the functionalist purpose of urban water infrastructure. It is an approach that has also been echoed in establishing the river Tiber's value to Rome, with some writers rationalising it as primarily a supply route for goods based upon the location of harbours along its course (see Malmberg 2015). Another off-shoot of this outlook is the discussion of the productive consumption of water, perhaps best understood in its agricultural usage in rural contexts (Wilson 1999). Yet, all of these approaches assume that Romans took a twentieth/twenty-first-century approach to water management, with the proportion of water supplied directly correspondent to practical requirements. The only real divergence from these approaches has been to highlight the symbolic potential of conspicuous consumption (Hodge 1992; Wilson 2012), which still relies on a modern conception of what would constitute water waste.

Thinking through Water: Issues of Agency and Dependency

This supposedly dominant and human-orientated relationship to water in the ancient past does not reflect the full scope of our evidence. One can make a robust debate that such circumstances have never truly existed in modernity and that the dominance of nature is certain to become an obsolete perspective in the face of climate change. Indeed, Daniel Miller's (1987) suggestion that the less we notice things, the more constraints they put upon us, is a particularly apt observation in the case of water. Human life is deeply entangled with water and characterising this as merely opposition, or as humans mastering the power of nature, is reductive in the extreme. The German dyke building crazes of the 1800s, mentioned above, may have seemed like a human victory at the time, but they eventually led to extensive flooding in different areas and dramatically altered the agricultural cycle for people living at these locations (Blackbourn 2007: 66–67).

Another example of the inherent complexity of water is the Yellow River in China. Along with the Yangtze River, this watercourse has a strong tendency to flood. So marked and vital are the flood events of these rivers that they have been cornerstones of Chinese politics, art, religion, and economics for centuries. The Yellow River is characterised by an unusual amount of sediment, some of which settles along the bed, elevating the river over time (Ball 2016: 371). Once the flood season comes, with increased rainfall and snowmelt from higher ground, the river inevitably bursts its banks. For generations, farmers have reacted to this by building larger and larger dykes on the banks; resulting in a strange aqueduct-like structure, suspending the river at a higher level, some 15 metres above the surrounding planes (Ball 2016: 372). Whenever these dykes fail, the water escapes and pools into large lakes, and is unable to return to its original course, leading to a continually changing riverscape.

Matt Edgeworth (2011: 77) describes the Yellow River as a hybrid – neither a natural river, nor an entirely human creation. Philip Scarpino (1997: 5) also notes that many rivers of the modern world are akin to cyborgs, somewhere between definitions of human or natural. Human actions may have manipulated the circumstances of water, but there is no binary sense of dominance. These developments have likely created a more volatile presence of water in the future. As Tim Ingold (2013) notes, there is a 'meshwork' of interactions on display here, without a clear-cut divide between culture and nature. This complexity is the reality of what we should expect when analysing water. As will be outlined below, in the Roman world there were robust local beliefs attached to water in the classical and provincial traditions. As such, substantial changes in Roman waterscapes were marked by a sense of negotiation with divine forces, rather than outright marginalisation and domination. Key to modifying our views of water is truly acknowledging its agency within traditionally humanised settings like cities.

This volume represents a collection of contributions that move away from reductive ideas about human agency as the overriding perspective of our approach to the past. In recent years, there have been many discussions about the agency of other aspects of the 'natural world' that were traditionally not even considered 'sentient', such as plants (see Head *et al.* 2012; Van der Veen 2014; Lodwick in this volume). Nevertheless, while we may have become open to discussing how the requirements of plants have shaped landscapes, water is still considered to have only a passive influence, just as it had in discussions of human agency. Yet, water debatably exhibits a more tangible sense of agency than even plants. At a chemical level, it possesses a bond that creates the phenomenon of surface tension; it resists gravity to remain bonded, and when separated it is quickly found coalescing once more. It is an attribute that has made life possible on Earth, but its ubiquity has lessened its impact.

This strength of flow towards larger bodies of water creates such physical force that it can destroy surrounding landscapes. Of course, we often see events like flooding as products of other processes, but it is the unique nature of water that makes them so destructive. As with the Yellow River, the variable composition of what we classify as a body of water can have a marked effect on the way it behaves. Regardless, it still retains the ability to utterly transform human landscapes on multiple levels, making a mockery of any sense of ownership or control over it. In a matter of minutes, flood events can eradicate the urban infrastructure that defines our modern way of life. Over a longer timescale, the erosion of limestone rock by water can even undermine the very foundations of our cityscapes, creating gaping sinkholes in the ground. Even at the molecular level, water is forcing its will upon any physical constraints. There is also the fact that human settlement and expansion has done much to further this agency of water. Deforestation, elimination of certain animal species, and the non-porous nature of our concrete cities are agreed to have increased its destructive power (see Sedlak 2015). If anything, the modern city provides a platform for water to have a more notable impact on humans in the near future.

Bodies of water can even self-regulate the impact of humans to a certain extent. For instance, a flowing river can process and purify sewage surprisingly efficiently, thanks to other elements in the river and the action of sunlight over a prolonged period of transit. This was the premise upon which many of the early sewage systems of the US were based, and it only became problematic when the volume of waste increased exponentially with the development of industry (Sedlak 2015: 65). In other areas of the world, particular waters have been identified as self-purifying based on their bacteriophage levels. Phages are viral organisms that attack bacteria. The Ganges river in India, for instance, has been the object of much scientific debate since English Bacteriologist Ernest Hankin (1896) noted the antimicrobial properties of the water in the late 1800s. Due to the bacteriophage concentrations, the river could kill the causative bacteria of Cholera within three hours. It is easy to see how such properties could drive dependencies in communities. The unique attributes of the waters of the Ganges lend themselves to healing, therefore driving more human interaction, and fortifying wider belief systems surrounding the river.

Of course, in modern Western thought, we find it harder to attribute this type of action to the actual 'will' of a substance like water. It seems to defy our 'rational' ideas about consciousness. However, there is evidence that other cultures around the world have looked into aspects of the non-human world as having distinct independent agency. The Japanese tradition of *Yōkai* is one of the most striking examples of this sort of belief system, and it endures even to the modern day. The translated term roughly equates to 'monsters', but these creatures represent a range of beings or spirits that are an integral part of the world and that can greatly affect the human experience of places and objects. They stem from the broad sense of animism in Japanese belief; an idea that all things possess a spirit or life-force

(Foster 2015: 86). It is an outlook that has immediate relevance to this discussion of posthumanism. In the world of *Yōkai*, after a period of time, human-made objects can gain a spirit and become *Tsukumogami* ('Haunted tools') (Foster 2015: 240). The mundane items of the home like umbrellas, brooms, brushes, and needles are then able to operate in a potentially malevolent fashion. As such, even today, in Japan there are memorial services (*kuyō*) held for loyal household objects (Foster 2015: 241). Even larger buildings can be imbued with the agency of a *Yōkai*. The poor heat retention of a room with a high ceiling is explained by the presence of the *Tenjoname* ('Ceiling licker'), rather than the design (Foster 2015: 233). Similarly, the unexplainable creaking and rattling sounds of an old house are the work of the *Yanari* (Foster 2015: 228).

However, *Yōkai* are also found representing the wider materiality and agency of the natural world. Water is a particularly rich source for this folklore tradition. The *Kappa* is one of the most notorious *Yōkai* and is thought to reside in rivers and wet places (Foster 2015: 157). So pervasive is its presence in the consciousness of the Japanese that it remains pictured on warning signs close to water to this day (Foster 2015: 163). In many ways, the *Kappa* represents the alluring and dangerous agency of water – they are known to lure people and animals towards rivers before drowning them. However, they also represent other aspects of water. Their favourite past time is sumo wrestling, and if an individual beats them at this then they can secure their ongoing good-will (Foster 2015: 163). This process is akin to the entanglement between humans and watercourses, physically confronting them so as to create better conditions. Indeed, when they are bested at wrestling, *Kappa* have then been known to help with the irrigation of farmland (Foster 2015: 161).

Agents of Roman Water: Deities in the Deep

At this point, it is worth returning to the assertion made above that Roman water interactions were seen in a different way to the great water projects of Western modernity. There has been much work on the 'exploitation' of water resources (for a recent discussion using such language, see Erdkamp *et al.* 2015). There have also been significant contributions that highlight how Roman control of water was a prominent source of power and symbol of conquest (see Purcell 1990; Campbell 2012). Yet, what needs to be emphasised that power was not derived from silencing and marginalising water, as is often seen in those post-Enlightenment accounts mentioned above. There was a far greater sense of negotiation in the Roman period, and something more akin to the examples of water agency from Japan.

There is no doubt that water was seen as a way for Roman rulers to prove their strength and power. Brian Campbell (2012: 370) notes how the struggle between the embodiment of the *Res Romana*, the Emperor, and the force of rivers was something emphasised by even the most powerful rulers. Yet, even when a great river was overcome, such as when Trajan crossed the Danube and conquered Dacia, it is rare that the water deities were forgotten or marginalised. Moreover, they were rarely seen as a humiliated foe, in contrast to defeated armies. Instead, they were often highlighted as participating in the Roman conquest itself, welcoming Roman influence into their domain. Trajan even minted a series of coins that depicted the personified Danube with its hand around Dacia's throat (Campbell 2012: 378). The local river had thus been recruited to, and joined, the Roman war effort. However, this was an alliance and it could be broken; a strong emperor was required to keep such power on the Roman side (see Plin. *Pan.* 82.4–5). These beliefs manifested themselves in a deep respect for provincial water practices. For example, Campbell (2012: 385) is right to point out that Arrian, during his governorship of Cappadocia, goes out of his way to communicate the intricacies of local religious practices relating to the river Phasis to Emperor Hadrian (Arr. *Peripl. M. Eux.* 7–8). Even the conquest of Britain was likely seen in such terms. David Braund (1996) notes that the Claudian conquest was portrayed as winning Ocean, father of all rivers, over to the Roman cause. Ocean frequently appears in provincial art, akin to a celebrated ally rather than in the form of a vanquished foe (Braund 1996: 15).

This respect for the agency of water was not just a facet of war; it was a foundational aspect of the Roman tradition. Tiberinus (Tiber), for instance, is particularly prominent in the historical foundation myths of Rome. Plutarch notes that when the infant founders of the city, Romulus and Remus, were placed on the edge of the Tiber, it rose up and gently took them downstream before safely depositing them near to a fig tree (Plut. *Vit. Rom.* 3–4). After this intervention, the infants are discovered by the She-Wolf and set on the path to greatness. Similarly, in Book Eight of the *Aeneid*, the Tiber comes to the protagonist Aeneas in a dream and guides him towards Latium, and the eventual site of Rome (Verg. *Aen.* 8.26–67). Again, this intervention occurs at a pivotal point in the narrative and, in this case, gives Aeneas a distinct focus on his eventual goal.

However, while the Tiber inevitably holds a special place in the mythic origins of Rome, other rivers were also portrayed as far more than simple elements of geography. In one of his letters, Pliny the Younger (*Ep.* 8.8) describes the Italian River Clitumnus (the Clitunno, Umbria) in a purple-bordered toga – a clear sign of authority. Likewise, in the *Amores*, Ovid depicts the River Anio consoling the character of Ilia, offering her refuge within his kingdom (Ov. *Am.* 3.6). Ilia is a pivotal individual, being the mother of Romulus and Remus as well as the descendant of Aeneas.

This power of water to influence space and people is also witnessed in the treatment of underground water sources.

Due to the continued popularity of spa sites in Europe, many people already know about their prominent history in the Roman period – for instance, Bath in the UK (*Aquae Sulis*), Aix-En-Provence in France (*Aquae Sextiae*), and Wiesbaden in Germany (*Aquae Mattiacorum*). However, Servius famously proclaimed that 'no spring is not sacred' (*Nullus enim fons non sacer*, Serv. Verg. *Aen.* 7.84). This was in reference to the much earlier comments of Virgil in his *Aeneid* (*Aen.* 7.84), showing an enduring reverence for all types of springs. While the Tiber is the most prominent water feature of Rome, many springs throughout the city were sites of worship. Debatably the most important of these was that of Juturna, located adjacent to the Forum. Again, this water feature is woven into the fabric of Roman history, identified as the place where Castor and Pollux watered their horses after the Battle of Lake Regillus (Plut. *Vit. Cor.* 3.4). There was also a spring near the Porta Capena, where the legendary King of Rome, Numa Pompilius, is said to have consulted with the water nymph Egeria on many of his religious reforms, and thus the input of water deities is tightly woven into the mythic narrative of the city. Furthermore, even pragmatic writers, like Vitruvius, reveal to us a world where springs can turn people foolish, make all their teeth fall out, make them abstemious or, indeed, give them better singing voices (Vitr. *De arch.* 8.22–24). All these examples combined present water as a varied and influential force that can entrap and influence human behaviour.

Complexity in Classical Accounts of Urban Water Infrastructure

The powerfulness and complexity of water has yet to influence our understanding of Roman urban water infrastructure like aqueducts. Despite the above classical references, some scholars may note that the Roman sources which discuss such subjects appear to be far more technical and functionalist in their approach. The account of Frontinus (*De Aquaeductu*) is one of the most detailed accounts of classical water supply that we possess, and the touchstone for any discussion of this subject. This text has largely been taken at face value as a technical handbook of Rome's water supply (Goodyear 1983: 672; Hodge 1992: 16). If this was the intention, it has been noted that the treatise is rather lacking in detail (Bruun 2012: 16–18). Alternatively, Janet DeLaine (1996) proposes that it could be a piece of rhetoric designed to highlight the achievements of Frontinus during his consulship (which he shared with the eventual Emperor Trajan), possibly spoken aloud in front of the Senate. That aside, previous scholarship has undoubtedly been fascinated by the structural details Frontinus highlights, rather than his various accounts of the entanglement of infrastructure with a meaning-laden natural world.

For instance, he informs us of the controversial introduction of the Aqua Marcia, where the Sibylline Books were required to be consulted, and it was initially deemed wrong for the Marcian waters to be brought into the capital (Frontin. *Aq.* 1.7). If one portrays the aqueducts as purely functional, this episode is slightly puzzling. There seems little reason for these oracular projections to deny the supply of freshwater. Yet, if one emphasises the cultural associations of water, as discussed above, then the first waters brought into Rome from the outside would have had great significance. In this light, it would be understandable if a conservative document like the Sibylline Books would inspire resistance to such a dramatic change. Rome's waterscape was fundamental to the religious traditions of the city and was enshrined in the mythic tales of the archaic kings like Numa Pompilius and Tarquinius. Bringing new waters to this area, laden with their unique meaning, was a profound act.

Similarly, while telling the Aqua Virgo's foundation story, Frontinus writes that the waters of this aqueduct first entered the city on the ninth of June (Frontin. *Aq.* 1.9–10); this coincides with the *Vestalia*, a significant festival held in honour of the goddess Vesta. This was one of the oldest celebrations in the Roman ritual calendar and was connected to the prosperity of the city itself and the duties of the sacred priestesses of Rome, the Vestal Virgins. Their duties included collecting sacred water from the aforementioned spring of Egeria for various ritual processes. The addition of the Aqua Virgo to the celebration of Vesta was likely a deliberate addition to these water rites, further underlining the non-practical and spiritual importance of water in the city.

The vast amount of water that was brought to Rome through its aqueducts was eventually channelled into the Tiber through the Cloaca Maxima. The entanglement of a 'human-made' conduit with a 'natural' watercourse is acutely expressed in the development of this sewer. Initially, it appears likely that the drain followed the course of a small stream that ran through what would later become the Forum (Hopkins 2007: 2). As time moved on, this feature was given a structural framework to help drain the flood-prone areas close to the Tiber. Pliny the Elder (*HN* 36.105) notes how the early Cloaca Maxima would have collected water from seven tributaries. This origin as a stream is also reflected in the winding course of the sewer, which remained unaltered despite a later renovation in the Republican and Imperial periods; the total length of the sewer was 1600 metres, but the actual distance covered was closer to 900 metres (Aldrete 2007: 171).

This connection to the early streams of the Roman flood-plain also linked the sewer to foundational religious traditions. The shrine of Venus Cloacina in the Forum is a testament to its importance in this regard. Scholars have also suggested connections between the sewer, the office of Pontifex Maximus, and archaic Roman deities like Janus (see Holland 1961; Coarelli 1986). It has also been said that Imperial era adjustments to the course of the sewer may have had direct religious connections with the buildings above ground; for instance, a section that underlies the Temple of Minerva was constructed in *lapis albanus* mirroring the material used in the temple above-ground (Hopkins 2012: 190).

However, even in more humble water infrastructure features we can find aspects of complexity. Seneca mentions the sinking of wells on a number of occasions. In the first, he describes how in a dry area a well can be sunk to a depth of 60 or 90 metres and still find 'living water' (*vivam aquam*, Sen. *QNat*. 3.7.3). The use of this term is interesting because it is often deployed in the description of springs and water concerned with ritual in the Roman belief system. The second mention occurs when Seneca tells us how wells and lakes disappeared on the island of Crete because the land ceased to be tilled (Sen. *QNat*. 3.11.5). Again, we are given an example where the wells are taken together as 'natural water', thus equally deserving of veneration. He continues by noting how 'some wells are full for six hours and dry six alternately' *(Sed quare quidam fontes senis horis pleni senisque sicci sunt*, Sen. *QNat.* 3.16.1); the explanation, according to Seneca, shows wells and rivers have a similar source, which also run dry at some points during the year. He also refers to certain wells that 'throw up not merely mud but also leaves, and bits of crockery and any other filthy things that have accumulated in them' (*Hoc quibusdam locis fontes faciunt, ut non tantum lutum sed folia testasque et quicquid putre iacuit expellant*, Sen. *QNat.* 3.26.7). This implies that these features also had the power to cleanse themselves and reject unwanted materials.

A chief aspect of these accounts is a sense of wells being entangled with the divine agency that has been mentioned previously. There appear to be several occasions where a certain action was needed, otherwise a negative outcome would result. Therefore, if the fields were not tilled appropriately, the wells and lakes would disappear, or if water sources were subject to extensive amounts of refuse they would reject this material through the wells. Even Seneca's account of wells being full and dry alternatively for six hours conjures images of mischievous non-human agency. These accounts reflect that the act of well construction may have involved a degree of negotiation and balance with the natural world if one was to secure an enduring water source. It reflects the possibility that any failure was probably not seen in purely practical terms, but also as a product of not satisfying or placating the local deity of the water.

The above descriptions do not describe a world where water is held in opposition to human activity. The water here is an influential presence with its own agency, which can transform the meaning of space and create variability in meaning at the local level. This should make it hard to talk about water infrastructure in generalised terms. For instance, it is clear from Frontinus' account that the waters of the various aqueducts of Rome were seen as possessing different associations, whether that was the aforementioned ritual celebrations to which they were connected or just their comparable tastes (see Frontin. *Aq*. 1.14). Therefore, it seems overly simplistic to then project a uniformity of meaning to water infrastructure located in more far-flung provincial territories.

Prehistorians and Progressive Approaches to Waterscapes

It is vital to acknowledge that Roman archaeologists have been markedly reticent to change the ways they interpret water in settlements, especially in provinces like Britain where scant evidence can be extrapolated into grand narratives of engagement with the rest of the Roman world. Prehistorians working on the evidence of temperate European sites, by contrast, have been far more progressive. This is perhaps due to the greater interpretive freedom offered by the Pre-Roman period, where the evidence is not as easily equated to modern equivalents, and has fostered the growth of very different theoretical traditions. Nonetheless, the acknowledgement of a far more diverse and strange conception of water has been a long-held consensus among these scholars.

To some extent, this has been inspired by the many deposits of material culture in springs, rivers, lakes, marshes, and islands (Fitzpatrick 1984; Aldhouse-Green 1986; Bradley 1990; Webster 1995; Willis 1999; Hingley 2006; Yates and Bradley 2010). Such activity is characteristic of sites from the Bronze Age through to the Late Iron Age. As the appearance of these items in the archaeological record during these periods cannot often be explained in a purely practical sense, archaeologists have looked to symbolism and ritual as key aspects that help us understand the relationship people had to these places. This non-functionalist significance of water is so entrenched within the interpretative framework of prehistorians that some thirty years ago Andrew Fitzpatrick (1984: 179) described it as 'unsurprising'. It is largely agreed that, throughout prehistory, people all over temperate Europe acknowledged the ritual and symbolic potency of engaging with waterscapes (Bradley 1990; Coles 2001; Larsson 2001).

However, while it is fair to say that water remained meaning-laden throughout this period from the Bronze Age to the Late Iron Age, the specific ways that people acknowledged its power did vary over time and between place. Emphasis has been placed on the deposit of weaponry into watery contexts, and this is certainly clear in the Bronze Age evidence (Bradley 1990). Iron Age sites such as La Tène, in Switzerland, with its rich metalwork (particularly weaponry) finds discovered in watery contexts seems to reflect similar values to those found from Bronze Age sites, albeit with the type of metal changing. Yet, as Richard Bradley (1990) notes, this obscured our understanding of the many ways in which the evidence of the Late Iron Age differed from earlier periods.

Even at La Tène, there was a breadth of different items recovered that were not weaponry, with coins and currency bars being two of the more prominent find types. This variety of finds is also reflected in other in the watery contexts of Britain during the Middle to Late Iron Age (Bradley 1990: 73; Hingley 1990). There is also the fact that food-related items increasingly became involved in rituals during the Late Iron Age, perhaps signifying elements of fertility and prosperity. Fitzpatrick (1984: 179) mentions how such organic votive deposits were unlikely to have been recovered by archaeologists from these watery contexts and yet could have played an increasingly prominent role during this period. His analysis of Late Iron Age finds from the River Thames also interpreted a possible votive deposit of items like bronze cauldrons, tankards, bowls, and wood sculptures (Fitzpatrick 1984: 166).

To some extent the recovery of these finds might depend on the circumstances of the site's discovery, if it was a chance find rather than a planned excavation, there is a greater potential for evidence to be lost (Bradley 2016: 60). Nevertheless, there is increasing evidence of locations where metal deposits played a smaller role, such as the Swedish site of Röekillorna. Here the prehistoric spring deposit only included four metal artefacts, but there was a significant collection of worked wood, consisting of *c.* 4000 animal bones and 44 human bones (Stjernquist *et al.* 1997). Similarly, at Oberdorla in north-east Germany, extensive deposits of animal bones, 30 or more wooden artefacts (interpreted as anthropomorphic idols), and human remains were discovered (Behm-Blanke *et al.* 2003). This diversity of find types reflects a deeper engagement and entanglement with water for varied ritual and symbolic reasons.

This more ambiguous range of deposits can also help us move away from just considering what an item says about the people who are depositing it; with weapons, the temptation has been to talk about warrior values or potential battles having taken place nearby. Yet, the human action of deposition into these contexts is part of an overall belief in the agency of water to transform events, memories, and time in the world of the individual or group. The above references to human bones also highlight the widespread deposition of people, or representations of them, in Antiquity. These practices bring the complexity of water's agency into focus. There is a growing acknowledgement of a substantive connection between death and the rivers and ocean in Iron Age Britain (Willis 2007) – the prehistoric waterscape of London, for example, may have been particularly entangled with burial practices as evidenced by the significant number of remains recovered from the rivers of the area (Hingley 2018). Furthermore, and perhaps more striking, are the bodies found in peat bogs in a number of places in northern Europe which have been interpreted in many different ways – sacrifices (perhaps due to physical differences), displays of community punishment, or high status captives that were executed (Giles 2009: 85). Nevertheless, all these motives involve sending an individual away into another world, out of sight. Similarly, in the Roman tradition, the practice of *poena post mortem* ('punishment after death') could sometimes involve the deposition of a person or effigy into water as part of a process of *damnatio memoriae* (Varner 2001: 59). In both these traditions, there was an idea that the power of water could dispose or consume individuals, perhaps removing them and their deeds from the historical record; throwing them into a portal and therefore into a different world. Interestingly, we are on the other side this portal, with a manipulation of time strikingly apparent in the 'unnatural' preservation of deposits like the bog bodies. Melanie Giles (2009: 90) and Christina Fredengren (2016) both remark that modern audiences are so fascinated with these bodies because they almost witness time folding, unveiling a person that could have died in the much more recent past. Perhaps contrary to the wishes of people in the past, the agency of water has revealed things that were meant to have been forgotten.

Hydraulic Communities of the Iron Age

There was also increasing structural interaction with waterscapes in the Iron Age (Bradley 1990). The site of La Tène is a prime example of this, with the majority of votive deposits discovered between two large timber bridge/platform features. They are not isolated instances, and similar features can be found at sites in Britain such as Fiskerton (Field and Parker-Pearson 2003); the Fen area of East Anglia also has precedent in the late Bronze Age, and at sites like Flag Fen such activity continues through to the Iron Age (Pryor 1992). Other interactions with waterscapes in this period such as pit-alignments and earthworks have left us with even more pronounced human evidence, but which can be highly ambiguous, while making significant communal entanglement with waterscapes. While both feature types may have signalled land organisation between communities, it was the agency of water that brokered these connections (Bryant 2007; Chadwick 2007; Rylatt and Bevan 2007).

In many ways, these developments represent increased complexity in the waterscapes of Britain by the Late Iron Age. They had become a mixture of 'human-made', 'natural', practical, symbolic, and ritual aspects that formed as an integral part of the life for local communities. Some of these structures mentioned above mirror the discussion of bridges by Martin Heidegger in 'Building Dwelling Thinking' (1971). He notes that the human construction of a bridge is a 'thing' which 'gathers to itself in its own way earth and sky, divinities and mortals' (Heidegger 1971: 153). The human-made bridge is a type of confluence, pulling together all elements of the 'fourfold' and creating deep entanglement and dependencies between these forces. In this sense, the bridge becomes more than just an aspect of human agency.

Prehistorians have been increasingly interested in how human engagement with water could have defined the identity of groups in the past, creating 'Hydraulic Communities' that were deeply bound to their waterscapes on many levels and rehearsed this connection through various communal endeavours (see Tilley 1994; Evans 1997; Bryant 2007; Rylatt and Bevan 2007). It is a point of view which contrasts sharply with the work of Roman archaeologists, who have been satisfied to suggest that increased engagement leads to humanisation and rationalisation, that would erode the special nature of a substance like water. In the work of prehistorians, there is a sense that greater human interaction with water led to an enhanced acknowledgement of its presence and importance, rather than dominance and marginalisation.

Case Study: Roman Lincoln – A Water Colony

The complex nature of water which emerges from the above discussion runs contrary to the pervading view of water infrastructure in Roman cities. Such developments have been interpreted through the prism of human domination. Work on Roman Britain has been particularly exposed to the disadvantages of such an approach. If one emphasises just human-made features, rather than water, then the evidence of infrastructure in Roman Britain is relatively inconsequential (see Stephens 1985: 203). Britain, unlike areas of France, Spain, Germany, and Italy, presents us with archaeology that is distinctly less grand; instead of aqueducts with the lofty arcades of the Pont du Gard, for example, the majority of British aqueducts were leat structures that ran at ground level (Burgers 2001). Therefore, discussions of this infrastructure are invariably distilled into somewhat colonial ideas of incompetent provincial engineers, or a lack of the necessary wealth to recreate the continental examples.

Many towns in Roman Britain appear to have been deeply entangled with watery settings and archaeologists are starting to acknowledge the complexity of this relationship (see Rogers 2013). However, there is still a tendency to over-emphasise the human side of these developments, whether that be through discussions of urban water infrastructure as 'artificial' (Rogers 2013: 129); or the continued emphasis of it being part of a generalised Roman 'identity package' that could be easily exported (Mattingly 2007: 280). As a result, it is worth spending time looking at a specific case study to understand how our views of water can greatly affect the way we interpret such spaces in the Roman period. However, the circumstances discussed below are not unique to the site of Lincoln. Richard Hingley (2018) has recently provided a synthesis of evidence at Roman London that bears significant comparison to what follows. Moreover, there is compelling evidence for a more complex relationship to water being proposed for the Roman towns at Canterbury, Chichester, Colchester, Dorchester, St. Albans, and Winchester (for a full discussion see Ingate 2019).

The first large-scale settlement at the site of modern Lincoln was established in the Roman period. Its name was Lindum Colonia. The term '*colonia*' acknowledges the status of the town and its population of Roman citizens. Lindum roughly translates as 'Dark Pool' and is almost certainly referencing the Brayford Pool (see Rivet and Smith 1979: 392–393). This is a large body of water directly adjacent to the settlement which formed at the confluence between the Rivers Till and Witham, at the heart of a more extensive waterlogged area. The name is particularly relevant for this volume as it neatly encapsulates the tension between human influence and a dynamic natural waterscape. With Lincoln, that human aspect has been the prime focus for archaeologists discussing the developments from the Roman period right through to modern times (see Wacher 1975). In such accounts, the Roman period represents a taming and harnessing of natural elements to the advantage of a new settlement through human technology and ingenuity. All aspects of the Roman urban water infrastructure have been explained in such terms, processing the water of this setting and humanising it. However, in line with the discussions above, it is questionable whether this was a reality of the Roman period.

The topography of Lincoln is particularly striking. The notable elevation of the site, where the original Roman

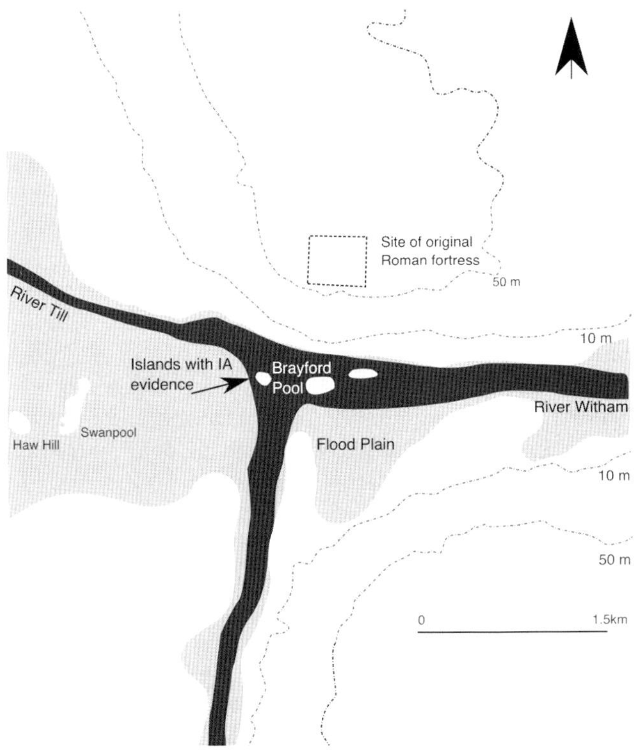

Figure 8.1: The landscape and waterscape of the Lincoln area (Drawn by author after Jones et al. 2003a).

Neronian era fortress was built, contrasts with the surrounding flat landscape (Fig. 8.1) (Rogers 2013: 69). This is a product of a glacial gap in the Limestone ridge that defines the geology of the area. The Witham runs through this gap and is part of a geographical bottleneck that lends itself to strategic and economic interpretations. These circumstances certainly made establishing a settlement problematic – the low-lying valley was prone to flooding, and the clay hillside was riddled with springs. However, in many ways, this combination of features meant the site was a nodal point in the wider waterscape.

It is important to highlight that this was a waterscape steeped in meaning throughout prehistory. On the Witham, there are prominent ritual causeway features at Fiskerton, Washingborough, Brigg, and Stamp End (Stocker and Everson 2003). These are all examples of the extraordinary reverence afforded to the local waterscape – the latter also being the location of remarkable metalwork deposits containing objects like the Witham Shield. Furthermore, there are numerous Bronze Age barrows that aligned with these causeway features, showing a long-lived, but developing, relationship to water in the extended landscape (May 1976; 1988; Stocker and Everson 2003: 280). Indeed, this water was so crucial to the people here it may well have defined them – the Corieltauvi has been interpreted as 'the land of the people of many rivers' (Tomlin 1983; Breeze 2002). Combine this with the fact that deposits at Fiskerton, and surrounding areas, continue into the Roman period and one must start to consider a more nuanced approach to the meaning of water in the settlement.

The principal evidence of Iron Age occupation at Lincoln has been located on sandy islands in the centre of the Brayford Pool (Jones *et al.* 2003a: 26). This consists of some roundhouse features that, considering their liminal location, have been interpreted as the centre of ritual activity. While this does not amount to a substantial human occupation of the landscape, the structures may indicate the broader importance of Lincoln's particular waterscape as a meeting place. These dwellings are paralleled by small-scale activity on the nearby hilltop (where the fortress was built) – with the possibility of a well feature that will be mentioned below. The marginalisation of this prehistoric landscape/waterscape narrative in the ensuing Roman period is entirely based on its lack of large-scale human engagement. However, as has been proposed for other sites like London (Rogers 2013; Hingley 2018; Ingate 2019), this is not an accurate way to assess the importance of this natural landscape to the local community and its ability to manipulate human activity in the long-term.

During the Roman period, a bridge (the Wigford Causeway) was built across the Brayford Pool and the sandy islands at its centre. The tradition mentioned above of ritual causeways in the immediate landscape would suggest that this was far more than just a practical structure for the town (even if it also had such advantages) and indeed could have been another aspect of the entanglement between the water and human occupation of this area. However, the most prominent discussion of this structure has been as a sign of domination/appropriation of this ritual site in the Brayford Pool by the colonising Roman force (Jones *et al.* 2003a: 97). As discussed briefly above, a view of bridges within a posthuman framework would suggest that they are not necessarily a feature solely aligned with human dominance. In many ways, the waters of the Brayford Pool would have been more accessible through the construction of the causeway; it would have allowed people to dwell above them, and also thoroughly incorporate them into the act of movement towards and away from Lincoln. There is an emerging consensus that much of the future work understanding the transition from an Iron Age settlement to a Roman town will come via a more in-depth study of the way this wet environment was treated (Jones *et al.* 2003a: 54; Rogers 2013). However, it is dangerous to rely on the dualisms of the past – whether that is Roman versus native or human versus natural.

Well Water on the High Ground

It is fair to say that the treatment of Roman water infrastructure at Lincoln has been almost entirely dependent on such traditional approaches. As mentioned above, the first Roman intervention in the landscape came in the form of the hilltop legionary fortress, in the Neronian period. As with all such military installations, the religious and administrative heart of the settlement would have been the *principia*. However, what is intriguing about this building in Lincoln is the incorporation of a well (now known as St. Paul's Well). This is not to say that it is unusual that a well would be located in such an area – Anne Johnson (1983: 106), for instance, notes other similar structures in *principia* courtyards. However, excavation in this area has found no proof that this well was a feature built at the same time as the surrounding fortress. It does not hold a symmetrical position within the *principia*, and thus is less likely to have been originally constructed in the Roman period (Jones *et al.* 2003b: 5.3). It was subsequently also incorporated into the Forum of the *colonia* and remained a prominent feature. It is an enigma that has been mostly ignored in the overall interpretation of the settlement.

It is perhaps not surprising that this well has had scarce analysis, considering its lack of eye-catching deposits. Of course, from the posthuman perspective we are exploring, the absence of such material is not problematic. This well already represents a deep entanglement between human activity and the natural context. However, the suggestion that this was an original Iron Age feature incorporated into the Roman period settlement warrants far more attention, especially considering the aforementioned local significance of water. If we acknowledge a broader importance of the well (outside of mere consumption), it would fit established patterns of sanctuaries on hilltops – like Nettleton on the Lincolnshire Wolds (Farley 2011). As with many sanctuaries in the prehistoric landscape, the Roman Forum would then have been built up around this focal point, and hence the monumental statues and structures increasingly framed the experience of drawing water (Steane *et al.* 2006: 187). The other known well of Roman Lincoln, the so-called 'Blind Well', was also located in the Upper City and has recently been considered in similar ideological terms (Steane *et al.* 2006: 187). While antiquarian excavations discovered this feature (Britton 1812: 600–601), it was purportedly a massive structure that could well have supplied the bathhouse.

However, moving away from just isolating the spatial impact of these features, there is also the question of quantifying the relationship between water on the hill and the Witham below. The hill that separates the Upper and Lower city at Lincoln has a steep incline which would have been 'riddled with springs' (Jones 2003: 111). Moreover, on this high ground one would have had some commanding views of the Trent Valley to the west and the Witham, plus potential sacred pools, to the south (Jones *et al.* 2003b: 5.4). The importance of such a visual link cannot be underplayed. The inclusion of the well on high ground gives us a sense of the centrality of Lincoln within a wider meaning-laden waterscape, rather than just a tactically secure location.

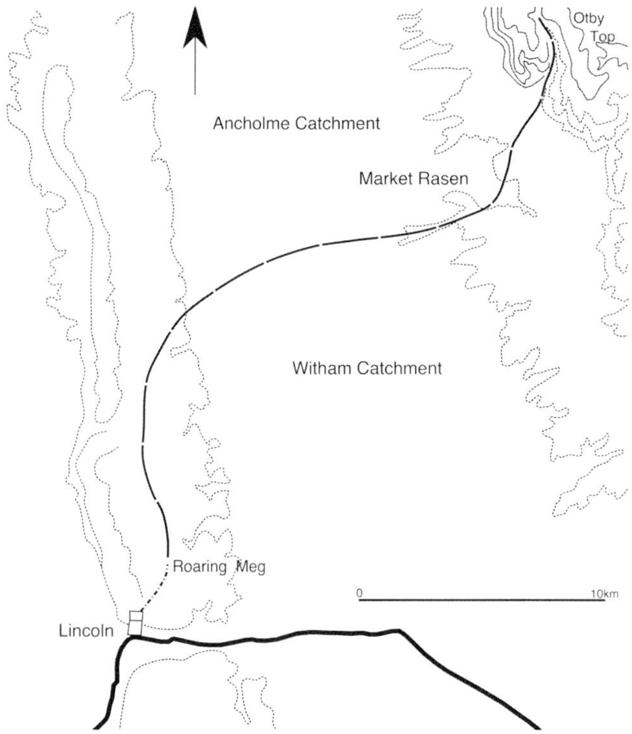

Figure 8.2: The possible course of Lincoln's Roman aqueduct (Drawn by author after Wacher 1975).

Piped Water Infrastructure

Lincoln's aqueduct has been a focus for many archaeologists investigating the town's development (see Thompson 1954; Wacher 1975; Lewis 1984; Hodge 1992). Accounts have invariably concentrated on the technicalities of engineering involved in supplying water to the Upper City of Lincoln. Interestingly, nearly all these writers have discussed the possibility that the aqueduct did not function; recent archaeological work, however, has shown this was not an issue (Williams 2006). Only recently have archaeologists begun to question whether assessing this structure in practical terms is limiting. Indeed, Michael Jones (2003) highlights how functionalist research into the purpose of the aqueduct has almost reached its practical end. Furthermore, as highlighted above, the Lincoln area was never really in need of extra water for consumption, its wells and numerous springs would surely have sufficed for this purpose.

Support for a non-practical reason for Lincoln's aqueduct is also found in the potential *nemeton* (sacred grove) at the Roaring Meg spring. The known trajectory of the aqueduct leads in this direction (Fig. 8.2). Furthermore, an inscription found in nearby Nettleham, north-east of the city, mentions the native god Mars Rigonemetos. This was part of a dedication on an arch at the entrance of a temple enclosure (Petch 1962). The inscription was found in a secondary location but has been interpreted as relating to activity at the spring site. That being said, it is by no means certain that the Roaring Meg spring was the source of the aqueduct; others have postulated sites as distant as Otby Top (Burgers 2001: 38), a prominent source of water in the second half of the twentieth century, north-east of Market Rasen. A third viable option for the aqueduct source, hitherto not suggested in the literature, is the next valley south of Otby Top. This is at the head of the River Rase, and it certainly has an appropriate elevation. Moreover, there is a Roman site here above a known spring source at Churn Water Heads (pers. comm. Steve Willis).

An aqueduct source at Otby Top or at the head of the River Rase would link the town to the dramatic natural potential of the Lincolnshire Wolds, which would have had a unique resonance in the local community. In particular, it is worth noting how areas such as Bain valley are known to be 'storm traps'. A 'cloudburst' recorded on 29th of May 1920 saw some 11 cm of rainfall in less than three hours, claiming twenty-three lives in Louth alone (Robinson 2009: 75). Interestingly, the drainage of these dramatic weather events would have been focused mostly towards the west (Smith 2009: 109). As such, the creation of an aqueduct would have been the only watercourse leading out of the Wolds towards the east and the settlement at Lincoln.

Roman Lincoln is also said to have possessed one of the best-developed sewer systems in Britain (Wacher 1975: 138). Part of this system was uncovered in the nineteenth century, primarily beneath the main north-south street of the Upper

City (Jones *et al.* 2003a: 61). In this area, the main conduit was large enough to be cleaned internally and was likely joined by numerous other drains from the east and west (Jones 2003: 117). Unfortunately, new excavations of these features are unlikely as there are many protected historic buildings from later periods in the area. Despite this, there have been traces of the drainage system located close to Steep Hill, meaning water would have drained into the Lower City and the Witham (Jones *et al.* 2003a: 61). This process meant that the aqueduct water, potentially derived from sacred sources in the urban periphery, would have joined the Brayford Pool, augmenting the message of the local waterscape.

Interestingly, there have been recent discussions about the potential of the aqueduct feeding water away from the town, perhaps to the sanctuary at Roaring Meg (Jones 2003; Jones *et al.* 2003b: 7.17). This would be a revelation that would be at odds with any 'consumer' models of water usage in Lincoln. However, it would certainly make sense in relation to the ideas of this chapter. The local meaning of Lincoln's water could have made such a project worthwhile. If true, it would be a prime example of how human interactions with water in this settlement were dictated by the beliefs surrounding the agency and power of water. That notwithstanding, without further evidence, it is hard to commit to such an interpretation fully.

Of course, one of the primary beneficiaries of any water infrastructure in this town would undoubtedly have been the public baths. They were situated in the north-east part of the Upper City, overlooking the Brayford Pool area. Despite the fact that the building has yet to be fully exposed, remains of several rooms with deep hypocausts and tessellated pavements seem to show this was a building of major significance (Jones *et al.* 2003a: 79). Indeed, these rooms covered an area of at least 60 metres by 45 metres and possessed clear evidence of extension after their initial construction. A major rebuilding or modification project looks to have taken place in the late Antonine period or soon after (Jones *et al.* 2003a: 80).

As mentioned previously, the Upper City of Lincoln had a multitude of water sources in the Roman period, and if the aqueduct did syphon water away from the town, it is possible these alternative sources supplied the bathhouse. With its potential beginnings as an Iron Age focal point and its later role as a central feature of the *principia* and forum, St. Paul's well is a highly significant feature. There could have been a connection between this well and the nearby bathhouse, potentially repackaging water rites taking place on the hilltop from prehistory. The massive 'Blind Well' was located within the same insula as the baths so its connection could have been even more important, despite our lack of surviving evidence (Abell and Chambers 1971: 19–20). There is also a potential that the bathhouse was a central place where all these waters from different sources were mixed; making it a microcosm of Lincoln's central positioning within the wider regional waterscape. As recent accounts have noted (Jones *et al.* 2003a: 7–22), such interpretations mean the Upper City could have been conceived of as a space more akin to a shrine than an administrative centre. Certainly, this is an interpretation that radically alters the purpose of the bathhouse itself, defining it through the agency of its water supply.

Thoughts on Lincoln and its Waterscape

Overall, Lincoln provides us with a powerful example of how our modern views on water can be transformative in the interpretation of key aspects of 'Roman' urban identity. If one interprets water as something with little agency, then the pervading interpretations of Roman Lincoln's water infrastructure create a compelling narrative of change that connects us to the modern day. Essentially, increasing structural influence subsumes the waterscape and redefines it to serve the town. It parallels a subscription to a uniform Roman identity, with archetypal infrastructure features like aqueducts appropriating any diversity of meaning.

Yet, when we consider the incoming traditions from Rome, alongside the known practices of prehistory in the Lincoln area, we should question whether such a dialogue is reliable. Human interactions with this waterscape changed throughout the course of the Bronze Age and Iron Age, but increased structural engagement did not negatively affect its importance and impact. While Roman period construction takes this activity to a new level, there is nothing to suggest that it would negate the pre-existing powerful associations of the water. If anything, the waterscape was more thoroughly a part of people's lives in the Roman period, with a greater sense of entanglement and dependency than had existed before.

For all of the obvious ways we can talk about water usage at sites like Roman Lincoln as the archetypal domination of human agency over natural context, we should dwell on the actual reality of that relationship. As mentioned above, Lincoln was a nodal point in a natural wider waterscape that formed as a product of glacial movements in deep history. At the height of the Roman colony, more water would have been accumulated in that place than at any time before. Moreover, the structures of the town made it easier than ever for water to coalesce and flow into the wider landscape. The human side of this equation was essentially an ever-deeper entrapment into the maintenance of this situation (Hodder 2012: 214). Aqueducts, bathhouses, and sewers would have all required regular upkeep, the avoidance of which would have created more problems for the settlement (Hodder 2012: 214). We should also not forget that this was more than just a matter of practical upkeep; it was a relationship based on religious belief. Accordingly, the humans in this landscape were entrapped spiritually and would suffer deeper consequences if they ignored their commitment.

Ian Hodder (2012: 209) highlights that the greater the entanglement, the greater the dependencies involved, and the stronger the likelihood of the framework falling apart. This is a particularly apt observation when applied to water infrastructure. As illustrated earlier, with the example of the Yellow River, there is a sense of entropy with water management that requires ever greater effort to maintain. If we think about the discrepant temporalities (Hodder 2012: 209) between water and human lives, then the primacy of water's agency is inevitable.

This feeling of inevitability should be particularly germane to the modern reader, with the increasing regularity we are witnessing flood and drought events as a part of the process of climate change. Yet, this also highlights the stark differences between modern and Roman views on water. There was a knowing interest in creating an ever-greater entanglement with water at Lincoln, because careful negotiation with this powerful and independent agency was a foundational aspect of local and incoming beliefs. Part of this entanglement was the practical necessity of water, but this served to further enhance the ideological potency of creating deeper connections between the town and its waterscape. It was a multifaceted relationship that cannot be satisfactorily encompassed in terms of humans exploiting a natural resource.

Indeed, the result of this active engagement with water was that when there was a breakdown of this system of dependency, a different framework was created. The Christianisation of the forum well (St. Pauls Well) and the establishment of Lincoln cathedral in the Upper City is a case in point. The agency of water was so prominent that it had to be accommodated in a new way to secure the prosperity of the community; the alacrity with which the Late Antique Ostrogoth rulers of Italy pursued revitalisation of water structures (see Marano 2015) shows that this was a widespread issue. Compare this to today, with our intransigence to change the status quo in the face of climate change, and we see the relevance of such historical enquiry. As David Sedlack (2015) previously remarked, one of the greatest challenges in creating a serviceable future relationship to water, is actually making people care.

Conclusion

Ultimately this chapter can only begin to question the logical framework upon which we interpret water. One of the critical results from taking a more complex view of the entanglement between humans and their waterscapes is that we can introduce a more thorough sense of local variability into the interpretation of urban space. If different types of water had an individual agency that was acknowledged by the communities of the past, no one aqueduct, well, or bathhouse can be accurately interpreted through generalisation. This is a perspective that is far more in-line with recent theoretical developments in Roman archaeology, which have emphasised discrepant experiences and variability in globalised similarities (see Hingley 2005; Mattingly 2007).

Hitherto, Roman archaeologists have been guilty of promoting a clear sense of dualism in discussing water, which mirrors our supposed twentieth and twenty-first century human dominance of nature. Yet, in the examples of this chapter, we can see that the Roman period evidence presents considerably more complexity. Instead of alienating us from the past, this difference could be a vital way that archaeologists can promote the wider relevance of such studies. In a straightforward sense, acknowledging change in the past, rather than continuity, communicates the likelihood that future developments will also be different from our current situation.

Instead of using evidence from Antiquity to bolster outdated attitudes, the 'strange' Roman municipal water presented in this chapter could help us engage with an even stranger future of urbanism. Clear ideas of what constitutes natural or human only serve to distance us from the realities of the environmental challenges we are beginning to face, and potential solutions we can put into action; the controversy around issues of 'Geoengineering' (Morton 2016) or 'Rewilding' (Monbiot 2014) are evidence of how we need to modify our current views. In some areas of the world discussions are already taking place on how a legal definition of water agency can protect the natural world; in New Zealand, for example, the Whanganui River was recently given the same legal rights as a human being on the basis of its cultural value to the Maori people (Warne 2019). It is a development which shows that sustainable future relationships to nature may require overt acknowledgement of non-human agency. The unique physical properties and variable local associations of people in the Roman period meant that water was a powerful and space-defining element of everyday life. Due to the necessity of its presence and the strength of these beliefs associated with it, the incorporation of water into various parts of the urban fabric was likely transformative. Accordingly, the non-human world was not a marginalised and subservient aspect of the Roman city, it was a partner with which humans constantly negotiated. Appreciating that aspect of dependency to the agency of water and the entanglement it created is more relevant than ever in the face of our current climate crisis.

School of Humanities,
Canterbury Christ Church University

Bibliography

Ancient Sources

Arrian (Translated by A. Liddle). 2003. *The Periplus of the Euxine Sea*. London: Bristol Classical Press.

Frontinus (Translated by M.B. McElwain). 1925. *On the Aqueducts of Rome*. London: Heinemann.
Ovid (Translated by G. Showerman). 1931. *Heroides and Amores*. London: Heinemann.
Pliny the Elder (Translated by H. Rackham). 1942. *Natural History*. London: Heinemann.
Pliny the Younger (Translated by B. Radice). 1969. *Letters and Panegyricus*. London: Heinemann.
Plutarch (Translated by B. Perrin). 1914. *Life of Romulus*. London: Heinemann.
Plutarch (Translated by B. Perrin). 1916. *Life of Coriolanus*. London: Heinemann.
Seneca (Translated by J. Clarke). 1910. *Natural Questions*. London: MacMillan.
Servius (Edited by G. Thilo and H. Hagen). 1961. *Commentary on Virgil*. Hildesheim: Georg Olms.
Virgil (Translated by D. West). 2003 *The Aeneid*. London: Penguin.
Vitruvius (Translated by F. Granger). 1931. *On Architecture*. London: Heinemann.

Modern Sources

Abell, E. and Chambers, J. 1971. *The Story of Lincoln*. 2nd edition. Wakefield: S.R. Publishers.
Ackroyd, P. 2008. *Thames: Sacred River*. London: Vintage.
Aldhouse-Green, M.J. 1986. *The Gods of the Celts*. Gloucester: A. Sutton.
Aldrete, G.S. 2007. *Floods of the Tiber in Ancient Rome*. Baltimore: Johns Hopkins University Press.
Ball, P. 2016. *The Water Kingdom: A Secret History of China*. Chicago: University of Chicago Press.
Behm-Blanke, G., Jacob, H. and Sušek, S. 2003. *Heiligtümer der Germanen und ihrer Vorgänger in Thüringen: die Kultstätte Oberdorla*. Stuttgart: Theiss.
Blackbourn, D. 2007. *The Conquest of Nature: Water, Landscape and the Making of Modern Germany*. New York: Norton.
Bradley, R. 1990. *The Passage of Arms: An Archaeological Analysis of Prehistoric Hoards and Votive Deposits*. Cambridge: Cambridge University Press.
Bradley, R. 2016. *A Geography of Offerings: Deposits of Valuables in the Landscapes of Ancient Europe*. Oxford: Oxbow Books.
Braund, D. 1996. *Ruling Roman Britain: Kings, Queens, Governors and Emperors from Julius Caesar to Agricola*. London: Routledge.
Breeze, A. 2002. Does Corieltavi mean 'army of many rivers'? *The Antiquaries Journal* 82: 307–309.
Britton, J. 1812. *The Beauties of England: Lincolnshire*. London: Thomas Maiden.
Bruun, C. 2012. Roman emperors and legislation on public water use in the Roman Empire: clarifications and problems. *Water History* 4 (1): 11–35.
Bryant, S. 2007. Central places or special places? The origins and development of 'oppida' in Hertfordshire. In C. Haselgrove and T. Moore (eds) *The Later Iron Age in Britain and Beyond*. Oxford: Oxbow Books: 62–81.
Burgers, A. 2001. *The Water Supplies and Related Structures of Roman Britain*. Oxford: J. and E. Hedges.
Campbell, B. 2012. *Rivers and the Power of Ancient Rome*. Chapel Hill: University of North Carolina Press.
Chadwick, A.M. 2007. Trackways, hooves and memory-days: human and animal movements and memories around the Iron Age and Romano-British rural landscapes of the English north midlands. In V. Cummings and R. Johnston (eds) *Prehistoric Journeys*. Oxford: Oxbow Books: 131–152.
Coarelli, F. 1986. *Il Foro Romano: Periodo Arcaico*. Roma: Edizione Quasar.
Coles, J. 2001. North European bronzes, rock art and wetlands: looking for context and relations. A preliminary study. In B. Purdy (ed.) *Enduring Records: The Environmental and Cultural Heritage of Wetlands*. Oxford: Oxbow Books: 148–157.
DeLaine, J. 1996. De aquis suis?: the commentarius of Frontinus. In C. Nicolet (ed.) *Les littératures techniques dans l'Antiquité romaine: statut, public et destination, tradition: sept exposés suivis de discussions, Vandoeuvres-Genève, 21–25 août 1995*. Genève: Fondation Hardt: 117–145.
Edgeworth, M. 2011. *Fluid Pasts: Archaeology of Flow*. London: Bristol Classical Press.
Erdkamp, P., Verboven, K. and Zuiderhoek, A. 2015. *Ownership and Exploitation of Land and Natural Resources in the Roman World*. Oxford: Oxford University Press.
Evans, C. 1997. Hydraulic communities: Iron Age enclosure in the East Anglian Fenlands. In A. Gwilt and C. Haselgrove (eds) *Reconstructing Iron Age Societies: New Approaches to the British Iron Age*. Oxford: Oxbow Books: 216–227.
Farley, J. 2011. The deposition of miniature weaponry in Iron Age Lincolnshire. *Pallas* 86: 97–121.
Field, N. and Parker-Pearson, M. 2003. *Fiskerton: An Iron Age Timber Causeway with Iron Age and Roman Votive Offerings – the 1981 Excavations*. Oxford: Oxbow Books.
Fitzpatrick, A.P. 1984. The deposition of La Tène Iron Age metalwork in watery contexts in Southern England. In B. Cunliffe and D. Miles (eds) *Aspects of the Iron Age in Central Southern Britain*. Oxford: Oxford University Committee for Archaeology, Institute of Archaeology: 178–190.
Foster, M.D. 2015. *The Book of Yōkai: Mysterious Creatures of Japanese Folklore*. Oakland: University of California Press.
Fredengren, C. 2016. Unexpected encounters with deep time enchantment. Bog bodies, crannogs and 'otherworldly' sites. The materializing powers of disjunctures in time. *World Archaeology* 48 (4): 482–499.
Giles, M. 2009. Iron Age bog bodies of north-western Europe. Representing the dead. *Archaeological Dialogues* 16 (1): 75–101.
Goodyear, F.R. 1983. Technical writing. In E.J. Kenney and W. Clausen (eds) *The Cambridge History of Classical Literature, Vol. II: Latin Literature*. Cambridge: Cambridge University Press: 639–666.
Hankin, M.E. 1896. The bactericidal action of the waters of the Jamuna and Ganges rivers on Cholera microbes. *Annales de l'Institut Pasteur* 10: 511–523.
Head, L., Atchison, J. and Gates, A. 2012. *Ingrained: A Human Bio-Geography of Wheat*. London/New York: Routledge.
Heidegger, M. 1971. Building dwelling thinking. In M. Heidegger (ed.) *Poetry, Language, Thought*. New York: Harper Collins: 141–161.
Hingley, R. 1990. Iron Age 'currency bars': the archaeological and social context. *Archaeological Journal* 147 (1): 91–117.
Hingley, R. 2005. *Globalizing Roman Culture: Unity, Diversity and Empire*. London: Routledge.

Hingley, R. 2006. The deposition of iron objects in Britain during the Later Prehistoric and Roman periods: contextual analysis and the significance of iron. *Britannia* 37: 213–257.

Hingley, R. 2018. *Londinium: A Biography*. London: Bloomsbury.

Hodder, I. 2012. *Entangled: An Archaeology of the Relationship between Humans and Things*. Chichester: Wiley-Blackwell.

Hodge, T. 1992. *Roman Aqueducts and Water Supply*. London: Duckworth.

Holland, L.A. 1961. *Janus and the Bridge*. Rome: American Academy in Rome.

Hopkins, J. 2007. The Cloaca Maxima and the monumental manipulation of water in Archaic Rome. *The Waters of Rome* 4: 1–15.

Hopkins, J. 2012. The sacred sewer: tradition and religion in the Cloaca Maxima. In M. Bradley (ed.) *Rome, Pollution and Propriety: Dirt, Disease and Hygiene in the Eternal City from Antiquity to Modernity*. Cambridge: Cambridge University Press: 48–74.

Ingate, J. 2019. *Water and Urbanism in Roman Britain: Hybridity and Identity*. London/New York: Routledge.

Ingold, T. 2013. *Making: Anthropology, Archaeology, Art and Architecture*. London/New York: Routledge.

Johnson, A. 1983. *Roman Forts of the 1st and 2nd centuries AD in Britain and the German Provinces*. London: Adam and Charles Black.

Jones, M.J. 2003. Sources of effluence: water through Roman Lincoln. In J. Wacher and P.R. Wilson (eds) *The Archaeology of Roman Towns: Studies in Honour of John S. Wacher*. Oxford: Oxbow Books: 111–128.

Jones, M.J., Stocker, D. and Vince, A.G. 2003a. *The City by the Pool: Assessing the Archaeology of the City of Lincoln*. Oxford: Oxbow Books.

Jones, M.J., Stocker, D., Vince, A.G., Powlesland, D. and Herridge J. 2003b. *Lincoln Archaeological Research Assessment: Research Agenda Zones, GIS and Interactive Database*. http://www.heritageconnectlincoln.com/ [Last Accessed 30/12/2018].

Kaika, M. 2005. *City of Flows: Modernity, Nature, and the City*. New York: Routledge.

Kaika, M. and Swyngedouw, E. 2000. Fetishizing the modern city: the phantasmagoria of urban technological networks. *IJUR International Journal of Urban and Regional Research* 24 (1): 120–138.

de Kleijn, G. 2001. *The Water Supply of Ancient Rome: City Area, Water, and Population*. Amsterdam: Gieben.

Krause, F. and Strang, V. 2016. Thinking relationships through water. *Society and Natural Resources* 29 (6): 633–638.

Larsson, L. 2001. South Scandinavian wetland sites and finds from the Mesolithic and the Neolithic. In B. Purdy (ed.) *Enduring Records: The Environmental and Cultural Heritage of Wetlands*. Oxford: Oxbow Books: 158–171.

Lewis, M.J.T. 1984. Our debt to Roman engineering: the water supply of Lincoln to the present day. *Industrial Archaeology Review* 7 (1): 57–73.

Malmberg, S. 2015. Ships are seen gliding swiftly along the sacred Tiber: the river as an artery of urban movement and development. In I. Östenberg, S. Malmberg and J. Bjørnebye (eds) *The Moving City: Processions, Passages and Promenades in Ancient Rome*. London: Bloomsbury: 187–202.

Marano, Y.A. 2015. 'Watered...with the life-giving wave': aqueducts and water management in Ostrogothic Italy. In P. Erdkamp, K. Verboven and A. Zuiderhoek (eds) *Ownership and Exploitation of Land and Natural Resources in the Roman World*. Oxford: Oxford University Press: 150–169.

Mattingly, D.J. 2007. *An Imperial Possession: Britain in the Roman Empire, 54 BC–AD 409*. London/New York: Penguin.

May, J. 1976. *Prehistoric Lincolnshire*. Lincoln: History of Lincolnshire Committee.

May, J. 1988. Iron Age Lincoln? The topographical and settlement evidence reviewed. *Britannia* 19: 50–57.

Miller, D. 1987. *Material Culture and Mass Consumption*. Oxford/New York: Blackwell.

Monbiot, G. 2014. *Feral: Rewilding the Land, the Sea, and Human Life*. Chicago: University of Chicago Press.

Morton, O. 2016. *The Planet Remade: How Geoengineering Could Change the World*. Princeton: Princeton University Press.

Mount, F. 2010. *Full Circle: How the Classical World Came Back to Us*. London: Simon and Schuster.

Myers, S. 2011. *Walking on Water: London's Hidden Rivers Revealed*. Stroud: Amberley.

Petch, D. 1962. A Roman inscription, Nettleham. *Lincolnshire Architecture and Archaeological Society Reports* 9 (2): 94–97.

Pryor, F. 1992. Discussion: the Fengate/Northey landscape. *Antiquity* 66 (251): 518–531.

Purcell, N. 1990. The creation of a provincial landscape: the Roman impact on Cisalpine Gaul. In T.F.C. Blagg and M. Millett (eds) *The Early Roman Empire in the West*. Oxford: Oxbow Books: 7–29.

Rivet, A.L.F. and Smith, C. 1979. *The Place-Names of Roman Britain*. Princeton: Princeton University Press.

Robinson, D.N. 2009. Storms of the Wolds. In D.N. Robinson (ed.) *The Lincolnshire Wolds*. Oxford: Windgather Press: 75–76.

Rogers, A. 2013. *Water and Roman Urbanism: Towns, Waterscapes, Land Transformation and Experience in Roman Britain*. Leiden: Brill.

Rylatt, J. and Bevan, B. 2007. Realigning the world: pit alignments and their landscape context. In C. Haselgrove and T. Moore (eds) *The Later Iron Age in Britain and Beyond*. Oxford: Oxbow Books: 219–234.

Scarpino, P.V. 1997. *Large Floodplain Rivers as Human Artifacts: A Historical Perspective on Ecological Integrity*. Ft. Belvoir: Defense Technical Information Centre.

Sedlak, D. 2015. *Water 4.0: The Past, Present, and Future of the World's Most Vital Resource*. New Haven: Yale University Press.

Smith, T. 2009. Restoring biodiversity. In D.N. Robinson (ed.) *The Lincolnshire Wolds*. Oxford: Windgather Press: 103–114.

Steane, K., Darling, M.J., Jones, M.J., Mann, J., Vince, A. and Young, J. 2006. *The Archaeology of the Upper City and Adjacent Suburbs*. Oxford: Oxbow Books.

Stephens, G.R. 1985. Civic aqueducts in Britain. *Britannia* 16: 197–208.

Stjernquist, B., Nilsson, T. and Møhl, U. 1997. *The Röekillorna Spring: Spring-Cults in Scandinavian Prehistory*. Stockholm: Almqvist and Wiksell International.

Stocker, D. and Everson, P. 2003. The straight and narrow way. Fenland causeways and the conversion of the landscape in the

Witham Valley, Lincolnshire. In M. Carver (ed.) *The Cross Goes North. Processes of Conversion in Northern Europe, AD 300 – 1300*. York: York Medieval Press: 271–288.

Thompson, F.H. 1954. The Roman aqueduct at Lincoln. *Archaeological Journal* 111 (1): 106–127.

Tilley, C. 1994. *A Phenomenology of Landscape: Places, Paths, and Monuments*. Oxford: Berg.

Tomlin, R.S.O. 1983. Non coritani sed corieltauvi. *The Antiquaries Journal* 63 (2): 353–355.

Van der Veen, M. 2014. The materiality of plants: plant-people entanglements. *World Archaeology* 46 (5): 799–812.

Varner, E. 2001. Punishment after death: mutilation of images and corpse abuse in ancient Rome. *Mortality* 6 (1): 45–64.

Wacher, J. 1975. *The Towns of Roman Britain*. London: Batsford.

Warne, K. 2019. A voice for nature. *National Geographic*. https://www.nationalgeographic.com/culture/2019/04/maori-river-in-new-zealand-is-a-legal-person [Last Accessed 10/05/2019].

Webster, J. 1995. Sanctuaries and sacred places. In M.J. Green (ed.) *The Celtic World*. London/New York: Routledge: 445–465.

Wildfang, R.L. 2006. *Rome's Vestal Virgins: A Study of Rome's Vestal Priestesses in the Late Republic and Early Empire*. London/New York: Routledge.

Williams, S. 2006. *93 Nettleham Road, Lincoln: Archaeological Investigation Report*. Lincoln: Pre-Construct Archaeology.

Willis, S. 1999. Without and within: aspects of culture and community in the Iron Age of North-Eastern England. In B. Bevan (ed.) *Northern Exposure: Interpretative Devolution and the Iron Ages in Britain*. Leicester: Leicester University Press: 81–110.

Willis, S. 2007. Sea, coast, estuary, land, and culture in Iron Age Britain. In C. Haselgrove and T. Moore (eds) *The Later Iron Age in Britain and Beyond*. Oxford: Oxbow Books, 107–130.

Wilson, A. 1999. Deliveries *extra urbem*: aqueducts and the countryside. *Journal of Roman Archaeology* 12: 314–331.

Wilson, A. 2012. Water, power and culture in the Roman and Byzantine worlds: an introduction. *Water History* 4: 1–9.

Wissowa, G. 1912. *Religion und Kultus der Römer*. Munchen: Beck.

Yates, D. and Bradley, R. 2010. Still water, hidden depths: the deposition of Bronze Age metalwork in the English Fenland, *Antiquity* 84: 405–415.

9

The Romans and the Anthropocene: Posthuman Provocations

Irene Selsvold and Lewis Webb[1]

The Anthropocene, Posthumanism, and the Romans

Human activities have developed into significant climatic and geological forces. The atmospheric chemist Paul Crutzen and ecologist Eugene Stoermer famously assigned the term 'Anthropocene' to the current geological period (formally known as the 'Holocene' epoch) due to increases in the following anthropogenic (human-caused) processes: chemical use, agriculture, animal husbandry, terraforming, deforestation, and fossil fuel burning (Crutzen and Stoermer 2000). All of these processes have greatly impacted the Earth's climate and geology on a global scale. While being open to other period assignments for the Anthropocene, these researchers defined the onset of this period as the latter part of the eighteenth century, which coincides with the Industrial Revolution and the invention of the steam engine in 1784 (Crutzen and Stoermer 2000: 17–18; Crutzen 2002; *cf.* Zalasiewicz *et al.* 2014: 3). The aim of assigning the term Anthropocene to this geological period was, according to Crutzen, to develop an Anthropocene ethic and 'a world-wide accepted strategy leading to sustainability of ecosystems' (Crutzen 2006: 17). To do so, he argues, requires 'intensive research efforts and wise application of the knowledge thus acquired' (Crutzen 2006: 17). The Anthropocene is one of the most prominent recent scholarly concepts that acknowledge the scale of anthropogenic impact on the Earth, alongside other concepts including the Capitalocene and Plantationocene (on which see, *e.g.* Haraway 2015; Moore 2016; but *cf.* absence of Anthropocene and its environmental and geological impact in a recent announcement of the Meghalayan age in Walker *et al.* 2018, noting critique of this announcement in Middleton 2018).

Scholars within the social sciences and humanities have taken up Crutzen's call for critical engagement with the causes and effects of the age of the Anthropocene and the realities of global environmental change, as well as with their ethical implications. Moreover, several of these scholars envision the Anthropocene discourse as a way to further disrupt the nature/culture dichotomy and interpret the human as but one (influential) actor in a network of geological, cultural, technological, and organic agents that together form the global condition (Braidotti 2013; 2016; Pálsson *et al.* 2013: 7–9; Ferrando 2016; Moore 2016; Ulmer 2017).

It may seem counterintuitive to focus on the Anthropocene in a volume on posthumanism and Roman archaeology. After all, posthumanism seeks to de-centre the human, while the Anthropocene centres the human. However, posthumanism has emerged as a major theoretical and ethical response to the Anthropocene (see Webb and Selsvold in this volume for a comprehensive definition of posthumanism). Indeed, Francesca Ferrando (2016) argues that the Anthropocene has emerged as a consequence of our anthropocentric *Weltanschauung* (worldview) and she envisions posthumanism as a necessary post-anthropocentric response to the causes and symptoms of the Anthropocene: '[…] the survival of the human species is related to the well-being of their environment, and that existence evolves in relational, symbiotic, entangled intra-acting processes. Post-humanism must happen now' (Ferrando 2016: 170–171; *cf.* Braidotti 2013: 5–6; 2016: 23; Ulmer 2017: 835). The Anthropocene provokes and even demands a posthuman worldview.

While the Anthropocene and its study centre *human* environmental impacts, they also encourage us to recognise the long-term consequences of anthropocentric exceptionalism, to consider the entanglement of human beings in networks of other beings, things, and environments (*cf.* Latour 2005; Hodder 2012), and to develop a post-anthropocentric worldview (Haraway 2015; Braidotti 2016; Ferrando 2016). Rosi Braidotti's 'critical posthumanism' (posthuman critical theory) offers a productive, post-anthropocentric perspective on these matters (Braidotti 2013; 2016; *cf.* Ferrando 2016). Her critical posthumanism is characterised by a relational ontology in which there is an 'enlarged sense of inter-connection between self and others, including the non-human or "earth" others' (Braidotti 2013: 50). In such a relational ontology, 'the relational capacity of the post-anthropocentric subject is not confined within our species, but it includes non-anthropomorphic elements'; this relational capacity 'cuts across and reconnects previously segregated species, categories, and domains' (Braidotti 2016: 22). Beyond a relational ontology, her critical posthumanism is driven by a relational ethic 'that values cross-species, transversal alliances with the productive and immanent force of [...] nonhuman life' and that 'requires a mutation of our shared understanding of what it means to be human' (Braidotti 2016: 23). This relational ontology and ethic provide Roman archaeologists with the critical apparatus to face the age of the Anthropocene and its implications.

Previous studies have explored the environmental impact of the Romans (*e.g.* Hughes 1996; 2003; 2014; Thommen 2012; Erdkamp *et al.* 2015 with bibliographies). In this chapter, we build on these prior studies and focus on the intersections among the Anthropocene, the Romans, and posthumanism. In particular, we investigate anthropogenic processes in the Roman period (primarily the Republic and Empire with examples from the early third century BC through to the late fourth century AD) in order to situate the Romans within the Anthropocene and to demonstrate the need for posthuman perspectives in Roman archaeology. We do not intend to re-date the onset of the Anthropocene to the Roman period, as various archaeological studies suggest that anthropogenic processes dating to millennia before the Roman period have contributed to the rise of the Anthropocene (*e.g.* Ruddiman 2003; 2007; Ruddiman *et al.* 2008; Ruddiman and Ellis 2009; Braje and Erlandson 2013a; Erlandson and Braje 2013; Smith and Zeder 2013; Butzer 2015: 1540). Rather, we suggest that the quantity and quality of surviving Roman archaeological and textual sources provide valuable insight into the development of the Anthropocene during the Roman period. Moreover, the Anthropocene provides a conceptually useful global and diachronic framework with which to synthesise these various sources and critically assess the environmental impact of the Romans.

By illuminating the extent of anthropogenic impacts on other beings and the environment in the Roman period, we aim to include the Romans in the rapidly growing Anthropocene discourse, to offer some insight into our present environmental concerns and conditions, and to encourage posthuman perspectives in the study of Roman archaeology. We begin with a discussion on the Anthropocene and anthropogenic impact as it relates to archaeology, then we turn to Roman conceptualisations and perceptions of nature, before we investigate anthropogenic processes in the Roman period in three case studies: Roman mining, exploitation of (non-human) animal populations, and agricultural expansion. We close with a discussion of the environmental impact of the Romans, the relationships between the age of the Anthropocene and the Romans, and the posthuman provocations of our findings.

The Anthropocene, Anthropogenic Impact, and Archaeology

Anthropogenic processes and their impact on the climate are at the heart of many Anthropocene enquiries, perhaps due to the popularisation of the term by climate scientists. Consequently, anthropogenic climate change has been the dominant identifier for the Anthropocene and has shaped the debate surrounding its onset. As we have seen, Crutzen and Stoermer (2000: 17–18) defined its onset as latter part of the eighteenth century. Scientists from other disciplines have argued for earlier and later dates based on evidence from their own disciplines. Some have argued for an even later onset after WWII (the 'Great Acceleration'), based on the great increase in human population and resultant carbon dioxide emissions, intensification of agriculture, globalisation, and other anthropogenic transformations of the environment since the war (Steffen *et al.* 2007; Graves-Brown 2014: 80; Zalasiewicz *et al.* 2015; Braje 2016: 505–506). Archaeologists have argued for far earlier onsets of the Anthropocene (Butzer 2015), pointing towards the extinction of terrestrial megafauna 50000 years ago (Braje and Erlandson 2013a), as well as the initial domestication of plants and animals, development of agricultural landscapes, and agricultural economies (Ruddiman 2003; 2007; Ruddiman *et al.* 2008; Ruddiman and Ellis 2009; Erlandson and Braje 2013; Smith and Zeder 2013). The appearance and continued growth of urbanism has been emphasised as another defining factor (Zalasiewicz *et al.* 2011: 836; Braje and Erlandson 2013b: 118; Butzer 2015: 1540). Simultaneously, archaeologists are concerned with the current environmental impact of plastic and garbage (*e.g.* Pétursdóttir 2017) and the role and fate of material heritage in the Anthropocene (Solli *et al.* 2011). While the debate surrounding the onset of the Anthropocene is nowhere near concluded, we as archaeologists are in a key position to contribute to the understanding of how the Anthropocene came into being, and its development and symptoms over time (*cf.* Pétursdóttir 2017: 178–183).

As seen above, an influx of archaeological enquiries into anthropogenic processes and their impact in the past have demonstrated that the current human domination of the Earth is the result of a long line of anthropogenic processes that span millennia. Karl Butzer argues that limiting the onset of the Anthropocene to the Industrial Revolution or thereafter would exclude millennia of anthropogenic activity and 'ignore regional and environmental outcomes' (Butzer 2015: 1540). One way of broadening our understanding of the Anthropocene, he argues, is precisely to include archaeology more intimately in Anthropocene enquiries (Butzer 2015: 1540).

The Anthropocene can be studied archaeologically by tracing anthropogenic impacts on ecosystems. Ecosystems consist of biotic organisms, such as plant and animal communities (humans included), and abiotic environments. Ecosystems are therefore assemblages bound together in sets of relationships. Due to these relationships, change in one element of an ecosystem will cause change to other elements. All ecosystems are subject to internal and external stress and the balance and survival of an ecosystem are dependent on its resilience and resistance to stress (Redman 1999: 36–39). Ecosystems often adapt when subjected to such stress, but they may not always be able to maintain an adequate balance themselves (Redman 1999: 48). Relevant to this study are anthropogenic imbalances in ecosystems, as human activities can be a major stressor. Charles Redman (Redman 1999) has studied the anthropogenic impact on ancient environments through case studies of animal exploitation, agrarian systems, and urbanism. Moreover, Butzer (2015) argues that the Anthropocene should be studied through early urban settlements and mining. Our selection of the case studies of mining, animal exploitation, and agricultural expansion is informed by Butzer's and Redman's challenges and perspectives.

Roman Conceptualisations and Perceptions of Nature

Roman conceptualisations and perceptions of nature offer some useful contemporary perspectives on anthropogenic processes and impacts, as well as on our case studies. There was no single, coherent, all-encompassing Roman attitude towards nature and its myriad aspects (environment and beings). Throughout the Republic and Empire, Romans attempted to conquer, control, cultivate, and exploit different aspects of nature, distrusting and even fearing uncontrolled nature (see, *e.g.* Purcell 1987; Beagon 1996: 286; Campbell 2012: 369–388; Thommen 2012: 76–78; Hughes 2014: 43–67; Shelton 2014; Erdkamp *et al.* 2015; Hutchins 2017; Östenberg 2018). At the same time, some Romans venerated nature, were aware of the human impact on nature, and even advocated human responsibility towards nature (Beagon 1996; Hutchins 2017). Two prominent Roman authors, Lucretius and Pliny the Elder, articulate these multivalent attitudes well and presage contemporary Anthropocene and posthuman ethical debates, albeit from Epicurean and Stoic perspectives respectively (on Greek and Roman philosophical concepts and Roman attitudes towards human impact on nature see, *e.g.* Thommen 2012: 76–78; Hughes 2014: 43–67, esp. 63–65).

For both Lucretius and Pliny, nature is *terra mater*, Mother Earth, a numinous parent and provider for living beings (*e.g.* Lucr. 2.993, 998, 5.795–6, 821–2; Plin. *HN* 2.154–9, 208). Lucretius recounts a kind of reciprocal gift-giving between early humans and *terra mater* (Lucr. 5.937–8, 970–1), describing an animal contract whereby some animals (namely dogs, burden-bearing animals, livestock, and oxen) were entrusted into human guardianship and for human use by *terra mater*, and claims that humans provided these animals with peace and plentiful fodder in exchange for their usefulness (Lucr. 5.855–77 with Hutchins 2017). He also criticises human abuse and destructive impact on animals – the use of animals in war and interspecies violence – and details how such discord produces animal revolts and a breakdown of the animal contract (Lucr. 5.1297–1349 with Hutchins 2017). In these and other ways, Lucretius advocates human responsibility for the protection and existence of other animals, precisely because of the power imbalance between us (Hutchins 2017; esp. 97, 108). For Pliny, nature is life itself, a divine power diffused throughout everything, a kind of distributed agency (Plin. *HN praef.*13; 2.208), and, as *mater* and *ancilla*, nature provides and gifts humans with everything they need (Plin. *HN* 2.154–9). While praising some human use and control of nature (*e.g.* Plin. *HN* 3.54, 5.71, 17.58, 17.96, 35.116, 36.101), Pliny criticises the impact of warfare on the landscape and humans (Plin. *HN* 6.182, 7.5, 34.138) and lambasts humans for their avarice (*avaritia*) for minerals (*e.g.* gold, silver, electrum, copper, pigments) and their mineral exploitation of nature (Plin. *HN* 33.1–3, esp. 3 with Beagon 1996). In a remarkably prescient passage, Pliny claims these minerals destroy (*perimere*) humans, and he ponders what the limit (*finis*) in all the ages (*omnia saecula*) of exhausting (*exhaurire*) nature will be (Plin. *HN* 33.3). Moreover, he wishes for a world where humans coveted (*concupiscere*) nothing but what is above ground (*supra terras*), and, indeed, nothing not at hand (*secum*, Plin. *HN* 33.3).

While not representative of Roman attitudes in general, Lucretius and Pliny demonstrate an acute awareness of negative human impacts on other beings and on nature, and both advocate a human responsibility toward nature. In this way, these authors presage contemporary Anthropocene and posthuman debates on, *inter alia*, animal ethics, exploitation of nature, and sustainability. For present purposes, Lucretius and Pliny also offer us a point of departure and comparison for our analysis of anthropogenic processes and their impact in the Roman period. In our case studies that follow, we will frequently return to these authors' perspectives.

Case Study One: Roman Mining

During the Roman period, there was a significant increase in metal production compared to earlier periods, with large mining ventures throughout the empire (Craddock 2009). In this case study, we explore the effect of anthropogenic mining activity during the Republic and Empire and discusses its local and global consequences.

Analysis of ice cores from the Greenland ice indicates that Pliny's concerns about mining were well founded, even if he did not have access to these data. The Greenland core shows a high concentration of copper resulting from anthropogenic atmospheric emissions in the Roman period, with a noticeable peak around the Augustan period. The high values recorded were principally due to anthropogenic activities – mainly copper mining and smelting. The emissions during the Roman period were high enough to result in significant pollution of the atmosphere in the northern hemisphere. The total amount of copper mined and smelted during the Roman period has been calculated to be *c.* 5 million metric tons in total, with an annual production of 15000 metric tons of copper during the peak period, resulting in annual atmospheric copper emissions of *c.* 2300 metric tons. After *c.* AD 400, this level of atmospheric copper emissions was not reached again until the Industrial Revolution (Hong *et al.* 1996: 247–249). Present in the Greenland core is also evidence of large-scale anthropogenic atmospheric pollution due to emissions of lead in the Late Republic and early Empire (Rosman *et al.* 1997: 3413). As with copper, the atmospheric lead emissions peaked around the Augustan period, with an annual production of *c.* 80000 metric tons of lead-silver, resulting in annual atmospheric lead emissions of *c.* 4000 metric tons. The atmospheric lead emission levels remained high until the mid-second century AD; similar emission levels were not reached until the Industrial Revolution (Hong *et al.* 1994: 1842; McConnell *et al.* 2018).

Considering the high amounts of atmospheric emissions, the pollution resulting from mining activity was tangible on a regional and local scale. Silver and copper mining affected the local environment through the release of noxious fumes, particularly sulphuric oxide in the vicinity of the mines, and through the release of poisonous heavy metals, including lead and cadmium into the local biosphere (Craddock 2009: 105). The environmental effects of fume releases were tangible, as referred to by Strabo in his discussion of the deadly fumes released from silver-smelting in the Iberian Peninsula (Strab. *Geog.* 3.2.8; *cf.* Xen. *Mem.* 3.6.12). The local effects of such metal pollution had the potential to leave significant and lasting footprints on the local environment (Pyatt *et al.* 2000: 773; Craddock 2009: 105). Accumulation of heavy metals in the soil in the environs of the mines had a cascade effect on living beings through bioaccumulation: metals including lead and copper bioaccumulate in vegetation, humans and animals ingesting the vegetation, potentially leading to sickness and death following metal poisoning (Pyatt *et al.* 2000: 776). Studies of the environmental impact of lead and copper mining in Wadi Faynan in southern Jordan in the Nabatean to Byzantine period (Pyatt *et al.* 2000; 2002; 2005; Pyatt and Grattan 2001) and on Cyprus from the Iron Age to the late Byzantine period (Pyatt 2001) suggest that the accumulation of heavy metals in soil derived from ancient mining and smelting activity has led to the heavy metal poisoning of living beings even today. Note that these studies have recently been reassessed and partially contradicted for Wadi Faynan specifically (Knabb *et al.* 2016).

Lead emission from lead-silver mining and smelting activity and copper emission from copper mining and smelting both originated predominantly in the Iberian Peninsula (Hong *et al.* 1996: 248; McConnell *et al.* 2018). As a consequence of this large-scale mining venture, the increasing Roman presence on the Iberian Peninsula impacted the environment beyond atmospheric emissions. The Iberian Peninsula has recently been the focus of several paleoenvironmental studies demonstrating the wide-ranging effects of Roman activity on the peninsula.

Massive amounts of wood and timber were used for construction and for charcoal in the mines, and heather (*erica*) was used in gold extraction. At the same time, agricultural production in the areas surrounding the mines increased. Together, these activities led to short-term deforestation and the emergence of permanent open (agricultural) landscapes in the region (Currás *et al.* 2012: 48–49; López-Merino *et al.* 2014: 214–215). When mining activity dwindled and farming activity declined in the fourth century AD, the lowland areas were reforested. The highland pinewoods, however, did not recover until between *c.* AD 580 and 715 when the population in the area had decreased substantially (Currás *et al.* 2012: 48–49).

Pliny's account of gold mining methods reveals anthropogenic terraforming on a massive scale in the gold mining efforts in north-western Hispania (Plin. *HN* 33.66–79, esp. 70–79). The mines here were called *arrugiae*, after a mining technique involving hydraulic extraction of gold in alluvial deposits (Plin. *HN* 33.70). In the *arrugiae*, deep shafts were dug to undermine the hillside. The shafts were thereafter intentionally collapsed before the gold was washed out by hushing. Hushing was a process where water was collected in reservoirs and released, and the power of the massive amounts of rushing water broke down the deposits and washed out the gold (Healy 1978: 87; Healy 1999: 169). The anthropogenic imprint the *arrugiae* made is apparent in Pliny's description of the mining method as the ruin of mountains (*ruina montium*, Plin. *HN* 33.66). Pliny describes a violent process in which 'a fractured mountain falls widely asunder with a crash which the human mind cannot conceive' (*mons fractus cadit ab sese longe fragore qui concipi humana mente non possit*, Plin. *HN* 33.73). The miners, he says, gazed upon this ruin of nature (*ruina naturae*) as conquerors (*victores*), even if there was no guarantee that gold was retrieved during all this destruction (Plin. *HN* 33.73 with Thommen 2012: 122–123). The small chance of finding precious metals to use for personal gain, then, was justification enough to ruin mountains. Pliny was not alone in his critique of ruining nature for gain; Sallust, Ovid, and Seneca the Younger criticise the exploitation of nature and natural resources for the sake of wealth (Sall. *Cat.* 13.1; Ov. *Met.*

Figure 9.1: Present-day view of the mining landscape of Las Médulas, Spain. (Wikimedia Commons: Rafael Ibáñez Fernández [CC BY-SA 3.0]).

1.138–140; Sen. *Ep.* 89.21; 122.8 with Thommen 2012: 122–123; Fargnoli 2015: 15–17).

In order to use the hydraulic technique, aqueducts were built and channels and trenches dug to lead the water to the mountain-top reservoirs. According to Pliny, the water was rerouted from sources up to 100 miles away. This harnessing of water and subsequent ruin of mountains (*ruina montium*) led to irrevocable geomorphological changes to the landscape in the north-western parts of the Iberian Peninsula, changes which are still highly visible today (López-Merino *et al.* 2014: 209; *cf.* Fig. 9.1). In Las Médulas alone, around fifty terraced open-pit mining sites are visible (Thommen 2012: 121).

As mentioned above, Pliny was critical of the mining of *terra mater* in the hunt for precious metals. We should be content with what we find above ground, he argued, and not drive into the depths of *terra mater* and exhaust her – and destroy ourselves in the process with our avarice (Plin. *HN* 33.1–4; *cf.* Ov. *Met.* 1.137–150). As these few examples have shown, Roman mining ventures had a substantial impact on landscapes, humans, and other living beings. Some of these effects, like deforestation, were local or regional, and albeit being noticeable and dramatic for several generations, the incidents of deforestation discussed here were eventually reversed. The consequences of anthropogenic emissions into the atmosphere are more uncertain, but with the large amounts of atmospheric emissions, the more local and immediate effects of the emitted fumes must have been tangible, as Strabo pointed out. Released fumes into the air and toxic metal into the surrounding soil made humans and other beings sick, and in the case of the soil poisoning, may continue to do so today in some places. The large-scale mining ventures, particularly those on the Iberian Peninsula, made irreversible changes to the landscape and environment.

Case Study Two: Roman Exploitation of Animal Populations

The Romans exploited animals on an epic scale (Jennison 1937; Hughes 2003; MacKinnon 2006; Shelton 2014). In what follows, we trace several examples of the exploitation of animals in the Roman Republic and Empire. Here we focus on one case, Roman animal spectacles, and closely consider the impact of public hunts (*venationes*) on animal populations and ecosystems.

From at least the early third century BC onwards, numerous non-indigenous (exotic) animals were introduced to Italy for public spectacles of 'animal abuse' (Shelton 2014: 466–475). The most notable early introduction and spectacle was of elephants, who were first displayed as captives in Rome in the consul Manius Curius Dentatus' triumph over the Samnites and King Pyrrhus in 275 BC (Sen. *Brev.* 13.3; Plin. *HN* 8.16; Florus 1.13.26–28 with Östenberg 2014: 499–500; Shelton 2014: 469). According to Florus, 'nothing was more pleasing for the Roman People than to view these [elephants]' (*nihil libentius populus Romanus aspexit quam illas*, Florus 1.13.28). Dentatus' spectacle of animal abuse was superseded and amplified by one enacted by the proconsul Lucius Caecilius Metellus after he displayed a large number of elephants (*c.* 120–142) as captives for his triumph over the Carthaginians in 250 BC (Varro *apud* Plin. *HN* 18.17; Sen. *Brev.* 13.8; Plin. *HN* 7.139, 8.16–17 with Östenberg 2014: 500). After the triumphal procession, two different traditions record the subsequent abuse the Romans enacted on these elephants: Lucius Calpurnius Piso Frugi records that the elephants 'were simply led into the Circus and, in order to increase contempt for them, driven around the whole Circus by workers with button-tipped spears' (*inductos dumtaxat in circum atque, ut contemptus eorum incresceret, ab operariis hastas praepilatas habentibus per circum totum actos*, L. Calpurnius Piso Frugi fr. 32 *FrRH* = Plin. *HN* 8.17), while Verrius Flaccus records that 'they fought in the Circus and were killed with javelins' (*eos pugnasse in circo interfectosque iaculis*, Verrius Flaccus fr. 3 Egger = Plin. *HN* 8.17). As Shelton argues, such abuse and/or killing served several purposes, including entertainment as well as a recreation of Roman conquests, where the elephants represented and embodied the conquered enemy humans; their abuse and/or death (re)exemplified the defeat of enemies (Shelton 2014: 469).

Beyond the abuse of elephants, the Romans held rural and urban *venationes*, encompassing the elite practice of hunting animals in the countryside and the broader practice of urban *venationes* involving staged hunts of numerous animals in front of spectators (*e.g.* Varro, *Rust.* 3.13.3 with Shelton 2014: 467; *cf.* Fig. 9.2). These latter *venationes* – which in Rome were initially held in the Circus Maximus and later in various other fora – were enormously popular, such that already in Mid-Republican Rome the Roman Senate provided financial support for such games (*ludi*) and individual members of the elite sponsored lavish *ludi*/*venationes* to celebrate their own victories and enhance their chances for electoral success by pleasing the people (*e.g.* Varro, *Rust.* 3.13.3; Cic. *Fam.* 7.1.2–3; Livy 39.22.2; Plin. *HN* 8.19–22 with Shelton 2014: 467–471).

According to Livy, one of the first major *venationes* was held in 186 BC, sponsored by the former consul Marcus Fulvius Nobilior as part of his ten days of votive games after his triumph over the Aetolians and Cephallenia (Kefalonia) in 187 BC (Livy 39.22.1–3). Nobilior's votive games were the first to stage athletic competitions and a *venatio* that included the killing of lions and leopards (Livy 39.22.2 with MacKinnon 2006: 141; Shelton 2014: 469). The scale of these *venationes* continued to increase throughout the Republic and into the Empire. Several additional examples will suffice to demonstrate this expansion. Livy remarks that in 169 BC, 'as display was then increasing, it is recorded that, in the *ludi circenses* of the curule aediles Publius Cornelius Scipio Nasica and Publius [Cornelius] Lentulus, 63 leopards, 40 bears, and elephants performed' (*et iam magnificentia crescente notatum est ludis circensibus P. Corneli Scipionis Nasicae et P. Lentuli aedilium curulium sexaginta tres Africanas et quadraginta ursos et elephantos lusisse*, Livy 44.18.8). As praetor in 93 BC, the famous Lucius Cornelius Sulla held a *venatio* that included 100 maned lions (Plin. *HN* 8.53; *cf.* Sen. *Brev.* 13.6), while, as curule aedile in 58 BC, Marcus Aemilius Scaurus sent 150 female leopards to die in one *venatio* (Plin. *HN* 8.64) and was the first to send in a hippopotamus and 5 crocodiles (Plin. *HN* 8.96; *cf.* Amm. Marc. 22.15.24).

As in many other ways, Cnaeus Pompeius Magnus (Pompey), Caius Iulius Caesar (Caesar), and Caius Iulius Caesar/Augustus exceeded these excesses of violence in their *venationes*. As consul in 55 BC and as part of the votive games for the dedication of the temple of Venus Victrix, Pompey sponsored *venationes* wherein *c.* 17–20 elephants were sent to die (Plin. *HN* 8.19–20; Dio 39.38.2–3), as well as *c.* 500–600 lions (Plin. *HN* 8.53; Dio 39.38.2), 410 female leopards (Plin. *HN* 8.64), lynxes, apes, and a rhinoceros (Plin. *HN* 8.70–71). Similarly, for his triumphs and as votive games for his dedication of the temple of Venus Genetrix and the Forum Iulium in 46 BC, the dictator and consul Caesar held *venationes* including 400 lions (Plin. *HN* 8.53), Thessalian bulls (Plin. *HN* 8.182–183), 40 elephants, and a giraffe (Plin. *HN* 8.69; Dio 43.22.2–23.3, esp. 23.1, 23.3 with Shelton 2014: 470; Östenberg 2014: 498).

On the cusp of the transition from Republic to Empire, in 29 BC after his triple triumph and as votive games for the dedication of the temple of Divus Iulius, the consul Caius Iulius Caesar (formerly Caius Octavius, later Augustus) held *venationes* that included numerous animals, but especially a rhinoceros and hippopotamus (Dio 51.22.4–6 with Östenberg 2014: 498). Moreover, after he became Augustus, he boasted in his *Res Gestae* that 'in my own name or the name of my sons or grandsons I gave 26 *venationes* of African animals to the people in the Circus, Forum, or Amphitheatre, in which about 3500 animals were executed' (*Venationes best(ia)- | rum Africanarum meo nomine aut filio(ru)m meorum et nepotum in ci(r)- | co aut (i)n foro aut

Figure 9.2: Marble relief fragment depicting venatio, *Roman, c. first to second century AD. Found in Sardis in 1912, now in the Metropolitan Museum of Art. Accession number: 26.199.63 (Public domain [CC0 1.0 Universal]).*

in amphitheatris popul(o d)edi sexiens et viciens, quibus | confecta sunt bestiarum circiter tria m(ill)ia et quingentae, Aug. *RG* 4.39–42; *cf.* Suet. *Aug.* 43.1 with Shelton 2014: 470). Under subsequent emperors, the sponsoring of such games became an imperial affair, and the volume of killing increased until animal populations began to decline (Jennison 1937: 60–98; Bomgardner 2000: 214–216; MacKinnon 2006: 141–142; Shelton 2014: esp. 470–473). For example, at the dedication of the Colosseum in AD 80, the emperor Titus held *venationes* in which 9000 animals were killed, including 5000 in one day (Suet. *Tit.* 7.3; Dio 66.25.2), and for his triumph over the Dacians in AD 107, the emperor Trajan held *venationes* over 123 days wherein 11000 animals were killed (Dio 68.15.1). But enough of this litany of deaths. The initial abuse of the elephants and the scale of the public *venationes* that followed are powerful indicators of the extent of Roman exploitation and consumption of animals and of the broader Roman desire to control and dominate nature (Shelton 2014: 475).

The scale of the exploitation of these animal populations naturally led to their decline (Bomgardner 2000: 214–216). Already, by the time of Cicero in the Late Republic, there was an awareness among the Roman elite of a reduction in the population sizes of these animals. This is evinced by the extensive communications regarding Anatolian leopards (perhaps *Panthera pardus tulliana*) between Cicero and the curule aedile for 50 BC, Marcus Caelius Rufus (Cic. *Att.* 6.1.21; *Fam.* 2.11.2, 8.2.2, 8.4.5, 8.6.5, 8.8.10, 8.9.3; Plut. *Vit. Cic.* 36.6). In this correspondence, Marcus Caelius Rufus pleads with Cicero to provide him with leopards from Cibyra (now in south-western Turkey) for the *venationes* that he would hold during his curule aedileship. Cicero, who was from 51–50 BC proconsul in the province of Cilicia (now south-eastern Turkey), replied that 'but they [leopards] are in remarkable scarcity, and those we have are said to vigorously complain that traps/ambushes are made for nobody except themselves in my province' (*sed mira paucitas est, et eas quae sunt valde aiunt queri quod nihil cuiquam insidiarum in mea provincia nisi sibi fiat*, Cic. *Fam.* 2.11.2; *cf.* Plut. *Vit. Cic.* 36.6). Moreover, Cicero reports that 'accordingly it is said they [the leopards] decided to leave my province for Caria' (now western Turkey) (*itaque constituisse dicuntur in Cariam ex nostra provincia decedere*, Cic. *Fam.* 2.11.2; *cf.* Plut. *Vit. Cic.* 36.6). Unless Cicero is dissembling, he provides an early indication that at least some animal populations were on the decline throughout one Roman province in the Late Republic (*cf.* Hughes 2003: 30).

Four further examples provide evidence of a wider scale decline in animal populations in the later Empire: the comparatively small number of animals reputedly used by the emperor Philip I for the *venationes* for the Saecular Games of AD 248 in Rome (SHA *Gord.* 33.1–3 with Östenberg 2014: 497), the astronomical prices for such animals in the emperor Diocletian's *Edictum de pretiis rerum venalium* of AD 301 (*cf.* Bomgardner 2000: 215–216), Themistius' reference to possible elephant, lion, and hippopotamus extinctions in his tenth oration of AD 370 (Themistius *Orationes*, 10.140a with Thommen 2012: 95–96), and Ammianus Marcellinus' reference to *venationes* and possible hippopotamus extinctions in his *Res Gestae* of *c.* AD 390s (Amm. Marc. 22.15.24 with Thommen 2012: 95–96).

In contrast with Trajan's 11000 animals, Philip I's *venationes* for the Saecular Games of AD 248 reputedly included only 32 elephants, 10 elk, 10 tigers, 60 tame lions, 30 tame leopards, 10 hyenas, 6 hippopotami, 1 rhinoceros, 10 wild lions, 10 giraffes, 20 onagers (wild ass), 40 wild horses, and various other animals (SHA *Gord.* 33.1–2); our textual source for this event is unreliable, but coins minted for the occasion bear images of, *inter alia*, lions, stags, antelope, and elk (*e.g. RIC* IV.3.12, 20, 23, 158, 160a, 160b, 161 in Mattingly *et al.* 1949). Firmer evidence exists in Diocletian's *Edictum de pretiis rerum venalium* of AD 301, wherein the maximum price for various wild animals from Africa is set; a sample of prices include: 150,000 denarii for a first class lion (*leo formae primae*), 125,000 for a first class lioness (*lea formae primae*), 100,000 for a first class leopard (*leopardus formae primae*), 5000 for an ostrich (*struthio*), 25000 for a first class bear (*ursus formae primae*), 6,000 for a first class wild boar (*aper formae primae*), 3000 for a first class stag (*cervus formae primae*), and 5000 for an onager (*onager*) (Diocletian, *Edictum de pretiis rerum venalium*, 34.1a, 3, 5, 7, 8a, 10, 12, 14 with Lauffer 1971: 193; Crawford and Reynolds 1979: 179). These animal prices dwarf the contemporaneous daily wage of *e.g.*, 25 denarii per day for a rural worker (*operarius rusticus*), 150 denarii per day (plus maintenance) for a figure painter (*pictor imaginarius*), or

200 denarii for a single student for a month for a teacher of Greek/Latin and geometry (*grammaticus Graecus sive Latinus et geometres*) (Diocletian, *Edictum de pretiis rerum venalium*, 7.1a, 9, 71). The reduced number of animals at Philip I's *venationes* and these astronomical prices suggest that such animals were scarce and highly valuable from at least the mid third century AD onwards (Bomgardner 2000: 215–216).

Supporting evidence exists in Themistius' tenth oration (Ἐπὶ τῆς εἰρήνης Οὐάλεντι, On the peace of Valens) of AD 370, wherein in a brief aside on the merits of not entirely destroying humans and animals during conquest, Themistius mentions that elephants have been completely removed (ἐξελέσθαι) from Libya, lions from Thessaly, and hippopotami from the marshes (ἕλεᾰ) of the Nile in Egypt (Themistius *Orationes*, 10.140a with Thommen 2012: 95–96). As mentioned previously, all three of these types of animals were used for *venationes*, which must have contributed to their population decline and possible extinction in these areas (Thommen 2012: 95–96). Finally, in Ammianus Marcellinus' *Res Gestae* of *c*. AD 390s, Ammianus provides supporting evidence that, since the first appearance of hippopotami in Scaurus' *venatio* of 58 BC, 'for ages thereafter more had been bought frequently here [to Rome]' (*per aetetas exinde plures saepe huc ducti*) for *venationes*, such that by Ammianus' time hippopotami 'could now nowhere be found' (*nunc inveniri nusquam possunt*) in Egypt (Amm. Marc. 22.15.24, for Egypt and hippopotami *cf.* 22.15.14, 21 with Thommen 2012: 95–96). Taken together, this evidence suggests that the Romans' *venationes* (alongside other factors) had a significant negative impact on animal populations from the Republic through the Empire.

For Rome itself, there exists zooarchaeological evidence for the impact of *venationes*. Early excavations from the nineteenth and early twentieth centuries made reference to remains of, *inter alia*, lions and tigers found near the Colosseum, while recent excavations around the Meta Sudans area (near the Colosseum) found a few remains of animals (lions, tigers, leopards, hyenas, wolves, horses, asses, bears, goats, and ostriches) in a fourth to seventh century AD context that can be linked with the *venationes* held at the Colosseum (MacKinnon 2006: 154–155; Sparreboom 2016: 70). This is admittedly sparse evidence, but the remains may have typically been disposed of elsewhere inside or outside of Rome, or distributed throughout the Roman populace as food (*cf.* consumption of such meat in Tert. *Apol*. 9.11 with Kyle 1998: 184–194; MacKinnon 2006: 155; Sparreboom 2016: 70). Perhaps, as with the remains of excess meat from banquets, criminals, and gladiators, any unconsumed non-animal remains were disposed of in the Tiber, and thus are no longer available to us (*e.g.* Plut. *Vit. Sull.* 35.1; Tac. *Ann.* 6.19; Suet. *Tib.* 75.1; *Vit.* 17.2 with Kyle 1998: 213–228). Evidence of the remains of animals used for *venationes* (including lions, elephants, bears, gazelles, wild boars, deer, camels, ostriches, wild goats, sheep) also exists in Northern Africa (*e.g.* Thamusida, Carthage), while the bones of an elephant have been found in Ostia (MacKinnon 2006: 151–153; Sparreboom 2016: 70). The small amount of currently available evidence may be due to previous disinterest or misidentification of the zooarchaeological material among archaeologists, and the Roman forms of distribution and disposal of animal remains (Kyle 1998: 184–194, 213–228; MacKinnon 2006: 155; Sparreboom 2016: 70).

Beyond the specific decline in population sizes of the animals used in the *venationes*, the decline in the number of apex predators, especially lions and leopards, would have had significant ecosystem cascade effects and ramifications. Such apex predators regulate and control entire ecosystems through the trophic cascade, impacting other predators and various animals and plants etc. (Ripple *et al.* 2014: esp. 2, 6). The decline in the population sizes of apex predators produces consequent changes in 'plant species diversity, biomass, and productivity', 'species abundance', 'food-web networks', and numerous other ecological processes (Ripple *et al.* 2014: 8). For example, William Ripple and others have demonstrated that a recent reduction in African lion (*Panthera leo*) and leopard (*Panthera pardus*) population sizes in West Africa produced a consequent increase in the population size of olive baboons (*Papio anubis*), and that the increase in population size of these baboons produced a decline in population sizes of small ungulates (hoofed mammals) and primates, as well as posing significant threats to livestock and crops (Ripple *et al.* 2014: 2, 4). Consider, then, the reduction in population size of the (possibly) Anatolian leopard (*Panthera pardus tulliana*) evinced by Cicero (Cic. *Fam.* 2.11.2) and of the lions of Thessaly evinced by Themistius (Themistius, *Orationes* 10.140a). These declines would have had major regional ecosystem effects, including impacting population abundance of other animals and plant diversity (*cf.* Ripple *et al.* 2014: 2, 8–9). Thence, the Roman *venationes* would have not only destroyed numerous populations of animals but also reshaped and significantly impacted various ecosystems.

The human impact on and destruction of animals in *venationes* did not escape the notice of Roman authors. Lucretius' criticism of interspecies violence in his *De Rerum Natura* – especially the visceral descriptions of the combined ruin (*permixtae ruinae*) resulting from lions, lionesses, bulls, horses, elephants, and boars fighting humans and each other – immediately recalls the *venationes* and may have been modelled on them (Lucr. 5.1308–1340; *cf.* 4.1011–1017 with Gale 2018: esp. 68, 68 n. 19, 70, 78). Such acts of violence and animal abuse broke the animal contract. But did other Romans notice? One *venatio* caused a widespread emotional reaction and sense of empathy in a Roman audience. This was the famous aforementioned *venatio* sponsored by Pompey in 55 BC, one that Lucretius himself might have witnessed (Gale 2018: 68 n. 19) and one that Cicero certainly witnessed (Cic. *Fam.* 7.1.3). As mentioned previously, this *venatio* included *c.* 17–20 elephants (Plin. *HN* 8.20; Dio 39.38.2–3). According to Cicero, the crowd did not enjoy the spectacle of the elephants: 'the last was the day of the elephants; on which the great admiration of the common crowd arose, but no enjoyment at all' (*extremus elephantorum dies fuit. in quo admiratio magna vulgi atque turbae, delectatio nulla exstitit*, Cic. *Fam.* 7.1.3). Indeed, Cicero writes that 'instead, even a certain compassion followed, and opinion was of this sort, that this beast (elephants) has some kind of fellowship with humankind' (*quin etiam misericordia quaedam consecuta est atque opinio eius modi, esse quandam illi belvae cum genere humano societatem*, Cic. *Fam.* 7.1.3). This moment of human to animal affinity in this *venatio* is rendered with even more *pathos* by Pliny and Dio, who write of the elephants' wailing, which produces a sympathetic reaction in the crowd (Plin. *HN* 8.20; Dio 39.38.2–3). Clearly, some Romans thought about the destructive impact of these *venationes* and (occasionally) the abuse and killing of animals produced compassion in some Romans. However, such opinions and emotions were exceptional, for, in general, the Romans revelled in their *venationes* (Thommen 2012: 96).

In summary, the exploitation and consumption of animals in the Roman *venationes* would have produced major declines in animal populations and had consequent cascade effects on numerous ecosystems. Some of these animals may have become extinct locally or globally due to these practices, notably the (probably) Anatolian leopards of Cibyra, elephants of Libya, lions of Thessaly, and some hippopotami around the Nile in Egypt. Such extinctions would have had lasting impacts on ecosystems, impacts that may last to this day.

Case Study Three: Roman Agricultural Expansion

The Mediterranean landscape today is highly sensitive to climate change (Nunes *et al.* 2008), and it has been argued that this is partially because of past modifications of the landscape, mainly through agricultural activity, grazing, and deforestation (Dusar *et al.* 2011: 138).

We have indicated earlier that an indirect consequence of Roman mining ventures in the Iberian Peninsula was the creation of a permanent open agricultural landscape. Agricultural expansion is a powerful anthropogenic geomorphic agent, one that became prominent in the Roman period. The process of agricultural expansion changes ecosystems, as it clears indigenous plants and replaces them with domesticated species (Redman 1999: 45). As the empire grew during the Republic and Empire, the agricultural development of land grew with it. The Punic Wars led to the inclusion of massive areas of Carthaginian agricultural land into Roman territories, and Egypt, with its fertile lands, came under Roman control at the conclusion of the Civil Wars. These areas became massive granaries for the Romans. When the areas north of the Alps were incorporated into the Roman territories, they were subject to intensive agricultural expansion (Thommen 2012: 70–71). The first century AD represented something of an 'agricultural revolution'. Smaller agricultural estates (*villae rusticae*) were replaced by massive estates owned by fewer men, and primarily worked by slaves (*latifundia*); the latter predominantly in Italy and Spain. The estates continued to grow, and the landowners became fewer. From the second century AD onwards, tenant farming increased rapidly. In the provinces, land was given to army veterans, but was beyond that mainly under the ownership of the local and imperial authorities, the senatorial order, other wealthy landowners, and later the Church (Jones 1964: 794; Rees 1987: 482–484; Thommen 2012: 79–84). Following Geoffrey Kron, the intensive farming of the Roman Empire matched the performance of early modern and modern agriculture up until the nineteenth century, in some cases even the twentieth century:

> As late as the 1880s, cattle of comparable size could be found only in England, Holland, and in a few scattered regions of advanced farming (Kron 2012: 158).
>
> Romans' wheat yields matched or exceeded the performance of the most intensive Medieval or Modern agriculture, or that of Italy as a whole in the 1970s (Kron 2012: 159).
>
> French yields did not match the benchmarks of the Roman agronomists until after World War II, when winemakers began fertilizing their vineyards in earnest (Kron 2012: 160).

Such agriculture accounted for a large part of the Roman economy, calculated to be around 80% of the value of overall 'production' (Bowman and Wilson 2013: 4).

Agricultural practices varied in different parts of the empire depending on local agricultural traditions, climate, and natural conditions including topography, soil type, and so forth. The cooler and wetter north provinces demanded different agricultural strategies than the dryer and warmer Mediterranean areas (Grey 2007: 363; Rees 1987: 481–482). Agricultural expansion in marginal areas like North Africa, Syria and so forth demanded substantial adaptation in the form of terracing, the establishment of canal systems, dykes and basins for irrigation, and construction of catchments for prevention of soil erosion (Rees 1987: 496). Agricultural development demands the removal of forests and groves, removal of vegetation, and often redistribution of water for drainage and irrigation. Needless to say, the Roman agricultural venture that in many ways could match the agricultural production of the industrial age, would have a great impact on environments and ecosystems. Large areas could be drained for the establishment or effectivisation of agriculture; Marcus Aemilius Scaurus' drainage scheme in the Po Valley in the late second century BC transformed the area into one of the richest agricultural regions in Italy. Similarly, irrigation was supplied by the redirection of water using aqueducts (Kron 2012: 166–167; Rees 1987: 487–488). Roger Hooke's calculations show that accelerated erosion caused by agriculture peaked in the Roman period when measured as tons per capita per year (Hooke 2000: 845, fig. 2). Drainage of a scale such as the Po Valley scheme would result in changes in hydrology, geomorphology, nutrient cycling, and sediment dynamics, which cumulatively would have had 'profound implications for aquatic ecosystems and biodiversity' (Blann *et al.* 2009: 910). Ploughing, grazing, and logging lead to accelerated land erosion. Eroded sediment ends up as colluvium (on hillslopes) and alluvium (floodplains) or is carried away by streams and rivers and slowly deposited along the river and the mouth of the river (Hooke *et al.* 2012: 4).

The widespread consequences of agriculture on the environment and ultimately even the human populations have been demonstrated in a recent study of the sediments in the Roman harbour of Ephesus (Stock *et al.* 2016). The study demonstrated that agriculture along the Kaystros river (now Küçük Menderes) significantly impacted the environment. While Ephesus was a port in Antiquity, the archaeological site is today situated *c.* 5 km from the seashore partially due to eustatic and climatic disturbance, seismic disturbances, but also due to alluvial deposits from the Kaystros (Scherrer 2000: 8). The harbour of Ephesus became something of a battleground between humans and the Kaystros river and its ever-flowing stream of alluvial deposits throughout the Greek and Roman periods. The harbour was dredged several times and moved several times (Kraft *et al.* 2011). A breakwater (mole) was built to enclose and protect the harbour. According to Strabo, the mole was something of an engineering mistake, however, as it accelerated the sedimentation and made the harbour shallower than it was before the mole was built (Strab. *Geog.* 14.1.24). Ultimately, the humans lost the battle of the Ephesus harbours, as the river delta of the Kaystros slowly but inevitably filled in the gulf with sediments (Kraft *et al.* 2011: 36).

The analyses of Stock and others showed that the sedimentation of the harbour area in Ephesus increased after the area was inhabited by humans, from 1 mm/yr before the first millennium BC to c. 6 mm/yr in the fourth/third century BC (Stock *et al.* 2016). The sedimentation rapidly increased to 30 mm/yr in the Roman period (Stock *et al.* 2016: 991). The samples contained pollen from species first and foremost associated with agriculture, such as olive (*olea*), hemp (*cannabis*), legumes (*fabaceae*), ribwort plantain (*plantago lanceolata*, a weed), various cereals, and spores from the aquatic/semiaquatic quillwort plant (*isoetes*). The pollen grains showed signs of decay, indicating that they had been transported some distance down the river before being deposited. Increase in pine (*pinea*) in the charcoal record from Ephesus in the Roman period indicate that the surrounding woodland resources were under pressure (Stock *et al.* 2016: 991–992). The transported pollen from plants associated with agriculture and grazing, combined with deforestation, increased the erosion that led to increased alluvial sedimentation in the harbour of Ephesus (Stock *et al.* 2016: 992). In the end, it seems that the increasing struggle the humans of Ephesus had with the Kaystros to keep the harbour open was mostly a product of their own presence and activity. Ephesus was not unique, however. Similar cases of human-made deltas in the Roman period have been documented at the neighbouring Maeander river (Büyük Menderes), the Tiber, Po, and Rhône, among others (Stock *et al.* 2016: 992 with references).

Roman agronomic experts from Cato onwards discussed the scale and impact of their agricultural practices. In his *De Agricultura*, Cato details the profit-based nature of Mid-Republican agricultural practices (Cato, *Agr.* 1.3, 2.7, 3.2), as affirmed by Varro in his exposition on Late-Republican agricultural practices in his *De Re Rustica* (Varro, *Rust.* 1.2.8, 1.7.9–10, 3.5.9–17). This profit-based nature is exemplified by Cato's statements that 'it is necessary for the father of a family to be a selling man, not a buying man' (*patrem familias vendacem, non emacem esse oportet*, Cato, *Agr.* 2.7), and that 'it is useful for the father of the family to have a well-built farm house/villa, an oil cellar, wine cellar, many storage jars, so that it may be pleasing to await a high price: it will be a source of wealth, virtue, and glory' (*patrem familiae villam rusticam bene aedificatam habere expedit, cellam oleariam, vinariam, dolia multa, uti lubeat caritatem expectare: et rei et virtuti et gloriae erit*, Cato, *Agr.* 3.2). Agricultural practices included intercropping from at least Cato's time (Cato, *Agr.* 33; Plin. *HN* 17.196–198; Columella, *Rust.* 5.6.5, 5.9.12–13) and potential farmers were advised by Roman agronomic experts to engage in many different types of agriculture at once and aim for the most profitable output (Cato, *Agr.* 1.7; Varro, *Rust.* 1.7.9–10; Columella, *Rust.* 3.3). By the agronomic expert Columella's time in the first century AD, commercial agriculture was large-scale and enormously profitable, especially viticulture (Columella, *Rust.* 3.3 with Roselaar 2010, esp. 154–209; Kron 2012). Pliny himself recognised the impact of such intense, exploitative agriculture, writing that such practices removed the life from the land (*extrahant sucum*, Plin. *HN* 18.296), but his comments are exceptional, and Roman agronomic experts tended to frame agriculture positively (Roselaar 2010; Kron 2012).

Beyond the direct impact of *venationes* on animal populations, agricultural practices in their natural habitats also produced declines in their populations. This phenomenon is well illustrated by an anonymous epigram retained in the

Anthologia Graeca, which details the impact of such practices on the population of lions and other animals in Libya:

> O Nasamonian frontiers of Libya, no longer are your mainland expanses burdened with tribes of beasts, nor do you rebound in echo to the remote roars of lions even beyond the sands of the Nomads, for their countless race, trapped in foot-fetters, Caesar the son/boy has put before spearmen; the mountain-ridges, formerly lairs for wild-dwelling beasts, are now the cattle pastures of men.
>
> Ἐσχατιαὶ Λιβύων Νασαμωνίδες, οὐκέτι θηρῶν / ἔθνεσιν ἠπείρου νῶτα βαρυνόμεναι, ἠχοῖ ἐρημαίαισιν ἐπηπύσεσθε λεόντων / ὠρυγαῖς ψαμάθους ἄχρις ὑπὲρ Νομάδων, / φῦλον ἐπεὶ νήριθμον ἐν ἰχνοπέδαισιν ἀγρευθὲν / ἐς μίαν αἰχμηταῖς Καῖσαρ ἔθηκεν ὁ παῖς· / αἱ δὲ πρὶν ἀγραύλων ἐγκοιτάδες ἀκρώρειαι / θηρῶν, νῦν ἀνδρῶν εἰσὶ βοηλασίαι (*Anth. Gr.* 7.626).

Not only does this epigram reaffirm the destructive consequences of *venationes* for lions and other animals in Libya, but it outlines how agricultural expansion had rendered their habitat unliveable. Additionally, both Strabo (Strab. *Geog.* 2.5.33) and Luxorius (*Anth. Lat.* 346 R) allude to an attitude that the agricultural ventures were hampered by the indigenous wildlife populations, as herbivores fed on the agricultural crops and carnivores posed a threat to the human populations (Bomgardner 2000: 216–217). Marginal lands in several places in the empire, including North Africa, underwent heavy agricultural development from the second century AD to produce crops like grain, olives, and grapes. The intensification of agricultural development in the area led to the destruction of the natural habitats of the animals used in the *venationes*. The agricultural expansion correlates with reduced appearance of carnivores in the *venationes* and a greater supplement of herbivores, including gazelles, mouflons, and antelopes from North Africa (Bomgardner 2000: 214). The agricultural ventures in the marginal lands of North Africa thus impacted the animal populations here both directly through active removal of animals for the benefits of crops and humans, and indirectly through destruction of their habitats.

Conclusions

In this chapter, we have demonstrated that the Romans produced substantial changes in landscapes and ecosystems in the Mediterranean and beyond through mining, exploitation of animals, and agricultural expansion. Roman mining had a major impact on landscapes, humans, and other living beings; it led to deforestation, soil and air toxicity, terraformed landscapes, and atmospheric pollution. Such mining has produced the most visibly lasting changes on landscapes in the Mediterranean. The Roman exploitation of animals through animal spectacles led to declines in their populations and possible local extinctions. In particular, the decline in population sizes for apex predators would have had significant ramifications for ecosystems, as such predators regulated and controlled entire ecosystems. Beyond mining and the direct exploitation of animals, we have shown that Roman agricultural expansion also had a large-scale impact on ecosystems and environments due to the widespread modification of landscapes and the consequent cascade of environmental effects. Notably, such agricultural expansion would have enhanced anthropogenic declines in animal populations via habitat destruction.

Humans produced irreversible or at least lasting changes in the Earth's environment and ecosystems during the Roman period. Our study – by no means comprehensive – indicates that the Anthropocene is a conceptually useful framework with which to synthesise our examined archaeological and textual sources and to critically assess the environmental impact of the Romans from a global and diachronic perspective. We have demonstrated that Roman authors, particularly Lucretius and Pliny, show some awareness of the consequences of human exploitation of other living beings and nature more generally. Our findings suggest that we must look to the ancient past, not just the Industrial Revolution, to obtain a comprehensive understanding of the extent and longevity of human impacts on the Earth. Future studies should map the numerous ways in which the Romans produced changes in the environment and various ecosystems. As Hooke and others have argued, global changes are not just those that alter the atmosphere and oceans, but also those local changes that 'are so common as to be, collectively, of global importance; these include changes in climate, in composition of air and water, in biodiversity, and in land use' (Hooke *et al.* 2012: 4). Collectively, the local changes we have highlighted in this study – the impact of mining, exploitation of animals, agricultural expansion, and the cascade effects thereof – contributed to global changes, changes that were tangible to the Romans themselves and that persist today. We propose that anthropogenic processes that contributed to the age of the Anthropocene can be found in the Roman period. We are not suggesting the age of the Anthropocene began with the Romans, but, rather, that it was well underway in the Roman period, and that the Romans were significant (but not the only) contributors in its development. As Butzer argues, to truly understand the Anthropocene, we must look back beyond recent anthropogenic climate change to earlier anthropogenic processes in urban settlements like Rome (Butzer 2015). In their pursuit of empire, resources, and entertainment, the Romans shaped and reshaped the world around them, as we continue to do so today.

Studying the environmental impact of the Romans provides us with keen insight into our present environmental concerns and conditions. As we have demonstrated, Roman anthropogenic processes had a considerable and lasting impact on the Earth. Lucretius warned of the *permixtae ruinae* that results from interspecies violence, while Pliny warned of the *ruina naturae* that results from the over-exploitation of resources. In many ways, these two Roman authors were prophetic. Due, in part, to the Romans, we live in the age of the Anthropocene, an age produced by an abundance of anthropogenic violence and exploitation. Humans are entangled in a delicate and fragile network of living and non-living beings. Anthropocene enquiries demonstrate how fragile this network is and how our human actions can disrupt its balance. By reflecting on the environmental impact of past societies, here exemplified by the Romans, we submit that we can better understand the magnitude of the impact of our own present, even more violent and destructive existence. To even begin to repair such damage, we as humans (and as animals) need a different way of thinking about ourselves in relation to other living beings and the broader environment. We submit that the age of the Anthropocene and its implications provoke new ways of thinking about Roman archaeology, about who and what we study in the Roman past, and how we go about it. Indeed, the Anthropocene demands that we, as Roman archaeologists, reflect on the consequences of anthropocentric exceptionalism, and acknowledge and consider the entanglement of humans in networks of other non-human beings, things, and environments in the Roman period. As mentioned previously, the relational ontology and ethic of Rosi Braidotti's critical posthumanism provides Roman archaeologists with the critical apparatus with which to face the age of the Anthropocene and its implications. By considering and valuing the entanglement of humans and living and non-living others in the Roman period, we can pose new questions of the past, produce new forms of knowledge, and move towards a post-anthropocentric worldview. We know that *permixtae ruinae* and *ruina naturae* lie behind and before us: posthumanism offers a way forward.

Department of Historical Studies,
University of Gothenburg

Acknowledgements

The authors would like to thank the TRAC Standing Committee for all their support and assistance, the Royal Swedish Academy of Letters, History, and Antiquities for financial support (Stiftelsen Enboms Donationsfond), Ingalill Thorsell for hosting us at Drakamöllan's Nordic Forum for Culture and Research where we first wrote and presented this chapter, and to Ida Östenberg for her support. We would also like to thank the anonymous reviewers and Christian Isendahl for their constructive and incisive comments.

Note

1. Irene Selsvold and Lewis Webb are equal co-editors and co-authors in this volume.

Bibliography

Ancient Sources

Ammianus Marcellinus, *Res Gestae*.
Anthologia Graeca.
Anthologia Latina.
Augustus, *Res Gestae*.
Cassius Dio, *Historia Romana*.
Cato, *De Agricultura*.
Cicero, *Epistulae ad Atticum*.
Cicero, *Epistulae ad Familiares*.
Columella, *De Re Rustica*.
Diocletian, *Edictum de pretiis rerum venalium*.
Florus, *Epitomae de Tito Livio Bellorum Omnium Annorum DCC*.
Livy, *Ab Urbe Condita*.
Lucretius, *De Rerum Natura*.
Ovid, *Metamorphoses*.
Pliny the Elder, *Naturalis Historia*.
Plutarch, Vitae *Parallelae. Cicero*.
Plutarch, *Vitae Parallelae. Sulla*.
Sallust, *Bellum Catilinae*.
Scriptores Historiae Augustae, *Historia Augusta. Gordiani Tres*.
Seneca the Younger, *De Brevitate Vitae*.
Seneca the Younger, *Epistulae*.
Strabo, *Geographia*.
Suetonius, *Divus Augustus*.
Suetonius, *Divus Titus*.
Suetonius, *Tiberius*.
Suetonius, *Vitellius*.
Tacitus, *Annales*.
Tertullian, *Apologeticus*.
Themistius, *Orationes*.
Varro, *De Re Rustica*.
Xenophon, *Memorabilia*.
(All translations by L. Webb)

Modern Sources

Beagon, M. 1996. Nature and views of her landscapes in Pliny the Elder. In G. Shipley and J. Salmon (eds) *Human Landscapes in Classical Antiquity. Environment and Culture*. London: Routledge: 284–309.

Blann, K.L., Anderson, J.L., Sands, G.L. and Vondracek, B. 2009. Effects of agricultural drainage on aquatic ecosystems: a review. *Critical Reviews in Environmental Science and Technology* 39 (11): 909–1001.

Bomgardner, D. 2000. *The Story of the Roman Amphitheatre*. London: Routledge.

Bowman, A. and Wilson, A. 2013. Introduction: quantifying Roman agriculture. In A. Bowman and A. Wilson (eds) *The Roman Agricultural Economy: Organisation, Investment, and Production*. Oxford: Oxford University Press: 1–32.

Braidotti, R. 2013. *The Posthuman*. Cambridge: Polity Press.

Braidotti, R. 2016. Posthuman critical theory. In D. Banjeri and M.R. Paranjape (eds) *Critical Posthumanism and Planetary Futures*. New Delhi: Springer: 13–32.

Braje, T.J. 2016. Evaluating the Anthropocene: is there something useful about a geological epoch of humans? *Antiquity* 90: 504–512.

Braje, T.J. and Erlandson, J.M. 2013a. Human acceleration of animal and plant extinctions: a late Pleistocene, Holocene, and Anthropocene continuum. *Anthropocene* 4: 14–25.

Braje, T.J. and Erlandson, J.M. 2013b. Looking forward, looking back: humans, anthropogenic change, and the Anthropocene. *Anthropocene* 4: 116–121.

Butzer, K. 2015. Anthropocene as an evolving paradigm. *The Holocene* 25 (10): 1539–1541.

Campbell, B. 2012. *Rivers and the Power of Ancient Rome*. Chapel Hill: The University of North Carolina Press.

Cornell, T. (ed.) 2013. *The Fragments of the Roman Historians. Three Volumes*. Oxford: Oxford University Press.

Craddock, P.T. 2009. Mining and metallurgy. In J.P. Oleson (ed.) *The Oxford Handbook of Engineering and Technology in the Classical World*. Oxford: Oxford University Press: 93–120.

Crawford, M. and Reynolds, J. 1979. The Aezani copy of the prices edict. *Zeitschrift für Papyrologie und Epigraphik* 34: 163–210.

Crutzen, P. 2002. Geology of Mankind. *Nature* 415: 23.

Crutzen, P. 2006. The 'Anthropocene'. In E. Ehlers and T. Krafft (eds) *Earth System Science in the Anthropocene*. Berlin: Springer: 13–18.

Crutzen, P. and Stoermer, E.F. 2000. The 'Anthropocene'. *IGBP Newsletter* 41: 17–18.

Currás, A., Zamora, L., Reed, J.M., García-Soto, E., Ferrero, S., Armengol, X., Mezquita-Joanes, F., Marqués, M.A., Riera, S. and Julià, R. 2012. Climate change and human impact in central Spain during Roman times: high-resolution multi-proxy analysis of a tufa lake record (Somolinos, 1280 m asl). *Catena* 89: 31–53.

Dusar, B., Verstraeten, G., Notebaert, B. and Bakker, J. 2011. Holocene environmental change and its impact on sediment dynamics in the Eastern Mediterranean. *Earth-Science Review* 108: 137–157.

Erdkamp, P., Verboven, K. and Zuiderhoek, A. (eds) 2015. *Ownership and Exploitation of Land and Natural Resources in the Roman World*. Oxford: Oxford University Press.

Erlandson, J.M. and Braje, T.J. 2013. Archaeology and the Anthropocene. *Anthropocene* 4: 1–7.

Fargnoli, I. 2015. *Ruina naturae* e diritto Romano. *Teoria e Storia del Diritto Privato* 8: 1–34.

Ferrando, F. 2016. The party of the Anthropocene: post-humanism, environmentalism and the post-anthropocentric paradigm shift. *Relations* 4 (2): 159–173.

Gale, M. 2018. Contemplating violence: Lucretius' *De rerum natura*. In M. Gale and J. Scourfield (eds) *Texts and Violence in the Roman World*. Cambridge: Cambridge University Press: 63–87.

Graves-Brown, P. 2014. When was the Anthropocene? (and why?). *Journal of Contemporary Archaeology* 1 (1): 77–81.

Grey, C. 2007. Revisiting the 'problem' of *agri deserti* in the late Roman Empire. *Journal of Roman Archaeology* 20: 362–376.

Haraway, D. 2015. Anthropocene, Capitalocene, Plantationocene, Chthulucene: making kin. *Environmental Humanities* 6: 159–165.

Healy, J.F. 1978. *Mining and Metallurgy in the Greek and Roman World*. London: Thames and Hudson.

Healy, J.F. 1999. *Pliny the Elder on Science and Technology*. Oxford: Oxford University Press.

Hodder, I. 2012. *Entangled. An Archaeology of the Relationships between Humans and Things*. Chichester: Wiley-Blackwell.

Hong, S., Candelone, J-P., Patterson, C.C. and Boutron, C.F. 1994. Greenland ice evidence of hemispheric lead pollution two millennia ago by Greek and Roman civilizations. *Science* 265: 1841–1843.

Hong, S., Candelone, J-P., Patterson, C.C. and Boutron, C.F. 1996. History of ancient copper smelting pollution during Roman and Medieval times recorded in Greenland ice. *Science* 272: 246–249.

Hooke, R. 2000. On the history of humans as geomorphic agents. *Geology* 28 (9): 843–846.

Hooke, R., Martín-Duque, J.F. and Pedraza, J. 2012. Land transformation by humans: a review. *Geological Society of America Today* 22 (12): 4–10.

Hughes, J. 1996. *Pan's Travail: Environmental Problems of the Ancient Greeks and Romans*. Baltimore: Johns Hopkins University Press.

Hughes, J. 2003. Europe as consumer of exotic biodiversity: Greek and Roman times. *Landscape Research* 28 (1): 22–31.

Hughes, J. 2014. *Environmental Problems of the Greeks and Romans: Ecology in the Ancient Mediterranean*. Baltimore: Johns Hopkins University Press.

Hutchins, R. 2017. Interspecies ethics and collaborative survival in Lucretius' *De Rerum Natura*. In C. Schliephake (ed.) *Ecocriticism, Ecology, and the Cultures of Antiquity*. Lanham: Lexington Books: 91–111.

Jennison, G. 1937. *Animals for Show and Pleasure in Ancient Rome*. Manchester: Manchester University Press.

Jones, A.H.M. 1964. *The Later Roman Empire, 284–602: A Social, Economic and Administrative Survey*. Oxford: Blackwell.

Knabb, K., Tirosh, O., Erel, Y., Rittenour, T., Laparidou, S., Mohammad, N. and Levy, T.E. 2016. Environmental impacts of ancient copper mining and metallurgy: multi-proxy investigation of human-landscape dynamics in the Faynan valley, Southern Jordan. *Journal of Archaeological Science* 76: 85–101.

Kraft, J.C., Rapp, G., Brückner, H. and Kayan, I. 2011. Result of the struggle at Ephesus: natural processes 1, human intervention 0. In L. Wilson (ed.) *Human Interaction with the Biosphere: The Geoarchaeological Perspective*. London: The Geological Society of London: 27–36.

Kron, G. 2012. Techniques, agronomic expertise, and productivity. In W. Scheidel (ed.) *The Cambridge Companion to Roman Economy*. Cambridge: Cambridge University Press: 157–174.

Kyle, D.G. 1998. *Spectacles of Death in Ancient Rome*. London/New York: Routledge.

Latour, B. 2005. *Reassembling the Social: An Introduction to Actor-Network-Theory*. Oxford: Oxford University Press.

Lauffer, S. 1971. *Diokletians Preisedikt*. Berlin: Walter de Gruyter.

López-Merino, L., Martínez Cortizas, A., Reher, G.S., López-Sáez, J.A., Mighall, T.M. and Bindler, R. 2014. Reconstructing the impact of human activities in a NW Iberian Roman mining landscape for the last 2500 years. *Journal of Archaeological Science* 50: 208–218.

MacKinnon, M. 2006. Supplying exotic animals for the Roman amphitheatre games: new reconstructions combining archaeological, ancient textual, historical and ethnographic data. *Mouseion* 6 (2): 137–61.

McConnell, J.R., Wilson, A.I., Stohl, A., Arienzo, M.M., Chellman, N.J., Eckhardt, S., Thompson, E.M., Pollard, A.M. and Steffensen, J.P. 2018. Lead pollution recorded in Greenland ice indicates European emissions tracked plagues, wars, and imperial expansion during Antiquity. *Proceedings of the National Academy of Sciences* 115 (22): 5726–5731; DOI: 10.1073/pnas.1721818115 [Last Accessed 21/12/2018].

Mattingly, H., Sydenham, E., and Sutherland, C. 1949. *The Roman Imperial Coinage. Volume IV. Part III. Gordian III – Uranius Antoninus*. London: Spink and Son.

Middleton, G.J. 2018. Bang or whimper? The evidence for collapse of human civilizations at the start of the recently defined Meghalayan age is equivocal. *Science* 361: 1204–1205.

Moore, A. (ed.) 2016. *Anthropocene or Capitalocene? Nature, History, and the Crisis of Capitalism*. Oakland, CA: PM Press.

Nunes, J.P., Seixas, J. and Pacheco, N.R. 2008. Vulnerability of water resources, vegetation productivity and soil erosion to climate change in the Mediterranean watersheds. *Hydrological Processes* 22 (16): 3115–3134.

Östenberg, I. 2014. Animals and triumphs. In G. Campbell (ed.) *The Oxford Handbook of Animals in Classical Thought and Life*. Oxford: Oxford University Press: 491–506.

Östenberg, I. 2018. Defeated by the forest, the pass, the wind: nature as an enemy of Rome. In J. Clark and B. Turner (eds) *Brill's Companion to Military Defeat in Ancient Mediterranean Society*. Leiden: Brill: 240–261.

Pálsson, G., Szerzsynski, B., Sörlin, S., Marks, J., Avril, B., Crumley, C., Hackmann, H., Holm, P., Ingram, J., Kirman, A., Buendía, M.P. and Weehuizen, R. 2013. Reconceptualizing the 'Anthropos' in the Anthropocene: integrating the social sciences and humanities in global environmental change research. *Environmental Science and Policy* 28: 3–13.

Pétursdóttir, Þ. 2017. Climate change? Archaeology and Anthropocene. *Archaeological Dialogues* 24 (2): 175–205.

Purcell, N. 1987. Town in country and country in town. In E. MacDougall (ed.) *Ancient Roman Villa Gardens*. Washington D.C.: Dumbarton Oaks: 187–203.

Pyatt, F.B. 2001. Copper and lead bioaccumulation by Acacia retinodes and Eucalyptus torquata in sites contaminated as a consequence of extensive ancient mining activities in Cyprus. *Ecotoxicology and Environmental Safety* 50 (1): 60–64.

Pyatt, F.B., Amos, D., Grattan, J.P., Pyatt, A.J. and Terrell-Nield, C.E. 2002. Invertebrates of ancient heavy metal spoil and smelting tip sites in southern Jordan: their distribution and use as bioindicators of metalliferous pollution derived from ancient sources. *Journal of Arid Environments* 52 (1): 53–62.

Pyatt, F.B., Gilmore, G., Grattan, J.P., Hunt, C.O. and McLaren, S. 2000. An Imperial legacy? An exploration of the environmental impact of ancient mining and smelting in southern Jordan. *Journal of Archaeological Science* 27 (9): 771–778.

Pyatt, F.B. and Grattan, J.P. 2001. Some consequences of ancient mining activities on the health of ancient and modern human populations. *Journal of Public Health* 23 (3): 235–236.

Pyatt, F.B., Pyatt, A.J., Walker, C., Sheen, T. and Grattan, J.P. 2005. The heavy metal content of skeletons from an ancient metalliferous polluted area in southern Jordan with particular reference to bioaccumulation and human health. *Ecotoxicology and Environmental Safety* 60: 295–300.

Redman, C.L. 1999. *Human Impact on Ancient Environments*. Tucson: The University of Arizona Press.

Rees, S. 1987. Agriculture and horticulture. In J. Wacher (ed.) *The Roman World, Volume II*. London/New York: Routledge: 481–503.

Ripple, W., Estes, J., Beschta, R., Wilmers, C., Ritchie, E., Hebblewhite, M., Berger, J., Elmhagen, B., Letnic, M., Nelson, M., Schmitz, O., Smith, D., Wallach, A. and Wirsing, A. 2014. Status and ecological effects of the world's largest carnivores. *Science* 343: 1–11.

Roselaar, S. 2010. *Public Land in the Roman Republic. A Social and Economic History of Ager Publicus in Italy, 396–89 BC*. Oxford: Oxford University Press.

Rosman, K.J.R., Chisholm, W., Hong, S., Candelone, J-P. and Boutron, C.F. 1997. Lead from Carthaginian and Roman Spanish mines isotopically identified in Greenland ice dated from 600 BC to 300 AD. *Environmental Science and Technology* 31: 3413–3416.

Ruddiman, W.F. 2003. The Anthropogenic greenhouse era began thousands of years ago. *Climatic Change* 61: 261–293.

Ruddiman, W.F. 2007. The early anthropogenic hypothesis: challenges and responses. *Reviews of Geophysics* 45: 1–37.

Ruddiman W.F. and Ellis, E. 2009. Effect of per-capita land-use changes on Holocene forest cover and CO_2 emissions. *Quaternary Science Reviews* 28: 3011–3015.

Ruddiman, W.F., Guo, Z., Shou, X., Wu, H. and Yu, Y. 2008. Early rice farming and anomalous methane trends. *Quaternary Science Reviews* 27: 1291–1295.

Scherrer, P. 2000. *Ephesus: The New Guide*. Istanbul: Ege Yayınları

Shelton, J.-A. 2014. Spectacles of animal abuse. In G. Campbell (ed.) *The Oxford Handbook of Animals in Classical Thought and Life*. Oxford: Oxford University Press: 461–477.

Smith, B.D. and Zeder, M.A. 2013. The onset of the Anthropocene. *Anthropocene* 4: 8–13.

Solli, B., Burström, M., Domanska, E., Edgeworth, M., González-Ruibal, A., Holtorf, C., Lucas, G., Østigård, T., Smith, L. and Witmore, C. 2011. Some reflections on heritage and archaeology in the Anthropocene. *Norwegian Archaeological Review* 44 (1): 40–88.

Sparreboom, A. 2016. *Venationes Africanae: Hunting Spectacles in Roman North Africa: Cultural Significance and Social Function*. PhD Thesis. University of Amsterdam.

Steffen, W., Crutzen, P. and McNeill, J. 2007. The Anthropocene: are humans now overwhelming the great forces of nature? *Ambio* 36 (8): 614–621.

Steffen, W., Grinewald, J., Crutzen, P. and McNeill J. 2011. The Anthropocene: conceptual and historical perspectives. *Philosophical Transactions of the Royal Society A, Mathematical, Physical and Engineering Sciences* 369: 842–867.

Stock, F., Knipping, M., Pint, A., Ladstätter, S., Delile, H., Heiss, A.G., Laermanns, H., Mitchell, P.D., Ployer, R., Steskal, M., Thanheiser, U., Urz, R., Wennrich, V. and Brückner, H. 2016. Human impact on Holocene sediment dynamics in the Eastern Mediterranean: the example of the Roman harbour in Ephesus. *Earth Surface Processes and Landforms* 41: 980–996.

Thommen, L. 2012. *An Environmental History of Ancient Greece and Rome*. Cambridge: Cambridge University Press.

Ulmer, J.M. 2017. Posthumanism as research methodology: inquiry in the Anthropocene. *International Journal of Qualitative Studies in Education* 30 (9): 832–848.

Walker, M., Head, M.J., Berkelhammer, M., Björck, S., Cheng, H., Cwynar, L., Fisher, D., Gkinis, V., Long, A., Lowe, J., Newnham, R., Rasmussen, S.O. and Weiss, H. 2018. Formal ratification of the subdivision of the Holocene series/epoch (quaternary system/period): two new global boundary stratotype sections and points (GSSPs) and three new stages/subseries. *Episodes* 41 (4): 1–11.

Zalasiewicz, J., Waters, C.N., Williams, M., Barnosky, A.D., Cearreta, A., Crutzen, P., Ellis, E., Ellis M.A., Fairchild, I.J., Grinevald, J., Haff, P.K., Hajdas, I., Leinfelder, R., McNeill, J., Odada, E.O., Poirier, C., Richter, D., Steffen, W., Summerhayes, C., Syvitski, J.P.M., Vidas, D., Wagreich, M., Wing, S.L., Wolfe, A.P., Zhisheng, A. and Oreskes, N. 2015. When did the Anthropocene begin? A mid-twentieth century boundary level is stratigraphically optimal. *Quaternary International* 383: 196–203.

Zalasiewicz, J., Williams, M., Haywood, A. and Ellis, M. 2011. The Anthropocene: a new epoch of geological time? *Philosophical Transactions of the Royal Society A, Mathematical, Physical and Engineering Sciences* 369: 835–841.

Abbreviations

FrRH	*Fragments of the Roman Historians*	Cornell 2013.
RIC VI	*Roman Imperial Coinage*	Mattingly *et al.* 1949.

10

Commentary: Pathways to Posthumanism

Oliver J.T. Harris

Introduction

It is a privilege to offer a brief commentary on the chapters contained within this volume. Together they present an intriguing contribution to debates around posthumanism in archaeology. Posthumanism, as the editors note in their introduction to the volume, represents a banner term for a host of different approaches, but is in general committed to a shifting of focus away from an ahistorical, transcendent, vision of the human, towards an approach which emphasises difference, historical specificity and emergence. As the chapters in this volume show us, this can take a number of different forms, but in all its varieties it is the challenge to anthropocentrism that is most critical. Posthumanism recognises, first and foremost, that not only have traditional approaches privileged human beings, but they also have privileged very specific forms of being human, ones that are male, straight, able-bodied, white, and so on (Braidotti 2013). By insisting on historical immanence and difference, posthumanism challenges the underlying dichotomies such as nature and culture, human and world, which underpin such essentialism. Going beyond the traditional anthropological celebration of cultural difference, posthumanism offers us a more radical contrast with our familiar worlds. In its various forms it chooses to emphasise the emergence of animals, objects, plants, landscapes, matter itself and more. In each case the elevation of an element of the world acts to undercut the position of the human at the ontological apex and to open up new ways of thinking about past and present.

The multiplicity of approaches one can bundle together under posthumanism is one of the strengths of this particular approach. In their introduction, the editors do an excellent job of tracing the history of the term, so only a few other remarks are needed here to set the scene for my commentary. In general, both within archaeology and more widely, one can draw a clear division between two forms of posthumanism. On the one side you have a range of approaches that tend to stress the importance of relations. These stretch from new materialism, with its emphasis on the vibrant force of matter (*e.g.* Conneller 2011; Jones 2012), via multispecies approaches that force us to reconsider the contribution of animals and plants to history (*e.g.* Overton and Hamilakis 2013), to those theories that emphasise a strong form of ontological difference (*e.g.* Alberti and Marshall 2009). On the other hand, approaches rooted in Object Orientated Ontology argue that things have withdrawn essences, and cannot be understood primarily in relational terms (*e.g.* Olsen 2010). These latter approaches in archaeology rarely deal with historical periods as we would traditionally understand them, and I will put them to one side in the commentary that follows. Both sets of approaches, however, clearly offer us a range of resources which we can develop in archaeology to provide new ways of thinking.

Each of the chapters in this volume starts us on a journey towards particular forms of posthumanism; routes towards opening up more complex understandings of the Roman world as well as other times and places. A turn to posthumanism, however, is not a revolutionary gesture. Unlike claims of modernist paradigm shifts, one does not simply abandon past understandings to embrace a new world order (Harris and Cipolla 2017). Instead, posthumanism represents a shifting process of becoming; it takes multiple moves and hard work to move the standard tropes of a discipline away from their foundations in anthropocentric Cartesian dualisms. The chapters in this volume begin to promote discussions in a number of interesting directions. In my concluding commentary, I suggest we can identify three different paths that the chapters start us on, and sketch out some ways in which these ideas could be developed to further enhance their posthumanist qualities. I shall term the three pathways new materialism, becoming animal and becoming plant, and ontological difference. Each draws on different elements of posthumanist thought, using these excellent chapters as a springboard.

Pathway 1: New Materialism

A number of the chapters in this volume start us down a direction that moves in a new materialist direction to a greater or lesser extent (*e.g.* chapters by Mihajlović, Zapelloni Pavia, Iara, and Ingate). New materialism is perhaps the most popular form of posthumanism, certainly in archaeology (for general introductions see Coole and Frost 2010; Dolphijn and Van der Tuin 2012). The central premise of new materialism is that matter, as Jane Bennett (2010) would put it, is vibrant. That is that matter and material things are active players in the emergence of the world. This means when we consider material culture, pottery for example, we need to think not only about the human being making the pot, but the way the material itself contributes to the emergence of specific forms. In archaeology, Chantal Conneller (2011) has considered the contribution materials make to the emergence of form in Palaeolithic material culture, and Andrew Meirion Jones and Marta Díaz-Guardamino (2019) have done the same with Neolithic art objects. Within archaeology, the most prevalent form of new materialism is assemblage theory. The notion of assemblage, taken originally from Gilles Deleuze and Félix Guattari (2004) and developed most notably by Manuel DeLanda (*e.g.* 2016) views the entities of the world, whether people, pots, landscapes, houses or anything else, as particular gatherings of different elements and relationships into more or less bounded agglomerations. These agglomerations, these assemblages, are historically emergent and more than the sum of their parts. In archaeology this idea has been used to rethink the nature of change (Crellin 2017), to reconceptualise medieval urbanism (Jervis 2016), and to transform concepts like typology (Fowler 2017).

One of the important moves new materialism makes is to democratise the range of historical actors at play in any particular context. So whereas in traditional archaeological approaches material things, for example, were cultural adaptations, or expressions of the identity or beliefs of the people who made them, within new materialism material things become more active players in historical processes. They move from being simply the focus of human strategies of representation to playing a more independent historical role. Vladimir Mihajlović's chapter on epigraphic funerary markers (EFMs) demonstrates this neatly. Mihajlović examines how by rethinking EFMs through Karen Barad's (2007) agential realism, alongside older ideas of relational personhood (*e.g.* Strathern 1988; Fowler 2004), we can transform the way we conceptualise EFMs from being representations of human identity to being active agents that have an impact on the world *regardless* of what human beings think of them. Arianna Zapelloni Pavia similarly recognises the importance of figurines in the rituals that took place in Umbrian sanctuaries, as does Kristine Iara in her discussion of figurative and non-figurative images of gods in Roman religion.

These chapters challenge us to reposition objects as central to their worlds, shaping, as well as being shaped by, the encounters between humans, things, and places. There are perhaps further directions we could explore down this path, however. The first connects to the question of agency. To what extent is it useful to accord agency to individual objects like EFMs, figurines or statues? Such an approach tends to draw on ideas from Alfred Gell (1998), who set out an argument for what he termed object agency (see also Feider *et al.* in this volume). A more useful approach may be, however, to consider how agency emerges relationally. In such an approach agency does not belong to anyone or anything – there is only agency that emerges through particular sets of relations (Latour 1999). Thus a figurine plays a role in producing particular forms of sanctuary-specific agency, or agency emerges in the relations an EFM has with other parts of the world (including human beings). Such a view allows for more subtle and contextual readings of the emergence of specific forms of agency, which shift as the relations around the specific objects change.

Similarly, a second new materialist direction to follow would be to develop an attention to the materials themselves. By treating objects as particular forms of assemblages, new materialism acts to map their histories and the processes through which they emerge, and indeed to examine the ways in which materials themselves contribute to these processes. Here we might consider how the stone itself contributes to the ways in which EFMs can affect the world, or indeed how this might differ with EFMs made from other materials. This might also allow us to reposition our understanding of how the transition in materials used in figurines in Grotta Bella from bronze and lead to terracotta. Whilst Zapelloni Pavia may well be right to flag the economic reasons behind this, the attention new materialism draws to the materials themselves may allow us to map out other connections and relations and new properties that were drawn upon in this transition. Iara hints at this in her description of the different materials present in the Forum in Rome, but there is surely more to say here.

The chapter that goes furthest down the new materialist pathway in the volume, however, is clearly Jay Ingate's discussion of water. Water is proving to be a useful material for new materialists to think through, as chapters in Susan Alt and Timothy Pauketat's (2019) recent edited volume show. Ingate, in a precisely new materialist fashion, stresses the constant movement of water and our need to think beyond human dominance if we want to understand its role in the Roman world. Ingate also shows us how water can be differentiated into multiple forms; he cites the idea of 'living water'. Here a singular category is revealed to contain multiple assemblages, which in turn allows us to further historicise a specific material and through that to understand its role in the production of past worlds. Ingate's detailed attention to water shows us how much we can learn when we focus on how materials emerge in historically specific ways, and as such, can make historically specific contributions.

Pathway 2: Becoming with Animals, Becoming with Plants

If materials offer one route towards posthumanism, the emphasis on the importance of animals and plants offers us another. From Donna Haraway's (2008) critical analysis of the ways in which humans and animals 'become with' one another, via Eduardo Kohn's (2013) analysis of how forests think, to Anna Tsing's (2015) magisterial account of matsutake mushrooms, anthropologists and archaeologists are making space for animals and plants in new ways. Some of the chapters in this volume do this too. Mike Feider, Ellen Hambleton, and Mark Maltby, for example, direct our attention to the humble chicken, and its appearance on coinage in Iron Age Gaul and Southern England. They trace how these animals seeped 'into the social consciousness', and thus came to be imprinted on coinage. Key here, for the authors, is what these coins with chickens on them were meant to do. Yet there may be ways to push this further. The authors seek to stress the secondary agency of coins, that is how their agency derives from the people who made them. Yet we might wonder, as we saw above, what a more relational take on agency might do, one that examined how coins, humans, chickens, and religious sites together allowed new forms of action to come into being. Further, we might think more about the hybridity of the images on the coins and, for example, the fact that many of the Gaulish examples have one side showing a chicken with a human face on the stomach, as indeed do the British Chichester 'cock bronze' type. Feider *et al.* propose a number of ways in which the coins may represent a symbolic link between humans and chickens, perhaps associated with shamanistic practices. When we develop a posthumanist approach, though, we might want to think more about the ways in which thinkers like Deleuze and Guattari (2004) write about becoming animal. For Deleuze and Guattari, drawing on Baruch Spinoza, a body (whether human, animal or anything else) is not defined by a list of essentialised criteria but rather by its affects, that is how it is capable of affecting the world, and being affected by it in turn. Famously, Deleuze (1988: 124) argues that an ox has more in common with a draft horse than a draft horse does with a racehorse, because the two former animals, although different species, act in much more similar ways. The archaeologist Chantal Conneller (2004) has drawn on this notion to think through how Mesolithic people at the site of Star Carr created masks from antler frontlets in order to take on deer-like *affects*, that is to 'become deer'. How might the hybrid images from the coins speak of a process of 'becoming chicken'? Or the inverse, given the images show chickens with human faces in their stomachs, might this be a case of chickens-becoming-humans? The aim here needs to be to identify what it is chicken bodies could do in the Iron Age world. What affects were they capable of? How then could they be taken up by others through processes of relation, depiction and hybridisation? Here we can also think of the Nero-becoming-animal as discussed by Filippo Carlà-Uhink, which we will return to when we consider ontological difference below.

Where Feider *et al.* focus primarily on the coins, rather than the chickens, plants themselves take centre stage in the excellent chapter on weeds by Lisa Lodwick. Her chapter stresses the specific capacities of weeds to act in the world, and the way in which they do so without necessarily requiring the intervention of human beings. Just as Ingate's chapter breaks down the material category of water, so Lodwick seeks to analyse particular types of weed, tracing the properties of Corncockle, *Atropa*, and others. Lodwick's work sends us down a posthumanist direction by making us attend to the ways in which plants occupy Roman worlds, both in the country and the city, in their own ways. How could we push this further? Ironically the answer here might be by returning to think through human beings. Lodwick argues that relational approaches risk entities like plants losing their specific and unique properties, yet this need not be the case. As Tsing (2015) shows with mushrooms, for example, the specific properties of things in the world – whether fungi or plants – emerge through their relations. The key direction here is flagged by Lodwick in the conclusion of her chapter, where she stresses the need to situate weeds with broader assemblages, an argument which runs slightly counter to her earlier critique of relations. The key, I would suggest, is not to begin with an analysis that presumes the existence of people, as one kind of bounded entity, and weeds, as another, and then seeks to explore how they connect. Instead, we need to start with the relations themselves, which include elements we might categorise as biological or material, and from that trace how particular assemblages of humans and weeds emerge together, with their own immanent historical capabilities. It is here that we can map a Roman world in which humans become with plants, just as plants become with humans.

A final chapter that deals with animals is the posthuman provocations of our editors, Irene Selsvold and Lewis Webb. They examine the ways in which animal populations were transformed through Roman intervention. Their account is clearly relational in its description of the way Roman *venationes* had an enormous impact on animal populations, and critically how the knock-on effects of the reduction in some animal species, such as leopards and lions, had on wider forms of ecology. This means they are well-positioned to appreciate the cascading effects that change has when one takes a relational perspective. Yet we might wonder if the discussion of *Roman* impact on animals leaves the agency rather one-sided, and raises the criticism that many have made of the term Anthropocene that the authors seek to address: that at the very moment we have realised how devastating the consequences of our anthropocentrism is, it might be slightly counterproductive to name a geological period after ourselves. Whilst the desire to identify the dramatic transformation of the planet at a geological scale is laudable, can we really understand the nature of these changes if we continue to oppose human beings and the world in a dualistic fashion? Whilst the authors' appeal to posthuman literature shows they are aware of this risk, we might be able to develop this further by refocusing away from the changes Romans had by themselves, towards thinking more about the way change occurred in the Roman period through a host of intersecting relations of animals, plants, people, and landscape. This fascinating chapter poses important questions about how we understand the Anthropocene. The question is, could an approach be developed that refocuses our understanding of emergent cause away from the human and so produce both a more posthumanist understanding of the Roman world *and* better position us to understand how to challenge the climate crisis in the present (*cf.* Carter and Harris *forthcoming*)?

Pathway 3: Ontological Difference

Starting us on a pathway to ontological difference is Filippo Carlà-Uhink's study of Caligula and Nero. Carlà-Uhink sets out how these two emperors sought to claim a divine nature, or as he puts it a 'bigger-than-human nature' through representational strategies such as impersonating different deities, in Caligula's case, or physically shaping the world and crossing human-animal boundaries through wearing animal furs, in the form of Nero. Carlà-Uhink's eye-opening chapter asks us to think through these moves as political strategies central to the performances of these emperors. How could we make this narrative more posthuman?

The question we might pose here, is what would happen if we took the claims the emperors are making seriously? That is, what if granted them ontological weight? What would happen if instead of reducing the claims they made to ones that make sense to us (and to some of their contemporaries) – that Caligula was *impersonating* gods for example – we considered them as actually taking place? What happens if we open up the possibility that Caligula became a God when he dressed as one, that Nero became the women he loved? The gap between the claim and our understanding of it reveals the ruptures between the concepts at play and the difficulties and issues of ontological translation. As archaeologists like Benjamin Alberti (2016) and Darryl Wilkinson (2017) have shown, it is in these moments of radical difference, of alterity, that new understandings can emerge. Drawing on anthropologists like Eduardo Viveiros de Castro (1998) and Martin Holbraad (2007), these authors have argued that moments of dissonance like this – between our conceptions and those of the people we study – can have radical implications for understanding the complex differences between worlds. What does it mean to be in a world where an emperor can shape the earth or become an animal? These differences become not just issues of cultural contrast, but actual, *ontological*, differences that require us to rethink the form of our own worlds – a truly posthumanist consequence.

What perhaps is most fascinating in terms of the potential here, however, is that Carlà-Uhink's chapter captures internal ontological dissonance within the Roman world. Does Caligula turn into a God or Nero into an animal? Yes for some people, some of the time. Here then we see not just a singular ontology, but rather an example of what John Robb and I call multimodal ontologies, the capacity for more than one form of world to co-exist within a time and place (Harris and Robb 2012). Here the capacity to work between the strange and the familiar, the known world and the unknown, a realm of ontological similarity and difference opens itself up to us. Such a conception would allow us to push the work in other chapters further too. Iara for example, switches between emphasising the feeling and experience of a god's presence in ritual experience, or in a statue, and referring to this as simple belief. What would happen if we took the presence of Saturn seriously in his temple? If we understood the statue as being able to walk? This position that Roman archaeology can open up – with text, but with difference – allows for a different form of ontological enquiry, one that can mediate between anthropologically informed accounts from societies with Indigenous descendants, and ones where no such modern connection exists (*cf.* Harris and Crellin 2018). Here posthuman Roman archaeology can enter the ontological debate and make a sustained and important contribution.

The same point could be made of the discussion in the Selsvold and Webb's final chapter in their account of the impact of hunting and trapping practices on leopards. They cite Cicero who proclaims that leopards are complaining about the traps and ambushes set for them and that the leopards have decided to leave Cicilia as a result. Where the authors treat this as evidence for the decline in animal populations, and reasonably so, one might also wonder if this opens up a moment of radical difference, a world in which leopards speak and express a view on their conditions. One can imagine how differently anthropologists in the Amazon would treat such discussions. How is our understanding of the Roman world changed if we open ourselves up to consider how it might work if leopards can speak? How does this change broader conceptions of human/animal relations, the notion of sentience and with it what it means to be human? What might this say about the process of conceptual translation? There are further posthuman questions of ontological difference to explore here.

Conclusion

The cover image of this volume, with which the editors begin their introduction, is the Great Artemis from Ephesus, a figure so rich in connection to both human and non-human that it becomes hard to see where one begins and the other ends. And so it should be. Posthumanism forces us to move away from the bounded individuals, the straightforward humans, the easy oppositions that we have been trained, throughout our lives, to detect. Instead it forces us to recognise how we all, from archaeologist to ancient Roman, are products, like Artemis, of countless relations. Critically, however, relations change through time, humans today are not the humans of the Roman world, not just culturally, as though this were a layer we could drape over ourselves to clothe the naked body beneath, but at a much more fundamental level. Posthumanism demands that we respect these differences, that we map these differences, that we ask what it was that bodies, whether human or non-human, could do at particular points in time, and to map the relations that made those capacities possible (Deleuze 1988).

What these chapters offer us, is the first hints of what a posthumanist Roman archaeology might be capable of: the range of affects, the forms of difference, the powerful roles of materials, plants and animals upon which new theoretical approaches can shed light. Given the ubiquity with which Roman archaeology is used to sustain the claims of presidents and prime ministers in the present, or the manner in which our politics is compared continuously to that of Ancient Rome, I can think of no period more in need of, or that could contribute so much to, a posthumanist archaeology. Indeed, given the manner in which our anthropocentric concerns have driven us towards climate crisis and potential species extinction, the need for posthumanism across the humanities has never been greater (Braidotti 2019). Selsvold and Webb are surely correct that only posthumanism can give us a reasonable insight into the potential for dealing with the Anthropocene, and the chances of making life, and understanding pasts, on an already ruined planet.

School of Archaeology and Ancient History,
University of Leicester

Acknowledgements

Thanks are due to Irene Selsvold and Lewis Webb for their kind invitation to a non-Romanist to contribute to such a fascinating volume. The topics I discuss here have hugely benefited from discussions with Ben Alberti, Emily Banfield, Craig Cipolla, Hannah Cobb, Rachel Crellin, Chris Fowler, Ben Jervis, Yvonne O'Dell, John Robb and Darryl Wilkinson among many others. None of course should be asked to answer for errors I have made. This commentary was written during a period of leave funded by the Leverhulme Trust through a Philip Leverhulme Prize (PLP-2016-109).

Bibliography

Alberti, B. 2016. Archaeologies of ontology. *Annual Review of Anthropology* 45: 163–179.

Alberti, B. and Marshall, Y. 2009. Animating archaeology: local theories and conceptually open-ended methodologies. *Cambridge Archaeological Journal* 19: 344–356.

Alt, S.M. and Pauketat, T.R. (eds) 2019. *New Materialims Ancient Urbanisms*. London: Routledge.

Barad, K. 2007. *Meeting the Universe Halfway: Quantum Physics and the Entanglement of Matter and Meaning*. Durham, NC: Duke University Press.

Bennett, J. 2010. *Vibrant Matter: A Political Ecology of Things*. London: Duke University Press.

Braidotti, R. 2013. *The Posthuman*. London: Polity.

Braidotti, R. 2019. A theoretical framework for the critical posthumanities. *Theory, Culture and Society (Special Issue: Transversal Posthumanities)* 36 (6): 31–61.

Carter, B. and Harris, O.J.T. *forthcoming*. The end of Normal Politics: assemblages, nonhumans and international relations. In J. Castro Pereira and A. Saramago (eds) *Non-Human Nature in World Politics*. New York: Springer.

Conneller, C. 2004. Becoming deer: corporeal transformations at Star Carr. *Archaeological Dialogues* 11: 37–56.

Conneller, C. 2011. *An Archaeology of Materials: Substantial Transformations in Early Prehistoric Europe*. London: Routledge.

Coole, D. and Frost, S. 2010. Introducing the new materialisms. In D. Coole and S. Frost (eds) *New Materialisms: Ontology, Agency and Politics*. Durham, NC: Duke University Press: 1–43.

Crellin, R.J. 2017. Changing assemblages: vibrant matter in burial assemblages. *Cambridge Archaeological Journal* 27: 111–125.

DeLanda, M. 2016. *Assemblage Theory*. Edinburgh: Edinburgh University Press.

Deleuze, G. 1988. *Spinoza: Practical Philosophy*. San Francisco: City Lights Books.

Deleuze, G. and Guattari, F. 2004. *A Thousand Plateaus: Capitalism and Schizophrenia*. London: Continuum.

Dolphijn, R. and Van der Tuin, I. (eds) 2012. *New Materialism: Interviews and Cartographies*. Ann Arbor: Open Humanities Press.

Fowler, C. 2004. *The Archaeology of Personhood: An Anthropological Approach*. London: Routledge.

Fowler, C. 2017. Relational typologies, assemblage theory and Early Bronze Age burials. *Cambridge Archaeological Journal* 27: 95–109.

Gell, A. 1998. *Art and Agency: An Anthropological Theory*. Oxford: Clarendon Press.

Haraway, D. 2008. *When Species Meet*. Minneapolis: University of Minnesota Press.

Harris, O.J.T. and Cipolla, C.N. 2017. *Archaeological Theory in the New Millennium: Introducing Current Perspectives*. Abingdon/New York: Routledge.

Harris, O.J.T. and Crellin, R.J. 2018. Assembling new ontologies from old materials: towards multiplicity. In M. Astor-Aguilera and G. Harvey (eds) *Rethinking Relations and Animism: Personhood and Materiality*. Abingdon/New York: Routledge: 55–74.

Harris, O.J.T. and Robb, J. 2012. Multiple ontologies and the problem of the body in history. *American Anthropologist* 114: 668–679.

Holbraad, M. 2007. The power of powder: multiplicity and motion in the divinatory cosmology of Cuban Ifá (or *mana*, again). In A. Henare, M. Holbraad and S. Wastell (eds) *Thinking Through Things: Theorising Artefacts Ethnographically*. Abingdon/New York: Routledge: 189–225.

Jervis, B. 2016. Assemblage theory and town foundation in Medieval England. *Cambridge Archaeological Journal* 26: 381–395.

Jones, A.M. 2012. *Prehistoric Materialities: Becoming Material in Prehistoric Britain and Ireland.* Oxford: Oxford University Press.

Jones, A.M. and Díaz-Guardamino, M. 2019. *Making a Mark: Image and Process in Neolithic Britain and Ireland.* Oxford: Oxbow Books.

Kohn, E. 2013. *How Forests Think: Towards an Anthropology Beyond the Human.* London: University of California Press.

Latour, B. 1999. *Pandora's Hope: Essays on the Reality of Science Studies.* Cambridge, MA: Harvard University Press.

Olsen, B. 2010. *In Defense of Things: Archaeology and the Ontology of Objects.* Plymouth: Altamira Press.

Overton, N. and Hamilakis, Y. 2013. A manifesto for a social zooarchaeology. Swans and other beings in the Mesolithic. *Archaeological Dialogues* 20: 111–136.

Strathern, M. 1988. *The Gender of the Gift: Problems with Women and Problems with Society in Melanesia.* Cambridge: Cambridge University Press.

Tsing, A.L. 2015. *The Mushroom at the End of the World: On the Possibility of Life in Capitalist Ruins.* Princeton: Princeton University Press.

Viveiros de Castro, E. 1998. Cosmological deixis and Amerindian perspectivism. *Journal of the Royal Anthropological Institute* 4: 469–488.

Wilkinson, D. 2017. Is there such a thing as animism? *Journal of the American Academy of Religion* 85: 289–311.